"Are you and the *señora* doing penance?"
the Spanish man asked.

"What's that?"

"Are you repenting by walking and carrying
those heavy burdens?" He looked at our back
packs and seemed to feel sorry for us.
"Are you being punished?"

"No, we are not being punished," I said.
"We are being blessed."

Please turn the page
to see what all America is saying about

THE
WALK
WEST

A WALK
ACROSS AMERICA 2

THE WALK WEST

A WALK ACROSS AMERICA 2

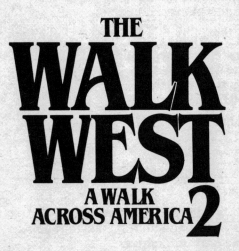

THE WALK WEST

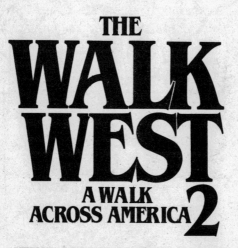

A WALK ACROSS AMERICA 2

JANUARY 15, 1979 Prineville

Florence

John Day

Boise

Twin Falls

Salt Lake City

Sandy

Green River

Lake City

SLUMGULLION PASS

San Luis

Clayton

Borger

Gilliland

Olney

Paul M. Breeden

The Walk West

A Walk Across America 2

Peter and Barbara Jenkins

Fawcett Crest • **New York**

Dallas

Westlake
Lake Charles

New
Orleans
JULY 5, 1976

Contents

To the United States of America

Acknowledgments

We walked thousands of miles and would not have made it without all the people who reached out to us along the way. We would not have been able to experience all that we did without those generous Americans. They gave us food when we needed it and work when we were out of money. There were those who gave us their love, time, support, advice and their life's story. Some prayed for us.

Our parents deserve much in the way of thanks and special recognition. We hope our long walk didn't keep them from losing too much sleep, or from getting too many more gray hairs.

There are other men and women who deserve to be noticed. They are the professionals who taught us how to take pictures, write stories, capture our experiences and then to share all we found in our books and articles.

We have so many friends who became a part of this walk that we will have to list them by state so they can find their names.

Louisiana: Rev. Charles Green and the members of the Word of Faith Temple, New Orleans. This is for you, Bobbie, thanks to Linda, David and Stephen. Rex Deaton, Rita Hauptman, Teddy Gabb, Larry and Diana Baker, Bud and Sandy Kelly, Bill and Sherry McInnis, Michael Green, David and

Ina Newell, Wally and Brenda Hebert, Welch and Gina Hill, New Orleans Baptist Theological Seminary, Dr. J. Stanley Watson, Ann Green Broughton, Virgil and Erlene Stiles, Dr. Jack Andonie, Dr. Allan Cougle, Joe and Eddie Fair, the Bennetts in Rayne, Rev. C. L. Moore, Marie and Rev. Garlon Pemberton, Larry and Debbie Gantenbein, Lee and Dawn Como, Charles and Jackie Pavur, George and Jackie Dantin, Jim and Nancy Cannella. (Friends across the border in Mississippi are Jan and Bob Taggart, Dorothy Prassenos, John and Charlotte Stack.) Walter Landry and family, Allen Bodin and family, Boy's Village, Rufus Landry, Rosalind Maricelli, C. J. Scheufens, John Wright and all the guys at the sign of the Shell, Dave Tayrien, C.C., F.E., and Richard at Amoco, and Gambino's Restaurant (super shrimp).

Texas: Don, Sara, Douglas and Saralee Stevens, Jay Dickman, Skeeter and Becky Hagler, Lyn, John, Tread Sheffield, Shelley, Sue, Ann Mayfield, Bettie and Otis Gafford, Leroy and Iva Mae Gibson, Thom and Jane Marshall, Ron and Kathy Hall, Don and Doris Jackson, Uncle George and Aunt Chaine Robie, Jack and Jerri Gross, Lambert's Grocery, Dr. Bruce and Lawanna McIver, Jim Pratt, Erven and Reba Tooley, Joe and Margaret Wells, the Roberts in Benjamin, Dale and Helen Lynch, watermelon from the Montgomerys, the Hammers, E. E. Grimes, Woody and Lois Egan, Christ for the Nations School, Jim Bob Nation, Randy and Jan Ammons, Tom and Polly Higley, the Coxes, Rev. Pettigrew Hamilton, Vivian Castleberry, Maggie Kennedy, Patty and Danny Snider, Wyman and Sara Meinzer and the coyote necklace, The Lighthouse Christian Center, Rev. Buster Kennedy, Jim and Alice Brown and their bologna sandwiches, Sam Burns, Larry and Margo Gerbrant, Peggy Taylor, Grand Avenue Baptist Church, R. C. and Wanda Gunter. The Joyces in Newton, Marine Drilling, Pat, Matthew and John McBryde, Chicken Fried Steak, Sammy Munsey, Bill and Billie Penn, Eddie and Catherine Pennell, Rev. James Robison, Lucille and Rev. Bob Sanders, Gil and Ann Strickland.

New Mexico: Pat and Jerry Smith and the antique spurs,

Gilbert Virgil and his royal elk, the wonderful picnic at Red River, Gladstone Mercantile, and the land of enchantment.

Colorado: V. G. Fitzgerald, Bill and Fay Chappell, Phil and Carolyn Virden, Chap and Alice Rowe, Harley and Caryl Rudofsky, Bud and Irene Weems, Dr. Harold and Barbara Parker, Beverly and Bonnie Vickers, Thom and Ruth Drabek, Bob and Betty Ortenburger, Frank and Elizabeth Pool and their mountain home with the eagle's view, Bob Hall, Tom and Midge Murphy, Larry Stukey, Bill and Ruthanna Hall, the Jacksons, the Skerrys, the Hegartys, Gary and Jean Wysocki, and little Angela Marie. Thanks to all the dogs of Lake City, too numerous to mention. The First Assembly of God and Pastor Cope in Grand Junction, Tom and Gwen Baer, Jerry and Micki Crutchfield, Carl Akers, Sandra Toohy, Evelyn Vickers, The Western Belle, First Presbyterian Church of Lake City, Mary Vernon at Pioneer Savings and Loan, Doug and Carol Hartman, John and Ann Parker, Grant Houston, Ron and Kitty Maupin, Lester and Emily Roberts, and Rev. Dillard Roberts.

Utah: Fred and Gladys Voll, Frank and Mary Jerant, Joe Rolando, Rell Francis, Dr. Larry Francis, the man with the silk pillow in Sandy, Lorene and Martin Rasmussen, Lola Redford, Myrtle Barker, and a lot of punch at BYU.

Idaho: Jack and Lucy Ramsey, Guy Ramsey, Tom Ramsey. A special thanks to Camille Ramsey. Ken and Helen Henderson, Joni and Jason and Nathan Ramsey, Grannie Ramsey, Dot and Dick Hagerman, Roger Simmons, and the "keep on stompin'" T-shirts.

Oregon: Lawrence and Trudy McCracken, Rollin and Bertha Bunker, Ironside, Burton's Sunset Motel, Jerry and Nancy Alford, Reba and Rev. Warren Cornelius and their Oregon hospitality, Tex Hagar and Driftwood Shores, and the folks of Florence. Smokey and Loretta Overton, David and Don Franke and their families. Thanks to all the logging trucks that didn't splash slush on us, the Kites, and the helpful people of John Day.

There are other special people who live in such places as Mukilteo, Washington; Jackson, Mississippi; and on Sutton Place. Thanks to Skip Yowell, Murray McCory and all our friends at JanSport. Also, Morgan Jenkins and Paul and Ann Breeden and all the kids on the Breeden ranch. Your maps and drawings in both books, Paul, are great. Glenn and Karen Brendle, Phil and Janet Yancey. Our typists, Mary Baker, B.J., Sarie Doty-Hamlin. Ben and Norma Hager and Ben's dancing, School of the Ozarks and Alfred University. All our friends up in Nashville at the S.S.B. of the Southern Baptist Convention. Our friends in Ashland, Ohio, and Spokane, Washington. David Cupp, Charlie Daniels and his band for super music. Bill and Camille Morris and their little southern belles. The fine folks at Fawcett, Reader's Digest Condensed Books, Fleming H. Revell, *Guideposts,* Lion and Scheider-Buch. Bruce Lood and Quadras, USIA, Danny Wilson, CBS, Bernie Sofronski, and Uncle Bruce.

Joan Stewart, our agent at the William Morris Agency, is a true friend. Her advice, wisdom, jokes, and protection of us have been intensely appreciated. Thanks again to Fred Mustard Stewart.

A special note of appreciation to all book people everywhere. Tiny book shops, stores the size of grocery stores, printers, wholesalers, chains and all those committed to people reading books.

This book is a tribute to the enduring family. All our love to Fred and Mary, Scott, Freddy, Betsi and Abbi Jenkins; Randy and Winky Rice, too. And to Ernie, Betty, Jim and Elaine Pennell. Sunny and Vicky Archer, and Grandma Pennell.

Many people at *National Geographic* magazine had a major impact on our walk. We'll never forget all they did for us. I must thank Tom Smith, especially. He taught me as much as any man ever could about photography and, more important, about life and living every moment to its ultimate. Bob Patton, thank you for your good counsel. Also, Gil Grosvenor, Bill Garrett, Elaine Ames, Don Frederick, Guy Starling, Joe Judge, Lou Mazzatenta, Jean McConnville, Gus Rutins, Carolyn Patterson, Pritt Vesiliand, Bentley Andrews, Cotton Coulson, Mary Smith and our friend, Harvey Arden.

Thanks to our friends at MTSU. Harold Smith for getting the secluded cabin on the lake in Tennessee. Also thanks to his wife Judy. Cliff and Gayle Gillespie were very understanding. Thanks to Joe Nunley. Also thanks to the nice folks of Smithville. Art and Jo Eidman. Laverne, Nancy and Kim S., Ken and Betty E., and David Johnson and family and their cabin. Also, thanks to Rev. Roger Pursley for inviting us to Destin, Florida, and the Clarys, Charlie, Sr., Carolyn, Charlie and Beth for giving us a spot on the white beaches. Thanks also to 10 Sidney Place, 68 Pemberwick Road, 45 Alexander Street, and 110 Doubloon Drive.

There's much more involved in bringing this book to you than writing it. We love our publisher, William Morrow, and all those who have given so much to this book and to *A Walk Across America*. We must mention our gifted editor, Pat Golbitz, who has brilliant instincts and has given all she had to make this book all it could be. We must thank our friend and Pat's assistant, Naomi Cutner. She's a real sweetheart. Special thanks to Larry Hughes, Hillel Black, Al Marchioni, Sherry Arden, John Ball, Victoria Klose, Mike Simons, Mary Kay Magner, Rich Davis, Cheryl Asherman, the Morrow sales people and all the ladies and gentlemen who make Morrow one of the top publishers anywhere. Don Patterson, that train ride to New Jersey was worth it. We love the title you came up with.

If there's anyone in the U.S.A. we forgot, we want to hear from you. AMEN.

1

Engineer Pass

Barbara climbed up the white wall and stood on top of the snow while I followed. I looked straight ahead to far-off cliffs piled with snowdrifts thirty to forty feet deep. We would head for them. They were the only way over these impassable peaks.

What I saw was like a hallucination. Just two days before, down in the mountain-walled valley, it had been a balmy 75 degrees. Up here, in the bitter cold, the sun shone with blinding clarity. The cold and the startling blue of the mountain sky could wake up an exhausted man.

We had chosen this route over some of the Rockies' tallest mountains and were headed for western Colorado and beyond. I looked at the mountaintops before us that were covered with millions of tons of snow and wished we could turn back.

The dirt path we had been climbing for the past two days had disappeared under a blanket of rocks and snow. With the trail gone, I doubted that we could find our way, but we had to try. We weren't prepared for cold weather. I had no long pants, we had one coat between us, and Barbara was wearing that. We used wool socks to protect our numb fingers and tied handkerchiefs across our wind-cut faces.

The driven snow blew against my unprotected legs, sting-

OPPOSITE: *We discovered an abandoned log cabin in New Mexico*

1

ing them red and raw. The wind slapped as though it were trying to push us back into the valley. It came at us, howling and mean, never ending its attack. We leaned our bodies forward and moved slowly as the flying snow hit our skin like a thousand burning needles. I wondered how many others had tried to cross these peaks, never to be heard of again.

After a quarter hour of climbing I began to fall through the snow. I put one foot forward, broke through the crust, and went down. The first time I sank, it felt like going down into quicksand. I couldn't get back up because if I pushed with my arms, they broke the crust, too, and I went even deeper. Barbara had to pull me out. I was amazed at how strong she was. I looked to see how far that wall was. What if I disappeared altogether? We kept on.

Sometimes with every step I'd sink into the crusted snow. Other times I'd make fifty yards. Barbara weighed just the right amount and only broke through once or twice. Anger did no good, my temper could do nothing with snowfields. After what seemed like a half day, we made it to the base of the peaks. Ahead was another wall of snow. If only we had an ice pick, we could tie ourselves together and I could pull us up. We could not wait; the sun was heating up the snow faster by the minute. The angle of this huge snowbank was such that I was afraid that it might cave in or break in half with us on it.

Yesterday, when walking near the ghost town of Capitol City, we had seen the signs of destruction leveled by an avalanche last winter. The snow had begun falling from the mountaintops and had flattened and disintegrated every tree, rock and living thing in its wide path. Large aspen trees were broken off by the thousands as if a half-mile-wide lawn mower had cut them down. They looked like giant toothpicks snapped in two. Rocks the size of cars were swept down with the avalanche, blocking the road below.

The power of the runaway snow was unimaginable to me. Could our weight trigger this almost vertical snowbank into sliding off the mountain? The winds cried louder, and every story of death by avalanche replayed itself. Two college students had been swept away while cross-country skiing near Crested Butte. They still had not found their bodies. A snowplow driver was caught in a tidal wave of snow and ice while plowing a stretch of highway near Ouray. Ouray was the next town we'd come to, if we got over this pass.

We started up. I knew if we could make the top, we'd see a view that would end all we'd ever seen. I sank in five straight steps. We kept going.

There was a deafening wail just twenty feet farther—we were cresting the top. As we stood on the summit, we saw an endless vista. Out there were Utah, California, Arizona, Idaho, the ocean. It seemed as though we could see all the way to the Pacific. To our right were peaks too high for even the elusive bull elk to scale: Uncompahgre, Wetterhorn, and a hundred others. The elevation of Engineer Mountain was 12,800 feet, the highest we'd ever been.

The extraordinary beauty of the view made us forget the wind. What force it exerted! What a humbling and dangerous concentration of power these mountains wielded! We could stop for only a moment. So far we had not started an avalanche.

Now that we had made it to the top, the road, which was more like a trail for the Abominable Snowman, was blown clear of snow. It was a blessing that we hadn't lost our way. But when we began our descent, the trail was soon covered with snow again. This time the snowfield sloped dangerously down, then fell off a cliff that dropped hundreds of feet to the Uncompahgre River. I asked Barbara if she wanted to hold on. She said no. At least she had mountain boots on. The track shoes I wore gave no traction on snow.

I led the way. The wind made talking impossible. Shouting, mouth to ear, was the only way to communicate. I looked back to see how Barbara was doing. She slipped and began sliding down the snowfield, almost as fast as a toboggan on ice. I screamed, "Dig your pack into the snow!" If she couldn't stop herself, she would slide all the way down the snow and off the cliff, falling hundreds of feet to her death on jagged rocks. She tried to dig her feet in. That just spun her around so that she was sliding headfirst. She desperately clawed with her hands. It made her roll like a runaway snowball. I shouted, "Dig your pack into the snow!" I knew she could not hear me.

This might be her end. We'd come so far. "DIG YOUR PACK INTO THE SNOW." Thirty feet before she ran out of snow, she dug the aluminum frame into the snow, just enough, and stopped.

She just lay there, stunned, for fifteen minutes. I lunged to go after her and slipped. I was sliding but stopped after fifty feet. She would have to make it back up on her own. She seemed to lie there a long time. Then, foot by foot, she dug one boot after the other into the snow, leaning forward. She made it back. We sat in the snow, breathing deep, knowing we'd almost lost one another.

I noticed a wide and red scrape mark on Barbara's face. A protruding rock must have cut her when she was falling. She looked so strong, so independent and confident of herself. After coming within feet of death, she was just sitting quietly, letting her body recover from the fall. It was almost impossible to remember the way Barbara was when we first began walking together from New Orleans, almost two years ago.

Barbara had changed in even more ways than the 2,000 miles we had walked. She'd come so far. And so had I. I had been walking across this country now for almost five years, and it had become a way of life. Sitting on top of these Rocky Mountains, I realized that I was so used to adventure that it took something dramatic to make me remember just how far I'd come, how much I'd changed.

I began my walk after graduating from a university in upper New York State, on October 15, 1973. Now it was the end of June 1978. I'd discovered more by walking across the country and living and working with all kinds of people than I would have dreamed possible. I guess that was because I'd known so little about what this country was all about. I'd also known little about myself.

After living with a mountain man named Homer on top of the Appalachians and working in a sawmill with a poor black family in North Carolina, I'd only begun. From North Carolina I'd walked to the "largest long-haired commune" in the world, called the Farm. I walked through Alabama. I'd expected a redneck war zone and discovered something shockingly opposite. I was totally amazed by Alabama and a rancher named M. C. Jenkins. Then I'd walked into New Orleans, after having come face-to-face with God in Mobile, Alabama. I settled down in the sultry, enchanting city of New Orleans and fell in love with a girl who looked like an angel. Her name was Barbara Jo Pennell and she thought she was in New Orleans to get her master's degree. After knowing her a month, I knew she was there to marry me, so we could walk to the Pacific together.

She had never seen a backpack in her life, never been or wanted to go camping. I'd never met a woman like her. She was so different from me in so many ways. I guess the best way for you to meet Barbara is for her to tell you herself.

Barbara

Most people say they feel like they know me. Peter likes to call me B.J., others call me Barb, and then some call me Barbara Jo. I am Barbara Jo Pennell Jenkins and you are meeting me for the first time. I want to tell you about myself, where I'm from, and my background.

Peter used to call me "country girl" and it would surprise me because I never considered myself one. He came from Greenwich, Connecticut, outside New York City, so my background seemed very countrified to him. I grew up in a small midwestern, almost southern, town in the foothills of the Ozark Mountains. Poplar Bluff, Missouri, was on the southern edge of the Show Me State, not far from the Arkansas border, and it was made up mostly of farmers and railroad people.

One of the biggest events of my childhood was the Sale Barn, a livestock auction and flea market held every Friday. Farmers came from miles around to dicker over the price of a hog, see who could tell the biggest hound-dog story, spit tobacco, and talk about how expensive everything was, the weather and crops.

When school was out for the summer, I would walk to the Sale Barn on Friday mornings. It was only about a mile from our house. One time I bought my mother a set of six glass saucers for twenty-five cents because she needed them in the kitchen. I had saved up the money. We lived on the other side of the tracks from the big houses. The Missouri Pacific Railroad switchyard was behind our house and we were so used to the noises of locomotives, revved-up engines and switching trains, banging into each other, that it was like background music. The only things that separated our house from the five lanes of railroads were our big garden and the outdoor toilet, a two-seater. We didn't have indoor plumbing until I was about ten years old.

Our small white frame house was located on South Eleventh Street. Granny and Grandad lived next door to us all of my childhood, so their house was as much home as my own. "Bar-bre-e-e-" Grandad would holler at me the same way he yelled at his hogs. He never did get my name right because he was hard-of-hearing and already an old man when I was born. He liked to grumble and fuss at Jimmy, my brother, about doing more work and less play, or at Vicky, my sister, for not helping more with the housework. He didn't scold me as much as his other grandchildren and I didn't find out why for many years. It was because I reminded him of his dear Mildred, his daughter who died a long time ago, when she was only eighteen.

The chicken yard was where Grandad spent most of his time, scratching around with his hens and one mean rooster, quarreling at the hens for not laying more. I remember his narrow, sky blue eyes, squinted from more than seventy years of tilling the earth in the bright sun. When he looked up and saw me coming home from school, hopping over the railroad tracks and dodging boxcars, he would stand motionless, his shoulders and back stooped, waiting for me. On his meager old-age pension of less then eighty dollars a month, he would slip me a dime for a "sodie."

Those farming roots went deep, from my granny and grandad down to my parents and then to me, Jimmy and Vicky. My parents were the first ones to have running water and gas heat inside their home. Granny and Grandad never knew what it was to turn a thermostat, only what it was to wake up to a cold house, chop wood, build a fire, shovel ashes, then throw them across the garden, where they helped replenish the soil. I remember sleeping with Granny in her giant feather bed, smothered in her homemade patch quilts. On cool fall mornings I remember hearing the meadowlarks sing me awake, while Granny fried bacon in the kitchen on her wood stove. She never had anything new or fancy, but inside her old gray house that leaned to one side, everything was shined and as neat as a dollhouse. She could make the best flaky blackberry cobblers, right out of the oven from her wood stove, that made even old-timers brag.

While Grandad quarreled at his hens, and Granny cooked and baked pies, my own parents were busy next door, working and struggling to raise a family and make ends meet. Everyone called my daddy Ernie. He owned Ernie's Motorway, a truck stop and gas station south of town, and worked as a mechanic ten to twelve hours a day. His thick, laboring hands were always as black as his hair, smudged with grit and car grease, and his uniform smelled of diesel fuel. Neither of my parents had much formal education, finishing only the eighth grade. Yet they were smart, well read, and full of country gumption. Although my parents did not get a high school education because they had to help work on their parents' farms, Mother and Daddy were determined that we children would get good educations.

Betty Jo, my mother, had bright red hair and a fiery temper to match. She was always in motion, spouting orders: "Barbara, set the table, stir the fried potatoes, get the clothes off the line, sweep the floor," etc. There was a lot of work to be done before Daddy got home and she liked to have everything ready. "It's no sin to be poor, but it is to be dirty or lazy," she would say to me over and over.

My cousins lived in big cities, in nicer homes, and had newer cars than we did. My family seemed much poorer than our relatives and I dreamed of having better and finer things in life, more education, more culture and more fun. My dreams were my parents' dreams, too, but I didn't know it for many years. Sometimes I despised the whining music, steel guitars and nasal singers that came over Poplar Bluff's one radio station because they wailed out the hard times and dreary tunes.

But one country ballad I loved was "On the Wings of a Snow White Dove," which I heard every morning of my childhood. Life was as hard as the rocky hills in this part of Missouri, but it was our family—Granny, Grandad, Vicky, Jimmy, Mother, Daddy—all of us working together, planting and plowing or hoeing in the bean patch, and the silent love between us that made my simple roots rewarding and wonderful memories.

I can still see my mother helping our neighbors on South Eleventh Street read their mail and pay their bills because the Lipscombs, Switzers and Larsens could not read or write. And Mother also had time for the strays. We called them hoboes. They would jump off the trains behind our house, work their way through the garden, and ask for food. Mother was proud to give them our leftover cornbread and beans and never sent anyone away hungry. I remember we would peek out at the hoboes from behind the smokehouse. My brother, Jimmy, would hide because he thought they were looking for him. It was one of his favorite pastimes to throw rocks at the open boxcars, hoping to hit a hobo.

Back in those days it was Uncle Lavelle who made us all happy. He was the preacher of the family and had got a college education during the Great Depression in the 1930's. That was a big accomplishment. He and Aunt Lillie would come down from St. Louis with their daughter, Velma Jean, and we would spend the holidays together. When we would all gather around Granny's old oak table for one of her wood stove meals, Uncle Lavelle would say the prettiest prayer. Before he could pray, Granny would scold Vicky and me as we shoved each other to get closer to the cobbler: "Hush up, younguns, so Lavelle can pray."

"Thank you for thy providence, Dear Lord. We are grateful for this bountiful supply of food and bless it to our bodies and we will be mindful to give you the praise and glory. Thou art all-powerful and merciful and we ask thy blessings in Jesus Christ's name, amen." He would rock back and forth on his heels, confident that God heard. "My, my. This looks wonderful," he would say.

Something drew me to Uncle Lavelle more than to anyone else in the family. He was the kind of man who kept quiet when other people screamed, fought and swore. He was the kind who studied the Bible and prayed instead of preaching hell and damnation and the kind who encouraged others all during the day. He lived a genuine faith. It was Uncle Lavelle's influence that would one day prompt me to study for a master's degree in religious education at the New Orleans Baptist Theological Seminary. And it was Uncle Lavelle's soft-spoken quotations from the Bible that would come back to me, through the years, over and over. "Trust in the Lord and lean not unto thine own understanding, and He shall direct thy paths."

It was here at the seminary in New Orleans that the pathway of my life took a new and unexpected turn. This was where I met Peter and fell in love. This was where Peter asked me to marry him, and I didn't know what to do because marrying Peter meant that I would have to leave the seminary and join him for the rest of the walk across America. Then, on a sunny, cold day in November 1975, I heard the piercing sermon at the Word of Faith Temple by Mom Beall. The sermon was called "Will You Go with This Man?" Out of all the millions of sermons from the Bible, and after praying for a sign all night in my dormitory the night before, I knew this was for me.

I knew I would go with Peter. I knew there would be a lot of dramatic changes in my life and a lot of unknowns, but I would trust God to guide me on the way.

Peter will be telling you most of the things that happened to us during our walk west, but every once in a while there will be people and adventures I want to tell you about in my own words and in my own way. So I will.

2

The J. Storm I

The seas had been extra-rough earlier in the evening. I was looking forward to a deep night's sleep, for when the Gulf was like this, the waves would crash against the four steel legs of our offshore oil rig and sway the rig back and forth, rocking like a cradle. When the twenty of us were not working our twelve-hour night shift, we would lounge around after dinner. But tonight was funny because most of the guys drifted off to their bunks early.

The oil rigger's life was lived half at sea and half free. Seven days on the rig, seven days on land. I had been working out here less than a week as galley hand and roustabout. I shared a room with Doug, the welder, and Jimmie, a galley hand. Doug was a thick-waisted, red-cheeked Texan from a small town near Houston. He didn't have that long, lean West Texas build that was right for the roping, rodeo kind of cowboy, but it didn't really mean much out here. A man needed all the muscle and bulk he could get. Jimmie was a short black guy, in his early thirties, from near Corpus Christi, and the first thing he said to me was: "Hey, man, call me Boots."

Tonight Boots must have been in a stupor over our wall-

Off-shore oil rig, the J. Storm I

paper because he was quieter than normal. Most of the other rooms on the rig had pine-stained simulated wood paneling from Sears. Our room was papered by a collage of female centerfolds.

Tonight Jimmie didn't talk and I pulled the sheet over my face, lulled and swayed in the arms of the sea. Before I knew it, I was dreaming. For some reason on nights like this I usually dreamed about happy childhood summers, my first bicycle, learning to swim on my dad's back, and throwing firecrackers at my sisters. My bunk swayed and swayed and swayed.

Someone must have finally turned off the lights because I remember uncovering my face and seeing total black. Deep in these steel caverns, night and day were the same. After twelve hours of the most demanding work, roughnecking, scrubbing floors, painting, lifting heavy equipment, and steaming dirty dishes, a gravelike sleep was the only way to get ready for the next day. But even in my sleep, I could still see the glare of the hot sun reflecting off the Gulf and feel the wind's resistance making extra work for our tired bodies.

Our rig, the J. Storm I, just kept rocking all of us. Back and forth, back and forth. Forward and backward.

"Wo-O-O-sh-sh . . . wo-O-O-sh-sh," said the Gulf in slow motion.

"FIRE!" someone screamed. Slow to come around, I figured I was having a nightmare.

"The rig's on fire. Peter, Doug, hurry! Been a blowout on the rig. The whole damn deck's on fire!" The shouting continued. The voices were beginning to sound familiar.

Still sluggish, I lifted my head in the darkness and heard people running up the metal stairs toward the open deck, one story above us. Where was Barbara? I reached for her, but my hand hit the wall hard. Where am I? I'm not home. I'm in the top bunk, on the rig.

"Hurry, Pete, there's a blowout. A big fire. Get up. You're gonna get your butt burnt if you don't."

My eyes popped wide open.

"A BLOWOUT."

This was what all offshore workers fear the most. Of course, they would never admit they were afraid of anything, but the truth was, they all feared it in the deepest and most secret way. Just two days ago the boss had given me a special lesson on blowouts.

"You ever see a blowout, boy?" Grady Cockerham asked.

"No, don't even know what one is," I answered.

"It's when thousands of pounds of gas and oil pressure, from thousands of feet down, builds up and blows out the top. You know what that means, boy?"

"No, what?" I was amazed at how close to death we always seemed to be.

"Can you imagine how much those thousands of feet of steel pipe must weigh? Think how much power it would take to blow it five thousand feet up through the earth and then up and out of the water. Tons and tons of pressure from free gas, oil, and salt water that could kill every one of us."

"You ever been on a rig when it blew out?" I asked.

"Where you born?" He sneered. Grady acted mean and hateful, but his face and eyes told a different story.

"How do we get off if there is a blowout?"

"There's a survival capsule hanging off the side; you must of seen it by now."

"Yeah, it's orange, right?" I'd noticed it right away. It hung like an enclosed cork, sixty feet above the Gulf, just like the rest of us.

"A lot of these guys will try to use it 'cause they know how many sharks and barracuda there are down below, but if I was you and still alive when it blows, I'd jump."

"J-u-u-mp?"

"With the explosion, and this small platform, and fire that could be raging, you just better run to the edge and jump. And pray on your way down."

"You think it could happen here, to us?"

"Listen, boy, it could happen anywhere, anytime. No one knows for sure what we're drillin' through." Grady didn't try to soften the reality of our offshore world. We looked at each other and then sat still a few moments while his words hung in the air over us.

All that Grady had said and more flashed before my mind as I lay ready to run and jump the sixty feet down into the Gulf. I wouldn't mess with the panic of trying to get into the survival capsule. Besides, I better let the older men with families use that thing. I reached under my pillow for Barbara's letters and lunged, really jumped, toward the floor.

My head and arms were the only things that went in the direction of the tiled floor. My feet and ankles were tied to the footboard. I was confused, still half asleep. The running up the stairs had stopped and no one was yelling to hurry up and get out of there. I knew all the other men were already off the rig. I yanked, pulled and fought at my legs. What are my legs doing tied? I pulled harder, ripping off the blanket and sheet.

Right at that moment the fluorescent light came on, and standing in the doorway were about ten men, all huddled in their stained overalls. They laughed so loud it echoed off the centerfold walls.

"What's goin' on?" I shouted, dizzy from hanging by my feet, looking up at the men, upside down. They kept laughing, louder and louder.

"There is a blowout, a fire," Red, the crane operator, said cutely. They were hollering for everyone else to wake up and come see the fire.

The boss man, Grady, had been standing in the background. He pushed his way through as they continued their hysteria, and without a smile he untied my feet, which had somehow been bound with torn sheets while I slept. When he finished, I landed in a heap on the foor and he handed me his strong right hand. He lifted me to my feet. I stood there in my underwear.

"You keep this up, Pete, and you'll be one of us."

Turning toward the door full of men, Grady told them to get back upstairs. He shut the door behind him, leaving me standing there under the air-conditioning duct with a frozen stare on my face.

It was 4:00 A.M. as I climbed back in my bunk to try to relax for an hour before normal wake-up time. The swaying rig did nothing for me now. All I could hear, repeating like a stuck record, was: "Fire, blowout, fire, blowout."

Since I couldn't sleep, I went out on the rig floor, which is like a deck through the middle of the rig, with the kitchen and the helicopter pad rising on one side and the drilling floor and the derrick rising on the other.

The morning Gulf breezes began to blow, and at times like this I could almost block out all the machine noises, the grinds of the drilling, and the lights for the night shift work. Staring out, I could see nothing but sea. I could understand why these dry-land Texans took to all of this. It was like living way out in the flats of West Texas on a ranch where your closest neighbor lived maybe ten miles down a rutted dirt road. The basic difference out here was that we couldn't visit the neighbors. It was just the twenty-nine of us.

I liked to dare the sun to sneak up before I saw it first. I scanned the horizon, not knowing exactly where it planned to make its appearance. The sun rises differently at sea from on land. Before it shows, it sends up a glow from behind the horizon. Sometimes the glow extends half the circumference of the sea because unlike on land, there's nothing to stop its spread. So you never can pinpoint just where it is going to come up.

The pink-orange light of this Gulf of Mexico morning brightened ever so slowly. It was as though God had His own dimmer switch and were waking this part of the earth gently.

Instead of the normal swells and wave action of most days, ten-foot-high translucent waves came rolling in from the east . . . one after the other, each trying to be more perfectly shaped than the last. I'd seen the sea do this before, but never had I seen with such clarity through the waves themselves. This morning they looked like thinly carved Oriental jade.

The sun was still low and the light made the waves glow. In the middle of one I saw something flash silver-gray.

Before I could see what it was, the arching wave went under the rig and so did whatever had been surfing. Then something laughed. I'd heard that laugh before, or thought I had. How could a laugh coming from the rolling waves sound familiar? Then I saw them—they were porpoises or dolphins, the humans of the sea, and they were laughing.

Another group of transparent waves came in, carrying along two more porpoises. They were surfing, playing, moving so sleek and efficient in these crashing waters. They didn't just swim the water; they owned it. As they passed under me, their continual clicky talk reverberated off the steel platform.

I saw them, but I didn't, couldn't believe it. They couldn't be this close to all these rigs. Inspiring sunsets were halfway expected. So was the danger of the man-crushing drill pipe. Even getting tied in bed. But surfing dolphins? I've been out at sea too long.

There was more. As the sun lifted up farther, shafts of

white light lit the high waves more clearly. From my million-dollar seat (actually the rig was worth closer to $25 million), I could see their every fleeting pass.

Then an entire school of porpoises surfaced. They had been driving food fish to the top of the water because now thousands of panicking silver fish broke the surface of the green waters. Whole schools of fish ejected from the waves. Out on the top of the waves they rocketed, swimming, now flying for their lives. The dolphins flew after them.

The fish they caught were big and some looked well over twenty pounds. I looked out to the east, to the south. There must have been a hundred of these awe-inspiring hunters. They were always smiling.

They surfed for about a half hour. Some were adolescents still being fed by their mothers or fathers. They'd surf within inches of each other on these morning waves, moving and shifting together as if they were one. When one of their parents had a foot-long chunk of silver food in its mouth, the youngster would literally flip out of the back of the wave. It would flip as if its job were to be sea jester: Do a trick and get a fish.

They all stuck around, surfing the perfect waves of morning, and eating all they could, and playing. Some were paired and from the way they swam so closely together, I thought maybe they were mates. Every movement was beyond grace, as they accelerated to get out of the wave before it smashed them into some unforgiving steel. They far exceeded anything human with their tranquil power.

The sun forced a squint to my eyes. When I was able to look again, the dolphins had disappeared. It would soon be time to get back to our living quarters for my next twelve-hour shift. I scanned the Gulf one last time. If only they would do one more wave, let me see them one last time. I looked to the east, nothing. I looked to the north, toward the bank, nothing. I couldn't see to the west, but when I looked to the south out toward the Gulf Stream, there they were, a curving line in and out of the water, just cruising away to somewhere.

All that day, from 6:00 A.M. to 6:00 P.M., I washed hundreds of unbreakable tan plastic dishes. All day, too, Slick or Zak, A.J. or Red would sneak up behind me and whisper, "Fire." Tomorrow was going-home day and everybody was in a messing-around mood. There was no end to what these guys could dream up.

My first shift was over; I'd made $400, most of which I would save toward the day Barbara and I would begin our walk together. It was still a long way off. We had months of training ahead of us. Someone yelled, "The crew boat's here!" It took time because we could unload only four guys at a time, while the crew boat bounced below the rig, sixty to seventy feet down. Red, our crane operator, whose red-haired arms were as big as some legs, had to lower an open basket to the deck and lift the guys up on a swinging cable. There had been many cases of men who quit the job because they would not even go near that basket. After my first ride I knew why. One slip from the crane operator or by my greasy hand and I would fall into the barracuda-filled water.

Going home, I was scrubbed clean but still had my working clothes on. I was proud of my jeans with their ground-in streaks of grease and rust from rubbing up against the railings. Every other member of the crew looked like a different person. Their faces were shaved as close as a clean mirror and reflected the glow of endless splashes of aftershave. They wore western-cut jeans, favorite cowboy hats and hand-tooled buckled belts with turquoise stars. No one could mistake them for anything but Texans.

We had spent seven days together and on the three-hour boat ride home there was little talking. We were all talked out. The riggers sat with their shiny lizard, shark or alligator skin boots propped up anywhere they could. I thought about seeing Barbara's soft face and they certainly thought about their women. We would land in Dulac, Louisiana, and they had a long bus ride back to Texas.

3

"Noo Awlins"
Running

Carefully I stepped off the still-rocking boat, hit the wooden dock and then the ground. My legs felt so good. I had no idea how tight and sore they'd become on our steel island. Seeing green leaves, dragonflies, dirt, cars, new faces made me feel alive and happy. I kind of pranced to the car.

Barbara was so anxious to see me she ran from the VW. "How was your week? Why has it taken so long to get in from the rig? I thought it would be only an hour ride. Are these the guys you work with?"

"Hold it a second." I smiled.

I wanted to hustle home, so we got the red VW into gear. We were south of Houma and about as far south as anybody could be in Louisiana. New Orleans was more than fifty miles north.

Highway 57 was shaded by live oaks that had probably sheltered their share of pirates. Every so often we'd have to stop as a silver drawbridge went up and shrimp boats idled by.

Downshifting into second gear, we came to another stop so two very round, black ladies could walk across the street to their favorite roadside fishing spot. They had on loose print dresses and carried homegrown bamboo poles, which were more than ten feet long. In a few short hours they'd have caught lunch and dinner.

"Barbara Jo." I spoke semiloud over the wind coming

18

in her window. "We have got to start some serious training while I'm home. What do you think, you want to start tomorrow?"

"Well, I was hoping that we could just relax. We haven't been married more than a few weeks, and well, do we have to start thinking about all that so soon?"

We had never really talked about just how much training we would need to get us across the West. I knew that it was going to be much harder than walking the territory east of the Mississippi. I thought that Barbara would let me work out a training program for us. Now I realized she didn't really want to think about it.

All through our swirling romance I had neglected to bring up the demands and dangers of this walk of mine. Maybe I had not been fair with her. I'd always told stories about the great times. But for every incredible experience there were lonely cold nights in a dark tent. For every Mary Elizabeth there were those who were suspicious of my backpacking lifestyle. For every owl flying in the moonlight there were mean hunting dogs that needed rocks to keep them away.

We drove along. Why couldn't I just let it go and forget about training? I couldn't. I felt a pressure about getting Barbara prepared because I knew what could happen if she weren't.

Standing under the shade of an umbrellalike mimosa tree, I stretched out my oil-rig-tightened muscles. I began running slowly, letting a sweat lightly coat my body. After a few hundred yards my stride was long. I was covering space, running smooth and fast enough so that I was leaving little sweat behind.

I ran past block after block of immaculately landscaped homes. I was almost back to the apartment, just one block off Gentilly Boulevard, when I realized that I'd been so absorbed in my own floating stride and rushes of movement that I had not paid attention to setting up a route. It seemed like such an effort to always translate everything from *me* to *us*. Before, it was only Cooper and I. To Cooper anything that I wanted to do was OK as long as I did not put any kind of leash on him. But Barbara had her own opinions.

I rounded the corner and stopped. I walked over to our door and saw Barbara sitting right by the air conditioner, reading her Bible. I jittered and high-stepped at the door, waiting for her like an excited horse that couldn't slow down.

"Hurry, Peter, close the door, quick. All the cold air is going to get out. Why don't you go into the bathroom and wash off. Can't you see how much you're sweating?... Come on, look, you're sweating all over the sofa."

I reached over toward her. I was overflowing with excitement as well as the quarts of sweat that soaked my hair, clothes, and leaked all over the living room. She backed away.

"Listen, I was so into running that I didn't have the time to measure out a route. It looks good, though, down through that black neighborhood toward Lake Pontchartrain. You want to get dressed and we'll run it together?"

She grasped her red leather-covered Bible tight and said, "Not right now. I'm right in the middle of reading this great stuff in Proverbs, Chapter Fourteen. . . . You want to hear this, listen!" She opened up to where her hand had been holding her place: "Every wise woman buildeth her house: but the foolish plucketh it down with her hands." She glanced quickly for my reaction and then said, "Peter, when do you think I will be able to build my house? I want our own house real bad."

I walked slowly toward the door, and gripping it, my hand slipped from the still-streaming sweat. "Enjoy your reading. I'm going back out running . . . be back later."

As soon as I hit the sidewalk straightaway, I sprinted. I ran till I groaned and my body hurt. I didn't really want to think about anything but figuring out how we were going to get into shape. So I ran down about three-quarters of a mile till I got to the golf course, then went right around the end of it another half mile. Then it was back by Southern University, headed away from the lake toward the river, the Mississippi. Everything in New Orleans seemed to be measured by its distance from the lake and from the river. From now on everything for Barbara and me would be measured between the river and the ocean: the Mississippi and the Pacific.

All in all the route was about four miles long. It could

never compare with the steep hills and dirt logging roads of
Mount California and my first training time in upper New York
State, but it would have to do. I felt so generous, giving her
only a four-mile route. It was all flat, side-walked and half as
long as the one Cooper and I had run.

When I got home this time, Barbara was lying by the
pool, reading the *Times-Picayune,* the city's newspaper.

The next morning was to be the start of our training. I
hoped that in two months Barbara would be running this four-
mile course nonstop. To begin, we would try walking one
block and running the next. I wanted to start early that morning
while it was still cool and build up to running in the heat of
the day.

Barbara put on some shorts and some new track shoes
called Tigers and an old sweat shirt from college. She watched
me to see how I was reacting and smiled self-consciously.

I looked over her body, judging her shape for the road.
Were her legs well built, not for a bathing suit or clogs but
for walking across America? How strong were her ankles?
Could they support a thirty-, maybe even forty-pound backpack? And what about her back and shoulders? Her arms and
neck?

My analytical stare seemed to make Barbara nervous.
"Well, let's get going. If we have to be out in this, I might as
well try to enjoy it."

"We can't just take off. I've got to teach you how to
warm up . . . to stretch some of those muscles that you've probably never used. Just try to do what I do. Don't bend hard and
please try not to bounce. . . . Just ease down . . . yeah, that's
right, honey. . . ."

She was bending at the waist, some of the muscles of
her long legs showing definition, some natural spring.

"Is this all right?" she said, sort of interested now.

"That's excellent. . . . Now let's try standing up, that's
right; now reach up to the tree branches. You'll never reach
them, but I want you to feel the muscles in your stomach, in
your arms, in your neck. Now bend a bit and you will feel the
muscles in your back. Can you feel it?"

"No, what do you mean? I'm reaching, aren't I?"

As she reached without pushing hard enough, I saw her in a new way. Her legs that I thought were wonderful in a skirt were plenty strong-looking. She didn't have those "preppy" bird legs, so thin with their veins showing. They were legs that reflected her pioneer-farmer heritage.

"Look, watch me, Barbara Jo," I asked. "When you reach towards the sky, begin slowly. Spread your hands and fingers wide; then begin to reach; push your hands and then your arms up. Yeah . . . Can you feel the muscles in your arms? Now stretch your stomach muscles. Can you feel them?"

"Yes, I can feel a pulling sensation right here under my rib cage."

"Now let's sit on the grass, and put your right leg out in front of you . . . like this. See, you straighten it out and point your toes out . . ."

"Like this," she said, getting it right. She was displaying a natural athletic grace I'd not seen before.

"Right. Without straining I want you to bend your back and try to touch your head to your knee. You should feel some long muscles in the back of your leg. Now you try it. Be careful, take it real easy. . . ."

At the angle I sat I could see her back. It was long and strong. As she tried to touch her chin to her knee, which she did with ease, she reached her angular arms toward her toes. Everything looked good with her body.

"Now what I want to try to do is get out on the sidewalk and just kind of run this first block. Then we will walk the next one, and then we will run the next one. Let's go. . . ." I had learned long ago on the track team how to get into an efficient ground-covering stride within, say, three strides. I took off, and with ten steps I was twice as far down the sidewalk as she was. She looked confused.

I stopped and waited for her to catch up. She did, but it seemed to take a long time. She alternated between keeping her head down and looking up.

"Why did you run off and leave me like that?" she said.

"Well, we are never going to do any good running if we don't really get after it. You have to learn to really stretch out your legs. This is not jogging. We would have to run too far for too long to get in the kind of shape that we need to be in. . . ." I found myself getting frustrated, just a bit.

"So," she said, "please teach me how to run like you were doing."

I reached over and put one of my arms around her. "What I'll do is begin slowly and you just take off with me. Then I will speed up and you can tell me when we are going fast enough."

I began slowly and no sooner had I gotten in the groove than she said that we were going fast enough.

I felt so high-strung with the pressure of having to get us both prepared to walk across the West that I just stopped. I had learned while living with my black family in North Carolina how to stop abruptly on the basketball court, and I did that. She kept going; in fact, she sped up as if to aggravate me even more. When she finally slowed down, she didn't look back; she kept walking, fast. A black man in his fifties was getting into his purple Mark V, and when I glanced in his direction, he smiled a knowing smile.

When I caught up with her, she wouldn't look at me and would not slow down. I thought, out of my frustration: At least I know that I can get her to walk across America mad.

"Why are you acting like this!" I shouted.

Barbara kept walking fast and wouldn't answer, as though I were supposed to know exactly what she was feeling. I didn't have any idea, so I asked again: "Why are you acting like this?"

"Because," she hissed with the cutting power of a thin-bladed stiletto, "I can't keep up with you and I don't like all this stretching out, running and training. Why do we have to torture ourselves now when we have all of Louisiana and Texas to break us in?"

We walked the rest of the way home at a pace that was slower than a New Orleans jazz funeral. There was no jazz in either of our steps. I couldn't stand it and Barbara did not say another word until she had showered and had dinner cooking on the stove.

4

Professor Grady

When I left to go back to the J. Storm I, many miles out in the Gulf, I was relieved that I had a job to do, a boss to answer to, and more thinking time. Maybe I could come up with a better way to handle this training. I knew that without it there would be no hope of our making it across the country.

As was always the case with the Gulf and its friend the sky, things had changed dramatically since I'd left them last week. The canvas of glaring blue, sun and glassy green was now fists of black-gray, lightning streaks and waves like mountains.

The first thing Zak, the cook, said to me was, "I hope you ain't ate much this morning 'cause if you did, you gonna give it to the Gulf."

Our crew boat was designed like a World War II PT boat. Everyone was there, except Grady, our boss. I was trying to stay seated next to Zak, who was reading. "Hey, Zak," I roared over the competing crashes of the seas, "how does Grady get out to the rig?"

"Him being the boss man, he's the only one of us hands that gets to take a helicopter."

"I wish I were on a helicopter right now, don't you?"

Grady

My stomach crept closer, in shades of purple and green, to spilling out all over everyone.

Zak shook his head. "You know how many of us offshore workers have got killed on them damn copters...hundreds, probably thousands. Me, I only take them things when they tell me I have to." His face turned green as the boat went head down and slipped to the right like it was going to flip. "Ol' Grady, he'll be Texas-lucky if he even makes it out to the rig today. When the wind's over thirty-five mph, they can't even land them things. You know how many helicopters been blowed off them landing pads? Into the Gulf?...Plenty."

That sea really threw our boat around, and everyone, including me, struggled to find a place to soften the lurches, swells and hull-splitting smashes. I tried lying down on some marine plywood seats. It didn't work. I tried standing up, in the middle of the straining boat, gripping with all I had to a

life jacket rack. The rack ripped off the wall. Sitting inside the
cabin with its overwhelming smells of sloshing diesel fuel,
sweating, nervous men and frantic cigarette smoke drove me
outside to the deck. Salt water washed over it. Blowing winds
forced themselves down my throat and fought back the urge
to throw up my stomach.

"Pete, you crazy damn Yankee," Red, our crane operator, who had the reputation as the meanest man in the oil
field, shouted, "get your ass inside this cabin.... You'll get
washed overboard!"

"I can't stand being inside that cabin, Red."

"You crazy airhead Yankee." Red slammed shut the steel
door as we fell from another wave, with his ever-present hand-
rolled cigarette looking like a toothpick in his drill-bit-sized
hand.

Thunderbolts lit up the sky like giant Kodak flashbulbs.
Every once in a while the bolts would seem to strike the rigs
we were passing. How the captain saw where we were going
I had no idea. I couldn't see over the next wave. Then Red's
warning came true. I shifted my grip and one of the waves
that we were trying to get over instead came over the side and
hit me like a plate of glass...UHNN! I was knocked on my
back. It pushed me back and I was caught up to my neck in
a river on the back deck.

I guess ol' Red had been watching me because his crane-
strong arm reached forward. He grabbed me, all 185 pounds,
lifted me up and out of the water, and threw me through the
doors. I landed in the brightly lit cabin. The air was knocked
from my lungs. I felt I had nothing left inside me.

To these guys all danger, all life-threatening experiences
seemed so casual. They stayed relaxed, no one asking me why
I was so wet.

Red, in his faded jeans and water-buffalo-skin cowboy
boots, now soaked, sat there still holding his drenched cigarette. "Pete, I don't know about you, son...you still got a
long ways before you become one of us, boy. From now on,
when I tawk to you, Yankee, you better open your ears. If you
don't, you may find your ass gettin' fired."

To change the subject, I asked Richard, our motorman,

"How far we got to go before we get there?"

He never answered. He rushed off to the tiny bathroom.

In between splashes on the small round windows I saw the towering legs of the J. Storm I. The boat's diesel engines slowed to an idle. The waves punched us back. The captain, a young black-bearded Cajun who looked like the descendant of a pirate, shoved the control lever into fast forward and we stood still. How could they ever get us off this boat's deck up seventy feet to the rig's floor? Going up in that small basket was bad enough in nice glass-calm weather. We all had seen the barracudas loafing around our rig. How would the crane operator get us off this lurching boat, through winds, and onto the swaying rig?

I guess I should have known that the crew up there was ready to leave. They had been at work in these storms all week. Their only thoughts were of cold beers, their women and home. They would get us off the boat or have to stay another week.

The crane operator dropped the circular basket onto the deck of our crew boat. Four men threw their luggage into the middle of the basket, balanced themselves on the outer edge of the saucerlike bottom of the basket and held onto the nylon ropes. The basket snapped in the wind as the crane operator pulled them up, slowly, higher and higher into the air until they reached the rig, some seventy feet up. I gained a lot of respect for those operators' fantastic skill, especially when my life depended on it.

It was a few hours before the other crew was all gone. I was put to work making salad enough for thirty men. There was a door right by where I washed the countless dishes and Red came through it. The wind followed him. It blew away our only newspaper, last week's *Star*.

Red held his hands carefully cupped. What kind of craziness is he up to now? I wondered. He sat down and told me, ordered me, to get him a cup. That meant the eye-electrifying coffee we all drank. It was as strong as a drug.

He opened his mean hands slowly, and inside them were what looked like some feathers . . . yellowish, blue-green. Then there was an excited buzzlike chirp, and huddled together, still wet, were two small songbirds dwarfed inside his opened fists.

"You see these birds, Pete. They're golden-winged warblers. They got blowed out here by them damn winds. I found them hiding in one of the pipes. Always some kind of birds get blowed out to sea in these rough storms." His work-battered face lit up gently. "I've found hummingbirds, arctic terns, even a red-headed woodpecker on rigs over the years during storms." Red abruptly got up and left the room.

"Pete," Zak called, "come on and get after it, son. I need that salad."

Tossing all that lettuce, I asked Zak, "What's Red going to do with those birds?"

"Oh, he'll make them a warm place down in his rooms, keep them fed with warm milk and stuff, and if they ain't too weak, he'll bring them back with us on the boat next week. You know, I've seen a time or two when he gave a bird to one of the helicopter pilots to bring back to the shore."

After the salad was made, I began making Kool-Aid for forty, then coffee for thirty. Our kitchen was being rocked by the Gulf, and it felt as if I were working on a rocking chair or a giant porch swing. There were two long plywood tables built to withstand these men . . . men to whom hard, highly dangerous work seemed a requirement, even a necessity. Sitting in the middle of the front table was an aluminum hard hat. To leave anything lying around was grounds for serious trouble, much more serious than any mother's temper. These guys wanted everything neat, so that there would be less to get uptight about.

There was something special about this hard hat. As I looked closer, I saw that it had been intricately carved with Persian designs. A scene had been carved of the J. Storm I, with huge, carefully etched waves, sharks, porpoises, work boats, helicopters, workers, and cranes. Whose is this? I wondered as I filled up all the sugar bowls.

When I finished filling the milk machines, Grady walked in, his normally slick-combed hair windblown. He had just come in from the helicopter and right after him came the red-headed pilot, a Georgia farm boy and Vietnam vet.

"Pete, get me a cup of that horrendous coffee Zak makes, will ya, please?" This must be the first part of the week, I knew. Grady *asked* me to do something and said "please."

Zak took in Grady's compliment, leaning over huge cast-iron skillets filled with pork chops, and said, "Glad you made it, boss. How was your week on the bank?"

Grady lived in what seemed like an unlikely place to me, sixty miles north of Dallas, in Bonham, Texas. To get home every week, he had at least 600 miles.

Grady didn't answer; he just drank his coffee, real slow. He was the kind of man who thought about things and events and people for days, weeks, months till he figured out whatever it was he wanted to figure.

Everyone on the J. Storm I respected him, although many kept a respectful distance. Especially those who didn't want Grady's probing shrewdness coming too close. I knew he'd been studying my every action with his undistractable face that had studied its way from a teenage roughneck to tool pusher of a multimillion-dollar rig. In essence, we were a separate country on our movable steel island and he was king. It didn't really bother me because although Grady tried to hide it, he had eyes that showed that friendship was possible, if earned. Grady didn't believe in anyone getting anything free. "Everything you get in life, son, it's got a price. The more you get, the more the price."

While I was still filling up the milk machines with wax-coated boxes filled with plastic bags of cold milk, Grady spoke. The pilot was sitting back in his chair, planning to spend the night. The storm wailed outside. "Pete, you know, I've been thinkin' about you all week."

"What for?" I asked. He seemed so serious and I knew that seriousness was not allowed out here except in blowouts, family tragedies and hurricanes.

"Do you know how we get the oil and gas out of the ground?" He stared, still serious.

"To be honest with you, Grady, no . . ."

His eyes squinted down on me, as if he were about to draw his gun and the sun was too bright. "That's why I been thinkin' 'bout you all week, boy. You're ignorant."

*Allen just gaffed this
medium-sized ling*

His eyes cooled a bit, to my relief. "You tell us you're walkin' across America, tryin' to understand this country of ours, right?"

"Yeah, that's what I said."

"In my figurin' I decided that it's 'bout time you understand what goes on in findin' oil and gas. Do you know that we use more oil and gas than Russia, England, Japan and West Germany combined?"

"No, I had no idea."

"Well, you're going to get an idea, as good a one as I can give you," Grady said as he reached down, lifted one of his small clothes bags onto the scrubbed shiny table, and pulled out two books.

Zak was leaning over the serving window, watching, letting the other galley hand, G. L. Countryman, tend to the pork chops. There were three roustabouts and their boss, Allen, a stubby-built redhead, standing in the doorway. Allen, who was no taller than some of the five-and-a-half-foot fish they caught out here, prided himself in being able to break any young smart #!*#!. He was at least forty and most of the guys that worked for him were in their twenties. He didn't care who they sent 'im: cowboy, farm boy, hippie, black, Cajun. Give ol' Allen a week and he'd have 'em broke or fire 'em. . . . Just like breakin' a mule, 'cept mules took longer. "You can't fire a mule!"

"Now I want to ask you one more question," the boss man said. Everyone stood, rarely silent, loving every minute of this.

"Pete, do you know what these terms mean in relation to the exploration, discovery and completion of an oil or gas well?" Even Grady was now smiling, if only out of the left side of his mouth.

"Come on, Grady," I pleaded, "don't make me look like a fool in front of all the guys." I spoke softly enough, hoping they would not hear me.

"Go ahead, Grady." Allen sneered through the stubble of his beard, red and scruffy. "He's a typical know-it-all, rich boy from up North."

Our tiny offshore oil rig was in a mean mood and so early in the week. There was absolutely no escaping whatever these oil field men wanted to do to me.

Grady spoke up. "Look, this boy's tryin' to be one of us. He's workin' here like all the rest of us and doin' his job and takin' all we give 'im. He wants to find out just how we get the oil out. . . . *Get back to work,* NOW!"

They all left, and Zak, too, went back to cooking. It was just me, Grady and the helicopter pilot. Grady got back to his question. "Now one more time . . . I want you to tell me what these words mean in relation to the exploration, discovery and completion of an oil and or gas well?" It always amazed me how Grady could switch back and forth from the glazed-look country boy to brilliant-minded. "Zak, give me your pen . . . I want him to write these down. . . ." I wrote them on an empty box of Sugar Frosted Flakes. "OK, you're ready. The words are: seismograph, long string . . . bit record . . . barite . . .

Schlumberger...workover...kelly cock...fishing tools...
Christmas tree and mud." He had written them down on a small
pad and would glance down every so often.

"Wait a minute, Grady...how do you spell Schlumberger?"

"By the end of the week, you better know what those
words mean and what order they come in, you hear me?" Grady
said.

I put the list in my back pocket. I guesed I'd have to
read those books.

Our first day back passed with no more confrontations.
When Grady wanted someone left alone by the guys, they
obeyed. Day 2 was time for my first test. I awoke earlier than
five. My subconscious kept replaying all those words—seismograph, barite...seismograph...fishing tools...fishing
tools...workover. At least I understood now what a seismograph was and what it did. Since I couldn't sleep, I went
up on the rig floor. I'd been rocked to sleep that night by the
Gulf, but that rocking had stopped sometime in the middle of
the night.

When I got up into the salt air, it was enclosing everything. The Gulf, lit like candlelight, was as dead as Plexiglas.

As I sat dangling my legs, waiting for the occasional
breeze, I thought about Barbara. I knew she would still be
asleep back in New Orleans. My mind drifted back to the
inspired times of the walk. How much I enjoyed being alone,
waking when I wanted, walking at whatever pace I wanted,
stopping and working when I wanted. Swimming where I
wanted, getting interested in the things that I was attracted to.
Never being slowed down or interfered with, or if I was interfered with, I could always leave. Our first attempts at training had not worked out well. She didn't seem to want to go
at any pace and seemed to disdain sweating and hard physical
work, everything that was part of getting across the West.
Voices of warning and advice from friends, family and others
came back in full sentences. Everyone seemed to have an
opinion about the walk, and only a few of them agreed with
me and thought that we should continue the walk together.

Sitting on the rig alone, I now had to remember that my life, my search now included Barbara. My thoughts were disrupted by the screeching of steel cable that sounded ready to snap. The men were pulling out their last stand of drill pipe and it banged against the side of the hole as it came out. It was ninety feet long. A.J., the night shift driller, started down the bright yellow steel stairs for breakfast. I was late! I jumped up and ran to the galley. Being late for a shift was cause to get fired. This rig reminded me of an orbiting space station because every inch of horizontal and vertical space was used for some kind of machine, motor, tool, light or storage tank. It left just the bare minimum for its men to do their work.

Grady was sitting in his usual seat, his forty-four-year-old body packed in strong over six feet of squint-eyed Texan. "Pete, come over here. . . . It's test time."

"Test time, what do you mean, Grady?" I sat down.

"What is a seismograph, boy?" He couldn't tell if I was for real or not. . . .

"Never heard of that word before, Grady. Did you know that I had some strange dreams last night?"

"Pete, I ain't gonna mess with you, this morning or anytime. . . . Now tell me what it is, NOW."

"I don't know what you're talking about, really, boss," I said.

Grady stood up slowly and started toward me. By now the whole night shift drilling crew was inside, lined up getting their horse-sized breakfast.

"Sit down, Grady. Now can't you take a joke from a 'dumb' Yankee?" The whole crew looked at each other, looked at Grady, who smiled slightly, and laughed.

"A seismograph," I said, "is a device for detecting vibrations in the earth. Did you know that's how they find out what kind of oil or gas strata is down deep in the earth? . . . On land they bore shallow holes and discharge explosives. The vibrations that come back to the seismograph, they go through the earth and bounce back, give the geologists an idea of that particular section of the earth. If it looks a certain way, then there might be oil down there. . . ."

The crew, now sitting all around me, dropped their hungry forks in unison and started clapping.

"And furthermore, Mr. Cockerham"—that was Grady's last name—"in my required reading I found out some more. When Jed Clampett of *The Beverly Hillbillies* shot into the ground hunting and found all that oil, he didn't have a seismograph; he was just a lucky country boy!"

"Very good, Mr. Jenkins," Grady said while he lifted a sausage to his mouth.

"And I also learned that they don't set off explosives out at sea when they explore. These boats I've been seeing going around in circles all day—they aren't drunk Panamanian captains in banana boats; they are seismic boats making surveys. Those devices pick up the returning energy waves and record them. It makes a picture that can tell all about what's down there. The only way to find out what is really down there, though, is to send one of our rigs to drill test holes and see for sure."

Shift change was the busiest time for us working in the kitchen. I was back washing dishes when I remembered one of the things that I'd learned reading. . . . I figured I'd tell Grady.

"Grady." I finally had to shout to interrupt all the talk. They were mostly talking about how great the fishing was going to be today after its being so stormy for the past days. "You want to know something I learned?" Grady didn't look up from a pile of eggs. "You know I can barely believe that I was this stupid."

"I can," Grady said with his mouth full.

"You know, I always thought that the oil was in a big pool, like a cave, all black and smelly, somewhere down there." There had been someone walking down the narrow dark hall when I had begun talking and he had stopped before he'd come into view, listening.

"Well, that's how it is, Pete," Grady said.

"Did you know, of course you do, that the oil and gas are suspended in microscopic spaces between the stone that they are in? How could they ever get that stuff out?"

Before my question was answered, stout Allen stepped

from behind the door, where he'd been standing, listening. If he had come in, I probably would not have admitted my ignorance.

His face was still puffy from sleep. How could anyone be so mean, so intense right after waking up? He charged toward me and stood just a foot from my face and turned me from the sink and made me face him. He hadn't brushed his teeth or combed his sun-blond thick red hair.

"You #!*# hippie, Yankee, college boy... you're just like everyone of them #!#*! up North and in Washington that wants to take over the oil fields. You don't know your #!*#!* lame brain from a piece of melted Jell-O. You people put us down while we work our butts off, trying to keep you driving all them big foreign cars and keeping your kids in private schools." He was so mad I felt I was about to become the punching bag for all his years of frustrations. He held his sunburned fists at his sides, but they were clenched and trembling.

"Grady," Allen pleaded, "just let me sink my fist in his face... just once... I'll do it for all of us who would like to kick a fool Yankee ass. Just once... I'll break his damn jaw."

"No," Grady said in a voice that seemed too quiet.

"Come on, Grady, just one punch. He's not the type to squeal." Allen was closer now and held one fist, his right one, in my face. It had white scars on it and had obviously been smashed into a lot of faces.

"Allen, leave him alone. Now get your breakfast. I told you I'm going to teach him what he needs to know." Again Grady's voice seemed not firm enough.

Allen didn't move. Grady had worked with Allen a long time and knew him. That was his job to know, after much testing, what his men could and could not take. "Allen, I've worked with you a long time.... You touch him and there will be a helicopter out here in an hour to take you home. There will never be a fight on any J. Storm rig... MOVE!"

The short bull-necked Allen moved, his steps sullen, shuffling over to dish out a bowl of oatmeal. With a very large pocket knife he sliced three bananas on top of it.

5

Hammerhead

Our welder came through the side door. He was breathless. All he could say was: "There's a hammerhead. It's the biggest shark I ever seen. . . . It's right down there . . . Hell, the thang's got to be over eight feet long."

Zak looked over at Grady. "I told you there'd be some good fishin' today, didn't I?"

Doug, who was new at working offshore, ran back outside. Grady and Zak finished what they were doing and strolled out. As they left, they both motioned for me to come with them. "Do you good to see one of these monsters," Zak said.

By now all the crew who didn't absolutely have to be working were leaning on the railing on the west side of the rig. The ocean was in a gentle mood, so deep and clear you could see almost to the bottom.

Doug, trying to restrain his excitement, spoke, "Where did that thang go? . . . I mean it, Grady, I saw this huge shark down there. Looked like it was layin' over on its side. It had a weird-lookin' head like an anvil . . . I ain't seein' things, am I?"

"Who knows, boy? We've had guys out here, being alone on the rig without no drink, no family, cramped up like this. It goes to their head. . . . They start seein' things—"

"*There* it is," I said. At first glance it looked like a small gray submarine. It swam slowly, as though it were bored. All that moved was its tail in wavy, tranquilized motions. The closer it got to the surface, the more detail we could see on its long, sleek body.

Grady and Zak conferred for a minute. Zak spoke up. "Pete, that's one of the biggest sharks we've seen. You want to try and catch it? You brought a pole with you this shift, didn't you?"

"Yeah, I bought what they called a deep-sea rod. . . . Bought some big hooks, too." Maybe now I was going to get my chance to do my first deep-sea fishing. The biggest fish I'd ever caught was a three-pound large-mouth bass.

"Well, get your gear, boy." Grady smiled. "You hurry up and we might catch this ol' shark."

I ran down into our sleeping quarters and got all my gear out of the closet. Back on the deck I put the biggest hook I had on the swivel.

"What'll I use for bait?" I asked. The shark was still just lazing around, letting his battleship gray fin break the blue waters.

"Look down by that pipe. I put a couple of eight-pound bluefish down there this morning. I was going to use them for cut bait. . . . Grady, give me your knife." Zak cut the fish in half, four pounds of bait! That was bigger than the biggest fish I'd ever caught. "Now put your hook through the back . . . yeah, like that."

Zak looked over to Grady and he nodded his approval. There was an entire school of huge spadefish. They looked like five-pound versions of the angelfish I used to have in a fish tank, just flashing their flat spade-shaped bodies toward the sun. Now they must have been nervous because they were in the shape of a fish tornado, countless thousands of them. They twirled around and around, swirling, reflecting the sun in slashes of silver. It was a thing of profound beauty till the hammerhead attacked them. It tore into those fish and turned the water red.

"Now cast the bait down there on the outside of where the shark's feeding. . . . Here, let me do it," Zak said as I fumbled nervously.

Zak cast the bait perfectly. It struck the water with a slap. After all, we were seventy feet higher than the water. I was glad we were. The shark continued tearing apart fish.

"Now pull that thing through the water. . . . Make noise with it. Lift it out of the water. . . . That's it. . . . Now drop it back in. Them big sharks, they're attracted to noise."

The shark emerged from the midst of the bloodied water. It still had fish in its teeth and it shook its head violently. It would circle the bluefish bait like a big cat, would dart toward it, then slow down and keep circling.

Other sharks were now tearing at the school of spadefish. They weren't half as big and not hammerheads. Our hammerhead went under and after several minutes Grady said it had left. I didn't want to believe that. I was tensed and ready to set a hook in a shark. I waited another minute and it reappeared. It went right for the bait that I was tugging and slapping in the water. Right at the last second it stopped, seemed to sniff the thing and turned back around; then it made another dash and grabbed the chunk of bait. It slowed almost immediately.

"Now, Pete . . . keep your cool, boy. This is when it gets hairy. . . . Just let it mouth the thang for a bit; then set that hook like you never set a hook before. That's one horse of a shark. OK, do it, Pete. Set that hook, PULL!"

I pulled and set that hook. It pulled and I was headed over the railing. Zak grabbed my belt from behind. "Pete, don't go swimmin' right now, OK!"

When the shark took off, it was like holding onto a rodeo bull with a shoestring. I tried to stop it from taking me, the rod, Zak and whatever else into the Gulf. It was headed for Mexico. My pole bent in half; then some of the chromed eyes that guided the 100-pound test line popped off.

"What'll I do now? It feels like the whole pole's going to break. . . . *Come on,* Zak . . . my arms are going to break. . . ."

"Just do the best you can, Pete. You can't be an offshore oil rig hand and not know how to handle a decent-sized fish. Now sock it to 'em."

"OK." I strained as sweat from exertion and fear streamed down my face. I heaved at the pole, pulled and grunted. The line began singing through the water, back and forth. Then it went down.

I tried to stop it from going down because Grady yelled, "Pete, now's your last chance. Stop it or it's gonna get tangled down under in the legs of the rig. *Pull* with all you got. . . . There it goes." I pulled like they said and there went my pole. It broke in half, my line snapped, and I fell backwards.

"Now, if I ain't mistaken, that thang's comin' back. Doug, go get that hook you welded. A.J., get me that old cable you got downstairs. We gonna show Pete how to get one of these monsters."

Doug had a hook almost as thick as an umbrella handle he'd made in the welding shop, its point shiny from all the polishing on the grinder. A.J. had steel cable as thick as my pinkie, about 200 feet of the stuff.

"Grady, why would that shark ever come back? It's got my hook in it!" I couldn't believe anything that large lived under me.

"That hook's nothin' to that shark. It's like a toothpick. I seen one of them things shot six times and never slow down."

Grady was out of idle and into passing gear. The thrill of the hunt was exciting him. "Doug, quick get me some of those leather welding gloves."

The boss man, beads of sweat appearing on his nose, squeezed the gloves on his big, hairy hands. With an intense deliberation, he pried each finger deep into its rough leather compartment. Then Grady squeezed his hands to a fist. He repeated this several times till he was satisfied with the fit. He rolled up the sleeves even further on his dark green work shirt, his white biceps in dramatic contrast to his Indian-tan forearms.

Before Grady threw the line over the side, the shark returned. The other sharks were gone and the spadefish tornado was back to its hypnotic swirling. How different a world it was down there! The shark swam to the south fifty feet, then back. Back and forth, so slow and patient and controlled. My measly hook and half of a bluefish had been only a tickle in its white throat.

When Grady threw his bait to the ugly king, it hit the water with a large thud, and the sun-rotted fish split in half and fell off. A small five-foot shark darted past the hammerhead, took the bluefish, and was gone. The hammerhead looked at the hook and went under. Grady dragged the heavy cable back up on deck and rebaited it with our last fish. He let it down slowly this time, eased it into the water, and let it sink out of sight. When it was far into the water, there came a hit like an electric jolt. It jerked Grady forward. I tried to reach out and help him. He scowled at me and whispered, "Get your hands off me. I'm gonna get this thang." His Texas temper was up, strong and vengeful.

He pulled easy on the cable, as if he were coaxing, and soon the dull silver bait came into view. Just below it was the shark, surfacing like a slow-motion rocket, twisting, turning, trying to get the big bait into its mouth. Grady sped up every time it came close. He wanted to play out this confrontation so all his men could see. Nothing threatened or challenged Grady around the J. Storm I.

When the bait rose to the surface, the hammerhead showed signs of frustration. Grady held the bait two or three feet out of the water while the shark would lunge upward, then belly-flop back in, twisting, with its mouth open. Its jaws looked disjointed, they opened so far.

Grady was just playing with it, knowing now that he would hook it but hoping to tire it out some. He also knew that once the shark was hooked, the real fight would begin. After five minutes of playing with the shark, Grady let the bait down and it disappeared instantly. It was hooked!

At first the shark continued to swim casually at the surface, just grooving around, rolling over on its side and grabbing chunks of spadefish. Its actions lulled all of us into relaxing. Not Grady . . . he kept jerking up on the hook, making sure the thing was hooked good. Every time he'd pull with all the force his 200-plus body could manage, the shark would thrash a little. Without warning the shark dove down.

The cable started disappearing from its coil. Grady had tied the end onto a support beam, eighteen inches wide, and just let it go. . . . "Everyone, get the hell out of the way of that cable! That gets wrapped around your leg and you're in the Gulf with that shark." He had said earlier that he had once tied a cable onto the railing when they had caught a manta ray, fifteen feet across, and it had popped a weld and broken the railing. That ray must have weighed over 1,000 pounds, he'd said.

When the cable was all pulled into the depths and stretched so tight it quivered, Grady clenched his gloved fist again. He kept doing it till he worked up another sweat and gripped, very carefully, the cable. The shark was darting frantically back and forth through the water—*wssh,* the cable would speed to the right, *wssh,* it would go straight out and away from the rig, and *wssh,* it would come back. . . .

"Grady," I blurted out, "what you going to do? That thing's going to get away. Aren't you going to bring him in?"

"Think I'll let you wear 'im down, Pete," Grady said, handing me the gloves.

"Come on, Pete." A.J. smiled. "You're big enough, just muscle 'im up to the surface."

I grabbed the cable; it had stopped singing through the water and everything seemed still. I started pulling, fast. It came up so easy, as if the shark had gotten away. I kept on, and more and more cable began coming out of the water and onto the deck. "Grady, the shark, it's gone," I said, the sweat evaporating from a strong west wind that was picking up.

"Well, just keep pulling, Pete. We got to get that cable of A.J.'s back anyhow . . . probably spit the hook out."

Grady turned toward Doug and reprimanded him. "Damn it, Doug, don't you know how to sharpen a hook?"

I turned to look at Doug, to frown at his ignorance. After all, it was my chance to have tangled with one of the biggest fishes in the . . . The cable thrust out of my hands, the leather on the gloves was smoking, and the cable whirred back into the Gulf! Boots, my roommate, had been standing on a piece of the cable and was thrown to the deck, swearing in soul talk. The cable went back into the water with such speed and force that it left a groove in the bottom of the tubular metal railings.

The shark had fooled me and Grady laughed. He had known it was there all along. "Pete, you've got to pay attention. If that thang had run in a different way, it could have caught your arm in the cable and broke it. Maybe ripped it off." I was awakened, every muscle tensed, my brain was stuck on "on" and my eyes were not distractable.

"Doug, give me your gloves," Zak commanded. "Pete, you and me are going to pull this thing in. We ain't got time to mess around. We got lunch to cook; these boys got oil to drill." So we both pulled, and for a bit the hammerhead would come along; then it would get mad and go to running down, in circles and everything else it could think of. It was hooked and we knew it and so did the shark. Pulling that shark was like trying to stop a pickup truck. My muscles in my arms got shaky; my stomach strained. Then it would give up and we'd make some headway. Without warning, it would charge straight down. The stiffening Gulf breezes camouflaged the sapping strength of the sun.

"I reckon we'd better take a break, Pete. Here, give me the cable. I'll just tie ol' hammerhead to the railing awhile, let him wear himself down. Let's go inside where it's air-conditioned and get some food ready for the men."

We cooked a lunch of the finest chicken south of the Mason-Dixon line. There were plates filled with smoked Cajun sausage with red beans and rice, cornbread and sweet-tasting coleslaw, and rivers of milk, coffee and orange juice. After washing the dishes in oil-rig-record time, I rushed back out to the center deck. The cable was still there and moving in slow circles. I leaned over the railing, trying to see the shark among the other large fish swimming around. Then a hand grabbed me from behind. It was Zak.

"Pete, let's get this over with. . . . We got to pull this cable up till that shark's head sticks out of the water. The shark's got to keep swimmin' to keep oxygen flowin' through them lungs. That's the only way we're gonna get that big thang up here."

"Up here?" I asked. "There's no way we can pull that monster up all that way from the Gulf. It's over sixty feet."

"Oh, keep forgettin'," Zak said as he slipped the gloves on. "You ain't never caught one of these bafore. We use that crane over there. That thang's over ten feet long. We don't just catch these thangs for fun, Pete. We get it up here and the men get to take home all the meat they could ever want. You ever skin a shark?"

"No, never have, Zak."

So we pulled the conquered hammerhead up to the surface. The cable slipped three times when it made unexpectedly powerful surges. Anything with as much power as this shark did exactly what it pleased in the oceans. I couldn't even bring myself to think what it might do to my body if it would ever get a hold on me.

Zak must have been reading my mind because he said, "You better be more careful than ever bafore when we get this thang up here. Even when it's almost dead, just by reflex it might bite your leg in two."

About then Grady appeared. He had such a wonderful sense of timing. "Where's Red?" he said, his blood circulating hard. "I need that basket hooked up to that crane."

"Grady, don't you do it. Send Allen or one of them down there." Zak was pleading.

"Got to, Zak . . . Pete needs to learn the right way. Before he leaves us, he'll be doin' this, too."

Doing what? I thought. What is he having the basket hooked onto the crane for? We only used that to come on and off the rig. But Red, our crane operator, started up the diesel engines of the crane with a black blast of smoke as a few of the roustabouts hooked up the basket. Grady got in and gestured with a few fingers to Red. Good Lord, Grady was getting lowered down to that shark! It was far from dead! It was still thrashing like a tropical storm hitting the coast!

What I hadn't seen was that they had also hooked another cable that had a loop in it like a steel lasso. When Red lowered him to about three feet above the water, Grady motioned to stop. Red operated that thing with the sensitivity of a surgeon. Then Grady motioned for a bunch of us to grab the cable and pull the shark out of the water. When we looked down at Grady, he looked less than half the size of the hammerhead. "It must be over twelve feet long," Zak muttered, his face turning as white as his cook's whites. And Grady was a *big* man.

The farther out of the water we pulled it, the crazier it went. All its frantic attempts to escape had attracted a ring of barracudas. They were probably four feet long, but they looked like nothing more than a dotted line surrounding the shark and Grady. They would have loved nothing more than to have

Grady fall in. All he had holding him in the basket was his left hand, which held white-knuckled onto the rope sides.

When we finally got the shark out of the water enough, Grady touched its side with a long gaff, which didn't look long enough. The hammerhead doubled up and and tried to lift its head and slashed rows of teeth toward the basket. It didn't miss by much. Grady swung back and forth as the barracudas closed in, making vicious attacks at the shark's side. Grady got the steel lasso around the hammerhead's powerful tail.

Grady screamed, "Now let go of the cable and let it fall into the water." We did, although I thought he was nuts. He motioned to Red to lift, and up came Grady and the shark. The diesel roared and jerked. The shark never quit its frenzied fighting even when it was lowered onto the dry steel deck. In fact, the second it hit the deck it went after three of the guys that were standing closest to it, slithering like the hugest, ugliest snake.

"Who wants this thang?" Grady asked, every success an understatement.

Boots, my roommate, said he did. It took him all that night to get it cut and wrapped and in our walk-in freezer. He brought home over 100 pounds of shark fillets and steaks that week. All the unwanted shark he threw over the side. It drew sharks and barracudas and schools of bluefish and other kinds of fish. They all stayed around for a couple of incredible days. At dinner that night Zak said to me, "I have seen more fish life and drama out here in the years I been working all over this beautiful Gulf than I could ever see in the Jacques Cousteau movies. I've never missed a one of his things. I like to compare what he does with what we do. We have more fun."

It was next to impossible to get out of bed the morning after the battle with the hammerhead. Each and every muscle in my back, arms and legs felt as if there were hooks pulling them in the wrong directions. In the bathroom that morning someone had made a cross on all the mirrors with shaving cream. Right under one of the hot-air hand dryers someone wrote in carefully printed Magic Marker, "Push for the latest word from Washington."

Grady didn't even wait for me to get upstairs that morning. He came from his room upstairs to shave. "What you lookin' in the mirror for, Pete? You gonna shave off that red briar patch on your face? You never know what you might find hidden in there." That was as funny as Grady got.

He washed off the shaving cream from his antique razor and put it back into his black toiletry bag. "After breakfast I'm gonna show you what happens around here."

"Test time." Zak smiled when he saw us walk into the kitchen.

"What's bit record mean, boy?" Grady asked.

"After the seismograph records come back, the earth formations are studied to determine if there is the possibility of oil or gas. Then the geologists and others decide whether to risk millions. If they decide to, they bring one of these rigs onto the scene to drill some test wells. There may be gas and oil down there, but there has to be enough to pay back the investment and then make a profit."

"Just out of curiosity, Pete, you know how much it costs to rent this rig, the J. Storm One? And this can't go out in deep water; it's one of the cheap models."

"No."

"Come on, take a guess," Zak intruded.

"Oh, maybe the oil company rents it for ten thousand a week."

"Try twenty thousand a day. And that's only for the rig, the men and the food we eat." Grady picked up another piece of bacon, the ever-present marine radio chatter from his office our background Muzak.

"May I continue with my test now?" I asked.

"Go ahead, college boy," Grady answered.

"Well, the bit record is first, the kind of drill bit used to cut through the earth. It probably will have many diamonds and cost about a thousand dollars each. These bits may last only ten hours; then again they may last twenty hours—"

"That ain't too long for something to last that costs a thousand bucks, is it, Pete?"

"No, it ain't," I mimicked.

"Don't get smart, now . . . I'll sic Allen on you."

I continued my answer. I hadn't been grilled like this since college. "The bit record also lists the type of formation drilled through and how many feet the bit is making an hour." I breathed deep. "The bit is a good word to start with because it is really the first thing that goes into the earth after the oil or gas."

"Very good, pupil," Grady said with a stiff upper lip, imitating an English accent. "You know I should have been a professor at the University of Texas, don't you think, mate?"

"No, Grady. How about Overboard U?"

"Let's go, Pete, time for your first tour. . . . By the way, when we get back, I want you to start painting every ceiling in the entire rig. They ain't been painted in a few years."

"Anything you say, prof, boss man." I learned more from Grady in a few weeks, information that would stick to my mind like gooey oatmeal, than I'd learned from some of my profs in a semester.

"Now I'm going to teach you about mud," Grady said. "You believe that?"

"Not really," I said, trying to keep up. That man could make time as he wove through the tight passageways stacked with pipe and old drill bits.

"Those bits had been invented awhile back by the young Howard Hughes," Grady said in passing.

We went under the drilling floor, where all the engines were. They were all worth multiplied thousands, Grady pointed out. "Fact is," he said, "we got a full-time motorman, you know, Richard, who does nothing but keep these things goin'. Just him alone, he makes maybe eight hundred dollars a week."

Here, in the rig's dungeons, were large, open vats of what looked like watery mud.

"There it is, the mud," Grady said reverently. This must be a joke. Maybe this is our sewage. I wouldn't put anything past Grady. "Now what does the mud do, Pete?"

"I don't know, yet . . . I have not read that far . . . I was too tired last night after catching that shark."

"Well, I'm gonna tell you . . . save you some reading." He looked up to see my expression. I was thinking.

"This here mud, it's like the oil that lubricates the engine of your car. It lubricates the drill bit and keeps it cool, prolongs its life. The mud also seals the strata until the casing is put in. That way no water or dangerous gases can seep in and up. Also, this mud supports the sides of the hole we are drilling and carries away chips of rock cut away by the bit." Grady grinned. "You know, Pete, I'm a lot smarter than I look."

He was smart and I respected him more than I let on.

"Pete, you know that college boy in the clean red overalls, well, he is our mud engineer, a specialist, went to college to study mud. Ain't that wild? All he does is monitor that mud, its density, strength, viscosity and all that scientific stuff. He sits in front of a wall filled with computerized gauges and adds to this stuff what's needed."

"What does he make a week, Grady?" I asked.

"I don't know, but I would imagine somewheres around twelve hundred dollars a week."

"You know, Grady, I'm beginning to fall in love with this mud."

"You see that barrel over there, Pete." Grady pointed to a forty-two-gallon barrel, the size they used to measure the production output of a well.

"Yes," I answered.

"That's some special additive. . . . It costs seven hundred dollars a barrel. That over in that bright orange barrel is some other kind. It's two-thirty a barrel. And we use thousands of barrels of this mud. Hell, regular ol' mud costs twenty dollars a barrel."

There was a shout. "Ling. . . . Ling!" A.J. called.

Grady took off, running up the steel stairs. "Now don't interrupt me, son," he yelled. "My babies done come to me!" Ling was Grady's favorite food and no one could catch these gourmet dinners of the sea like he could.

Each week as soon as we'd be lifted onto the rig from our crew boat, I'd take a pencil and on the outside of our kitchen, on the white steel walls, I'd draw a square, divide it off by days and record what we caught. Everything depended on the temperament of the Gulf and the temper tantrums of the winds. A fairly typical week read like this:

Tuesday—#8 spadefish (2–5 lbs.), #4 gaff-top catfish (up to 6 lbs.), #2 ling (Peter, 22 lbs.; Red, 28 lbs.), #1 shark (Doug). *Wednesday*—#3 ling (Peter, 32 & 25 lbs.; Zak, 51 lbs.), bunch of speckled trout (Grady, biggest 4 lbs.). *Thursday*—#2 amberjack (A.J. & Allen, both over 40 lbs.), #4 ling (Peter, 18 lbs.; Grady, 50 & 29 lbs.; Zak, 47 lbs.), #2 sharks (Slick); thought Slick was going to have a heart attack fighting that last shark—a long and skinny one. *Friday*—no fish, waves 8 ft. *Saturday*—#6 ling (Peter, 22 lbs.; Grady, 24, 25 & 53 lbs.; Boots, 50 lbs.; Zak, 47 lbs., bunch of triggerfish), #1 "Moby Dick" . . . I hooked fish that took off like a freight train, all my pulling never even slowed it down . . . new line needed. *Sunday*—about 30 BIG bluefish (some over 10 lbs.); they were attacking everything that moved like bloodthirsty piranha. *Monday*—#1 ling (Slick, 16 lbs.). *Tuesday*—#4 ling (Peter, 36 & 29 lbs.); #2 barracuda, teeth almost as long as my pinkie.

As I painted the ceiling the next day I thought about what I'd learned on this offshore jack-up oil rig. I knew a lot about the animals, birds and plant life on the bank.

But all this discovery, in such exciting real-life doses and in vividly told country-boy stories, made this Gulf come so alive. I painted on, remembering.

My first memories were those surfing porpoises. They surfed those jade waves with Oriental elegance, their sculptured bodies perfect; eating their fill. There was almost a sensory overload as I watched the Gulf. My eyes were riveted to its waters. How could I divert them? I might miss something like that sun-splashing fish tornado, those thousands of spadefish, tightening into a whirl, nervous, sensing some of them would die. Then to see speeding bullets that were five-foot sharks tear them apart. The electric green Gulf turning that rusty red color. Never could I erase that twelve-foot hammerhead shark with its supernatural-looking head and those voodoo eyes, hideous, unbelievably powerful, so oblivious to all intruders. Anything that could snap a deep-sea fishing rod like a decayed twig from a pine tree, well, let's just say I'd let it swim anywhere it pleased.

Then there were the lings. Some called them cobia. Grady's favorite, flakiest, whitest, mouth-melting fish. I loved watching them cruise in, almost always from the west, hunting the top of the Gulf, looking for smaller fish in the shadows of buoys, oil rigs. . . . They were the coyotes of the Gulf coast. They patrolled the whole thing, I learned, from Mexico through Texas and all the way around Florida; sometimes they made it as far as Rhode Island.

All these large fish—the porpoise, shark and ling—were attracted because the rig created its own environment, a separate ecosystem. One of the first things I had learned was that the Gulf around here did not have coral reefs, underwater rock outcroppings, or anything that created the start of an underwater ecosystem. All of this began with the barnacles and other microscopic organisms that attached themselves to the rigs. There were seaweeds, oysters, other sea life. Then small minnow-sized fish would come to feed on all this. Also, they'd find safety hiding around the legs and underwater structure of the rig. Attracted to these small minnows, the way I was attracted to a Whopper at Burger King, were the fish in the catching and eating range.

I caught these and learned that they were the tropical blue and yellow spotted triggerfish, with their tiny parrotlike mouths for biting off the shell-hard barnacles. Then there were the spadefish, looking like giant angelfish. Swimming with them were sheepsheads that looked nothing like sheep and loved to steal bait. I knew I was getting good when my hands got sensitive enough to feel those round and flat sheepsheads stealing my bait.

Bluefish swam as if they were hypnotized, in schools of thousands, their long, mirror-shiny bodies turning to the sun in unison. I'll never forget the first time I watched their trancelike swimming around and around the rig. I was about to go back inside when they went crazy and began attacking everything in sight: seaweed, cable, other fish (no matter what size), even themselves. When one grabbed one of their own, the whole school would tear them both apart in seconds. "Bluefish have no class," Zak would say.

Other schools of silver-sided, chrome-plated fish would come and go from rig to rig. There were bonitas, Spanish mackerels, sometimes even schools of small dolphins. The cowboys of the Gulf would say that when you pulled one of these dolphins out of the water, its side would turn every color of the rainbow.

Underneath, where none of us could see, although I tried, were other fish. We sent our hooks down to find out who was with us from one week to the next. Grady had said, "The great thing about this job is after we drill the wells, we move to another location. We might be out in two hundred feet of water for two months, right next to the Gulf Stream, and next month at the mouth of the Mississippi. Then it might be off the coast of Texas. . . . Son, you work out here long enough, you'll know the Gulf like I knew where the quail was when I was a boy on the family farm."

Feeding on the bottom of the Gulf were bull reds, some weighing up to fifty pounds. When you hooked one of these channel bass, you were guaranteed sore arms. Then speckled trouts might answer the hook, or sand trouts or huge flounders. Sometimes someone might hook into one giant eel, like hooking a snake monster. Then down deep there were the groupers and jewfish that could weigh over 300 pounds, not to mention pompanos, the delicacy of the Gulf. And there were floating blobs of tentacles and color called Portuguese men-of-war. Swimming in the midst of their poisonous tentacles were tiny harvest fish and others. Occasionally, depending on the mood of the winds, whole towns of jellyfish would blow by. Some were clear jelly and others had actual floats, with red and yellow tentacles.

"Pete, what you thinkin' 'bout, boy?" came the voice from the dark hall behind me. "You ain't got any drop cloths down on the floor under where you're paintin'." It was Grady.

I looked up, startled away from my thoughts of the Gulf. I'd been so absorbed that I had forgotten to put down a cloth. There were some small drops of white paint on the streaked floor.

"I don't care what you think about on your own time, boy, but there can be no daydreamin' on an oil rig. Now go get a razor and scrape all that paint off that floor . . . and stop thinkin'!"

On my knees I scraped off the hundreds of tiny white spots from the roller. I couldn't stop thinking.

Barracudas became as real in my eyes as any dog. They reminded me of greyhounds, except their teeth were much sharper. Amberjack, tripletail and wahoo became more than weird-sounding names. Instead of flocks of pigeons, we had manta rays flying in formation. No birds ever flapped their wings with such finesse. And there had been nothing since dinosaur birds that could compare with a twenty-foot-wide ray cruising by.

What held us all captive was the mystery of these roving fish. After all, we were only visitors on our steel island, one week with *them*, one week without *them*. We never knew who *them* would be when we got back.

When would the silver king, the tarpon, come to see us? Would the great white shark, all twenty feet of him or her, ever open its jaws in our direction? And what of the sailfish, were we close enough to the Gulf Stream? Then maybe the greatest of all would come calling, the blue marlin. Would a 500-pounder ever surface to dance on its tail for us working-men?

Normally, as our week progressed, the walls closed in, the other men's voices grated, and everything made me mad. This week ended and I was still painting ceilings white and thinking rainbow thoughts.

Right before it was my turn to take the basket down to the crew boat, Grady spoke. "Pete, your word for today was Schlumberger. What does it mean, in one hundred words or less?"

I grabbed the rope, threw my bags inside the open basket and stepped on. Mine was the only pair of feet not snug in some kind of cowboy boot. "Grady, you can take Schlumberger and use it for shark bait back in Texas. I'll see you next week."

6

Grandad's Chair

The ride from the docks in Dulac to "Noo Awlins," as the natives pronounced their beloved city, got shorter after every week at sea.

As we walked to the apartment, I asked Barbara if she had done any countrified cooking for my homecoming.

"No, I didn't have time," she said. Something was coming. She acted more restrained than ever.

"Well, what did you do all week? Did you do any training, running?" I asked as I opened the door, craning my neck, looking back at her.

"No...it was too hot...but you'll see what I did as soon as you get into the apartment."

I walked in and saw the floor and chairs covered with catalogs.

"They arrived the day after you left," Barbara said.

"Why are they all cut up?" I asked.

"You promise not to laugh if I tell you the truth?" she asked, her country-girl pure smile shining. That smile got whatever it wanted.

"I started trying to read these catalogs and I couldn't understand all that technical stuff about the loft of the down in sleeping bags. Then there were the advantages of box baffle construction versus the overlapping V tube baffle. Why do they worry about all the materials so much . . . arguing about this rip-stop nylon and these YKK zippers?"

"But why did you cut out the backpacks and tents from the catalog? Couldn't you see what they looked like?"

She grabbed my arm and sat me down at the table. She brought the cutouts and sat next to me. She had drawn a picture that looked a lot like her outline. "The reason I cut them out was I wanted to see how a backpack would look on me. I've never seen any girl wearing one . . . fact is, I've never seen you with yours on."

"Why didn't you try mine on? You know it's in the closet," I asked.

"I was going to, but when I got it out and those straps were so worn-out and had sweat stains on them . . . besides, it looked too big and I don't like the color."

Leaning against a dishwasher was my faded gold pack. It had been obviously overworked. The once-glistening golden nylon was worn. It looked as if it had been mashed and dragged over a quarry of granite. It had been on my back for the year and a half that it took me to walk and work my way down here to New Orleans. The shoulder straps had absorbed so much of my sweat that they looked rotted. Not only were they rotten, but they were worn through and foam stuck out the sides.

I looked at the mementos hanging from the pack. There was a broad, proud feather, orange-rust with a black strip at its bottom. I would never forget how I got that. I loved eagles, hawks, falcons, any kind of bird of prey. I'd always wished that I could have been an Indian youth who, to become a warrior, had to hide in a hole in the desert and attract the bald or golden eagle to fly down. When the eagle landed, the lad would have to pluck a feather from its tail. This would begin the young man's collection toward a full headdress. . . . Well, one day, while walking by a freshly cut hayfield in Tennessee, I saw a red-tailed hawk sitting on an extra-fat rabbit. It had obviously just killed it and was eating lunch. I took off my pack slowly and rushed that hungry hawk. It tried to take off with the rabbit, and the carcass was so heavy it couldn't get up too high. I kept running hard as it flapped its broad wings, trying to get some height. It flew to the end of the field, and just cleared the barbed-wire fence. The only thing that didn't clear the fence was this one tail feather. From that day till this one, I hung that single feather from my pack. Some days I looked at it, thought of that great hawk and it inspired me to keep flying down the road.

Then there was a deputy sheriff's badge pinned right under the Alpine Designs insignia. It had six points and was given to me by a country-calm man back in Robbinsville, North Carolina. After being run out of that town by others, I kept the silver star because it reminded me that just because some of the people didn't like me some of the time that didn't mean that all of them didn't like me.

Hanging from one of the drawstrings on the main compartment were two feathers that an Indian sculptor, John Wilnotty, had given me and wound with brass wire. He was a Cherokee and one of the best artists in the country. He lived in a small house, like a shack, next to a Smoky Mountain river on his people's North Carolina reservation. The two feathers were from a blue jay and a downy woodpecker. He said they both had a special meaning but never said what that was. I knew one thing about them: They didn't like company. I'd put hundreds of other feathers in with them. They always fell out. John had also melted down some old gold he'd had and fashioned a heart of gold out of it. When he gave it to me, he said that it should inspire me to find many hearts of gold.

Strung on a piece of fishing line was a glass bead given to me by a Georgia girl I met on the walk. The bead was black, with yellow and blue circles. It had fleeting memories, too fleeting to dwell on.

Almost all the things that were attached to the pack were sparks to good memories. One wasn't. It was a shiny canine tooth that I'd found one day while Cooper ran way ahead. It was stuck into a leather patch on my pack. All it did was remind me of Cooper. I just couldn't bring myself to remember him that day.

Barbara was spreading what was left of all the catalogs

on the table. "Trying to decide which pack I want to use reminds me of something my grandad did."

"Did your grandad do any backpacking?" I asked, knowing that was unlikely.

"Of course not. My grandad Crain farmed with mules, on some hill country at the edge of the Ozarks. They didn't need to get away from the city life. They cut wood every day to cook and carried their water from a well, burned kerosene lamps for light and went to all-night singings. When you think about it, they were already as far out in the wilderness as they ever wanted." She lifted her head high, her free-form black hair softened by the caressing humid light of a New Orleans afternoon. Her eyes shone with memories of the country past she held on to so tightly.

"I know this is hard for you to believe, knowing how energetic you are, being from the city and all, but one of my grandad's favorite things in the world was just to sit on the front porch after a long day plowin' or cultivating. He had a favorite chair and he'd sit out on the weathered porch and drink cold well water and listen."

"What would he listen to?" I asked. "The radio?"

"It would depend on the time of the year. In the fall he said he liked to hear the leaves from the oak trees blow across the dry ground. He also liked to listen for us kids coming down the road from school. He said that he could hear our voices echo through the trees. In the winter it would usually be too cold, but if the afternoon sun was warm enough, he liked to listen for the mailman's truck. He said that if the truck had chains on that day, he could hear it a mile away. In the spring he liked to try to figure out who was cuttin' the grass by the sounds of the lawn mowers. Only two or three had mowers with engines; the others had the kind you could push. He said he knew the sounds of all of them, the push kind and the power kind. The summer, especially August afternoons, were his favorite. I could tell 'cause he rocked his chair the fastest this time of year."

"What does all this have to do with our backpacks?" I asked.

"I'm getting there," Barbara said. She always told her

country stories slow and easy. "Grandad's favorite time of the year was late summer, especially in the green, cool afternoon, when he said he could point his ear just so and aim it in the direction of the swimming hole down on Logan Creek and tell what kids were swimming and whether they were diving off that big ol' scrub oak."

"Barbara, *please,* what does all that have to to with our backpacks?"

"Because reading all that about how important the pack would be for us reminded me of a story Grandad told me about his favorite chair—"

"What about his favorite chair?" I asked, wondering just how long she could draw this out.

"Someone gave Grandad this high-backed oak chair. Well, Grandad wouldn't sit in it 'cause he said that it was too darn stiff. He continued to sit in his chair, and it was so loose and old in the joints that it would squeak and sway in the slightest wind. Granny said she was scared Grandad would lean back one day and the chair would fall apart and he'd hurt himself." She looked up for a second to make sure that I was paying attention. I was. "Finally, one day, Grandad's ol' chair fell apart like Granny feared it might. Luckily it came apart when Grandad was not sitting and listening. Grandad always said that the Good Lord made the human body to fit into chairs and sofas and porch swings. He said that his backbone moved and so should anything he used. 'Ain't nothin' worse than a hard chair.' So he traded that new chair in on one that was laminated from oak. It fit his tall, raw-boned body, and the seat flexed.

"I figure that we should get backpacks that flex with our bodies, packs that fit the curves. Some of them look so rigid, like that straight-backed chair. What do you think, honey?"

I'd never looked at a backpack like that before, but it made a lot of sense. Barbara was constantly amazing me with the way she could reduce complex problems to countrified common sense. One time I asked her why she and many of the other country people I knew answered a hard question with a story. "That's how Jesus did it," she said, her Alice in Wonderland look beaming back.

"After looking at all these catalogs and cutting out the

packs and trying them on"—I laughed—"which type of pack looks like the one we should use?" Here I had walked all the way from upper New York State to New Orleans and I was asking Barbara, who'd never seen a pack till she met me.

We decided on JanSport packs, a D-5 for Barbara and a D-3 for me. The D-5 had 51,000 cubic centimeters of room. That would be a real challenge for B.J. to fit everything she would bring with her in 51,000 of anything, which seemed like a lot until I figured that it only equaled 3,111 cubic inches. That translated to just more than a piled-high bushel. It was less than half a barrel. Mine would hold 67,966 cubic centimeters. If all she could bring was just over a bushel, well, I decided to keep that from her till next week or the week after. . . .

"What are you figuring out, Peter?" she asked as I crumpled the paper I'd been multiplying on.

"Oh, nothing. . . ."

Running in New Orleans was a cross between sprinting and swimming. There was no escaping that wet heat.

"You stretched out, Barbara?" I asked.

"I feel good. I've never felt this feeling, though, that I have in the back of my legs. . . . Must be some new muscles telling me they're glad to be noticed."

"Today"—I sweated profusely already—"we are going to run our route, trying to walk a bit less. Let's go. . . ."

As we ran three blocks, I asked Barbara to notice the different parts of her body as we loped along.

"Can you feel your feet flexing on the pavement as each one hits?" I asked.

"Yeah, sort of." She smiled.

"If you can feel your feet, now try to notice if you are running on your toes, flat-footed, or what."

"I'm running on my toes . . . I think that I usually do till I get near the end of the route," she said. "Is that good?"

"That's good. . . . Now notice your calf muscles. Can you feel them tighten, then relax?" I asked, my body in a citywide sauna.

"Yes, I think so." She smiled. "I always thought you paid a lot of attention to my calves. Now I know why."

"Now let your mind follow up to your thighs. They are some of the strongest muscles we've got. They will be counted on to carry a lot of weight."

Barbara stopped suddenly. "Why are you saying all this about noticing our body and the different muscles? Isn't running enough?"

When I stopped, sweat splattered to the dry sidewalk. "Because I think that it is important for us to become very aware of our bodies, our muscles and what they do and what they can't do. You want to try it again?"

"Maybe, but let's walk an extra block. All that thinking made me forget how far we were running and I think that we ran four blocks further than our usual three, didn't we?"

"Yeah, we did."

She started running again, that invisible humidity in perpetual pursuit. "What do you want me to notice this stretch?"

"Since you asked, try to let your face just go loose, let your mouth fall open. Then see if you can hold your eyes still like a dulled gaze. See if you can feel your entire body becoming more like one . . ."

She was doing it. Instead of looking as if her body were not one flowing motion, she now moved it all together. Her self-consciousness had gone.

She ran toward a long straightaway on the golf course that was watered today with hundreds of sprinklers.

Normally, when I couldn't stand going at Barbara's pace any longer, I would sprint ahead. I needed to feel that pure rush of speed. Always before, when I looked back, she would be far behind, her head looking down at the sidewalk, mad that I would leave her behind.

This afternoon was different. When I looked, she wasn't there. I thought, Oh, no, she got mad and went home. It wouldn't have been the first time that happened. I looked across the street at the sidewalk: She wasn't there. I looked to the left. What I saw almost knocked me over with surprise. There was Barbara, her long white legs galloping. Her hair was now tied back, and the clean, clear sweat reflected her newfound exuberance. She was as happy as a quarter horse foal kicking up its heels, spinning around and around, rearing back its graceful neck. Not only was she running for the sheer bliss of it, but she was running through every sprinkler. These weren't the sputtering types of sprinkler used on tiny city lawns but ones that shot powerful streams of cool water for over 100 feet. . . . She'd begin at the end of the stream of water and run straight through it till she got to the end. After that it was on to the next sprinkler and the next. . . . When she got close to me, she pulled one out of the ground and drenched me, chasing me with it.

When she ran out of hose and could chase me no more, she fell to the grass. Steam rose from her T-shirt.

"Peter," she said, "this sweat is not so bad after all."

With that she jumped to her feet, her socks so wet that they hung over her Puma track shoes and dragged on the ground. She ran off, daring me to chase her.

One day it occurred to Barbara that we were concentrating on running when we would be *walking* across America. I told her that running was harder than walking, and therefore, that was our way of getting our bodies strong enough to handle the extra weight of our backpacks.

That week, I ordered two blue backpacks and two grape purple sleeping bags. They would keep us warm to −5°F. and would weigh only three pounds four ounces. Prime northern goose down was what would keep our body heat with us if we reached the Rockies. Until then we would just use sheets for sleeping on our foam pads. Since Barbara was almost five feet eight inches, I got her a regular size while I got a large. I was six feet and weighed about 180 pounds. B.J. weighed 126.

The Sierra Designs tent we chose weighed only seven pounds twelve ounces and had a height of forty-five inches. It had an alcove in the rear for cooking inside if one was stranded in a blizzard or days of rain and a tunnel door at the back, like an igloo, for crawling out if it was snowing hard. It had ventilation tubes on both top ends and I chose the light forest green color with a gray bottom. Unlike many campers who liked to have bright-colored tents to make a splash or in case they needed to be spotted, we needed to have a tent that would camouflage us and hide us from any harm. Most of the time we slept in farmers' fields, well off the road, and because of the time of the day we made camp or the location of the farmer's home, we could not find anyone to ask permission to camp.

Having Barbara along made me a lot more nervous about protecting her. We still planned to follow two rules that had helped to shape this walk so far. One is an Indian law that says, "With all beings and all things we shall be as relatives." The other is my own: "Distrub the land no more than a deer would in passing through." I'd seen many places in the deep woods where deer had slept for a night and all they left was an indentation in the grass or leaves where they had lain. That's all we would leave, an indentation from two tired bodies that would be gone by the time the sun was up and the grass had the time to stretch back toward it.

So our equipment was ordered and our bodies were almost trained. Once we crossed the Mississippi and set foot on its west bank, there would be no turning back.

7

Battle in a Basket

"Look, down on the surface!" Grady was yelling. It was a day of soft, crawling swells, hot and humid. "That's a huge ling. Pete, go get my pole. You know where it is!"

I ran off and was back. He had the bait ready. Someone always kept fresh bait and there was a bunch of it nearby.

He had the ling hooked fast. It was at least fifty pounds and thrashed at the top of the water like a poolful of kids. Its thrashing brought two more from the depths of the Gulf. Grady seemed to have forgotten his million-dollar worries and was thinking of nothing but fishing. Then a king ling came within a few feet of the one that Grady was fighting. Zak handed me his pole, already baited. "Pete, that may be the record." It looked like twice the size of Grady's.

At first I didn't want to take it. Grady might not like me catching a bigger fish than his in front of all the crew. Then, when I saw A.J. rear back and cast, I took the pole. The pole was black, threads had been popped, some eyes had been replaced, and Zak said he'd caught many thousands of pounds of fish with it. A.J.'s reel fouled and the line never made it down to the surface.

My cast landed too far to the right and the small ling made a dash for it. I pulled the bait out of the water with a jerk, and half of it fell off. Still, the king ling heard the splat of the bait and was coming, very slowly. It didn't get this big by being hasty to bite on a hook.

I slapped the water with the bait ever so gently. I tried to make it sound like an injured fish, trying to get away. Zak whispered in my ear, "Son, that's going to be real close to the rig record, maybe even for the entire Gulf."

I kept on, but the king ling did not get interested. Its friends now were both hooked and tearing up the surface, opening up the possibilities of shark attacks, bluefish frenzies, even barracuda dashes. Any of them could hit a fish of almost any size and leave nothing but a head in seconds. I kept caressing the water with my bait. Nothing. The big one went under.

I decided to take a chance. My subtle thrashing wasn't working, so I reeled up. This time I cast far out, maybe twenty feet from the thrashing ling. I hoped that the sound of the bait landing on the Gulf's quieter surface would be more attractive. It was. The fish came. Five feet from the bait it shoved its body into reverse and started backpedaling with its wide side fins. The ling seemed to be trying to figure the odds. Was this a free dinner or some kind of trick?

I moved the bait ever so slightly. Then I dashed it away. The ling came forward and took it gingerly in its wide, strong mouth. The way it took the bait, like a food critic sampling an hors d'oeuvre, I knew it was going to be hard to hook. Grady was yelling for Allen to get the basket ready, as Zak whispered again, "Pete, this one's real educated. Let it go down. When I yell, you let 'im have it good, awright?"

My mouth went dry, my arms and stomach shivered, and my back muscles jittered. Zak counted quietly to ten, then shouted, "GO FOR IT!"

I strained, ready for the equivalent force of a runaway bucking horse. There was the feeling of weightlessness in response—nothing. I pulled the bait to the surface, everything was still in place, and here came the ling.

This ling was extra-educated, having cruised through the Gulf for many years without being caught. As I lured it closer to the rig, I could see long scars on its back.

I jerked the bait through the water, trying to make the soggy fillet look like a crippled swimming fish. The king surged forward, then ambled, waving its strong tail, curving, acting only semi-interested. Again it rushed the bait, took it, and I let it go under. It just pointed its nose toward the bottom and let gravity take it down. It disappeared and this time I let it go. It was obviously mouthing the bait, trying to tell if it was artificial. I hoped it tasted as good as a T-bone. I let the line run freely.

After what seemed like too long, I knew I would never be able to get any leverage with this much line out. I pulled again; there was slack, nothing. I eased the pole and the line toward my chest and felt the slightest tension. I pulled again . . . more tension . . . again. There *was* something there. It didn't feel like anything more than a five-pound redfish, maybe even one of the trash fish we caught called a hardhead.

I began reeling in the line, over fifty yards, and at the end of it was the ling. It made that line sing through the water as it headed for the rig's legs. "Stop it, Pete . . . jerk straight up . . . stop it now," Zak shouted.

Allen was standing to my right. "Sock it to 'em, rough-neck," he shouted, even letting out a Texas victory shriek.

Red had come back from the crane. He got caught up, too. "Tighten down the drag a bit, son. You land this one, we might even make you a honorary Texan for the day. . . . Well, maybe half a day."

I kept fighting, reeling in some and then loosing more line. The ling with the scarred back and sensitive mouth was winning. Grady hung his fish up and walked over, his shirt streaked with sweat, his face red with victory. He put his arm around me and whispered, "Pete, you land this one and you're in!"

I intensified my concentration . . . just one forceful run toward the bottom, one moment of lapse in my vigilance, and I'd lose my big fish. It was important to me that these Gulf cowboys accept me as one of their own. From what I'd seen of how they'd gotten rid of plenty of hands after the first week for the smallest things, the slightest slip, I knew even landing this would be no guarantee.

For the first time, though, I sensed that the crew was standing up for me. They were now a choir offering all kinds of advice, support and Texas war cries.

After twenty minutes of long runs by the ling I got the fish to the surface. Without any time to savor the moment, Grady ordered Red into the crane's control cabin.

"Pete, give Zak that pole. Allen, give Pete that gaff. It's time this college boy finally becomes one of us. All the way for you...come here," he ordered. His breath was short, his eyes squeezed their most intense squint. "You hold on tighter to these ropes than anything you ever held on to... You ever rode a bull?"

"No, of course not. Why?" I asked.

"Because you need to hold on to those ropes tighter than anyone holds onto the rope on a mean rodeo bull. You fall in that water and that's it. How the hell we gonna get you out of that Gulf? You've seen what's down there. I can guarantee there's sharks after all this thrashing, those ling bleeding from the mouth. The barracuda, you can see them just out at the edge of the action."

I was beginning not to want to go down. "Grady, where do I gaff the fish?"

"Any damn place you can. You just hold on with your left arm, aim this thing and lift with all you got. This one's gonna fight you. Be ready for anything. You hear me," he blurted, pushing me toward the clearing where Red had rested the basket on the steel deck. It was there, next to that railing that kept us all from falling overboard. As I got inside the ropes, Grady came over, grabbed the gaff, felt to see if the point was sharp enough, then spoke one last time. No one else could hear him. "You caught this fish. It could be the big record. You *got* to land it. I know you can do it."

The crane's engines spewed black smoke. Red pulled the lever to lift me above the railing and moved the crane so that it hung me out over the Gulf. I was hanging eighty, ninety feet over the water, the last thing I wanted to imagine. Then Red did something that sent jolts of the most intense fright throughout my every cell. Every molecule of my body jumped away from each other. He let the basket drop, free-fall. Instead of letting it down slowly, the engine straining to the water's surface, he just let me fall like a 500-pound weight. I knew the controls had broken. I was amazed at how fast my mind played back my whole life.

There was a snap of cable. My legs wanted to break from the jolt of stopping. *Had I hit the water?* There was no water. The intensity of the stop forced me to my knees. I was not in the water. *I was alive!*

Then I saw the hooked ling. Down here the Gulf was an imposing force. I looked up and saw the tiny faces of the crew. They were so far away. I was on my own. The ling and I, swinging on a 100-foot steel cable, in a basket.

I saw Zak moving along the railing, bringing the ling toward me. Then the fish tried one last run under, but Zak held its frantically jerking head high and stopped it. I was dangling only a foot off the Gulf's surface. When swells rolled in, they washed over my track shoes, halfway up my calves. Then either the waves picked up or Red lowered me further. *"I'm low enough,"* I screamed. It was hard to see them. It must have been hard to see me. They could never hear me. I waved. Red lowered me farther into the water. Like an ol'-timey baptism I'd seen in Tennessee, he kept lowering me into the Gulf and then lifting me up. Red kept doing it, every time a bit lower. I saw something big on the second dip. After a few dips I was thinking I'd have to climb up the rope sides to keep from getting completely drowned. I didn't think it would end, but it did. Red turned me into the wind, and right in front of me was my ling. It was more than five feet long.

I'll never forget thinking, right before I gaffed it, how beautiful, how profoundly pure and salty the Gulf is when you stare at it only a foot away.

I gaffed my ling on the second lean. I was almost prone over the water, looking at it in the eye. It had big eyes. There was never a thought of letting it go. I'd been through too much for the months I worked, slaved, been tied in bed and much more. This was to be my final test and I was going to pass. I wanted to be a cowboy of the Gulf, not just because I thought so but because these great men thought so. Putting the gaff in its side was no simple task. It was like sticking a gaff into a moving car on the interstate and pulling it back in your lap. I got it into the basket. I was soaked. I shoved it with my right foot into the ropes and told them to lift me up. Red did and lowered me onto the rig floor. Red spoke first. "Boy, you did good."

Allen and Grady came over and tried to take the fish out of the basket. I pushed away their attempts. I cut the line, pulled it out, more like dragged it. It was either much heavier than any ling we'd caught or I was weak after that free-fall. I lifted it upright, trying to hook its mouth into the scales that we kept hanging. I couldn't do it. I tried again . . . still couldn't. Zak helped me lift, and the scales went shooting past fifty, past sixty, went past seventy, back to sixty-five, then settled on sixty-nine. Grady pushed it up and let it fall to make sure he was seeing what he thought he was seeing. It went back to sixty-eight. "Is this a record, Grady? What's the biggest ever caught on this rig?"

"Yes, sir, Pete, you did it . . . the whole thing. It's the new J. Storm One record. This huge thing's not that far off the Louisiana record. It wasn't long ago I heard it was seventy-three pounds. This here fish probably swam here from the Texas coast." The crew went back to work.

Grady stuck around. He wanted to see if what he'd taught me about cleaning a fish this size paid off. "I'm proud of what you done, Pete. Even if the rig record did have to get broken by a Yankee." He smiled a smile that told me I was now one of them, a cowboy of the Gulf. That smile made all I'd gone through worthwhile.

8

A Cajun Pearl

Today would be our last hard training run. Things had not worked out the way that I had wanted them to. Our bodies didn't have the crisp thoroughbred refining. This deadly combination of heat and humidity had sapped our strength.

As we ran, rivers of sweat poured down our foreheads. Barbara wasn't complaining and I wasn't mad. We finished off the first three miles. I lengthened it a mile and a half. Every time I saw Barbara running I thought the same thing: that sweat actually looked beautiful on her. Running next to her, on her right, and just slightly back, I would watch her. Whatever it was that made sweat beautiful on her had to do with the translucent whiteness of her skin, the purity of her thin, doll-like lips, and her eyebrows that had a perfect line.

There was one stretch of densely green field on our training route. It had a half-mile straightaway of grass. We often ended the run there, in order to let our bodies cool down before hitting the air conditioning. As we stepped from the hard bleached white concrete to the soft field, I stopped. Anytime I let up or stopped Barbara was guaranteed to do the same. Instead, she loped on by, lengthening out her strides. She was covering ground with a smile. I sprinted and caught up, letting my head feel the freedom, straining to lean as far forward as I could without falling down. For many strides we matched, stride after stride. It was one of those special moments between a man and a woman. I wanted it to last forever, to be always linked, streaming out behind the winds or some such.

There were forty-eight hours to go. Excitement and anticipation were winding tight. John and Charlotte Stack had a big attic and bigger hearts, and these Mississippi friends agreed to store our stuff. They would mail us our sleeping bags and jackets to General Delivery, Anywhere, U.S.A. That alone would save us four or five pounds each. Five excess pounds in a backpack could feel like fifty.

Those last twenty-four hours were difficult for Barbara. She tried to hide her feelings. She wasn't good at it, though. A lot of what Barbara thought and felt lived on her face. She had a closetful of lacy feminine dresses, blouses and skirts. Now they were all in eight big boxes. Her shoes filled the bottom of the closet like a pile of wood. Barbara loved shoes. They fitted in three boxes. Then there were boxes filled with delicately appointed slips, bras and piles of underthings, some silk, some extra-soft. She loved clothes that glided over her body and made her feel light. She was saying good-bye to all that now in more ways than she could have realized.

After she'd sealed the boxes against moths and mice, she began putting away her beloved books. She didn't have a few books; she had bookcases filled with them. She didn't have just one Bible; she must have had ten. There were three King James Versions. Then there was a Thompson Chain Reference with a red leather cover; I'd given it to her for her birthday. There were a couple of Living Bibles, a New American Standard and others. Then there were all kinds of novels, sociology textbooks and piles more. Commentaries of every book of the Old and New Testament, dictionaries, and all kinds of cassette tapes. Books were wonderful things, but they weighed too much. There would be little reading on the walk, I told her, and besides, we'd be reading the people, the land, and everything else that waited to be discovered.

"Do you think I have what I need?" Barbara asked with her forehead crinkled with concern.

Piled before her new blue pack were a yellow sleeping mat that blew up by itself; a couple of plastic dishes to eat out of; a knife, fork and spoon set; some waterproof matches; a roll of sealable Baggies out of the box surrounded by a rubber band. She had a roll of flowered toilet paper. The flowers were pink. She had two toothbrushes in case she lost one. She hated morning mouth. Toothpaste, combs, two brushes and Cutter's insect repellent, although, to repel the insects I'd heard about, we'd need a flamethrower and a planeload of DDT. I hadn't told her those stories, the ones the guys told me on the rig. They said that in the "invasion of '63" whole herds of cattle were killed by thousands of mosquitoes. If the bites didn't do it, they swarmed in such numbers on their noses and mouths that they smothered them. During that year they made official body counts of these salt-marsh monster mosquitoes. At any one time there would be 500 to 1,000 mosquitoes landing on one human leg.

She'd bought a first-aid kit, some moleskin for blisters, a snakebite kit and her own camera. She'd be using a Nikkormat camera body like mine and carry two Nikon lenses, a 35 mm and a 105 mm. For shoes she had decided to try my advice and use some Adidas cross-country running shoes. They were white with red stripes. She had a lot of socks. She'd said that she had not worn socks since she was in fifth grade. There were a couple of blue bandannas and a throwaway flashlight. Instead of double-thickness T-shirts or sweat shirts, she packed pretty cotton blouses. The only problem was they weren't made for walking across country; they'd disintegrate in a week. Her shorts were not made for walking either, but there was no way I could tell her that. I understood that she wanted to keep some degree of her femininity. After all, this was the former Barbara Jo Pennell, the Miss Priss of South Eleventh Street.

She had some candles, a pair of nice slacks and even a dress. There were a few used, threadbare towels and a bright green stuff sack filled with little plastic bottles of vitamin E cream, avocado face balm, Vaseline, extra bottles of contact lens solution, Shaklee mint foot creams and a lot more.

"I'll tell you what I think, B.J.," I said. "If we just relax, we'll find out what we need and don't need."

"That makes sense," she agreed. I hoped that we'd make it far enough to get all that worked out.

Midnight, July 4, 1976. It seemed that the entire country was partying, lighting off fireworks on the streets and celebrating. What were *we* doing? Psyching up to leave. Sitting in an empty apartment, seeing spider webs that I'd never seen before. I'd heard that people who spent Christmas alone had a hard time not getting depressed, and I could understand why.

We had chosen 3:00 A.M., just three hours after the Fourth and still close to the country's party, to start our walk. We'd be able to slip out of the city under the cover of the jungle-warm darkness. It seemed appropriate for this part of the country.

We chose 3:00 A.M. because we could take an anniversary stroll through the French Quarter. After all, our first walk through the French Quarter kicked off this whole thing between us. We'd let the gas lanterns flicker on us one last time.

Barbara was getting some sleep, although she kept tossing about. There was no way I could make myself sleep. At 2:00 A.M. I woke her with a whisper, and by 3:00 A.M. we were on the sidewalk heading west toward Chef Menteur Highway. Living things ran, scurried and crawled in the depths of dark, dank alleyways. It was gooey cool that humid night. There was no moon.

At four or five in the morning Bourbon Street was quiet. The barkers who stood at the bar doors and slurred out their invitations to come in with hoarse, ghoulish voices were gone. We saw only two men in the street, conventioneers, obviously.

Suddenly a pair of legs on a trapeze swing popped through a black curtain and swung out from a second-story window. I knew they were plastic, but the thigh-high black-lace garters sure made them look real. The two men behind us stopped and whistled. As we neared the intersection of Bourbon Street and Canal, I saw a man dressed in a frayed blue jean jacket. From the back I could see a long braid of hair and a leather bag hanging off his shoulder. In his left arm he carried what looked like a gun case.

He glanced back at us when he heard our steps. Anytime anyone heard fast steps coming up behind him in this city, he looked back. If he was smart, he ran or at least walked faster.

This guy glanced back casually, then kept walking. We were closing on him; it seemed that he had slowed down. Maybe he had no cares because of what was in that black case in his left arm. New Orleans had all kinds of hit men. Maybe this guy had just done a late-night job.

As we got closer still, I could see that the black case looked like a violin case. When we caught up with him, I recognized something about him. Maybe it was his brown hair and untrimmed beard that looked familiar. He was in his mid-twenties. Maybe his picture had been on the news; maybe Channel 4 had done a report on his latest murder!

He spoke first. "Where ya-all going? Isn't it a bit late to be out back-packing?" He smiled and his voice was soft. That didn't exactly reassure me. Lots of killers are soft-voiced. I decided if I told him the truth, he might be so surprised he'd be thrown off guard.

"As strange as this may seem, my wife and I are walking across the country." I looked into his brown eyes, which were trying to persuade me that he wasn't dangerous. "We plan to walk from here to the Pacific."

He stared at us thoughtfully and then asked, "Why are you heading down through this part of town?" He took the leather bag off his right shoulder and let it drop to the street. I listened for something hard like a pistol. Everything sounded soft, like clothing.

"We are going to cross the river on the Canal Street Ferry, on its first crossing," Barbara answered. She was looking at him as though she'd seen him, too.

"That sounds like a wonderful thing you both are about to do," he said, his eyes still the same. I knew I'd talked to him before, somewhere. It was hard to recall anything this time of the night-day.

"I've done a lot of traveling myself. All over the world, matter of fact."

"Really," I responded, somewhat afraid to ask where he'd traveled and why. One of my friends, a builder, told me about a retired hit man he was building a house for. He was so nice and gentle, and what a family man! When you talked to him, my friend said, he had such a quiet way about him it was hard to believe what he'd done for a living. It was funny how the subcontractors did such great work when my friend told them who they were working for.

"Tell me," the stranger said, his manner as silky as a magnolia flower, "are you walking cross-country just to see if you can do it, or are you getting to know the folks?" He acted as if he knew.

"We're walking so that we can meet people that we'd never meet otherwise. Walking makes us open to them, and them to us."

He placed his "violin case" on the road. Very carefully he reached out his right hand and offered it to me. "I don't know your name, brother, but what you and she are doing is something I can relate to." We shook hands. Then he bent down and laid the case on its side and opened it. His back was blocking my view. When I saw the back of his blue jean jacket and the Harley-Davidson patch, I remembered who he was.

He was a street musician unlike anyone I'd ever seen anywhere. Inside that case was a violin. In that leather bag was a small battery-powered amplifier that he plugged the violin into. The time we'd seen his astounding talents he'd been surrounded by over a hundred people. He needed that amp. Now it looked like he was going to play us a song, for free.

"Now I know who you are." I smiled. "We saw you some months ago, playing by the Café du Monde."

"What do you want me to play for you?" he asked, turning the tuning knobs. "I was headed home, I've got a small room down on Magazine Street. But anybody that's doing what you two are deserves a song. What'll it be?"

"How about 'Orange Blossom Special'?" I asked. I'd learned that this famed fiddle tune had been written by a man somewheres in the Deep South.

"You planning to walk fast?" He smiled. He rested his chin against the violin. It was dulled, scratched and darkened from constant use. He played it better than anyone I'd ever heard. His foot tapped fast on the empty road. It was after 5:00 A.M. He played the song that required an arm as quick as a hummingbird's wings for about five minutes. If I had not been in New Orleans, I would have known this was a dream. I don't think I could have ever even dreamed this. It was too perfect.

When he finished, he looked at Barbara and asked her what she wanted to hear.

"Would you play something beautiful for our first sunrise on the road?" Barbara asked.

"How about ol' Felix?" he said.

"Who's Felix?" I asked. It sounded like the name of a country-store fiddle player.

"Excuse me. That's Felix Mendelssohn. He wrote one of my favorite pieces, this here violin concerto."

And so he switched moods and played that beautiful concerto for Barbara and me and the moths that fluttered around the streetlight overhead. Every note was crisp. There was no screeching on the thin strings. This isn't happening, I kept thinking.

"If you don't mind my asking," I said, "how did you learn to play classical music like that and why are you playing in the streets of the French Quarter?"

He looked down at his worn-out shoes and spoke. "Well, I went to Juilliard but got tired of all that highbrow music. So I dropped out in '74 and moved into the hills of West Virginia. There I worked in a coal mine and learned how to play fiddle. You want to hear one of the first songs I learned?"

Before I could answer, he was playing "Amazing Grace" like I'd never heard it done. Then he went right into one of the all-time great bluegrass tunes, the kind that made me want to dance all the way to the Pacific. I don't remember the name of that one.

He spoke again. "After living in the hills for a while, I got to reading and found out that most of the tunes they played had come over here from Ireland, Scotland, the kingdom." His voice took on a slight brogue.

"You look like you have some Scottish blood. How about a Highland reel?" His right hand, the one that controlled the bow, spun over the strings. My heart danced and spun, too. Barbara had her pack off and was sitting on it, bouncing her feet on the pavement in time to the music.

It was getting close to six. "Listen, why don't I walk ya-all down to the ferry? I don't meet folks like ya-all every day." When we hit Canal Street, he played something by a Cajun fiddle player named Doug Kershaw. For the past three months he'd been studying and living with a bunch of Cajuns in southern Louisiana. "You know those Cajuns remind me of the Gypsies I traveled with in Germany, England and Greece. Listen to this." His dark eyes outdanced his bowing arms and leaping feet as the Gypsy spirit came from his heart into his hands and face. And so, as we walked toward the great, flowing Mississippi, this minstrel played us on our way. He switched from classical to country-western, from rock to Cajun, and from bluegrass to Gypsy to jazz. I shared with him some of the people I'd met. I told him briefly about Homer and Zack, about Cooper and the moonshiners; about the commune and the Black Belt. We traded the dearest memories we had with each other.

When we got to the river, our new friend sat with us till the ferry came. As it chugged across the river, I was still telling stories, he was still playing his fiddle. The last song he played I'll never forget. I had first heard it in the Smoky Mountains— it was Hank Williams's "I Saw the Light." He was still playing it as he walked away, the strains of the fading song mixing with the gentle lap of the Mississippi. Our journey had begun.

Early on a Mississippi River morning there were strong smells of the river mixing with the smells of the city. First came the smell of coffee, thousands of pounds being roasted all through New Orleans. The wind caught it and brought it to my nose, and it was almost as good as a cup of fresh. Then there came a heavy smell of tar. Tar was used to cover the pilings for the wharves, and there were millions of pilings sunk into this city of reclaimed swamp and river. Vague catfish scents milled throughout. The sun was rising.

Once our feet hit the west bank of the Mississippi, nothing but "everything" lay before us. The route we had chosen through Louisiana was old Highway 90. It went through the heart of Cajun country. People who knew said New Orleans was nothing like those parts of southern Louisiana that we were headed for.

We were warned, "It's nothing but swamp, snakes, bars with no windows, and mosquitoes. And that road is barely wide enough to drive two cars on. Too dangerous to walk. And those Cajuns aren't all that friendly to strangers. Besides, some of them don't even speak English. Some of them are a real mean type of people."

But ahead on Highway 90 waited places called Boutte, Des Allemands, Chacahoula, the Atchafalaya River, Lafourche Parish, Bayou Queue de Tortue and Avery Island. Southern Louisiana sounded like the most exotic menu and I was determined that we'd taste all of it.

We'd walked all that torturously hot morning and well into even hotter high noon. There were no shoulders on the road, and visions of being hit by one of the passing trucks kept us alert. The heat and its sadistic friend, the vapors of evaporating water, were like the palm of a giant's hands pressing us further into submission with every step we took.

We were somewhere between Des Allemands, Louisiana, the "Catfish Capital of the World," and Raceland, Louisiana. The sun reflected like a radiation gun off the white shells that were used instead of gravel on the sides of the roads. There was no way to open my eyes all the way. People in these parts had a perpetual squint and, after a few years, hundreds of lines around their eyes. Even the darkest sunglasses meant little.

A building stood alone off the side of the road. It would offer some shade. Maybe it would have a water hose. Even hot hose water would be OK. It was too bright to look up until we were right up on it.

We had learned the hard way, when we'd be walking in that life-sucking heat, to sit out in the shade for about ten minutes before we entered an air-conditioned place. That first day we'd walked right into a cold Exxon gas station and I almost passed out. I would have fallen to the floor if I had not grabbed the water fountain and held on. The shock of cooling off too fast was too much for my body.

After laying down our packs and cooling off, we went in. We stood still in the doorway to get accustomed to the dark. A dim light shone from a Dixie beer sign by the bar. Barbara sat down at a table and I went to the jukebox to see what was playing. It was a French song by Alan Fontenot and the Cajun Country Gentleman, called "Jolie Blon," which, from my high school French, meant "Beautiful Blonde."

The Cajun song, its lead instrument an electric accordion, was hard to compare to anything I'd ever heard. It sounded something like a polka, something like country swing, with a fast three-step thrown in. I put in twenty-five cents and played a Steely Dan tune and "Thank God I'm a Country Boy" by John Denver.

The waitress dealt us menus that were handwritten and sealed in plastic.

"You people from 'roun' here?" she asked in a French accent as guttural and tough as the oysters she shucked.

"No, we're just traveling through," Barbara answered.

"You college students travelin'?"

"Yes, something like that," I answered as everyone in the place had their ears turned our way. They knew anyone traveling through here had to have a good reason.

"You two ever eat da kind of seafoo' we eats down 'roun' here?"

"Not much," I said.

"Ya wan' me to tell yu what I tink you'd like?" She was warming up some. Her hair was black and wavy like a beautiful Spanish girl's. Most of the Cajuns had dark hair like hers.

"Sure," Barbara said, "what is your specialty?"

"Sometin' you got t' try is dat shrimps. We got dem boiled, fried and sun-dried. Me, I likes 'em boiled bes'. We got a platterful for a dollar fifty."

When she brought them, all the shrimp were still in their shells.

"Excuse me, but how do you eat these shrimp?" I asked.

The chef had left his kitchen and was standing by our table. "You mean you people never done ate no boiled shrimp before? Tha' ain't right." He grabbed one off my platter and peeled it with ease. "Listen here, after you peel dem shrimp, don't put dem shells back with de shrimp you ain't ate yet. Put de shells on de table in a pile, *comprenez-vous?*"

"*Oui, monsieur,*" I answered.

He picked up two more of my shrimp and popped them down like candy. "There ain't no better seafood in da worl' den 'roun' here. My frien' he bought a crab boat up in Alaska. They beautiful dem king crab, all da salmon, but dem peoples don't know how to cook. He sol' his boat and came home after year. He was makin' big money, too, and only workin' a few muns out da' year. You wanna know how we do it?" he asked, taking another shrimp and dipping it into the textured, snappy red sauce.

"Sure. You have a cookbook we can buy?"

"Shou, we don't use no books. I go by tase. Here. You come back into ar kitchon, OK?"

He opened a saltine and sent it down into his stomach to equalize things.

Back in the kitchen, it was cleaner than the restaurant, and cooler. There were no cookbooks of any kind.

"Dis stuff ri' here is wha' makes our cookin' the bes'." He pointed to a big cardboard box. "Dat stuff made by Zatarains. You throw it in da boiling pot. It got cayenne pepper, mustard seeds, bay leaves, dill, cloves and sometin' dey call coriander. It comes in dis see-tru bag. It's strong. Woo! Den we throw celery, a who' lots of lemons, salt, got to have lots of dat salt. Got to have big pots, bring 'em to a boil."

"What's in that red sauce?" I asked.

"All da is ketchup, strong horseradish, da kine dat can make you eyes water an' a few drops here Worcestershire sauce. Got to have it if you eatin' boiled shrimp."

"What else do you-all eat that we might not know about?" Barbara asked.

Behind us in a dry corner were bushels filled with blue crabs. They had been boiled and were ready for eating. I wondered what parts of those things they ate.

"Tell you frenly people sometin'. You go back out to d' table and I'm gonna cook yu everytin' we get out of deez waters dat's in season. You got some time for dis' trip you on?"

So we sat down again and finished up the shrimp. While we waited, they brought us a root beer called Barq's. It was made and bottled around the Gulf Coast and was a favorite of seafood connoisseurs. Our waitress said that we were really going to get the special treatment from the owner. She said that he had taken a liking to us. She also said that she had something *she* wanted to turn us on to.

The lines around her eyes were thin and finely etched and seemed to point in like arrows toward the warmth.

"Did you tu ever trink a bottled Coke dat had ice floatin' in it. It has to be jus' right in da cooler. Dere ain't no col' drink better dan a Coke in a tick glass bottle. Ya know da green bottle?"

"No, I can't say that I've ever noticed," I answered.

"Well, let me get you boat one. We got lotsa people dat will drink nothin' but, specially in da summer like now."

She was right, of course. It was like rolling some Rocky Mountain snow across a face that had turned as red as a boiled crawfish.

Then Randy, the chef, came back with a dozen raw oysters he shucked himself just seconds ago.

His fisherman's heritage showed still in his build. His body was thick and compact. His back was strong with long muscles. His arms gave him away. They were loose-hung and sturdy as a small crane. He must not have retired from fishing too long ago, I thought, as he returned with a plate filled with boiled crabs. The chef pulled up a seat.

"Why don' ya move ova," he asked me, "so I can seet in betweens you and show what all dis is?"

I felt as though we were in some province in the farthest reaches of the world or some hidden valley in Tibet where they ate roasted things that had no names in English.

"Da' right there is wha' we call gumbo. It ain't what dey put in Campbell soup cans. In dat particular gumbo I put pieces of crab, oysters, shrimps, okra, wop tomatoes and whatever else I was in da mood to pu' in. My gumbo change every day, dependin' on what I got 'roun' the kitchen." I tasted it carefully.

It was both spicy-hot and yet had a deceptive sweet taste coming from somewhere. I wanted to eat nothing else.

"In dat otha smaller bow' is fresh turtle soup. My boys, dey caught dem turtles. Guarantee dat some of da bes' in all d' country. My wife she add da spice." I was getting braver. Barbara was just getting to the gumbo and watching me extra-close as I contemplated the turtle soup. It had a reddish brown color. After tasting it, I was ready to eat nothing but turtle soup.

Up to this point I had had some boiled shrimp, seafood gumbo and turtle soup, and we still hadn't turned a bit of attention to the platters and raw oysters, *auggh*... Their huge shells, the size of a small child's foot, were pearly white on the inside and gross, rough and gray-black dirty on the outside. The raw cold oysters waited for the brave swallow. The chef picked up the biggest shell, slurped, and kind of shoveled it into his mouth.

"Dese oysters, when dey dis col', are d' bes'-tastin' of any dis stuff. Here, try one," he said as he handed me the next biggest one. I tried to look somewhere else, think about something else, and then thought it might be better to eat it with a fork. When that man saw me going for a fork, he shook his head. "Now don' be messin' up your firs' oyster with a metal fork. Jus' take it in your fingers. Da' fork will spoil da taste."

I slurped, trying to hold my breath and clog my nose. I downed it, every taste bud prewarned. It was a ravishing surprise. The cold, seafoody taste. It's a special sensation that can't be described. Eating a dozen cold raw oysters is something like dying and going to heaven. Thinking about it is the worst part.

"One ting 'bout eatin' dis food is you got to eat it in da right order. Nex' we try da crabs. Dey was alive dis mornin'." He grabbed one, said it was a female. He turned to Barbara and showed her how to hold it properly, in the palm of her hand. Then he popped the bright orange top shell off. Before he'd done that he'd broken off the big front claws. He would later crack them open with expert taps from the side of a cheap table knife. Then he pried out some highly seasoned morsels of the whitest of meat. Everything they ate was highly seasoned. Highly seasoned to *them* would have been so hot that it would have melted my eyelashes.

After popping the shell off, he broke the crab in half and began picking more white meat out of the insides. The first one I tried ended up a bunch of mashed shell, meat and other unknown things. By now many of the people in the restaurant had shifted their seats so they could watch us.

"What's next?" I wondered as I looked at the piled-high plates.

"How 'bout some bull frog's legs? We got some nice ones two nights ago. Four legs to da poun'. Go 'head, try one, Peter. Dey taste jus' like chicken, better, I tink." He grabbed one and cleaned it fast.

I started and just kept going. Then the chef got up and headed for the kitchen. "Come with me." He motioned my way.

I saw about thirty or forty Polaroid pictures tacked to the kitchen walls, some covered with a brown sheen of grease.

"Who are all these people?"

"Oh, dem are my family. Some are of some goo' deep-sea fishin' trips we had wit' my sons and brothers. Oders are of some jumbo-big crawfish boils we had las' spring."

"Who's this red-headed lady you're standing with in this picture?" I asked. As I asked, I remembered that one of my friends who had been raised in Cajun country warned me to be very careful about asking personal questions. He knew I was prone to pry and he knew that these people hated anybody getting nosy before they knew you real good. If he said it once, he said it twenty times: "Peter, these Cajun people of southern Louisiana aren't like those people you ran into in Alabama, North Carolina or Virginia. You just be very careful and quiet around them for as long as you can possibly stand it so that they can get a feel for you. They are a suspicious people at first, but if they take to you, if you can keep your mouth shut, they'll give you all they have. They can be quick to explode, fast to hate."

"Oh, she's my fourth wife. Dis bar business is awful bad on havin' a wife. You sure heard by now dat we have some a da mos' beautiful womans anywhere in the world in southern

Louisiana. I'm on my fourth woman now, back to a natural Cajun girl. She good to me."

"That's good." I breathed a sigh of relief.

"What I wan' to show you is dis. De whole secret to cookin' seafood, so it taste good, like you and her been eatin'. You wanna know?" He threw six more frog's legs into a deep frying unit.

"Yes, please," I answered.

"Firs' you take a self-rising flour and add some water in a nice solid bowl. Dat's what you dip the sof'-shell crabs and shrimps in firs'. Den you get a yellow meal called cream meal. It got to be real fresh. One trick, ain't never le' dat yellow meal get stale. Dat ruin all dat fres' seafood. After you dip dose sof'-shell crab in dat flour and water, den you dip 'em in dat cream meal. Roll 'em 'roun' real good wit' your hans." He turned the frog's legs over in the grease. They were sizzling real good, he said. "Nex' you grease is very, very importon. It got to be real clean. I empty mine twict a week. Dat grease it got to be aroun' three hundred fifty degrees."

We took out the frog's legs and laid them on some extra-thick paper towels in a green platter. He picked up some fresh oysters. "Mos' places dey buy all dere oysters fresh but already shucked in tin cans. Dey fresh, but dey ain't as fresh as mine. I got dis ol' black man use' to live up in Amite, where he was one a da bes' oyster shuckers in the plant. Now he retire and he shucks oysters for me, tree, four hours a day. Dese oysters dat I gonna fry are de freshest. I grew eatin' 'em right out the Gulf from my uncle's boat. Dat's da way I serve 'em to my people. Watch dis..."

He grabbed a big handful. "You don't put dese in da wet batter, jus' da dry. The trick is to fry dese things jus' so. Not too crispy on da outside, not too mushy on da inside. Go ahead, take dese frog's legs out to your table. I be out wit' da oysters."

Barbara and I chowed down on the frog's legs as if we'd been born Cajun. There were still some boiled shrimp left. They tasted better every time one went down into my born-again stomach. Then I dipped one in the homemade tartar sauce. Another discovery. There were fried shrimp on the platter we ate. There was some white and light-tasting catfish.

I never thought I'd be eating catfish. Now I was chewing with a smile on my face. For the first time since we'd come in, the jukebox was quiet. Most of the other customers had left.

When the chef came back out, we had cleaned the platters and I had seen to it that the raw oysters were gone, their shells pearly.

There was another platter in his right arm. How could we handle more? These were some pickled crawfish tails his mother had made for him. He broke open one of the jars. Then there were about a dozen freshly fried oysters, still hot on the tongue, crisp on the outside, inside juicy as the finest peach. He signaled to our waitress to get us some more Cokes with baby icebergs.

On my third or fourth fried oyster I bit down and felt as if my teeth on the right side of my mouth were going to split in half. Maybe it was a chunk of oystershell. I could feel it in there. I reached in and pulled out something that looked like a baby tooth. What was it? I put it in the center of my hand and held it toward the light.

The chef spoke. "What you bit down on? Let me see." I showed him. "Dat's wha' I thought. It's a pearl. Every so often we get dem. I got a small aspirin bottle filled wit' dem."

"Here, you take it then," I said.

"No, no, you keep it. May bring you luck."

After that pearl I could eat no more.

When I walked over to pay, the man said, "Jus' leave a tip for the girl. Dat food, it's my pleasure. I enjoys showin' peoples our ways down here in dese swamps." This man, the Cajun cook, asked if we'd send him some postcards as we walked through the West. When we all waved good-bye, we promised we would.

9

Needles in the Dark

Our squints returned as we walked west. We weren't a quarter mile away when I realized I didn't know the name of the place where I'd bitten down on that rough pearl. I looked back and could see nothing. The reflections from the oil-black road and white shells hazed everything into wavy oblivion. It was too hot to go back. I still had the pearl.

I was walking quite a ways in front of Barbara. After all those oysters, frog's legs, boiled shrimp, and iceberg Cokes I surged with power. The winds of freedom blew through me again and made me feel I could discover everything there was to know in an hour, made me shiver with overflowing energy. I felt I could walk across America this afternoon. It wasn't the sugar from the Cokes either. It was having everything I needed to live on my back. It was never rounding the same corner, never seeing the same face. It was a feeling as strong as a Gulf Coast lightning bolt. It was so good to be on the road again.

I had been soaring inside myself for what seemed like a moment; it may have been an hour. When I looked back for Barbara, she was way back. I stood still. There were no trees except the cypress and willows that grew out of swamps; I wasn't about to float under them for what little shade they might give. When she got closer, I could see that she was

83

favoring her feet, walking like the road was a café's grill heated
extra-hot for the lunch rush. She got closer; she was limping.

"B.J., what's wrong? You step on something?"

She could have cried, but she wouldn't. "My feet, they,
they hurt so bad. Are they always going to hurt like this on
the walk?" Her mouth was strung tense. I knew that although
she'd get used to it, there would always be some pain. I couldn't
tell her that, though.

"You know it's possible that your feet are not strong
enough to wear Adidas running shoes. When we get to Morgan
City, we'll get you a pair of boots. I'm sure that will make a
lot of difference, honey. That sound OK with you?"

"OK" she said, her voice trailing off into the pizza-soft
road. "Will you please tell me how long it's going to take us
to get to Morgan City?" she asked.

I swung my pack down to my feet and got out my 1976
Louisiana state map. Like most maps, the water was blue, the
land white, the roads black and the interstates red. The parish
boundary lines were yellow. But that map transmitted false
information. Most of the "land" was underwater, and the people
lived on their own islands. They had built them in the swamp
with imported dirt and sharp-edged white shells. Walking a
few hours on the shells was like walking on the dull edges of
a million razor blades.

Their islands were surrounded by huge expanses of the
greenest greens I'd ever seen. Lily pads reflected the sun like
round green mirrors and they served as these Cajun people's
grass. When the hyacinths flowered, they turned hundreds of
acres of bayous into a delicate purple field. There were trees,
undergrowth, vines, and weeds that choked out the light.

When we camped by these swamp thickets, I expected
to wake up with vines growing around our necks. A rabbit
would have had trouble going more than ten feet. There was
a lot of life in there; almost all of it slithered in the dark.

Three days later we half stumbled into Morgan City.
Barbara had to settle for a pair of boots that were black and
looked like Israeli combat boots. I tried to explain that they
needed to be broken in. She couldn't wait any longer. Her feet

had to have some support walking on the slanted sides of the road on the unstable shells. She said we'd have to pray for the best.

We crossed a high bridge into a little town. We'd been on the road now together for almost two intense weeks. Some of the places on the Louisiana map sounded menacing. Bayou Goula, Montegut and Grosse Tete were good places to detour.

On our left only a couple of hundred yards off the bridge was a building set maybe seventy-five feet back. There was a shell parking lot that looked like a bomb zone, it was littered with so many potholes. They were filled with hot, muddy water and probably filled with jiggling mosquito larvae. It was before midday and there was only one car parked under a sliver of shade.

A man, his face draped with saggy flesh, came out of the raised building. His skin was the color of a coffee milk shake; his hair, bleached rust red by the sun and thick as wool. I was looking at a bumper sticker that said something about Cajuns but was covered with oily dust. I asked him if I could wipe it off. His eyes were lily-pad green. It said, "Cajuns Live Longer . . . They'll Eat Anything."

"This place have anything to eat?" I asked.

"It depens," the man said. In some places in this country they would call this man a Creole, in others, a Cajun. Some would call him a mulatto, some a tan. Some could call him black. Others would call him nigger and there'd be fighting. In a few places he'd pass for white, especially if he stayed out of the sun. He had calf-high white rubber boots on, and that meant he worked fishing, shrimping, oystering or frogging.

"What does it depend on?" I asked.

"It ain' got notin' to do wit' your color. Da peoples dat run it dey black. Bu' da ol' lady in dere she jus' don' like certain peoples. If she don't, you betta leave, yu hear?" The heat of these southern Louisiana summers melted words together.

"Why does she not like certain people?" I wondered.

"I can't tell youse dat. Jus pay my words mind . . . pleez."

He sounded serious. He backed out carefully, avoiding all the potholes.

"Peter," Barbara said, having overheard us, "let's go further into town and find someplace else. That guy made me nervous. Why did he say what he did about some old lady?"

"Let's try this place since we're here. We can always leave," I said.

The weathered building had no sign to announce its intentions, only a plastic Coca-Cola sign in one of the dusty windows. There were stains of purple, pink and yellow that had once coated the bare wood. The dominant color now was wind- and rain-pelted gray.

There were two steps and a screen door for ventilation. There was no air conditioning and almost no light to see by. A big fan sat on the center table and went back and forth, back and forth. It had an old cord that looked frayed and was right next to the table we sat at.

There was no old woman in the place, only three black men. They weren't Creole; they were blacker than the dark room. As we sat down, one turned on a light. They could see us better, and we could see what else was in here. There were a few windows up high, making me think that this may have been an old country store before. This was sugarcane plantation area and maybe this had been one of the old plantation stores for the slaves. The high windows were covered thick with spider webs. The light filtered through the webs, covered with dust and moths, in opaque slivers. The floor gave when people walked.

The men sat with their strong backs to us. Behind the bar, surrounded by many half-emptied bottles of liquor, was a statue of Jesus. There were some candles. They were purple or black, standing in plates on both sides of the statue. There was a bowl of something that looked like white sugar. In the plates were all kinds of Mardi Gras beads and piles of other things I could not see from our table. There was a cheap metal peace sign hanging over the saint and a cutout picture of Jimi Hendrix with his face and puffy Afro colored by red and green lights. There was no jukebox, but in one far corner there was a table with an old mono-record player. It rested next to a pile of frayed album covers. On the back wall, taped with yellow Scotch tape, were many pictures of other saints. I could only recognize the Virgin Mary.

The more I saw, the less I wanted to stick around. But I was desperately thirsty and sitting down felt so good.

I kept smelling the stale air that had lingering odors of smoke, grease, some type of strange incense, chickens, body odor, fresh country air and food. Where is the person who runs this place? We'd been sitting here for about ten minutes. The men hadn't moved. Then from the back, where I guessed there might be a kitchen, came a loud noise. Something had been thrown into some very hot grease. Maybe they were a wire box of french fries or some delicious seafood, maybe shrimp. Never had I heard anything fry and pop and crackle so loud. What could possibly be frying so loudly?

From underneath the building came a scream. A shrill noise of something getting killed, bitten. Something jumped up from the earth underneath the building and hit the floor. There was a thump, then another squawking shriek. Then everything broke loose. "That dawg mus' not been fed again."

Now a woman's voice was screaming, her voice directed underneath the building to the dog that must have been killing all the chickens there. The back door opened and slammed again. It was one of those worn-out doors that begged not to be slammed. Maybe the spider webs held it together, too.

On another wall I saw a picture, all in vivid reds, blues, flesh tones and purples, of a heart. If I remembered right, it was the Sacred Heart of Jesus. What strange things to have in a seafood place.

Maybe it was one of those chickens that was in the deep fryer. It still crackled loudly. Out of the kitchen I heard steps coming, soft, but firm and padded. Neither of us had said anything. We were frozen in our seats. Swaying through the door was a wide-faced, blue-tongue Chow, one of the most ferocious dogs anywhere. It was red, like an Irish setter, except for a bald patch under its neck. Maybe it had been in a bad fight. These kinds of dogs were known to be very mean. Cooper

had fought a few of these dogs and won every fight but one.
I'll never forget the first time one attacked him. He was only
ten months old and that Chow tried to kill Cooper. We had
been having a Halloween party at college in a graveyard. We
were huddled around a fire when the Chow walked quietly up
to baby Cooper and wagged its tail. Then it went right for his
throat. I had no choice but to reach into that swirling pile of
dog muscle and hair and teeth to save Cooper. One of them
bit through my hands, but I kicked the Chow in the head and
held Cooper. He couldn't stop shaking from fright all that night
from that attack. I'd never liked Chows since. This one acted
as if it owned the building.

He smelled me first, stopped, looked in my eyes and
then went to Barbara. She was normally kind of nervous around
strange dogs, but this one she just stared at. It stared back like
no dog I'd ever seen. I'd seen dogs that thought they were
humans and looked at you that way, but this dog thought it
was something more. What, I didn't want to know. After
checking us out, it went back through the kitchen, stayed there
a minute or so, and then the back door slammed shut once
more. I wondered when that door was going to fall apart.

I turned to Barbara and was about to tell her that we'd
better leave when someone started moving through the kitchen.
I could see a shadow coming toward the brightly lit doorway
in the kitchen. The loud frying sounds had stopped. A black
woman came through the door. She was silhouetted against
the light so I could not see her face. She had a lithe body and
she looked somewhere in her thirties.

"What do you people want here?" she asked with a slight
French twang. Her diction was clear and her delivery dramatic.

"Could we see a menu?" I asked. She moved around so
that she was facing the bar.

"We don't have a menu. In fact, we don't serve food
here anymore." Her face was long with continually moving
white eyebrows that arched high against her cocoa-colored
skin. There were few wrinkles except for deep ones at the sides
of her mouth. She couldn't be in her thirties, I knew, now that
I could see her face and hands. Her hair was the whitest thing
in this place except for her teeth and the teeth of her Chow.

The dog was now back inside, lying against the front door. Anyone that came in or out would have to walk over it and brave its teeth.

"Do you have anything cold to drink?" I asked her. One of the men called her Miss Sweet when she first walked in. But there was nothing about her that seemed sweet. Her eyes pierced like a bayonet. Her voice was both whispery and grating. She didn't like us, and I didn't think it had anything to do with the fact that we were white.

"That depends what you drink," she answered, shifting her eyes from me to Barbara. Barbara had been very quiet since we'd come in. She looked my way, and I could tell this lady made her very uneasy. She wasn't about to go over that dog, though.

"We were hoping that you had some cold Cokes or maybe some orange juice. You see we've been out traveling in the heat all day."

"Yes, I know. We only have beer and I think," she was saying as she walked over to the bar, "we have a couple Seven-Ups. You want one, sir?"

"Thank you, I'll take one and also one for my wife." She gazed at Barbara.

"I only have three left. I'm not going to give one to her. I have to save two for others that might come here tonight." She lit one of the purple candles next to the strange statue. This just didn't seem like a place that would have a statue of Jesus. I'd never felt such strange feelings swirling around. They seemed to be generated by the woman and the dog. She brought the 7-Up over and gave it to me.

"That'll be a dollar fifty," she whispered.

I would never argue with someone like her. I pulled two dollars out of my pack. She didn't return the change; she just sat down in a chair at an empty corner table. She crossed her legs, the way only thin people can do, and stared. Mostly she wouldn't take her eyes off Barbara. I'd seen Barbara handle all kinds of weird people and I knew that sweet as she looked, she was afraid of no one. Barbara moved her eyes back and forth, first looking at me to make sure I was still there and then a quick glance to see if the strange woman was still staring

at her. She always was. The three black men at the bar did
not say a word.

Then there was a noise, footsteps, as someone came up
the back steps again. The woman, the skin pulled very tight
across her narrow face, still sat in the corner and bobbed her
leg up and down slowly. She had hold of her hands and was
taking each finger and squeezing it from the base to the tip.
Her hands were oddly much darker-colored than any other
visible part of her body.

When the back door closed, this time it didn't slam, and
no one came through into this main room. Miss Sweet got up
from her chair, keeping her eyes on us like a cowboy getting
up about to draw his gun.

I heard her speak to someone. She sounded mad.

"Wha' you boys doin' here?" she yelled as her way of
talking changed. "You suppos' to be in schoo'. You knows
you mama don't allow you here. Get out!"

"But, Maw Maw, we both gots a paddling at schoo' and
we rans from dere. We wanna be wit' you and watch you
doin'—"

She interrupted and it sounded as though she'd put her
hand over the mouth of the boy that was talking. "Shut up and
get *out* there and sit down."

"Yes, Maw Maw," the boys answered. Many kids in the
South called their grandmothers Maw Maw.

The boys were about fourteen. They were both thin as
sugarcane stalks and their presence added some degree of nor-
mality to this eerie place. By now we'd finished the 7-Up and
I was wanting to leave. The more aggressive boy walked over
to the old record player, like the kind we used to use as kids
and play Walt Disney records on. He took an album from the
top of the stack and put it on. The woman had gone over and
lit another candle, this time the black one. As soon as the
record dropped down and the first notes came out of the speaker,
she stood up abruptly and rushed over to it. The record sounded
like some kind of chanting or moaning. It was hard to really
tell because we didn't hear enough. She pulled one of the boys
into the back and I heard a loud slap. Sounded like he'd been

stunned to the face with her powerful hands. When he came back out, there were no tears, just a dazed look set deep in his eyes, as though this had happened many times before. He walked over to the stack of records and looked through them. When he found what he had been looking for, he put it on. It was a scratchy old James Brown album. His "get down and boogie" music lightened the heavy atmosphere.

Before he went back and sat down by his grandmother, I asked him if he would move the dog for us. He said he'd have to ask *her*.

He walked over to her where she sat like some queen. She said something, which took longer than "Yes, move that dog!" The boy, dressed in a striped T-shirt, jeans and orange sneakers, came back and pulled up a chair. He had a stare as vivid as a hex. He seemed to have inherited that from his grandmother. "She say I can move da dog, but firs' she wan' me to tell youse sometin'. She say dat you, mister, better leave. She don' like you eyes. She say dey too open."

With that we both got up very slowly. I had a feeling that there were invisible spirits zooming back and forth over our heads. It was a heavy feeling, almost cold. It made the back of my neck tight as a steel rod. It also made the front of my head pound. I'd heard of stories here and there about demons and possession. A few movies had made me shiver, but I always knew they were actors on a screen of light. But if any of it was possible, then there were demons banging on the ceiling and slithering on the floor in here. I wanted to break and run. Barbara's eyes figured out every exit. Since we'd been standing, she kept either her hand or shoulder touching me, as if she were afraid I'd disappear.

The sitting queen, as skinny as a caved-in black Barbie doll, stared, her legs still crossed, her boys guarding her sides, her blue-tongued Chow at her feet. They looked like they should have been in stone in front of some pyramid. I'd never felt any human, man or woman, that gathered a force about her by doing so little. The three men still sat at the bar.

We got to the door. I opened it and fought myself to hold it for Barbara. When she was safely in the potholed shell parking lot, I slammed it. I almost expected to have the building disappear and to wake up in the middle of some jungle thicket, sweating from a bad dream.

Normally, when we left a stopping place, it took a few minutes to get our packs on and every strap adjusted, the hip belt tightened and our shoelaces tightened. This time we both ran with our packs hanging off one shoulder. When we got back onto old Highway 90, I glanced back and saw and heard nothing. The place looked as if screams should have been echoing off the thickets of spider webs.

We were moving again. I told Barbara we were not going to stop anywhere else in this town. We'd gone a couple of hundred yards, and there was the rest of the town. A few harmless-looking gas stations, a small bank, an everything-for-everybody store that had groceries, clothes, bamboo fishing poles, some chicken feed piled up by the front door and rolls of chicken wire. An old black man, his skin shiny, rode by on a green and yellow John Deere tractor. He wasn't going that much faster than we were. Waxy-leafed magnolia trees stood among shacks and trailers in the middle of yards that were scratched bare of grass by chickens and rooting hogs.

We were leaving town and could see again the endless fields of cane. Someone called out from behind us. Sounded like a kid on a bicycle. We always attracted children on bicycles when we walked through towns. Often we gathered a small parade, and sometimes, when we got from one city limit sign to the other, there was an escort of ten bicycles.

"Hey, mister," someone said.

It was Maw Maw's two boys on bikes with high handlebars. One of them had a basketball in his right arm and pedaled with no hands.

When they caught up with us, they asked the usual first question. "Where you peoples headed?"

I gave the usual answer.

"You tinkin' 'bout movin' here?" They'd never seen anyone on foot with packs like us before, they said.

"No, we're just walkin' through town, headed for Texas." The sun was still midday-blinding and even with my mirrored mountain climber's sunglasses I had to squint some. They were in front of us, their backs to the west and the sun. I couldn't really see much but their outlines. They were both sugarcane thin.

"Whys you gonna go to Texas? Dem peoples ain't got notin' but desert, ain't dat right?" he said to his silent friend. "You peoples married?" The one talking had a small paper bag in his hand.

"Yep," I said.

"Ain't many strangers come tru dis place."

"Because it was on the road we had to take to walk across southern Louisiana. You ever been to New Orleans?" I asked.

"No, man, dat's way far from here."

Barbara still wanted to get far away from here and she had walked ahead. She stood under a grandmother live oak that sent its octopuslike branches out over the road.

"Do you boys have any more questions?" I said, looking toward Barbara and wanting her close to me in this hostile town.

"We come afta youse wit' sometin' to say. Dat lady back where you bought a Seven-Up, she says dat if youse a-plannin' to move here and tries to take over any of her territory, she says she gonna gets youse." I could see that the bag he had was stained with grease or something.

"What do you mean?" I demanded.

"My maw maw, she a powerful lady. Everyone 'roun' here is afraid of her, man. Youse bes' jus' get outta here."

"What kind of power you talking about?" Barbara was standing under the tree still, with her hand on her hip. I knew she was mad at me spending too much time talking to these boys. She was really in a hurry.

"She's got da voodoo powers. She can gets you, mister. Kills you, too." He said all this not vengefully, not boastingly, just stating facts, like he'd seen it happen many times before. "Youse betta not be movin' heres."

"I can guarantee to you we are just traveling through."

"I never seen my maw maw not likes two peoples so fas' as youse. She say dat you woman gots the spirits and tryin' to turn dem again' her. Ain't no one crazy 'nough to tries dat, mister." He shifted the bag to his other hand. "She say dat she put a hex on your wife. Youse betta gets outta heres, fas'."

I didn't need to hear any more. As I turned to leave, the boy, still sitting on the long seat of his bike, spoke again. This time there was hostility in his words. "Hey, mister. Where you goin', I ain't finish." His friend was backing up.

"I don't care whether you're finished or not." I turned around and began walking.

He rode up to me, pulled his small bike over and blocked my way. "You peoples don' acts like youse heard wha' I says 'bout my maw maw. She powerful: she say she can make devils go in peoples. She say she know Satan. I know she do."

I stepped around him again and began walking faster. He rode by me and pulled over again. "One las' ting, mister. She told me to giv' youse dis bag. Youse better takes it or sometin' double bad gonna happens." The bag was a regular grocery bag, medium-sized and filled with something. There was a rubber band holding it closed. He reached out to hand it to me and I saw there were red stains coming through the sides by the bottom. I touched the side and it was something kind of soft, something hard. I let it fall to the ground. The boy rode off. His friend, the silent one, had already gone.

I walked away from the bag as fast as I could. Then I thought, What am I afraid of? I've never run away from anything like this. I was letting that bag scare me and I had no idea what was in it. I turned around and walked back to it. I reached down to pick it up. What could it be? I straightened back up and decided to take my sunglasses off so I could see what was in there. I bent back down and again saw those stains. They were blood red; that was no ketchup leaking through. There was no way I was going to open that paper bag.

I overheard some men talking. I could pick up only a few words and when we opened the door to the small gas station, they switched in mid-sentence from English to Cajun French.

"What do you suspect those people are doing hiking through here this time of year?" one dark-haired farmer said in fast, clearly spoken French. If only I could have had an accent as pure as that when I took French in high school.

"Maybe they are crazy!" They roared, laughing with that French sparkle in their eyes, so typical of Cajuns.

I waited till they stopped laughing. *"Bonjour, comment vas-tu?"* That meant, "Hello, how are you doing?" *"Il est très chaud, oui?"* That meant, "It is very hot, yes?"

"Bonjour." The least shocked farmer smiled. *"Tu parle cajun?"* He had said hello, his tan face turning bronze red. Cajun is their special brand of French, mixed with some English, and Spanish. It was as blended as the best of their gumbo.

"Non," I answered, smiling. "I only speak a little French I learned in high school." I switched back to English.

"You sure caught us good that time." They all walked a bit closer to us.

"Can I ask you something?" I didn't bother making any small talk.

"Sure." When they spoke English, they had the faintest of French intonations.

"Something really strange happened to us back there. It looked like a bar or restaurant." Barbara was leaning against the front of the white painted building. We stood under a tin roof that shaded all of us.

"We stopped in this place and this old black woman, she was thin and had a dog, acted very strange. She wouldn't even sell my wife a soda, give us any water, or sell us food."

They looked at each other as though they knew who I was talking about.

"What's so odd about her not wanting to sell you a soda? Maybe she didn't like you being in there. That's mostly a place where black people go."

"That's only the beginning," I said, feeling those tightening muscles in my neck. "When we were there, she lit these candles that were in odd saucers filled with sugar or something."

"What color were the candles?" one interrupted, his eyebrows furrowed.

"One was black; the other was purple."

"I don't know about the purple one, but I know that the black candle has something to do with death. That lady is known all over, by black and white alike, as a voodoo queen.

That voodoo and hoodoo has been practiced in these parts for over a hundred years."

"What else did she do?" the thinnest farmer asked.

"Nothing except stare at us. That is, until we left. After we were about a half mile down the road from the place, her grandson and his friend rode up and asked us if we were planning to move there. Then he handed me a bag."

"Oh, mon Dieu!" one exclaimed. "That must have been bad!"

"Did you look to see what was in the bag?" the other man asked.

"No, I didn't open it. It felt kind of soft, though. Do you men have any idea what it was?"

"It could have been a chicken foot, a rooster's head or other things. She may have been trying to put a hex on you both."

"Have you ever seen any of these hexes work?" I pressed.

The thinnest farmer answered. "I used to laugh at all that when I was a young man. But I seen too much to laugh any more. I seen people go crazy and then found out one of the voodoos had put them under a hex. I've seen deaths and heard worse. Killing babies, even cutting cattle in horrible places as part of their rites. I still don't believe it, but I don't mess with them either. One of our neighbors supposedly had a cleaning lady who was one who claimed to have the powers. A lot of bad things happened to that couple when the wife began getting into the voodoo."

The other interrupted. "If I was you people, I'd just keep on going and forget about it." He glanced at his fellow farmers, giving them a silent message to quit talking. I thanked them for their time, wishing in a way that I'd forgotten about it before asking these men all the questions.

"There is no way that I'm going in there," Barbara said. It would be dark in an hour or so and we were about to enter the woods. It looked impenetrable.

"Barbara, we don't have any choice." I had to fight back the daggermean words that the clinging heat brought on. "We have got to camp soon, before dark, and this is the only place

platforms but usually in sun-bouncing bone-white tombs. The older ones were built with brick, covered with white plaster.

Sometimes these white tombs were so old that resurrection fern grew from the cracks in the plaster. This stunning green fern dried to an ugly brown when it was dry. When it rained, it resurrected. There was such little space between each tomb. Some just had concrete slabs holding the dead people inside. I heard something that sounded like rock against rock. I wouldn't have lived if someone had come out, resurrected! It was only a baby raccoon running over one of the graves.

"Barbara, I am not jiving with you, girl. GET OVER HERE. We must get our tent up!"

"I'm not camping in there." She crossed her arms. I hoped no police car would pass by. It would definitely stop.

"Where, then, do you think we should go!" I asked. I could barely keep myself together, such was the intensity of torture I experienced when attacked by mosquitoes.

"The only place I'll go is in the sugarcane fields. Look over there. There's some kind of tractor. Maybe they've been harvesting some. There may be a clearing."

We had to walk through the graveyard. There were rows of white crosses in the now-red sky. There were figurines of Jesus. There were statues of Mary and many angels flying.

As we walked through the city of death, I saw huge cockroaches scurry across the white and cracking plaster. They were as big as small mice. Barbara was holding on to my pack and I don't think she saw them. I hoped one would not jump on her.

On one of the biggest tombs, which seemed to house a whole family, the brick front was crumbling. Grass, weeds, ferns and vines grew from within, where the bodies were. If I'd had a flashlight, I'd never have looked inside. On a black wrought-iron cross four or five lizards were soaking up the last bit of heat. They were chameleons and they were all vivid green. The biggest one had half its tail missing. Barbara didn't see them either. Fortunately she didn't see too well when the light was dim.

We neared the fence that would hold no snakes back. It

would not keep back any lizards, opossums, roaches, rats or armadillos either. The darting blurs of nighthawks and bats replaced the white flocks of egrets that were already roosting. As I lifted my pack to the other side of the rusting fence, there was a neon green thing zipping toward me. It was a long snake, thin as a pen. When my pack hit the weedy ground, it turned back into the sugarcane field. The fence creaked as I climbed over. Everything metal seemed to be rusting down in this special world. Barbara didn't see the snake, thank God.

We found a road-wide section of the field that had been harvested. Maybe they'd taken it early as a test or something. Maybe this would be OK for sleeping. The nights in our tent without air conditioning in mid-July made Devils Island sound like paradise.

A closer look and I saw that the sugarcane was grown on mounds, and when it was cut, there was left a section of the stalk about three inches long. Its point was cut at an angle and became a spear. Sleeping on the mounds and the sugarcane was like being dropped into a pit in Vietnam filled with pungie sticks.

We had maybe five minutes to get into the tent, so I chose the flatter-looking mounds and pulled the tent out. At least we'd be hidden in case the voodoo lady came after us. I tried to center the tent so that we'd each lie in between the rows. The valleys weren't wide, but on our sides maybe... Well, I could set it up so that only one of us could have a valley. I let Barbara have it. Today had been extra-stressful on her and it showed in her eyes. There was no sparkle; even her delicate lips, which usually turned up in warmth, turned down. What an introduction to our first week of the walk! This section had been the most tormenting so far. I told her that, but she acted as if I were just trying to make excuses. I gave up and just hoped that she'd make it through these swamps, cockroaches and black candles.

Sleeping that night was impossible. It was like being on a bed of nails. Every time I would turn in another direction, another sugarcane spear would jab me somewhere. If it were just the spears, it would have been semi-bearable. But it never cooled off. It was so hot that if I had been tortured by an enemy, I would have told him anything for air conditioning, a cool shower, a dry sheet.

From the way our bodies were stabbed I knew the tent was being pierced too. I was worried that snakes would crawl in. Mosquitoes, fire ants and worse could attack. I couldn't share my nightmare fears with Barbara. We'd been lying next to each other for hours, both knowing we were awake, yet unable to speak. All I could hear were her lungs straining through the thick, slimy air.

Our night of agony, surrounded by tall sugarcane that blocked even the whispers of breeze, could have ended peacefully if only there had not been that sound outside the tent. At first I was so miserable that I didn't notice it. After I told myself to concentrate on anything but the spears and sweat-soaked tent, I heard it. It wasn't a sound that you would call loud, but one that began like a murmur and grew with concentration and imagination.

The first thing I heard was a kind of low hum. As I listened closer, trying to sort out the usual tree frog songs, it became a drone. The sound was steady and seemed to be moving around outside the tent like a misty ghost. I concentrated. After I had been on the walk for so long and living in the woods, my hearing had improved remarkably. I had become able to discern much in the night's soft sounds. I'd never heard this sound, though.

I turned and kind of leaned up against the tent walls. A second later it felt as if a hundred tiny needles were piercing my skin. Mosquitoes were biting me through the tent. All they wanted was for us to come out with them. That's why we couldn't escape this insect-droning night hell. The drone was the clouds of mosquitoes. There were so many out there waiting for our blood that we could actually hear them.

The more I tried to shut out their echoing drone, the louder it got. The harder I tried to lie still and sleep, the more conscious I became. The more I thought of waking Barbara and making a run for it, breaking into the church, even a tomb, the louder their noise became in my head.

The wicked clouds of bloodsuckers had eternal patience. They never gave up on our coming out to them. I knew that they had smothered and killed 2,000-pound cattle, swarming so thickly on their faces. I prayed and waited for the light, so that they would go back, like Dracula, when the light appeared. The light took over from the dark so slowly, so leisurely. I wanted to scream at it to rise faster, to burn away the clouds of blood-hungry insects.

There came a time that morning when we could stand being inside the stench of our nylon tent no longer. It was either our sanity or our blood. We talked about it and decided to give them some of our blood. I thought of even leaving the tent right where it stood and just running away. But then what would we do tomorrow night? So I told Barbara to get all her stuff packed up and get dressed in long pants and to sprint to the road and wait for me there. If need be, I said, just start walking and I'd catch up.

She got packed up and took off. A gray cloud followed her as she ran with that thirty-five pound pack. The cloud gave up on her halfway to the road and came back for me.

When I was packed, I reached my arm out into their midst. I opened the mosquito netting ever so slightly to unzip it so I could get out, and my arm was covered in seconds. It was like the commercial on TV where the man sticks his arm in a tent filled with mosquitoes and shows how great his repellent works. Mine never worked.

I reached up for the cool metal zipper to open the tent and I felt something slimy on it! I shook my hand in horror. It was a bright green tree frog.

I burst out and ripped at the pegs that held the tent in the ground. Some wouldn't come out, the ground was so hard. I slapped at the whirring insects that blackened my bare legs and my sunburned arms.

The mosquitoes flew in my eyes and I couldn't see. I rubbed at them: then there were dead pieces floating in my tears. They attacked my ears, flew up my nose. The mosquitoes didn't care whether I screamed or not.

I had half the tent down. Another cloud, like a wave of World War II bombers, came in from the dense sugarcane. I could not see Barbara. She must have been running down the road.

With my pack already on my back I slapped with my free hand continuously, my arms and legs were still covered, and the gorged mosquitoes were fat and red with my blood. Some even fell off dead, they drank so freely. I was so mad, trying to kill them, that I left welts and bruises on my skin. At last I made it to the road.

Dragging the tent down the road like an escaped patient from a padded room, I saw Barbara way down the road. The sun was up now, and the mosquitoes seemed to have thinned out.

As I rolled the tent up on the early-morning road, I thought for a moment that maybe we were crazy, subjecting ourselves to the kind of day and night we'd had yesterday. Then I thought of what lay ahead and behind and thought about what I'd be doing if I wasn't on the walk. I strapped the tent on top of my blue backpack and hit the road. It was a new day.

10

Babe Ruth, Joe DiMaggio and Preacher Hebert

There were many new days after that one. All of them pretty tough, but nothing in comparison to that day in the voodoo café and that night in the sugarcane fields by the white tombs.

We walked through many intriguing towns and cities and wide places in the road. We eased through New Iberia and by the turn-off to Avery Island, where all the tongue-sparking Tabasco sauce is made for the world by the McIlhenny family.

Then there was Lafayette, Louisiana. It was a city of riches made possible because of oil. I never knew till I got there that Louisiana was second only to Texas in oil and gas production in the U.S.A.

Barbara was walking next to me. She had pulled out a small Bible. She often read Proverbs and Psalms. The Bible soothed her the way classical music or a glass of fine wine calmed others.

"Peter," she said, "I have just found a scripture that we should use as *our* rule for the walk." She kept walking. Her voice was as soft as a child's cheek, so I had to stay next to her. "You remember how you told me that you had two rules that you followed on your walk?"

"Yeah, I remember."

"Well, I like this. It's from the Book of Isaiah in the

Old Testament," she said as she waited for a semi to groan by. "'They that wait upon the Lord shall renew their strength; they shall mount up with wings as eagles; they shall run, and not be weary; and they shall walk, and not faint.'"

Everything Barbara *wasn't* doing worried me. Normally when things got hard, I could count on Barbara to tell me about it. For the last three days nothing seemed to move her. "I don't feel like talking," she'd say, or she'd pretend she didn't hear me.

Her face had no fight left. Her mouth hung open as if she were having trouble breathing. She seemed trapped inside herself and she couldn't or wouldn't come out. She was so silent.

It was near night. For this time of year it was nice . . . cooler, less humid. On our left was an open body of water. It looked like a black mirror. From its center grew some cypress trees in a clump. The moss hung so thick it looked like silvery tinsel left there from ten Christmases. The sun's reflection was a wavy red brushstroke on the black-gold water.

"B.J., let's sit down for a few minutes?"

She never answered; she just stopped and stood still. Her eyes said nothing. She said nothing. I hoped that if we could sit down, maybe she'd talk to me about how she was feeling. Having another person on the walk was proving more of an adjustment than I thought it would be.

I sat down on some soft grass with my back to the east. She let her pack fall off her shoulder in a heap. Some of her things fell out of a small pocket on the pack that she had not closed. Forgetting to close something or being sloppy was just not like her. She sat down with her back to mine. I leaned close to her, back to back. Her back was so strong, yet her *will* seemed to be staggering.

We just sat and leaned against each other and let the tree's black reflections blend with the reflections of the electric pink clouds. These swamp waters were so soothing. Barbara sat still as an Indian on a cliff. I tried to ask her how she was feeling after about fifteen minutes, and she wouldn't answer. I'd heard of people becoming so withdrawn by pressures that they couldn't communicate. But I'd never seen anyone affected like that.

I quit thinking and looked toward the water. The more I looked, the more I saw. Gentle ripples intersected each other as a muskrat swam and a turtle headed for a mossy log. The colors of everything softened. Swallows flew so free that at times they seemed to fly through the glassy water. Dragonflies flapped their brittle wings in unison. I hoped this feeling of oneness, our back-to-back sitting was soothing her. It was working for me.

"Honey, do you want to talk some?" I asked quietly.

"Not right now." Her voice trailed off.

Then a great white egret glided over us. A breeze gave the surface of the water a slight roll, rippling the bird's angelic white reflection. The egret flew on.

Barbara turned her head to the sky to watch the bird fly away. It caught her attention, some.

"Peter," she said, "you remember Wally Hebert back in New Orleans?"

"Of course," I said. He had been one of our best friends in New Orleans. He was getting his master's at the seminary and then on to Tulane to get his Ph.D. in European history.

"Doesn't he come from around here somewhere?" she asked.

"Yeah, I think so."

"Didn't he say when we left that if we needed a place to wash up and rest, his parents would probably take us in for a night?"

"He said he would drop his folks a line telling them we might give them a call when we came through."

"Peter, I think that you should give them a call. I have got to rest."

It was not like Barbara to ask me to call strangers. She was very independent and proud, and would rather solve things on her own.

"As soon as we get close to where they live, I'll call them. How does that sound?" I was willing to do anything.

"You have got to tell them that I really need more than one day of rest. Peter, if I cannot get relief from the way I've been feeling, I may have to quit. Maybe I could go back and get a car and follow you like some people suggested. I'm not sure I can handle all this. It's much more than I thought it would be. There is never any relief."

I said nothing in defense. I held back from making any explanation. We got up and hit the road, looking for a place to camp. I promised her that we'd stop at the Heberts, or if they couldn't take us in, we'd get a room somewhere and let her rest and recover. I hoped that Wally Hebert's family would open up to us. Calling them out of the blue and asking them if we could come over and stay so Barbara could rest would be a hard phone call to make. I knew I had no choice. All they could do was say no.

We walked through Acadia and Jefferson Davis parishes quickly. Barbara was placid and restrained, her mind on nothing but getting to Westlake, Louisiana. The towns of Crowley, Jennings, Mermentau, Lacassine, Welsh and Iowa became as blurred as anyplace ever could for us. The Heberts would *have* to understand. The Lord had watched out for us throughout, and I knew He would now. Silently I thought of the possibility of the walk ending.

In a bit over a week we were crossing the Calcasieu River. Lake Charles was behind us; Westlake was on the other side.

At the west end of the bridge I went into a gas station and got the Westlake phone book. In this area the name Hebert took up pages and pages in the phone book. I had no idea what this Mr. Hebert's first name was or his address. I looked up and down the long lines and saw one that said Wallace Hebert, Sr. I looked at Barbara. She made the Mona Lisa look hyperactive. I called.

"Hello, is this the Hebert residence?" I asked.

"Yes, it is," a lady said. Her voice was guarded, like she was used to *knowing* all the voices that she talked to over the phone.

"Is this the Heberts that are the parents of Wally Hebert?"

"Which Wally Hebert are you speaking of?" she asked cautiously.

"I'm referring to the Wally Hebert who lives in New Orleans and is going to graduate school over there. He has two daughters, Andrea and Nicole, and—"

She interrupted. "Yes, that's our son. Can I help you with something, sir?"

"My name's Peter Jenkins. Has Wally told you about my wife and me?"

"Let me see." She paused. I could hear her put her hand over the phone and it sounded as if she were talking to someone else. "Yes, I think your name sounds familiar. You're the ones who are walking across America together, right?" She didn't seem very interested. Maybe she had somewhere to go. Maybe she didn't like my voice. Maybe she thought we were a bit strange, even crazy.

"Yes, that's us," I answered. "I met Wally and Brenda about the time I met my wife," I volunteered, trying to give her the chance to hear the sound of my voice and make some positive first impressions before I asked the big one.

"Do you need a place to stay?" she interrupted.

"Just tell us how to get there," I said, trying to disguise my relief.

We walked by a new Southern Baptist church set back off the road and eased on down the road past a stand of pines. They were as straight as pencils. Ahead I saw the road come to an end, curving hard to the left, just as Mrs. Hebert had said.

There was the place. It was a green one-story house on about a half acre. There was a big green garden out back. A Plymouth Duster and a well-broken-in green pickup truck in the carport. There was nothing that made this house stand out from thousands I'd seen. There was a yard, close-cut and very green. There were a few small pines in the front and some undergrowth that had been allowed to grow. It looked comfortable. There were dark green hedges around the front of the house.

I knocked on the door. The shades were drawn; the air conditioning worked overtime. We stood there waiting. I was thinking about Wally, my friend and the oldest son of five children. Wally had dark hair and often grew a scholarly black beard. It was Cajun black. So were his eyebrows. His eyes bounced with a glee for learning. His mind was a gift from God. He knew French, Romanian, Greek, Hebrew and Italian. He couldn't speak Cajun, though, and Hebert is as Cajun as boiled shrimp. Their name was pronounced "A-bear" in southern Louisiana. Where I came from, it would have been pronounced "He-burt."

I rang the bell. The woman who answered smiled and said, "I'm Wally's mother. Ya-all hurry up and get in here out of that heat." Her voice had a sweet ring to it, like a grandmother. Mrs. Hebert was about sixty-five but seemed more like thirty-five. There was something youthful and fresh about her. Her large friendly eyes took us in immediately, without any reservation.

We sat down on a green sofa. It was itchy and cold. Everyone kept shades drawn in midday because the sun reflected like a ray gun. "Ya-all thirsty, hungry?" she asked with a perfect southern drawl. "I don't see how in the world you stand that heat." She shook her head. Her white skin told us that she seldom got outdoors.

"I would love something cold to drink, Mrs. Hebert," Barbara said.

"Please call me Bobbie; everyone does."

We sat drinking iced tea in their daylit kitchen. We found out fast that Bobbie was not from Cajun country. All her people were Texan, to their dying breath, regardless of where they happened to live out their lives. While we were talking, Mr. Hebert woke up from a nap. I could hear big feet padding down the hallway. My first impression was that of a mild man with a tan that never faded. I knew he was in his late sixties. He said nothing, just bent down some to get through the door. Bobbie kept talking. I was watching him, looking for any hint that they might be nice enough to take us in for Barbara's sake. It would be hard, but I knew that I had no choice but to ask them soon.

I was about to pour out our problems when Mr. Hebert took a white towel off something on the countertop. They looked like two thawed-out ducks. He opened a well-worn drawer and pulled out two knives. The blades had been ground down, even looked homemade. The handles had been whittled down to fit. I figured he was getting things ready for Bobbie. Maybe it was a hint to her to stop talking and cook him some duck for dinner. Maybe that was his way of giving us the message to leave. They were very sharp knives.

"Bob"—he spoke with the faintest French swirl to his words—"are they going to stay for dinner?"

"Of course they are," she said, looking toward Barbara. Barbara looked like she would cry with relief.

Mr. Hebert picked up the knife as Bobbie started talking again. He had one duck cut up before I could focus. I couldn't keep my eyes off his hands. Never had I seen a pair of hands like these. Some people have incredible minds; some have honey blond perfect hair; others have eye-turning legs. Some could sing like Aretha Franklin, write music like John Lennon. But no one I'd seen had hands like these.

He cut, using both knives, switching back from one to the other. Bobbie and Barbara moved into the TV room, but I stayed in the kitchen with Mr. Hebert, who pulled out a bag of potatoes and reached in for another filed-down knife. It, too, had a hand-whittled handle. Soon, along with his sliced mallard, there would be home fries cooking with garden onions in a historic cast-iron skillet. The man had still not said a word.

That night I decided that if there was any way, we would stop here for more than a rest. This friend's father had caught me by surprise.

At four-thirty the next morning Mr. Hebert unrolled the tar-covered trolling net, and while steering his boat's small outboard motor with his knee, he eased the net into the water. We were going shrimping. The boat was a flat fourteen-footer that had been used so much that the green paint on the floor and seats was worn through to the shiny aluminum.

We would troll in circles in Calcasieu Lake. It was an open body of water surrounded by miles and miles of marsh. This close to the open Gulf there were few trees, just an occasional willow. The shrimp swam in the shallow waters of

*Mike and Preacher
pulling in the shrimp*

this lake, getting ready to breed. It was the tenth of August.

Mr. Hebert still did little talking. The sun, looking like an overripe Louisiana strawberry, came out of the lake. The water was quite rough and the ridges of the waves reflected a deep pink-red color.

"Either we've hit something with the trawl, or there is a big mess a shrimp in that net. Stop the motor, Mike." Michael Deaton was with us to do the hard work for his grandfather. Michael was fourteen, close to fifteen, and already about six feet tall. He never missed going with his grandad.

Mike and Mr. Hebert pulled the net in. Small jellyfish fell through the small holes; some of the big ones with orange spots fell onto the bottom of the boat. Something big, long and black was jammed sideways in the net.

"What is it?" I asked. Maybe it was a gator.

"It's a big clump of oyster shells. We're lucky the net wasn't ripped apart," Michael said to his grandad.

Mr. Hebert nodded while sitting down and opening up the end of the net. He pulled the hand-cutting clump of oysters out and poured out a mass of shaking small fish. They were baby croakers, Mike said. There were crabs crawling all over. Mike touched a few and smacked his tan lips. They were soft shells, he said. In with all that were some silver gray shrimp, their tails fluttering for the last time.

We'd put the net out, and after a half hour of circling a spot of the lake, we'd stop and pull it in. After four or five runs I convinced Mr. Hebert to let me pull the net in with Michael. It wasn't long before we had almost fifty pounds of shrimp tails. Mr. Hebert showed me how easy it was to grab the shrimp in one hand and pop the translucent head off. When I tried it, I stabbed myself with a barb that shrimp have sticking out of their heads like a jousting sword. Then their razor-sharp shells cut my hands and the salty water ran in the cuts. By the time I got twenty pounds of shrimp tails ready my hands were sliced up.

Mike asked his grandad if he could make a pass with the net and run the boat. Mr. Hebert turned off the motor, stepped over into Mike's center seat and, saying nothing, let him run the boat.

"Grandad?" Mike asked. "Tell Peter about when you were my age. You know, when you—"

"Now, Mike, I'm busy with this shrimping," he responded. Mr. Hebert was the kind of man who blushed when he talked about himself.

"Please, Grandad. Tell him about that summer, the summer of 1921," Mike remembered proudly.

"When that summer began, I was thirteen, Mike. That'd make me 'bout two years younger than you are now, right?" The net was out for a new run. There were more boats now, so we had to keep it in the water longer.

"Right," Mike said. I don't know how many times Mike had heard this, but he couldn't wait to hear it again.

He proceeded. The fact that this man had only been thirteen when it happened made it almost unbelievable to me. It was like hearing about a childhood from another planet.

"After school was out that year, I took a pirogue"—

which was a canoe-thin boat, hand-carved from a cypress log—
"a cast-iron skillet, a shotgun and some clothes." (I had heard
that to sit in a pirogue, much less paddle one through the
swamps, took a lot of coordination.)

"Grandad, tell him. You were all by yourself that whole
summer," Mike added.

"That's right. The reason I lived out there was because
back in '21, in these parts, money was real scarce. I was there
to hunt gators. Back then gators were as thick as birds. I lived
in a real old houseboat. It had a wood stove in it. I caught all
that I ate: fish, some duck, squirrel." (I looked at Michael,
thought of me at thirteen, fourteen, or even now, and tried to
imagine either one of us spending a summer hunting gator
alone, living in a swamp, catching all our food. No way.
Cutting grass and making a few bucks to get summer funky
were as far as I got. Michael played Babe Ruth baseball in the
summer and went to church camp.)

"Why did you spend the whole summer out there hunting
gator? Why didn't you go home every night?" Mike wanted
to scare himself again.

"The night was when I hunted them. See this wealthy
landowner, he lived in Lake Charles, well, back in them days
the fur-bearing animals like mink, muskrat and nutria were
worth a lot. Well, the gators weren't worth nothin', and they
ate little animals as fast as Mike eats my fried shrimp. Well,
this rich man, see, he put a price on them gators' hides. Five
fifty for everything from seven and a half feet to twenty feet.
Every gator from four feet to seven feet was a dollar fifty.
You know that in 1921, five dollars was like seventy-five
dollars today."

"Grandad, tell him about the time one gator over fifteen
feet knocked you into the water." Mike beamed.

Mr. Hebert just continued his story. He remembered it
all vividly.

"Gators don't come out much during the day. And besides, they might attack a man quicker in daylight. That pirogue
I paddled through the bayous and canals was pretty tippy."
(What he didn't say was that it could be tipped over by breathing too deeply.)

"In the blackness of nighttime I would move through the waters with a lantern and my shotgun. All the time, 'cept full moons, it was as dark as anything. No one lived within miles of the marsh and swamp I was huntin' in. I'd shine that lantern out in them canals and bayous and there would be nothin' shining back but eyes. Red gator eyes.

"I'd paddle within two and three feet of them gators' eyes, keepin' that light in them, and with my shotgun, I'd shoot 'em right between the eyes!"

He stopped talking because it was time to pull the net in again. There was a big bunch of shrimp, jiggling, trying to pop back into the water. The net was put back out, and Mr. Hebert, born on August 21, 1907, continued his story about the summer of '21.

"I had to be kinda careful the way I paddled my pirogue into position with them gators. Had to make sure that they were pointed the right way. Sometimes their heads could be sticking in one direction and their tails in another. When I shot, they'd jump and try to whip their tails around and knock me in the water with them." (The ultimate terror: being knocked into the black, bottomless bayou water in the darkness at thirteen.)

"Tell him what happened, Grandad," Mike said.

"After I'd shoot one, I'd paddle over to the bank, holding onto its mouth with one hand, and drag it out of the water. I'd leave it there till morning." (I could not imagine dragging a 300-, 400-, 500-pound gator out of the oozy, warm water at midnight.)

"In the morning I'd paddle back and skin the thing. Sometimes I'd skin all day long and hunt almost all night. Couldn't do that today. Hunt all night, skin all day." He paused briefly to watch some summer ducks fly over us. Said something about some thunderclouds might make us quit shrimping early. "I stored all them hides in wood barrels filled with brine. My dad would come pick 'em up some weekends. Kind of checked up on me. Brought me some more shells for the gun, maybe a cake my mama cooked. Boy, them cakes were good-tastin' after all that fish, duck and stuff."

"Grandad, tell him about getting attacked by that gator." Mike wanted to hear it again.

"Now, Mike, I wasn't attacked." Mr. Hebert pointed toward a shallow corner of Calcasieu Lake. There were thousands of shrimp exploding from the water. Maybe a big redfish after those shrimp, he said. The yakking sea gulls were flying into each other over the panicky shrimp. He headed the boat in that direction.

"I'll never forget goin' out in Lacassine Bayou to fish in the spring. We'd paddle up on a big shallow pond and we'd see maybe twenty bull gators and one female. Those bulls would bellow so loud you could hear it over the whole marsh. When they were bellowing like that, all the other animals hid out. Sometimes even the fish seemed to quit biting. The bigger gators"—there were a few fourteen-footers in that pond—"they would fight off the smaller ones for that female. The water would boil; they grab each other and twist and turn, tryin' to tear each other up. The way they bellowed, that sound they made, and the way they attacked anything that moved, now that was one time I was scared in the marsh." (If that had scared him, I would have died.)

"Grandad, please tell me about that time the gator got you."

"This particular night was extra-dark. It was one of those hot, foggy nights. A mist hung everywhere, real low. No clear, dark night. Fact is, my lantern would just shine out a little ways into the water. The gators seemed to be thicker and closer together on warm nights like this. There were those eyes all over. There was some terrible noises coming through the fog. I eased up on these eyes. From the size of the head the thing had to be at least ten feet long. One of them big-headed type of gators. Real wide head.

"So I let him have it, and before I knew it, my boat was turned over and me, the gun, my lantern, everything I had was in that water with the gators. There were plenty in there, jus' waitin' for a thrashin' man." (I could not let my imagination picture being knocked into a bayou by a gator. How did he have any idea in the dark where he was? How did he ever get out of the water? How did he get back to the houseboat that night? What about his gun? Were there huge chunks bitten from his pants-covered legs that I couldn't see?)

"I thought for a second of diving for that gun, but it was so dark. I couldn't see anything and all I could hear was that shot gator thrashing right next to me. The water was so warm it was hard to tell if anything was touching me. I just swam in the direction I thought the bank was, and when I felt the mud of land, I scrambled out. My boat floated over to the other side of the bayou; the gun, I guessed, it was sunk into the mud. All I could do was sit there and wait for daylight. I was scared them gators would come after me on the land. For some reason they didn't. Next mornin' I swam over and got my pirogue, dove down and found my shotgun and drug that gator out on the bank. It was a twelve-footer.

"When I came home after that summer, I had grown 'bout six inches and filled out real big. After dragging them gators out the water, seven days a week, turnin' over four-hundred-pound gators to skin 'em, why, that fall, when I went out for football, I had it easy. Tacklin' people and running over linebackers was nothin' much. You know, I'd grown so much my mama didn't recognize me when I came home that fall. I got almost three hundred gators that summer. That money sure helped out our family. We had six children."

We unloaded the nets into the light green pickup, iced down the shrimp and drove home. I was so tired I dozed off. Mike switched on the city's rock station, KLOU, real loud. Mr. Hebert didn't seem to mind. Fact is, he tapped his finger ever so subtly on the steering wheel. The man had soul.

There was a curly-haired baby in Mr. Hebert's lap. She threw another shrimp onto the ground. Barbara and I were at a Hebert shrimp boil and Grandad Hebert was trying to teach one of his many grandbabies to peel and eat boiled shrimp.

Mr. Hebert and Bobbie had prepared about forty pounds of our catch. Bobbie had cooked all kinds of other food and her daughter had brought some over, too. Everyone in the clan was there. No one would miss a shrimp boil like this.

The one thing that I could compare it to was an Italian wedding, but no one was getting married except me. I was marrying the boiled shrimp. Even while chewing, everyone smiled.

Robbie walked over with a plateful of food. He was not as tall as his younger brother, Mike, but he had the same thick, sun-browned, curly hair. Robbie was a long-distance runner, one of the best in the south of Louisiana, and like a lot of runners I knew, he was solitary and seemed to think about what he was going to say before he said it. Robbie's specialty was the two-mile run. He was five-seven or eight and weighed 135. There was a scar on his chest where he'd had heart surgery as a young boy. "Granpa?" Robbie spoke softly. I'd noticed since being in Louisiana that most of the men spoke softly, regardless of whether they drilled for oil, farmed rice, loaded ships at the port of Lake Charles or hunted.

"Yeah, Robbie," the man said.

"Granpa, after you spent that summer in the swamp trapping gators, it really built you up, made you a good athlete. How come, if you were all-state as a fullback, that you played baseball instead of football?" Being all-state fullback in Louisiana was as important as anything a young man could do. I didn't know Mr. Hebert had been a star in high school athletics.

We sat under the canopy of twisted pine branches, waiting for Mr. Hebert's answer.

"I began playing baseball way before I played football. We played in a field filled with stumps. Sometimes one of the boys would be chasin' a fly ball and almost disappear into a sinkhole. Finally, we all learned where those big ol' cypress stumps were and a few could run without even lookin'. They had 'em memorized where they were. Some days the guys would have to sidestep the snakes. Especially if we had high water."

"Did you know my granpa pitched against Babe Ruth?" Robbie asked me, interrupting Mr. Hebert.

"After high school I was working for Gulf States Utilities. It was a good job. Plenty money. We had a baseball team in the summer and one weekend in 1929 we were playin' Houston Electric. Anyway, that day I pitched a no-hit, no-run game.

There happened to be a pro scout there, watchin' some relative. They signed me in '30 to play Class C. It was the St. Louis Browns minor-league team. We played Joplin, Missouri; Fort Smith, Arkansas; Shawnee, Oklahoma; Independence, Kansas; and I think it was Springfield, Missouri. Small towns. Man, it was hot, too. Dry! Woo, yeah."

A man walked over to say hello briefly. He had one of those crying faces, as though life had overwhelmed him. I never did know who he was. It occurred to me then that these people with the French blood seemed to have faces like Mr. Hebert's or the stranger's. They were laughing or crying faces.

Mr. Hebert continued. "Playing ball's where I got my nickname. At first they called me Mississippi Mudcat. But seems to me some other pitcher had that name. Then they took to calling me Preacher. Never could figure that one out," he said, as though still surprised at the nickname which stuck to this day.

"Big as you are, Preacher, you must have been a fastball power pitcher?" I asked.

"I was more a control pitcher. I reckon, with my strength I coulda been physically overpowering. I used the curve, dry spitter, sinker, slider, knuckle ball and fastball. I had a pretty decent fastball. Mostly I studied the hitters I faced." He would watch for the subtlest changes in their stances. Maybe they showed weakness in handling certain combinations of pitches. Maybe they hated slow pitches, and when they got mad, they couldn't hit so well. Babe Ruth was that way, Preacher said.

He pitched to Ruth, Ted Williams, Joe DiMaggio, Lou Gehrig and hundreds of others. He pitched professionally for twelve to thirteen years. He saw as many types of hitters as he had ducks and geese.

"Babe Ruth, now, that man was a power hitter. All his power was in his upper body. He lunged at the ball. He hated slow-ball pitchers. Used to call 'em crap ball pitchers. Me, I just never pitched him the same way. Never threw the knuckle ball on strike three. Now anyone that knew Ruth could tell you some real wild stories 'bout the man. But I don't believe in all that. People should mind their own business. We stuck together in those days. Now they pose in underwear." Mr.

Preacher (left) with Ted Lyons of the White Sox, when he pitched for the old St. Louis Browns

Preacher's hands

Hebert raised his eyebrows and looked amazed. He thought for a while—maybe about Babe Ruth posing for an underwear ad, because he chuckled before he began again.

"To me, Lou Gehrig was one of the best hitters I ever pitched to. He hit flat-footed and had few weaknesses. He was quiet, but could *he* play.

"I'll never forget when Ted Williams broke into baseball. It was 1936. I was pitchin' with the San Diego Padres and Ted was seventeen years old. He was as thin as a willow branch. They used to say he could rattle them boards. He was such a pure hitter that when the ball left his bat, it took off low like a bullet and it would hit the boards at the back of the stadium and make the loudest noise. He was seventeen. I was twenty-nine. Ted was born and raised there in San Diego and they took him right out of high school. When the balls he hit started risin' just so, they'd land way beyond four hundred feet away. Those balls dented cars, broke windows. They weren't the kind of home-run ball that went way high and landed soft. Those pitchers that pitched him walked him 'bout every four times at bat. He had eyes like a telescope. Lots of times they'd walk him on purpose. He hated that, Ted did."

One great moment was a hot summer's day. It was June 20, 1932, and Preacher Hebert struck out Lou Gehrig and Babe Ruth that game. For many years he had more complete innings pitched than any pitcher ever in the Pacific Coast League. But to me, there's one story that best told the story of the man.

It was the first day of June. The year was 1941. Preacher was the starting pitcher for San Diego that day and the mound was fresh-raked. The place was Los Angeles. The team was the Los Angeles Angels. Preacher was pitching smoothly, efficiently, and he felt great. He had an eight-run lead. Although Preacher was a left-handed pitcher, he was never known as flaky, the way a lot of left-handers were. Everybody, including his manager, Cedric Durst, thought of him as an unshakable country boy. Well, Bobbie, his wife, was expecting their second child any day. The word came to the manager and to the press box, while he was on the mound, that sure enough Bobbie had had their second child.

The manager, having known Preacher for more than ten

years, decided that they'd let the play-by-play man announce it over the public address. They figured he'd get so fired up he'd pitch even *better*. Strike out everyone so he could get to the hospital and see his baby.

After the announcement and the applause from the crowd, Preacher never struck out another batter. They took him out of the game and ended up losing to the Angels.

When Preacher finally got home to San Diego and went to the hospital to see the baby, there were fans everywhere. They loved Preacher and Bobbie in San Diego. When Preacher looked down at Hillene and her big Cajun eyes, he melted.

By now Preacher had been making his living pitching baseballs for thirteen years and he missed the marshland of Louisiana. There was no ground anywhere in the world as fertile where he could grow tomatoes, okra, roasting ear corn, squash and his beloved rice so delicious. He couldn't hear a bull gator roar except if he went to the San Diego Zoo, nor could he watch the sky turn electric pink with flights of wild flamingos. The decision wasn't hard for Preacher and Bobbie to make. They went home.

11

Red Devil Eyes

There was nothing in front of us except two round red eyes. Everything else was a wet, humid black. The eyes glided forward, very slowly, and stopped. We eased forward and the iridescent eyes slid to the right, then closer to us. They held a steady and lethal stare. No movie of frantic possession had ever made me want to escape like I wanted to now, but there was nowhere to go.

The black silence broke with a splash and grabbed my throat.

"That one is over ten feet long," he said. "There's two more right in front of us, both more than ten feet long." He sounded raspy and full of excitement as he tried to keep his voice down.

I had been so tense that when he spoke, it was like another hand at my throat. I had forgotten there was someone else in the boat with me. We were floating down a slim, overgrown bayou, our backs to the end of the canal. We were facing four eyes that glowed like two demons. The man in the boat with me carefully pushed us further back. He was using his paddle to ease us along. The water was so black we couldn't tell where it ended, and all of a sudden we felt a bump.

Scratch. Bump. The willows and marsh grass rubbed against the boat and we could hear the water lap against the boat and the swampy bank. My nerves were already past the surface of my skin and I jumped in fright at the noise. Then we flushed some sleeping water birds and they screamed for me.

The bull alligators came even closer. Now they were only twenty feet from us, circling us in the waters that they owned. I knew they sensed they could conquer me. If only they could get me out of that short fourteen-foot aluminum boat. It had hopelessly low sides. They could easily explode from the water and land in the boat. And where could I go? There would be no running because these marsh grasses could only hold up egrets, muskrats and huge cottonmouths, as black and thick as tires. The four empty red eyes stalked closer.

The plotting gators were closer to each other and seemed to be deciding which one would eat me and which one would eat Mr. Hebert. Now they were splitting up. One moved silently a few feet closer to the boat, which was jammed as far as it could go into the end of the overgrown bayou. These bayous were like passageways through the endless marshes and swamps, but we had hit a dead-end one.

I must have been crazy to come out here on this moonless, flat black night to help search out the biggest alligators in southwestern Louisiana, especially with only an old car battery and headlight taped to a broken broom handle.

"Them bull gators, they so big they got green moss growin' on their backs," Mr. Hebert said.

This man wasn't afraid. He grew up in a boat. He would know what to do. Some people joked he was born in a boat. These southern Louisiana people were often teased about having web feet.

"It's not normal to see big gators together like this," this fearless man stuttered in his deep voice. "Usually they fight each other off or eat each other."

"You kidding?" I asked, turning around to see the outline of his face in the night.

"Yeah, Pete, I've seen 'em with their legs chewed off, no eyes, tails gone, and teeth marks a foot long down their sides."

I groaned. "What should we do?" I felt uneasy in a boat

in a pure lake where the water was nice and only had bass and pretty ducks in it, much less out here like this. "I think we ought to be going soon. Did you bring your rifle?" I asked.

He moved quickly, his hand scratching around on the plywood floor of the boat. That was unlike him because he usually moved as deliberately as the gators swam. He had forgotten whether he had stuck his 30-06 in the boat, about the only weapon that could stop one of the incredibly powerful gators. This man who lived for the marsh, the swamps, the shrimping, the skinning of gators, this man who had the eyesight of a duck hawk and who could outsee younger men with binoculars as ducks flew into the blinds, had forgotten his rifle. He was scared. I was beyond scared.

He looked back and re-aimed the headlight where they had been. They were gone, but I knew they were still out there close by. He moved the beam again, nervously jerking the ray of light back and forth, trying to find them. Still not there. Then he pulled the straight beam of white light in closer, but those red, possessing eyes did not answer back.

We sat there in silence with only the occasional slapping of the water against the boat. Then, for some strange reason, this quiet man began to tell me a story. I almost freaked out. It must have relieved some tension for him, but I wished I had never come out here. Why couldn't I be safe back in their air-conditioned house watching cable TV?

He turned the light in the direction behind us as if he were looking for a way out, a road or something man-made to help us escape. Of course, there wasn't anything. We were in the gator's world. Of all things, Mr. Hebert turned off the light.

"Turn that light back on!" I shrieked before I got control.

"Can't, Pete. Battery's about gone and then we will not have a light." He sounded a lot calmer than I did.

So he began his story.

"One time my brother-in-law, his name's Stoner, was out here fishin' for them big redfish. He loved catchin' those big reds, Stoner did. It was gettin' midday and they had a whole cooler full of them and should of quit. It was so hot, you know, beatin' down and their ice was meltin' in the cooler."

Normally one sentence every half hour was really running at the mouth for Mr. Hebert, so I knew he must have been real nervous to have said all that in one breath.

"Anyways, Stoner had a beauty hooked, seven- or eight-pounder, and he was payin' close attention not to lose this one." Mr. Hebert looked around, panning his head from side to side as he talked.

"Stoner's grandson, Todd, you remember, the little blond boy with him?"

"Yeah," I answered, not really paying attention.

"The grandboy was gettin' tired and wanted to go home, but Stoner wanted to stay. Can you believe a grandad was outfishin' his grandson?

"Well, all of a sudden the boy started yellin' for his grandad to look up, and there was one of the biggest ol' buck deer swimming across the bayou. He was swimmin' so fast that instead of his head and antlers stickin' out of the water, his whole front quarters were out."

"What happened?" I interrupted.

"His front legs were slappin' the water and he was jerkin' everywhere. The buck musta weighed over a hundred fifty pounds. He just disappeared in the bayou; all they saw was him twistin' like crazy.

"Did you know the water turned red and it wasn't long before everything was calm again? Stoner said he almost threw up his lunch when one of the buck's legs floated to the top. He started the motor to get out of there, and just as he did, a bull gator eased up real slowlike and grabbed that leg in one bite and went under."

How could he have turned out the light to tell that story? My imagination took over and I saw myself being dragged under in the slimy water, gators' teeth tightening around my body, and never coming up again. There could not be any worse end than being at the bottom of a warm mud bayou in the mouth of one of the kings of the swamp.

The ending to my mental horror movie stopped when Mr. Hebert turned on the light again. They were where he knew they would be, right next to the boat. The big one on the left was no more than four feet from me with only a thin aluminum boat wall separating us. I remembered from another one of his stories that they could bite through a boat like this. When the light flashed in my direction, those red eyes were staring at me.

"You see that?" Mr. Hebert whispered.

"What?" I flinched.

"Looks like there's more than a foot between them eyes."

I sat paralyzed. For the first time it was so close I could see the whole head. It was knobby, big and black, and ugly. I knew that behind those impassive, staring eyes a small brain was waiting to give the command to tear me apart, like that fattened buck deer.

"Sit still, and be quiet," Mr. Hebert ordered me. "If they sense you are scared, they might get more aggressive."

"More aggressive?" How could they get more aggressive? I shivered quietly in the over-90-degree night that surrounded me like a wet ghost. My stomach, my whole body jittered and I felt I was going to throw up. Nothing had ever overcome me with its presence like this.

I caught my breath and knew it was over. Mr. Hebert had picked up his favorite oar, old and battered, lifted it high over his head and brought it down on the bull gator that was closest to him, using all of the strength of his seventy years. *This is it.* They would be turning the boat over any second. The boat bounced back and forth, making it possible for the gator's head to be level with the top of the side wall. The way the gator moved, which is to say, barely, it must have felt as pleasurable as a back scratch.

I grabbed the light and beamed the light ray down nearest to the boat's sides. The eyes were there, waiting for their food to make the final mistake, to panic for the last time. One wrong move and we would be theirs.

"What are we going to do?"

"Stay calm."

"How are we going to get out of here?"

There was no time to answer. A loud thump hit the under side of the boat, and then another thud, louder this time, hit the back end of the boat. My God, they were attacking! Mr. Hebert began nervously fumbling around under him, and he turned over his tackle box, the ice chest and whatever else lay on the bottom of the boat. He jerked the lamp from my hand and flashed it at the gator nearest to me. It was about two feet away and I could have reached my hand in his direction and come back with no hand.

Those empty red eyes, like bright lights shining from a semi on the interstate, stared. Still waiting for me, its prey, to panic and do something that would put me in its water.

Mr. Hebert found an old glass bottle that he used for bait.

"I'm going to throw this to make him think there's something to eat back behind him, so watch out."

"No, don't throw it! He's too close!" The bottle splashed. That bull gator's whole body was aimed like a simmering rocket right at me and I knew if that bottle hit it, there would be a gator in my lap.

This was our last chance. The gator stayed still, never blinking an eye. Mr. Hebert reached below him again, shifting oars, gas cans and who knows what in the darkness. This time he held the light on the bottom of the boat. He found something else. It was an old plastic milk jug filled with ice that had been in the cooler.

With both big hands he flung the jug. *Splash*. It made a much bigger noise. Smoothly the gator turned to the right and glided toward the splash. It probably thought it was me. As the moss-covered monster swam through the water silently, Mr. Hebert handed me one of the oars and shouted for the first time. "Push. Push us out. Hurry."

He furiously ripped at the rope to start the black Mercury engine. The way he pulled it, I wondered if he would pull the cord out of the 9½-horsepower engine. For his age, this man of the swamps had a lot of power. It didn't start. He flashed the light over and the bull gator was turning around and heading back toward us. Again Mr. Hebert ripped at the cord.

"Can't get this oar to come loose, stuck in the mud," I screamed as I heaved to pull it out. The oar had gone down into the mud as easy as melted butter but wouldn't come out. A suction held it there.

"Stand up and pull harder," Mr. Hebert ordered as he gripped the cord again.

I should have known not to stand up too fast in a small boat. The boat rocked and I fell down hard on the metal and splintered wood. My left arm flopped into the darkness and down into the water. I knew there would be teeth around it in just seconds. I yanked my arm up as fast as I could, yet sharp psychic pains went through me as I thought about having it bitten off.

My arm was all right, but I felt light and dizzy as I threw all my weight against that stuck oar. There was a loud suction noise as the oar was released from that bottomless pit of rotted bones and stench and everything else that had turned to mud over the years.

I strained and pushed again, this time with the help of the weakened beam of light, and the boat moved. Mr. Hebert finally pulled the engine cord just right and it started. The engine sputtered and spit smoke as he threw it into reverse. We had to fight against trying to turn the boat around too fast because it could flip. Within seconds, what seemed like hours to me, we had the boat steered in the right direction, away from the dead-end marsh, away from those hungry swamp kings, and we were out of there.

We looked back; the gators were dropping farther and farther behind as we sped into the night winds blowing from the Gulf. The cool salt air on my face helped me relax again. I'm glad those four red eyes got no closer.

The sun was coming up. The Hebert camp, a cabin on pilings on top of a man-made island of white shells, was surrounded by thousands of square miles of marsh, waterways, canals and swamp that slithered with untold kinds of wildlife. Preacher and I had come to this camp two days earlier to hunt gator. Only the wildest life survived out here. The way to get to this camp was to take a four-mile boat trip through what was a maze of lily pads, aquatic growth and narrow bayous. Occasionally we came into open water. We had to cross the Intracoastal Waterway.

Marsh hens walked on top of lily pads, their steps deliberate. They didn't want to end up in some snapping turtle's jaws. It took very little for them to start shouting in their high-pitched voices. There were small oil platforms in these shallow marshes put there by Union 76. Terns and gulls used these rusted metal oil collection stations as clubhouses. Every time a boat went by they had to fly overhead to see if it was going somewhere that they might mooch some food. They flew over us once, got bored and flew back.

Pink ibis, long-lanky wading birds, flew over in diamond formations. Alligator garfish, some over 200 pounds, rolled on top of the water. Preacher told me that on particularly hot days they rolled a lot because the oxygen content of the water was lower than usual and that was their way of getting a deep breath. Whatever they were doing, they slapped their tails as loud as a rifle, and it made my heart pop.

Snakes of many colors swam on top of the water like so many hairs in a bathtub. Red-winged blackbirds sat on top of the tallest marsh grass and guarded their nests. The lily pads stretched endlessly with cantaloupe-sized white-yellow flowers. Bamboo poles, put there by people, marked the way through the scraggly water passageways. It reminded me of a mountain man's knife markings on trees leading to his cache of furs or maybe his still. I could never have found my way out here. Often we'd pass a thick fishing line tied to a stout branch hanging over the water. Preacher explained that they were trotlines, which were fishing lines stretched across a bayou with many fish hooks on them. Many marsh people ate much of what they did eat from what they caught on these.

On the camp's man-made island, there were two main cabins, the bigger one owned by the Heberts, and the other, smaller, was owned by a family that were their partners in rice farming. There were a few shacks with rusting tin roofs and a couple of boat sheds. They looked as if they had survived some hurricanes. There were huge piles of duck decoys and crabbing traps. There were poles for pushing the flatboats through low, muddy marsh water and snake skins everywhere. Snakes used this island for shedding their skins. The Heberts kept the grass cut as short as a marine's hair so that no one would step on any poison coral snakes or cottonmouths. Grass grew through the white shells and the sun reflected hot off the tin roof that was still silver. There were old decaying pieces of fishing line everywhere. The fishing poles were kept inside.

It snarled to life, sending deafening warnings through the marsh. This was morning, the opening of gator season, the only legal one in the U.S.A. *It* was the boat that we would use to cover the thousands of acres of marsh that they hunted. This boat was no shiny specialty model; the Heberts had made it themselves. It was a shallow-hulled wood boat, and instead of an outboard, it had a V-8 engine from some old car right in the middle of it. Oftentimes, Preacher explained, the water was only about six inches deep and *then* there was maybe three, four feet of mud. No boat could get through but this mud boat.

We were out alligator trapping when Glenn Hebert, a distant cousin of Preacher Hebert, held up a bamboo pole that had a long white nylon line attached to it. Glenn explained that they tied large fish hooks on the end of the line and used blackbirds for bait. The line was staked into the ground and the bamboo pole held the bird and the line suspended over the water. The bird dangled about eight inches off the surface. The line was held to the pole by the thinnest thread. That way only the gators would be able to reach the bait.

We set up about fifty poles and lines that day and covered many thousands of acres of marsh, weaving down one thin trail after another. We'd come out into open bodies of shallow water and Glenn would guide the boat with his built-in radar to the continuation of the trail on the other side, maybe three-quarters of a mile away.

As always, I had my dented Nikon camera around my neck. The sun was too bright to take any pictures now. Glenn, whose piercing stare made me a bit uneasy, kept looking at the camera. Maybe he'd never seen one like it before. "What's the real reason you're out here?" he said after hours of setting up the alligator traps.

The hot air that the boat kicked off had made me sleepy and I didn't answer right away.

"I asked you *why* you came out here during gator season, sir!" He slowed down the V-8 engine.

"I'm out here because I have always wanted to live out in the marsh." Glenn was the kind of man who wanted you to look him in the eyes when you spoke.

"You know, we make our living, just barely surviving a lot of time, off these marshes, bayous, swamps and Gulf. Hundreds of people in Washington try to tell us when to do this and that. How there ain't gators in the swamps when we know they are so thick they eat each other and are crawling into people's swimming pools. Eating people's dogs in their backyards, even go after their children. I heard one of those Washington people shouting about how we were barbarian, gun-shooting rednecks, killing gators just for fun, for sport. They were saying all this while wearing their gator-skinned shoes and carrying matching handbag or wallet. You don't see me wearing anything made of gator skin. We just been trappin' all our lives down here and it's a way to make a living."

Glenn had a preacher's zeal and he talked faster and faster. "They told us to stop trapping gator for twelve years because they said we were killing them off. They may have been doing that down in Florida, but we Cajuns, we take care of our wildlife. We don't abuse it. We've been living on these bayous for too many years, long before someone could sign up for food stamps and welfare. We stopped, left them alone until they overpopulated, till they got so thick they were eating all the other life in the marsh."

The mud boat scared about twenty long-legged wading birds that were sticking their long beaks into the shallow mud. They could have been curlews or sandpipers. Near here they said there were whooping cranes. These Cajun people were as connected to their environment as any people I knew.

Glenn was still talking. "This year we are allowed to trap a hundred fourteen gators. They all have to be at least six feet long. You know how they figured out a hundred fourteen? Now I think this method is a good thing for us and the gators.

"Well, they have some scientific way of flying over the marsh and counting up all the active nests. They do it during

nesting season, when all the females are laying on these big
mounds of grass they make. They say that by counting all the
nests, they can come very close to estimates of how many
gators are in this part of the marsh. Even those Washington
boys say there are five times more gators here now than back
when they stopped the huntin'. Anything to protect our marsh
is fine as long as they don't get air-headed about it. Sometimes
they do good; other times they don't."

That afternoon I found out a lot more about Glenn. He
was Preacher's fourth cousin. He had three children, farmed
1,600 acres of rice land, had worked on an offshore oil rig
and now, besides gator, trapped nutria, mink, muskrat and
raccoon. He also did a lot of duck and goose hunting.

Glenn had wanted to go by one of his favorite places at
the edge of the Sabine Refuge, to see how some nesting cranes
were getting along. He said he loved to watch the babies try
to walk on those spindly, bamboo-skinny legs. But there was
a black-gray cloud, raging and round, coming in fast from the
open Gulf. We were not more than three miles from the Gulf
as the sea gull flew. If it caught us, and those thunderheads
moved as fast and erratic as attacking Mongols, we could be
killed by striking lightning. More than a few people they knew
had been killed by lightning on the open water. Glenn put the
gas to the boat, and a rooster tail of mud raised behind us. We
were in the boat shed quickly. These swamp men were scared
of little, but killer lightning put the fear of God in them.

"One of the neighbor girls might have been about seven
years old, she got hurt real bad. Terrible," Preacher said. "She
had extra-thick black hair down past her back. I remember
'cause my sister and her used to play house."

We were both sitting in an elevated shack that was next
to the cabin that we slept in. Its wood siding looked like
reclaimed driftwood and a few warped windows let in what
little light there was. The place was filled with duck decoys,
rusty anchors and small weights that were used to hold the
floating decoys in place. There were piles of old nets. Fishing
lures missing their hooks hung from the wall. If Andrew Wyeth
painted Louisiana Americana, this interior would have been

one of his best. Preacher wore the room as if he were born in here. The light from the moldy windows was dimming; rain drummed on the tin roof. The summer storm had reminded Preacher of the small girl with the long hair.

"When the hurricane hit, there was nowhere to run. No one but Dr. Hawkins had a car. The little girl's daddy forced the whole family out of their house, crying. They wanted to bring their toys and pets. They all laid down by the strongest section of fence they could find. Anyway, when the worst of the winds blew over that family, they said that the little girl lost her grip on the fence and was saved only because her hair caught onto the barbed wire."

It was not too far past midday, but there was no light to see. Preacher lit a kerosene storm lamp. We weren't in there anymore to listen to the rain. It now sounded like the hardest rock group gone crazy. Even though we were just fifty feet from the cabin, we'd have been drenched if we'd tried to leave. Possibly struck by lightning.

"Her hair caught onto the fence.

"Her brother said that one of the times when he could see her, her body was almost straightened out by the winds. There was nothing he could do. It was all they could do to hold onto the fence. In the strongest gusts, her little body was parallel with the ground, held there by that long, tangled hair. Every one of them had broken bones, but they all lived." The rain now was blowing so hard that it was hitting the sides of the building more than the roof.

"Our best horse had a two-by-four blown through it. Our house was blown away."

I was sure he was talking about a hurricane he'd lived through, but I didn't want to ask any questions. It obviously had profound influences on his life.

"Because of that hurricane, our whole family had to move to the city [Lake Charles]. It wiped out, blew away and killed everything we'd worked for. It was the hurricane of 1918."

Preacher had a quiet way of letting me know how serious a hurricane could be, with winds over 100 mph, sometimes 200 mph. History seemed to be measured in southern Louisiana by the hurricanes that hit.

"The worst hurricane I can remember was Audrey back in 1957. What she did to the people in Cameron was the awfulest thing I ever seen in my whole life."

Preacher went silent, as though the memories of it were painful.

"I was working for Firestone at the time, and when we got word it was coming, the boss asked me and a few of the boys to stay with the plant through the hurricane. Well, the winds hit us at the plant real bad. We all thought the place would explode. After it passed, we heard that it had wiped Cameron [a coastal fishing and oil service town of about 9,000] off the face of the earth. The whole area was now the Gulf. A tidal wave had covered everything but a few of the highest peaked roofs. Well, my brother Charles lived down there, and so did other friends and relatives. We got in a boat and went down there. The planes that flew overhead said that all but a few people, a very few, would be drowned and worse."

Preacher turned ash gray. He looked the other way for a moment, and when he finally spoke again, it was as though he were talking to himself.

"Where the road had been, the Gulf covered it.

"Alligators swam crazy, panicked.

"Clothes, dead chickens, gas cans, everything floated by us.

"We ran over and by thousands of drowned cows, horses.

"Even thousands of birds, floating.

"Drowned cats, rats, garbage . . .

"Bodies . . ."

Raindrops kept crashing, giving emphasis to Preacher's every word.

"Stoner said it was worse than the war."

There was nothing more, only the sound of thunder for about fifteen minutes. I picked up a Ducks Unlimited baseball cap and pulled the bill over my eyes. I knew Preacher wouldn't want me to look at him now.

One night Preacher came over to the dock where I was baiting a line. He had told me that if I put out a line overnight,

I might catch one of those huge alligator gars. Some were ten feet long.

"Pete," he said, "I think we'll take the boat and go to the house for a few days tomorrow. I kinda miss the wife and I need to check on my garden. You want to come?"

"Sure, Preacher," I said.

Barbara was sitting with Bobbie in the den and she looked wonderfully rested. After lunch she said she wanted to go for a walk. It was the hottest time of the day. I knew she had something to say that would have an impact. There was a distinct possibility that all this rest and air-conditioned comfort had helped her to do what she had threatened. There was an angle to her jaw, a way in which she held her mouth, that I had not seen on her face since we'd begun the walk. Maybe she was going to tell me that the walk had to end. That she could take it no longer. That the whole thing was absurd, as some had suggested. Possibly she would suggest that she couldn't take the walking and camping and she would get a car and follow me from town to town. She had her mind made up about something.

"Peter." Barbara didn't wait long to make her point. "Am I going to be a total part of this walk or not?"

"Of course," I said.

"Are you and Preacher going back to the camp in the marsh?"

"Preacher is. I was planning to go back with him."

"I'm going back to the marsh with you." The thinnest smile broke through, the kind that meant Barbara was absolutely determined.

I could tell Barbara was surprised to see how tiny the island of shells was that held us all. The heavy smells came in hot gusts from the Gulf. Scents of fish, exposed mud, brackish water, oil and a lot more mingled into the perfume of the swamp.

Glenn was standing under the dominant willow tree, in his usual clean tan work shirt. His thick arms were crossed on his muscular chest. His face reacted openly and quickly to all life and he didn't look too excited to see Barbara. This was a man's island. It was for men who thrived on danger.

"Preacher, I'd like to talk to you," Glenn said immediately. Glenn's voice had the intensity of a marine.

I took Barbara over to Glenn's mother, who sat in her white metal chair under the willow, and introduced them. They seemed to like each other. Most people liked Barbara right away. Mrs. Elaine Hebert seemed glad to have another woman out here with her.

Glenn and Preacher stood over by the skinning shed talking.

After some Cajun coffee and a few pieces of toast Glenn, Stoner and I headed for the shed where the boat was kept. Barbara followed behind. I figured she was just wanting to see the mud boat with the V-8 car engine in the center. She did look at the boat. Then she got in and sat down. Still, no one said anything. Glenn was tight-lipped. So was Stoner. Barbara sat on the front bench and faced out proudly like one of the carved angels they used to attach to sailing ships.

I was expecting Glenn to say something, give Barbara some kind of guided tour. There was no such tour. I decided not to say anything either. The tension was thick. Nobody was smiling, especially Barbara.

12

The Letter

Barbara

Bobbie sat snoozing in the reclining chair, taking a break from her soap operas while the noonday news came on television. The volume was turned low. It was the steady humming of the air conditioner that lulled her to sleep. I sat quietly at the kitchen table, writing a letter to my old roommate, Ann Green, telling her I was going to quit the walk and come back to the seminary in New Orleans.

For the first time in weeks I felt rested and like my old self as I wrote the letter. It was good to feel normal again, dressed in clean clothes; my hair was bouncy and combed, I had on fresh makeup, my stomach was full, and best of all, I wasn't carrying forty pounds on my back. After walking the past two months from New Orleans to here, I had proven to myself that I could walk across America, but I didn't want to. I was tired of sore muscles and dirt. A concentration camp could not have been worse than the shock and strain I had been through, trekking in the stagnant humid heat, mosquitoes, blisters, choking on the fumes of honking cars and living out of a tent and backpack. Sensitive and self-conscious, I couldn't stand being watched and pointed at by the steady stream of passersby one more day. All I wanted to do was retreat to my secure dorm room back at the Baptist seminary and pretend this wasn't happening to me.

Yet I was haunted by the sermon that brought Peter and me together, "Will You Go with This Man?" That November day in 1975 in the Word of Faith Temple kept flashing in my mind because that sermon was supposed to be my sign from God. This was a mission for me. Or was it? Doubts crept into my every waking moment and I was tormented constantly. I reasoned that Peter should finish the walk alone and I would join him somewhere on the West Coast. I was making my newlywed husband miserable with all my complaints, self-pity and slower pace. I had never been camping before in my life, nor was I an outdoors person, but now I was out here, walking across American with almost 3,000 miles ahead of me. Nothing was going right, so I must have been confused about that sermon in church. How could anyone expect me to go through such hardships, even God?

When Moses led the Israelites out of Egypt to the Promised Land, it was a forty-year walk on foot. That was fine for church history, but God didn't call on modern Christians like me to do such things. Even the Baptists thought I was crazy. Walking across America for the Lord was the most foolish thing in the world and it sure didn't fit into any missionary program. This was all just a delusion of mine.

As soon as I could make arrangements, I would return to the seminary and admit my mistake. I would tell Peter when he came home. I licked the envelope and sealed it, feeling proud that I was doing what I really wanted to do. Just as I pressed a stamp on the envelope, Peter and Preacher burst through the front door, waking Bobbie from her nap and letting in a gush of steamy air. Peter was so excited he almost tripped and fell at my feet. I jumped up and quickly stuffed the letter in my pocket because this was not the time to tell him I was quitting the walk.

He was beaming as he stuck his face in front of mine, trying to muffle his loud voice that echoed throughout the house anyway.

"Honey. Honey," he gasped. "You won't believe it. There are literally hundreds of alligators out there. I've never seen anything like it in my life."

"That's nice," I said, feeling resentful that Peter was

having all the adventure while I stayed behind. All that this walk had meant to me so far was hardships. "I want to see them, too."

Before dawn the next morning we left Westlake for the alligator camp. I was quiet and withdrawn as we loaded our gear into the flatboat and began the six-mile boat ride into the swamps and toward the camp. Just as my eyes were coming awake and starting to focus, something deep inside me was waking up with excitement, but I didn't want Peter to know. He had never seen me truly excited since we had been on the walk and I wasn't about to let him see me get enthused now that I had made up my mind to quit. It was a mystery to me, however, why I would like being the first woman to hunt alligators with these men. Something strange was happening to me. The more I tried to understand this stirring inside me, the more it eluded me.

We reached the camp before the sun came up and transferred our gear into the mud boat, which was a special flatboat with a souped up Chevrolet engine that was water-cooled. The mud boat could go through shallow water and sludge to get to the gators and we had twenty-six sets to check on this morning, so we had to get moving. Glenn Hebert stood tall at the end of the boat and shouted, "Contact," as he started the high-powered engine and we began to slide through the narrow trails of marsh. Sprays of thick black mud and water spit out the back.

Glenn Hebert was kin to Preacher. He had permits for trapping 114 alligators on this swamp that had been issued by the Louisiana Wildlife and Fisheries Department. Glenn angled the boat to the right and then to the left through the thin trails as easily as if we were on an open lake. Peter and Preacher were near the front while I sat at the rear of the boat. This was another world as we glided through the endless maze of rushes, salt grass, whips, lily pads and other swamp grasses. A hazy mist hung over the still waters. The only division was going from one black pond to another and Glenn seemed to know where all the openings were.

Within thirty minutes we came upon the first set. These sets were really traps where a dead blackbird was used as bait with a giant hook hidden inside the bird. A long rope was attached to the blackbird. We knew we had a gator when we saw the bird gone and the rope was underwater. Glenn eased the boat into the right position while Preacher began to pull at the rope. I was spellbound. I had never seen such a thing, not even in movies. The thick burlap rope began to move and spin and weave from side to side. Then without warning the rope went away from us with such terrific speed and force it almost pulled Preacher into the water. Peter jumped up to help as Glenn stepped back and got his rifle ready to fire.

"Pull, pull," Glenn screamed. The rope was slipping through Peter's and Preacher's big hands, giving them burns as they fought to get the gator back toward the boat. They heaved and pulled, making the flatboat tip from side to side. I grabbed the end of the rope to help pull and keep them from tripping over the slack. Black water was splashing everywhere and mud sprinkled on everyone.

"Get his head up.... Watch out." Everyone was yelling at once as a huge, knotty head surfaced. There was no time to be scared. The giant swamp creature growled or snorted; I wasn't sure since it was a different sound from any I had ever heard. He opened his long jaws and at least 100 sharp teeth glistened against his red-pink mouth in the watery light. As quickly as he surfaced, the gator flung his long body back and forth, trying to maneuver around and hit the boat with his power-packed tail.

"He's a good five-hundred-pounder," Glenn shouted above the splashing water. "Easy. Easy." Glenn held his rifle between both hands, aimed at the water and waited for the bull gator to come up. With a strong effort Preacher and Peter braced themselves against the side of the boat and pulled with all their might. His head came up, twisting and angry, and then a loud crack wailed across the swamp. The fury lasted only seconds as the massive gator went down. Glenn had shot him between the eyes. Sounds of the shot echoed into silence. My heart was racing and every cell in my body surged with new energy and excitement.

There was no time to waste. "Hurry, get him up," Glenn commanded. The heavy body had to be lifted out of the waters and stretched across the front deck in order to be tagged. It took all three men to hoist the gator out of the water onto the boat, and after they did, Glenn was sure he weighed 500 pounds.

On this day we would fight and eventually catch six big alligators and not make it back to camp until sunset. We were tired as we watched a flock of white egrets usher us back to camp. A smile was fixed behind Peter's rust-colored beard and his face was red from a sunburn as well as the soft light of the setting sun. There was a faraway look in his blue eyes. Mud was all over him, and he looked stately and wonderfully barbaric to me. He was perched on the front of the boat as we made our way through the shadowy swamp and he reminded me of a courageous Viking at the moment.

A salty breeze moistened the drying effects of the hot sun on my face. I felt good, too, but strangely different. To my amazement I had not been afraid once today as I recalled each battle with the gators. I actually came alive at their challenge. For the first time since we left New Orleans, I felt positive because the walk had toughened me for what I had done today. It was as if a sleeping adventuress had been awakened.

I wished I had it all figured out, but maybe this walk across America really was right for me. There must be dozens of adventures just waiting down the road. I was learning how much taking risks, doing new things and not knowing what was ahead excited me and how unafraid I really was.

The mud boat knocked against the boardwalk and jarred me back to the camp. Long evening shadows covered the dock while each of us climbed out and put our feet on solid ground. Peter walked next to me and put his arm around my waist and gave me a little squeeze to let me know how glad he was I had shared this day with him. He still had that quiet grin in his eyes which made me smile back. He hurried away to help the men unload the gators as I turned and walked to the cabin to wash up. I felt the letter I had hidden in my pocket yesterday and immediately crumpled it and threw it in the weeds.

A woman had never been out in the mud boat after gator

with Glenn or Stoner before, and they seemed to think Barbara was just in the way.

Stoner was retired, maybe in his late sixties. He was about five-eight, had very little hair and what he had was cut very close. He looked like a Scottish Highlander who'd been transplanted. He used to own and operate a sporting goods store.

He was the kind of man who would tangle with anything. His feet moved quickly and his body was as sturdy as an I-beam. There was no meanness in him, just no *fear*. His job, when we got to a trapped gator, was to bring out the long wooden pole that was used to push through the shallows.

We had three gators in the boat. Barbara still sat and watched. Certainly she never, ever expected to be in a situation like this.

Glenn turned the boat toward the west and decided to make a check of his marsh traps. He was worried that poachers might have got to them. Unlike these men, who made their livings from these waters and conserved the animals, poachers didn't care what size gators they took. Anything that swam at night was shot and smuggled out of the country. I hoped we would not run into any poachers. There would certainly be a leveling of rifles.

There was one bird missing as we turned down a very narrow bayou. The white 1,000-pound test line was floating in the water limply. That was the way it looked when the bait had been stolen. Smart gators took the birds and held them in their teeth, then stripped them from the hooks and got a free snack. The bait was stolen about half the time.

Glenn jumped out of the boat onto a small chunk of ground that would hold him. He was planning to take up the stake and the rope and the pole.

"Stoner, pull in that rope, will you, please?" Glenn was bent down, pulling out the long steel stake.

Stoner pulled. The slack came in and then it stopped. "Glenn, it's caught on something. Probably one of those long-necked snapping turtles got ahold to it."

"The wind must've blown the bird into the water," Glenn responded, not looking. "If that thing won't come loose, I'll go in after it. They have a way of sittin' on the bottom like a lead weight."

Stoner had let up the tension on the rope when I saw a dark flash and a whole bunch of stirred-up mud. Something was moving. I could only see bits of a dark shape, but there was no way that the shape could have been a turtle. The pieces of dark form, under the water, stretched as long as the boat. No turtle was that long. Another swirl of mud was kicked up and Stoner shouted out pure pain. The rope was tearing through his calloused hands so fast it seemed that it would eat chunks of blood and flesh from his palms.

The force of whatever was at the end of that rope lurched the boat sideways and away from where Glenn was. Glenn, who had on the only pair of gloves, was too far from us to be of any help. It was just Stoner, Barbara and me. *And* whatever was at the bottom of that bayou. Not that I knew anything, but I doubted it could be a gator. None of the other gators did anything like this.

I had been standing with one leg resting on the back of the boat. The jolt knocked me down, denting my shins. Stoner was jerked off his feet and would have been pulled into the water if Barbara had not grabbed him from behind by his belt and held on with all her strength.

After falling, I got up and grabbed onto the rope. Stoner, who had some heart trouble, was turning sunburned red. The sweat poured down his clean-shaven face. I was afraid for him, considering his age and all. We both pulled with all the strength we had. It felt like it was snagged on a two-ton anchor. I knew it was attached to something alive.

Then the thing began to move, kicking up clouds of mud. It was coming back toward the boat, in a measured sort of crawl. It was crawling on the bottom, maybe slithering through the mud. I knew there were no monsters of the deep, or were there? No. Of course not.

Glenn was frustrated and mad, but he could do nothing till the boat was pulled back toward him. We could not start the engine for fear of cutting up the thing at the end of the rope. Stoner motioned for Barbara to come back over to where we stood and asked her to grab hold. "Let's stop this thing from coming this way." His voice was taut with fear. It was horrible to know that something was down there with such vicious power and we could not see it. We could not stop it from coming toward us.

It was now almost under the boat. Stoner tied the rope onto a piece of metal bracing, hoping to keep it close. Something hit the bottom of the boat. Preacher had told me that a big gator had been known to bite through an aluminum boat. What could one do to a wooden boat? It seemed to me that it had to be a huge gator or possibly a crazed one. Could gators get rabid like dogs? The thought didn't last as it hit the bottom of the boat again. It was trying to force itself under the boat.

The water broke with a torrent. Stoner untied the rope; he was afraid that it would pull so hard that it would tear the metal support piece out of the boat. He motioned to Barbara, again, to grab hold.

Glenn was back in the boat and now all four of us pulled. Glenn weighed about 175 pounds and was as strong as any 200-pounder. I was 185 pounds and able to hold my own. Stoner, although in his sixties, was stocky and tough. Barbara was a lot stronger than she looked.

Our first pull moved it toward us. Then it went berserk. It began twisting like a tornado. Warm water splashed all over us. Its tail came partially out of the water. It was a giant gator. Its tail looked as thick as a big telephone pole. Glenn had set the push pole by now and the gator decided to eat through it. Or something. It wrapped around it violently, came to the surface and tried to attack us in the boat. For the first time we saw its head. Its head looked five times bigger than the others I'd seen. Thrashing, its mouth opened, its teeth and jaws slapping shut, it tried to get in the boat. It looked three times the size of Stoner. I had no idea anything this big lived in the swamps.

It was now moving fast. The bull gator was so agile, so much quicker than I would have thought. When alligators oozed along on top of the water, they seemed so lazy and uncoordinated.

Again the bull gator pulled explosively. It almost yanked both Stoner and me into the water with it. Again Barbara grabbed ahold of Stoner's belt and my shirt, steadying us. The gator was creating waves.

Glenn finally shot it. We were all so drained of strength that we had to wait until we could get it in the boat, if we could. Whenever these men killed one of their creatures, there was never any glee or bragging. There was always a reverent period of quiet. As if they wished that there were no killing of the things that they loved and respected and knew so well. Even though they knew it was their heritage and way of making a living, there was a sadness in their silence.

With the taking of this king, there was a special mourning. He was too big to fit in the boat. Glenn had to lay him across the entire front of the boat. Stoner said that he was the biggest one he'd seen in many years. At least eleven, maybe twelve feet long. Probably weighed almost 500 pounds. To be that large, he had lived through maybe fifty years of the chase.

On the way home we saw marsh life flying in cloud-sized flocks. The top of the water was golden with reflections and interrupted everywhere with life swimming and squiggling and paddling. From underneath fish broke the orange-green reflections with a roll or a leap or a flip. If I could see hundreds, there must have been millions. It was almost dark when we got back to the island. There was still a red glow in the air and it lit up Barbara in a way I'd never seen. She looked charged, ready for anything.

We left Preacher and Bobbie's home late one morning. Barbara was anxious to hit the road and I was dragging. I hated good-byes. It was one of those moments between people who care a lot for each other. It could have turned into a lot of crying and weeping. Finally Hillene said, "Why don't we say a prayer?"

Everyone gathered in a circle. There was Preacher, Bobbie, Hillene, Barbara and me, and we held hands and all prayed. We'd been standing outside for almost half an hour. It was late-summer hot. I couldn't tell if what was coming down their faces were tears or sweat. I knew mine were mostly tears. Then we walked away from the Heberts' Louisiana home. The "country of Texas" was just across the Sabine River.

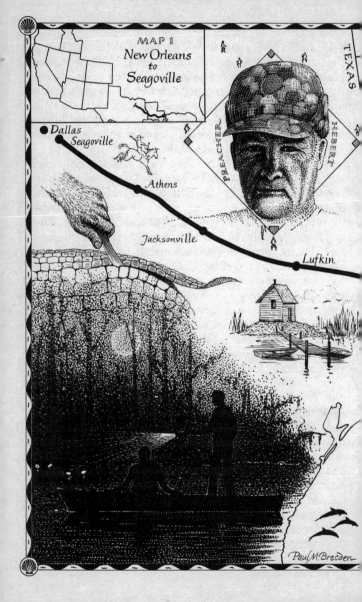

MAP 1
New Orleans
to
Seagoville

TEXAS

Dallas
Seagoville

PREACHER   HEBERT

Athens

Jacksonville

Lufkin

Paul M.Breeden

ARKANSAS
LOUISIANA

Mississippi River

NEW ORLEANS

Lafayette

Westlake

Lake Charles

GATOR CAMP

J. STORM I

13

T.E.X.A.S.

T.E.X.A.S. Every letter demanded to be in capitals. I'd seen enough in the movies to know what to expect. I imagined herds of longhorn cattle kicking up dust. I knew that cowboys would still be riding to the bank on their horses. They would have silver belt buckles shining from the middle of their lean bodies. They'd be dressed in faded jeans and blue plaid western shirts. I didn't want to think about it too hard, but I figured they'd be wearing pistols in easy reach of a quick draw. I knew most of Texas was a desert and I thought I was crazy for wanting to walk across it *all*.

I knew there would be glassy and growing cities somewhere, that there were places called Houston and Dallas. I knew John Wayne wasn't still at the Alamo, but I knew *some* Texan was. I pictured Texans taking on anyone who dared mess with the red, white and blue. I knew every Texan would be very tan and thin as a pitchfork handle. They all wore Stetsons and six-shooters.

My mind kept feeding me all this information about a place I had never been. Even though we were walking through a section of southwestern Louisiana that was very green and covered with huge pines, I knew that the second we crossed the state line, it would be different, just like the movies.

We were cruising down Route 190. Here was Texas between Newton and Jasper. There were no longhorns mooing across the plains. There were rolling hills everywhere and pines bigger than back in Louisiana. Before us was a country store, a watering hole for pickups and tractors. The parking lot, which was just dirt with some gravel spread here and there, was so big some city people would have thought it was a farm.

We took our packs off; our sweat had soaked through our clothes like a downpour. As I opened the screen door, someone said, "Ya-all come in, don't let any flies in, ya hear."

We walked over to an old refrigerator that had hundreds of bumper stickers stuck all over each other. The stickers boosted either the Houston Oilers or the Dallas Cowboys. It looked as if the Dallas Cowboys were winning. Above it all was a sign saying NO AMNESTY.

The farmers and just plain folks around this part of Texas were connoisseurs when it came to drinking Cokes, Dr Pepper, 7-Up and whatever. On a 99-degree day these people needed their soda just right. They wanted it to be in a bottle. Not the throwaway kind but the thick, green-colored, return type of bottle. Cans, forget it. These people were the most demanding connoisseurs, and when their throats were dry and dusty, the demands intensified. The Coke then had to be cooled enough so that there would be ice floating on top. Not frozen completely, of course, just some floating on top and ready to slide down into a hot throat.

Two light bulbs dangled from the ceiling and old farm calendars hung on the walls. There were a couple of men playing dominoes. A ceiling fan above was old but still stirring hot air. Everyone was talking.

"Here, take muh chair, sister," one of the men said to Barbara. The man got up from his game of dominoes.

Barbara sat down and nodded her thanks. They kept the dominoes in place. One of the men lounging against the counter spoke out. The other men flinched when he spoke. His face looked red and whiskey-sodden. "You people foreigners?" he said loud enough that everyone stopped talking.

The man who'd given Barbara his chair whispered to me

to ignore him. He was real mean, especially on days as hot as this. Barbara didn't hear him, though.

"No, sir." She smiled. Her loving-eyed smile calmed most people. It made the mean man more aggravated.

"Ya look like weird foreigners. Where you freaks from?" His words slurped from his loose mouth. "You sure as hell ain't from Texas." He muttered the foulest swear words as he slouched against a wall. I felt like throwing him out the window, head first.

"Where you headed?" one of the farmers asked politely. He adjusted his baseball cap. It was covered with dust from fertilizer.

"We're just traveling," I said.

"Hippie, welfare-grubbin' foreigner, lazy, good-fer-nothin'..." the puffy-faced slob mumbled. Everyone heard him. I glanced over at Barbara to give her the sign that we'd better leave when one of the farmers, who had not said a word, walked over to the man, still swearing under his breath, and grabbed him by the arm. He half dragged him out of the store. I heard a pickup truck door open and slam. The pickup wove down the road. The silent farmer walked back inside, said, "Sorry about him." The farmer looked apologetic as he said, "Ever since ol' Wilbur's wife died, he's been goin' downhill. Been drinkin' from sunrise to sunrise. They say two fifths a day. Lost most of his farm and even stopped comin' to church. He used to be a deacon in our church. Sad, ain't it?"

Everyone agreed; one person nodded. "Young lady, you people ever been in Texas bafore?" he asked. He looked like a Southern Baptist preacher.

"Can't say as we ever have," Barbara answered.

"Well, let me speak for everyone here and welcome you to the greatest state in the Union. Ain't nothin' like Texas." Everyone agreed. A bunch of them smiled. "Fact is, friends, we're glad you made it through Louisiana. Now that place don't even come close to comparin' with Texas. Ain't no place in the world that compares with Texas. If you people are lookin' for somethin', then you found it. We got everything there is to want and then some, don't we, boys?" He pointed his face into the west and all of Texas. Any real Texan would have stood to attention.

I walked over to the refrigerator to get another Dr Pepper. "Did you know Dr Pepper's from right here in Texas?" the preacher commented. I said no, I didn't.

On the side of the refrigerator was a yellowed sheet of paper that had been there for many years. The title was *A Communist Manifesto*. It was a sort of summary of the Marx and Engels theory. The man who owned the place noticed me reading it and spoke up.

"Now, boy, that's one document you need to memorize. You ever seen it bafore?"

"No, I haven't," I said.

"Well, if you were a Texan, you'd know what that said. That's how the communists plan to take over the country. Not one shot fired. They're doin' it, just exactly like it says on that sheet right today." His face was turning red with zeal.

A couple of farmers left. I watched one drive down the road on a big red and black Massey-Ferguson tractor.

"Those commies know they can't take over this country in a fight. They know that Texans still are ready to fight. Ain't we, boys?" His eyes held a straight-line stare out the dirty window. "Boy, you read this *Communist Manifesto* while you're a-travelin' . . . 'cause them people ain't gonna fire a shot. OK?"

"OK," I said.

Every ounce in my pack that pressed down on my shoulders and back mattered. Usually at the end of the day I was ready to throw away something, everything, to lessen the load. I always waited till the next morning, though.

One hard decision was to limit myself to one book. I'd started out with about three. One was a book by John Muir, one was a western by Louis L'Amour, and the other was a Bible. Barbara had left with only her Bible. It was too heavy for her, so I sent all my books back and we kept her Bible.

Usually each day we'd sit and read the Bible. We'd sit under a gnarled yellow pine, lean up against some fence post or sit in a fifties-cheerful café, eating chicken fried steak. On especially draining days we'd read from the Old Testament, either Psalms or Proverbs. Hearing those verses, more than 2,000 years old, had the most calming and centering effect on us. If I felt frayed, the Psalms calmed me. If Barbara was scared, the Psalms soothed and comforted her. I never got enough of them.

We had passed through Zavalla and Lufkin. To our north were the Texas-sized Toledo Bend Reservoir and Sam Rayburn Lake. We were walking along Highway 69. At the end of an East Texas day the sun took on a greenish tint, it filtered through so many pine needles. This was the best time of the day for walking. It was semicool and the winds smelled like pine oil. We usually made our best time right before dark because we knew we would soon be making camp. We were like horses heading toward the barn.

When I first began sleeping in the woods, I sometimes had a tense time getting to sleep. Even after walking thirty miles. My eyes were not secure in a darkness that blacked out everything like blindness. My ears turned every mouse into an attacking ghoul with neon eyes. Every owl that sounded! My heart touched my rib cage. And if something big, like a whitetail buck, should walk near me, down a narrow, hard-packed deer trail, then I knew I would be ending life in some torture.

After three years I still heard the sounds. The softest acorn landing still blasted like an amplifier burning out in my ear. But now I knew what each sound was and who or what was making it. I'd slept on the ground for so long that I slept better now on pine needles than a king-size bed with deluxe inner springs.

This night I could not keep my head down. Every bull that groaned a mile off, my head jerked up. My ears scanned. I even smelled for strange odors. Every insect that flew into the side of the tent, my eyes wedged open, afraid to blink or even to tear.

I lay my head down and closed my eyes. I was so tired my eyes hurt. Then with some whisper or dull noise my head went up. Listening, looking, though I could see nothing. Not even shades of black. I looked for a shaft of light I knew would come.

I fell asleep for a second, a minute. Some hours. My head sprang up again. There was a rustling. Loud, shuffling through the leaves of maples and oak. Breaking the branches of pine. It sounded like a man coming toward us. I wanted to open the flap of the tent and look out, but I was afraid to.

Whatever it was, it came right up to the tent. Then there were some scratching, clawing, grabbing sounds on a tree near us. Maybe climbing it. Maybe bending it into some kind of trap. My mind was too tired to think anything through. I just lay there, wishing I could wake Barbara up. What good would that do? None. Only frighten her.

"What is that noise?" Barbara said, sounding very awake.

"I don't know." I almost shrieked when she spoke, lying there too tired to lift her head, her head turned away from me. "Why don't you go back to sleep? I'll take care of us."

"I haven't been able to get to sleep," she said.

We both lay there, listening. Waiting for the worst. Trying to keep our imaginations from overdosing. Then the noises on the tree trunk stopped. It fell from the tree and hit the tent so hard that the back of the tent fell down on us. The night silenced. I might have slept some before dawn. I might not have.

A dry wind woke us early and got me out of the tent into the anxiety-relieving dawn. A sleepless night in the woods is a lot worse than a sleepless night in bed.

Route 69 wove gently in between the Neches River and the Angelina River. We were close to a town called Alto. All the French names were gone. Since crossing the Louisiana-Texas border, we had walked about half the way to Dallas and Texas still hadn't turned to desert and I hadn't seen an Appaloosa stallion tied to a rail in front of a bank yet. Where was the cactus? And the herds of longhorns, swimming across some river on their way to Kansas?

A few miles east of Alto, we passed a mill piled high with pine logs. They were made into fence posts. In front of one of the houses was a field of lush grass. Grazing in it were some of the most beautiful floppy-eared cattle. I'd never seen

Longhorn cattle

anything like them. They looked like a cross between elk, deer and buffalo. They seemed holy.

As far as I was concerned, cows and bulls were anything but holy. I knew that Texans thought cattle were holy, sort of. Well, at least held in the same company as bald eagles and babies. But these cattle were different from Herefords or Anguses or longhorns. A sign hung from a post: HICKS RED BRAHMAN RANCH.

These Red Brahman cattle were so captivating that I took off my pack and pulled out my camera. As they moved, their loose red and white skins bounced. They walked beside us for a while. We were a mile or so down the road when a pickup drove up.

"We noticed ya-all lookin' at our Brahmans," the teenage girl said in a thick East Texas accent. "Ya-all passin' through?" she asked shyly.

"Yeah," I drawled back.

The next thing I knew, Barbara and I piled into the cab of the truck beside the girl and headed up to the ranch house for supper. She said her daddy told her to come fetch us because he saw us taking pictures of their biggest bull.

When we sat down at their table, Mr. Hicks told us about Cherokee Arauto 1/783, their king bull worth about 100 times more than any ol' pickup. Fact is, the Hickses had just sold half of ol' Cherokee for $125,000. This meant that a rancher bought half interest in the bull and that half the year they used Cherokee to breed to their cows. They would also collect his sperm and sell it.

We spent the night, and before we hit the road, they loaded us down with extra-big postcards and calendars with pictures on them of Cherokee standing there, puffing out his chest. I wondered if they'd taken the picture since Cherokee had found out he was worth more than a quarter of a million dollars. As Leo Hicks said, "These here Brahman cattle are smarter than dogs. Even smarter than pigs."

Walking through Texas

14

Isaiah 40:31

Barbara

"You're so beautiful, B.J.," Peter whispered lovingly.

We were lying on our stomachs on the tent floor, perched on our elbows, looking out the door watching the drizzling rain. We had camped on a bed of fern under some tall trees. It was almost light, but we could still see the hungry mosquitoes and bugs looking for a way through the mesh-net door. It was zipped shut.

"I like you without all that makeup and phony junk on your face."

"What you see is what you get." I said it quick and mean. I hated my sweat-matted hair, dust-streaked face, wrinkled T-shirt and shorts, hairy legs and underarms, and my strong body odor from not having had a bath in more than three days. The two of us made the tent smell worse than any gym locker room.

"Come closer," Peter said in a low, husky voice, reaching to pull me next to him. I caught a whiff of his underarm and tried not to let him see I almost choked. I pretended I was clearing my throat. I gave him a push, and he puffed up and turned toward the outside wall of our tent, grumbling.

"Guess I might as well get used to this."

We were up, packed and on the road by 7:30 A.M. A fat

rabbit jumped across the road in front of us as if to say good morning and a bright yellow butterfly hovered around us, skipping from one tall weed to another. Flying grasshoppers sprayed through the grass. It was going to be a beautiful day, but I didn't much care.

My steps began wearing down after about two hours and five miles. It was getting sticky and muggy. At midmorning we still had not found anyplace to eat. I could have done without food; it was water that I needed most. It wasn't like I was back home where I could mosey into the kitchen and turn on the tap or open the refrigerator and pull out a cold Coke or jug of orange juice. Now getting a drink of water meant I had to walk five or ten miles after I woke up. Our quart-sized canteens had been empty since last night.

I swatted at my face with a red kerchief to shoo away the flies, gnats and mosquitoes, which must have been as thirsty as I was.

We walked on a busy highway facing traffic. My hip-bones felt they were being rubbed with sandpaper as the belt pads on the bottom of my pack dug deeper into my skin with each step. I usually walked at a slow pace in order to keep a momentum, lifting the heavy five-pound hiking boots one after another. My pace was never as fast as Peter's. He always walked several yards ahead of me. He had stopped now, turned back toward me.

"You act like a ninety-year-old woman, you are so slow," he hollered for the whole world to hear.

"I'm walking as fast as I can," I screamed. My feet felt like sore stumps and I was limping.

"We're almost in town so you can stop your limping act. *Hurry up.*" He sounded like General Patton commanding the troops across Africa.

"Go ahead. Leave me behind!" I howled. I really hobbled now, purposely trying to look even more miserable. Maybe he'd worry. Maybe he'd be sorry. Maybe he'd cry if I lay down and died.

"You should have won an Academy Award for your acting." He mocked me, cold and spiteful, as I limped toward him. He stood with his legs spread apart, waiting to strike. I could see the fire in his eyes. Just as I reached him, he grabbed me and pinched a chunk of my sunburned arm.

"Will you hurry up!" He gritted his teeth.

"Get your hands off me!" I yelled at the top of my lungs. He gripped my arm tighter, but I fought loose and slapped his face. Cars and trucks were slowing down beside us, honking and staring at us. I hit him again. That I couldn't even hurt him made me so mad. Some more cars slowed down. We must have looked like two bulls bashing into each other.

Peter was red with fury. He clamped down on my shoulders and pushed me backwards so hard I fell down on the ground. The tears began to fly and I rolled over, picked up a hard clump of stones and dirt and threw it at him as hard as I could.

"HITLER!" I screamed. "You are worse than Hitler!" I grabbed up more dirt and threw it.

"Hitler!" . . . Throw . . . "Hitler!" . . . Throw . . . "Hitler!" . . . *SPLAT!*

When that clump hit the back of his legs, Peter turned toward me. A big semi truck zoomed by and blew its horn.

"Why am I being tortured with this stubborn woman for a wife?" Peter shouted, lifting his hands toward heaven. He fired his eyes at me. He squared his massive shoulders and then stalked off toward town. He didn't care if he got a mile ahead of me because he never looked back.

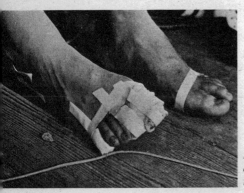

Barbara's blistered feet during the difficult first miles

Several hours later we were on our way to a Laundromat. Peter and I had cooled down our tempers by this time, but I was still the filthiest I had ever been. I longed for a cool, leisurely bath in an air-conditioned room. I was crusty with dirt and my face was streaked from the tears this morning. I was *desperate* for a bath. Most Laundromats had public bathrooms, but this one only had a stool, no sink and no running water where I could at least splash cold water on my face.

The longer I sat in the hot Laundromat in my own sweat and stench, the more desperate I became. I knew what I would do. I grabbed my handkerchief and locked the bathroom door behind me. I flushed the stained toilet bowl five times and could see the water was as clean as it would get. I dipped my cloth into the bowl and soaked it down. I squeezed the cool water down my legs and arms, flushing the toilet over and over to keep the water clean. Then I scooped up a handful and washed my face. My bar of Ivory soap covered up the smell of urine that penetrated the dirty room.

"Dear Lord, I've come a long way and changed a whole bunch to do this," I said out loud to myself.

Barbara said it was like walking into the Twilight Zone. The walls had little on them but faded-to-bleak paint. There were three calendars. The biggest one advertised the local funeral home. It was blinding, Texas-bright outside, but in this lobby it was hard to see. Everything was tinted reddish brown by a single light bulb that hung down from a ceiling fan. The fan turned slowly and seemed to stir up this hotel's strange history.

There was a man with sunken cheeks and a short-sleeved shirt and an older woman, over sixty, with dark hair and a sleeveless dress and blue sneakers. They were playing dominoes on a bare table. Either they didn't hear us come in or they wished we'd leave. We were in Athens, Texas. This antique-hotel was just off the square, a block from the courthouse.

I stood by the desk. It had the old-timey window with a small opening at the bottom. On the front, lettered in chipped gold, it said CASHIER. I tapped my feet, whistled and stared at the lady. She kept playing dominoes. I had never played and I didn't know if she couldn't leave till the game was over. She finally got up.

It had been six days since we left Cherokee and the Hicks ranch. We hadn't found any good lakes or rivers to take a bath in, so Barbara said this was as far as she was going to go. I had changed a lot even to consider staying in a motel. When I had begun the walk, I wouldn't have stayed in a motel because it would have made the walk too soft.

The domino lady said it would be $8.50 for the night. In our room upstairs there was a ceramic washbasin on an oak dresser with a mirror. The mirror had certainly seen many cowboys, outlaws and saloon ladies. No telling how many things it had seen. The bed was made of rusting iron curves, like a brass bed but a lot cheaper. The bed looked like it was right off the TV show *Rawhide*.

Barbara got undressed instantly. The bath water was running hot, clean and private. The parts of her body that weren't touched by the Texas sun were white. I pulled out my Texas map and our American Express traveler's checks. I wanted to see how we were doing for money. We'd left New Orleans three months ago with a little over $1,000. I figured we'd have plenty to get us through Dallas and Fort Worth. I pulled out the blue packets that contained the checks.

I figured we'd have about $150 to $200 left. Knowing the walk would be more expensive together, I'd hoped that we could still live cheaply. Most of our money would go for food and liquid. We had only $40 left. Just two traveler's checks. I put my hand on my chin and breathed heavy through my fingers. We might not make it to Dallas. Barbara was singing.

Few things in the world were more enjoyable to Barbara Jo than a *hot* bath. She took baths so hot that when she got out, her white skin was red. She especially loved old bathtubs that stood out from the wall and were deep and had iron feet like lions. I started to walk in and tell her about our money problems but decided to wait till she got out. I didn't want to interrupt her pleasure.

I lay on the old bed that was too soft and tried to figure out how long our $40 would last. We'd been on the road a

A dry-land homestead

little less than three months and spent almost $1,000. That meant we were spending $10 to $11 a day. Considering that we'd bought Barbara some new boots, that was not bad. At $10 a day, that meant we had about four days of food and then we'd be out. It was time for a job, sooner than I'd hoped. We had no choice. From Athens into downtown Dallas was about sixty-five miles, maybe seventy. In a car that was an hour. For us it was a good four days' walk. Sixteen, seventeen miles a day in the late-summer Texas heat was an accomplishment for us. Walking across America, I had learned that you can never really trust mileage figures on maps, on signs and from directions. Many maps did not count the miles through towns and cities. Many people had no concept of walking sixty blocks, much less sixty miles, and thought of it in terms of 60 mph, air conditioning and watching for speed traps.

    Wherever our money ran out would be where we would settle and get a job. If we made it to Dallas, that would be OK. It might be interesting to spend part of our walk in a big city. After all, I still thought there would be cowboys and cactus and barbed-wire fences, separating Main Street. If we ran out before Dallas, so be it.

    On the first half of the walk I'd kept a code for each day on my maps. I'd given that up for notes by sunset, sunrise or candlelight. I wrote on postcards and sent them to our friends in Meridian, Mississippi. I still wrote on my maps making little lines marking how far we walked each day. Barbara and I often talked instead of writing. I could have written ten pages on each day. Every day was a feast. Speaking of feasts, I decided that I would keep a record of how long it took us to spend the $40. How far could we make it stretch?

That bed in that antique motel in Athens felt too soft to me. I let Barbara stretch out and I slept on the floor. I was too used to sleeping on the pine-needle-coated ground. We had breakfast that morning in a café and ate country sausage, home-made biscuits, gravy, home fries, two eggs, OJ and coffee. We also got the Dallas *Times Herald*. It felt strange reading a big-city newspaper. I didn't see any pictures of cowboys any-where, and the ads for clothing looked very chic. Maybe I'd been in the country too long. The breakfast cost us $1.95 each, plus a tip. It came to $4.50. We had $35.50 left.

It was rare for us to eat a hot breakfast. We surged with power and walked through Eustace, ending our day in Mabank. We eased on down Highway 175. For lunch we stopped at a tiny café with red-checked curtains. I had chicken fried steak, green beans, cornbread, iced tea, fried okra and peach cobbler. Iced tea in Texas is almost as important as the Alamo. Barbara had fried catfish, cornbread, homemade mashed potatoes, ba-nana pudding and fresh tomato. All of that fuel cost $5.75. We had $29.75 left.

The next day we walked a bit past Kemp, Texas. Now we had only $18.26 left, give or take a few cents. We stopped for an afternoon rest in the shade. While resting, we searched through all the pockets of our packs for stray quarters, nickels, dimes or pennies. The end of the third day out of Athens we spent the night in Kaufman, Texas. We had been trying to eat less, but it was weakening us. I counted our money. We had $9.75.

A cluster of stores sat back from the road on our left. I could feel the pull of the big city, even though I could not see Dallas yet.

We took our packs off and I pulled out our money. Instead of $9.75, there was only $4.75. I must have misplaced a $5 bill. After emptying my pack, I knew it was gone. We bought a half gallon of orange juice, a box of Wheat Thins and a tiny chunk of cheese. We had $1.87 left.

The skies sizzled and a road runner flew across the road. The pine forests of East Texas were gone and the few trees were scrub oak and mesquite. The Wild West was finally beginning to look the way it was supposed to. The land wasn't ironing board flat; it waved like a sheet in a hot murmur of a breeze.

We had been walking as fast as we could. Our $1.87 could feed us one more meal. Almost through a town called Seagoville I stared west. I could see as far as a vulture on top of a phone pole. The sun had scorched the prairie grass yellow-brown and the gaslike swirls of a mirage whirled close to the ground. A steel and glass skyline grew from the midst of the mirage like a geometric cactus. Finally we'd seen a cactus and it was Dallas. It was growing before everyone's eyes.

I knew there were more than a million people living around that skyline. Feelings of loneliness surfaced in me. We knew no one. Normally not knowing anyone excited me. But this western city scared me. I had heard that cowboys had to make friends with loneliness. Maybe these open lands of no shade had that kind of effect on people. It was a new feeling for me. I was an "east of the Mississippi" boy and felt secure with trees and hills and sprawling old cities. The sky seemed too big; it made me feel vulnerable. There was too much space between things.

I couldn't take my mind away from the fact that we only had $1.87.

"Peter, are you worried?" Barbara spoke calmly.

"Yes, I don't know anything I can do to get us out of this. At least in Louisiana we could call our friend's parents." I was a combination of scared and worried. When I felt like this, I could be explosive.

"Peter"—Barbara's voice sounded too calm—"I have a scripture that I would like to read, all right?"

"OK." I really didn't want to hear it.

She pulled out her Bible from my pack and opened it to the front section. She knew where everything was. "Listen to this. This is beautiful. It's from the Book of Isaiah." We kept walking toward the lonely city. "They shall not hunger nor thirst; neither shall the heat nor sun smite them: for he that hath mercy on them shall lead them, even by the springs of water shall he guide them. And I will make all my mountains a way, and my highways shall be exalted."

She reached for my hand. "Why don't you say a prayer? There's nothing else we can do."

I asked God to help us. I thought of another scripture from the Old Testament that Barbara had said should be our motto: "They that wait upon the Lord shall renew their strength; they shall mount up with wings as eagles; they shall run, and not be weary; and they shall walk, and not faint."

Under my breath I said, "OK, God. Forget about soaring with the eagles. How about some food."

Highway 175 turned into a four-lane. All energy seemed to point toward Dallas. We walked on the quiet access road. Had anyone that we'd stayed with given us any addresses or phone numbers of people in Texas? My uncle Bud lived in Texas, but he lived in the Panhandle. That was many hundreds of miles from Dallas. Too far to call him. My cousin George— hadn't he gone to SMU in Dallas? Yes. But he was in medical school in Galveston. Too far away. My cousin Dick was in college in Texas somewhere, but where? At Texas Tech. And that, too, was in West Texas, closer to New Mexico than Dallas.

While I thought, some cows stood under the flimsy shade offered by some pale green mesquite trees. There was a light brown snake dead and flattened on the road. A man and a young girl rode by us on their bicycles. A male sparrow hawk perched on a dry gray fence post, eating a Texas-sized grasshopper.

"Hello," a voice from behind said. I looked back.

It was the man and the girl on the bikes.

"Hi," I said.

"I was driving to a car auction a few days ago and saw ya-all walking near Kaufman. You must be walking somewheres. If no one else has said it, let me welcome you to Texas." He looked like he was in his late twenties; his face was boyishly handsome and smooth. His brown eyes were penetrating and innocent. He acted very comfortable around us, as if he were accustomed to meeting lots of strangers.

"Thank you," Barbara said. The little girl, maybe eight, nine years old, looked like the man. She was thin and pretty, and she knew it. The girl, he called her Lisa, moved as if she'd entered many beauty contests. They looked like brother and sister.

"Sure is hot today," he said. "Ya-all been travelin' long?" He was the type who knew how to find out things about people, carefully.

"Pretty long," I answered. I wasn't sure how much I wanted to tell this stranger on the bike.

"Lisa"—he spoke to the captivating girl—"go ride on home and tell your mother these people are coming over. Tell her to cook some hamburgers."

"Yes, Daddy."

"Why don't you come home? We live just a half mile down this road. I'll ride along with you. We can talk. Is that all right with ya-all?" He looked at the both of us.

"Are you married?" he asked.

"We're married," Barbara said. It bothered Barbara that anyone would consider that she'd do this with me and not be married. "You can ride along with us." She was watching him carefully.

"Would you like to come have something to eat over at the house?" he finally asked.

"Why not?" Barbara smiled. She had remembered our prayer and forgot her suspicions. I glanced at the sky that moments before had felt overwhelming and too big. "Thanks for the food."

We kept walking. The man kept riding his bike slowly.

"Have you ever been to Texas before?"

"No, never have."

"Have ya ever eaten any good Mexican food?"

"No, I've never really eaten any real Mexican food except a few tacos at a Dairy Queen back East."

"Well, then," he said, his tan Texas face bragging, "we'll forget them hamburgers and go have us some Mexican food. My name's Ron Hall." He held out his hand. It's almost a state law to shake a stranger's hand.

15

Hot Breath

The restaurant's name was El Chico. It was in a mall called Town East. Ron said that we were in East Dallas and that North Dallas was where the people with the Texas-huge bank accounts lived. There wasn't a Neiman-Marcus in this mall. As we turned into Town East, it looked as if a spaceship, bigger than Captain Kirk's, had landed in the midst of a ranch-sized parking lot in the middle of the prairie.

El Chico was dark inside, decorated with black wrought iron and plastic plants and flowers. Ron said that since we didn't know what to order, he'd order for us.

First there came a few baskets of toasted tortilla chips, as fresh and as crisp as the freshest potato chip. They were warm. There was a thick glass bowl filled with red sauce with yellow seeds floating in it. Ron said to leave it alone. He practically drank the stuff. There was a tray with onions, carrots and peppers. Kathy, Ron's blond wife, interrupted me as I was about to eat some. She said that they were hot, too. I bit down anyway. I could have sold my breath to a power plant. I tried not to breathe on the plastic flowers in the straw baskets.

After a few minutes Lupe, the Mexican man who looked a lot like some of the Apache Indians I'd seen in westerns,

*The gringo waiter at
El Chico*

returned with a basket filled with steaming corn tortillas. He could see my eyes watering and Ron and Kathy laughing and said that these soft corn tortillas and the ice-cool butter were meant to soak up some of the flame from the hot sauce and hot carrots.

My stomach had never talked to me like this before. I couldn't understand what it was saying. Maybe it was trying to speak Spanish.

For my main dish I had something called chalupas Jalisco. They were large round tortillas toasted hard, yet fresh. They were coated with refried beans, which Ron said was Mexican peanut butter. On top of that were piles of shredded lettuce, chicken and cheese. It was topped with something called pico de gallo. On the plate was a burrito. Ron ordered Barbara a meat taco, bean and cheese enchilada combination plate. They ate this Mexican food, which was exotic to me, like so many chicken fried steaks and french fries.

Ron ordered dessert called sopapillas, pronounced "soap-a-pe-a." They were deep-fried and puffy the way no doughnut ever is. They gave us more butter and some honey and guaranteed that they would melt on our lips. When the first few sopapillas hit my stomach, it went wild. It started dancing, fast-stepping, hot and Latin and passionate. The sopapillas were as sweet as nectar and light as Texas cotton. It was still trying to tell me something, something important. *Finally* I understood what it was trying to say. "Peter," my stomach said, "you need a job, right? Well, get one *here!*"

I started as a busboy, at minimum wage, no tips. They said that since I had never worked in a restaurant, I would have to learn the business from the taco up. After hunting gator, working on an offshore oil rig, rough cuttin' logs in a sawmill and working on M.C.'s ranch in Alabama, this job was a real switch.

For weeks I wore a busboy's coat, blue pants with cuffs and black shoes. I cleared off tables, filled water glasses, brought extra butter, replaced silverware and set up hundreds of high chairs. El Chico was a middle-class restaurant and most people ate what they paid for. About ninety percent of its patrons were white. The rest were black folks and very few Mexican people. One of the waiters, Richard Estrello, said this food was Tex-Mex, part Mexican and part Texan. He said I'd have to go closer to the border to get the real thing. He usually ate fried chicken; his people had been citizens for more than fifty years. He was married to a very blond Anglo girl. They had two of the sweetest dark-haired daughters.

Richard, who reminded me of a Mexican version of Tony Orlando, the singer, took me under his care and showed me how to be classy. When we worked the same shifts, he taught me some of the tricks that he'd learned over many years of waiting on people. How to get assigned the best tables. How to get the big tips. How to give the generous types little extras. How to spot the cheap tippers and not waste time on them. How to get the busboys to do their work. How to flatter the ladies. I didn't have his Latin smoothness, but I listened and watched him. He could get twice the tips of other waiters.

Then it was my turn. I was a waiter. Like so many things in life that are first-time experiences, I remember my first day as a waiter most clearly. I had my own creamy-colored waiter's jacket with bright Mexican strips of fabric down the front.

Richard and Kathy and Robert and the others made it

look so easy. But I was learning that it wasn't as easy as it looked. It took good coordination to bring the right plate of hot or cold food at the right time to each eater. This wasn't the kind of place to get away with slurping the plates down and forgetting about the people. I was OK for my first few tables, with two to a table. Then the lunch rush hit. Richard had been watching me to make sure I was doing OK. Now he had to keep track of his own people. A group of six retired ladies came in from the bright lights of the mall. I prayed Lupe would give them to some other waiter. He set them down in the round booth in the corner. They were mine.

Richard said that he loved older ladies; he just didn't like waiting on them. Lupe wanted to break me in.

They were all very nice, smiled a lot and joked about how romantic and dark it was in their corner booth. They loved Mexican food. "You must be new here," one of them said. I told them that I was. Wasn't it a shame how prices were going up so fast?, they were saying. I lit their candle and brought them over an extra one.

"It's so hot out today. Please, son, bring us our water right away."

"Yes, ma'am," I said.

Today was their day. Every Wednesday they got together and went out and had their hair done. Some had theirs tinted. Then they would come to Town East to wander around. They almost always came to El Chico. All six of them had flowered or print blouses, and every one had a matching scarf tied in a bow. They all wore neat plain skirts.

When I returned with a platter of six full glasses of water, they were arguing about how badly the Dallas Cowboys needed a great running back. They all seemed to agree. I stood there balancing the tray in one hand, waiting for them to lean back some so I could serve them their water. The booth was very cozy.

I stood there longer than I wanted to because they got in a debate over which was the best collage football team in the conference: Texas or Baylor. It seemed that they would debate that from now till Texas became a country, so I stepped in and reached over the table to the soft-skinned white lady farthest away. Set her water down lightly, with grace. Two more of my tables had filled up with hungry people.

One lady asked if I was from Dallas. I said no. I picked up another glass and reached. The rest of the water glasses, including a plastic pitcher full, began to slide and then fall. They fell in all directions. So did the pitcher. One glass poured onto a lady's lap. Another bounced off the table and splashed all over. The third glass spilled onto the table, drowned the candle and leaked all over the lady on my right. The pitcher landed on the chest of the lady who loved Roger Staubach. There was about a half gallon of iced water down her blouse.

I wanted to die. The ladies all jumped up, grabbing the wet cloth napkins. They shouted for the manager. John wasn't there yet. Lupe came over, shaking his head, acting very upset. He motioned for me to go on back in the kitchen before the headlines read GRINGO WAITER DROWNED BY SENIOR CITIZENS AFTER HE DOUSES THEM WITH ICE WATER. They didn't stick around for their usual Wednesday lunch. I had baptized my first customers.

"Pedro." Lupe looked very serious. Normally his wavy black hair and red-tan skin outlined a perpetual white-toothed smile. His eyes tap-danced, always ready to help the most beautiful ladies. "Those ladies have been coming here for quite a few years. They said they would never come back. You know we have fired people for less, Pedro." He had a deep South Texas accent. "Jus' don' let e-it happen a-GEN," he said with a thick Spanish accent, smirking. "We need our token redheads, Pedro."

Saturdays were berserk at El Chico! It seemed that every famished family in Dallas lined up from the moment we opened till the time we closed the doors. The folks who ate paid for meals in cash. To get a dollar tip was not common. We were lucky if people tipped ten percent, much less fifteen percent. The only way to make any money was to keep those tortillas disappearing. Seat 'em, feed 'em and get 'em back to their shopping. Saturday was an eleven-hour sprint from the tables to the kitchen and back. Saturday was also the day that people lost their cool. Tempers exploded like tastebuds after a bite into a hot pepper.

"Bring me more tortillas." . . . "I need more tea." . . . "Would you be so kind as to bring us more butter?" (They'd gone through about a pound of patties already.) . . . "Another large Coke and three coffees." I'd give them the check added up. "Oh, we forgot . . . Sue wants another order of sopapillas." The water glasses emptied faster than a prisoner of war could eat his first hot dog. "Hey, darlin', our tortilla chips are cold. Bring us some hot ones." Then the darlin' and her five friends would leave me a twenty-five-cent tip. I felt like stuffing a basket of cold chips up her nose.

Like I said, Saturdays could really get on your nerves. I wouldn't have worked on Saturday except that it was the day that I could make some decent money. After all, I was doing everything I could to save money for the rest of the walk. All we were paid was $1.30 an hour, plus tips. Some Saturdays I could make as much as $45. After eleven hours of delivering plates of enchiladas and guacamole I felt like a taco that had fallen on the kitchen floor and had been stomped, ground into crumbs.

The cooks hated the way I pronounced the food I ordered. They especially loathed the way I pronounced "enchilada." On normal days they just hassled me in broken English.

"Say 'enchilada.'" They'd sneer. I'd say it with my Connecticut-nasal drone.

I'd smile at them and say, "Say 'Campbell's soup.'" They refused. "Say 'Massachusetts.'"

As this particular Saturday drew to a close, the crowd got worse. There was a line that wove out into the mall, people waiting to get a table. One waiter hadn't shown up, so we had more tables than usual. The tips were flowing, but back in the kitchen the cooks were getting mean. It was hot back there. The lights were operating-room bright and by the end of a rushed day the Texas streets felt cool in comparison.

I shouted over the rush when it was my turn.

"I need a beef burrito plate and three enchilada plates."

There were about five of us waiters lined up. They ignored me and served the two Mexican American waiters who were behind me in line.

I knew my tables were getting aggravated. "I said, I

need..." I repeated my order. They ignored me some more. Then another gringo came in, Kathy, a bleached blond waitress. They dished up her order. I shouted mine, staring at the main cook, who was waging a personal war against me, enjoying the battle. The only thing he was missing was a belt of bullets across his chest.

"Say 'enchilada' or you ain' gettin' no food," he spit out in his nastiest English.

I tried my best Spanish accent. It wasn't good enough. He repeated it. I refused to say anything more. He screamed out,"Say 'enchilada,' you gringo @$X!"

I just stood there. I was about to go out and get Lupe to come back and translate for me when he lunged at me with a butcher knife. I thrust out my metal platter, like a shield in a sword fight, and the knife made that noise of metal on metal. Lupe happened to come in at that moment. Someone had told him there was trouble. Lupe grabbed the cook by the hair and shirt and threw him out the back door. He took over the cooking.

When we closed the wrought-iron gates that night, Lupe played some songs by Freddie Fender. He said that he used to make music with Freddie down in South Texas, near the Rio Grande. Nobody but Lupe thought Freddie would make it so big in the music business. When I was on my way out, Lupe said, "Peter, your accent ain't much, but soon, *amigo,* you'll learn how to say 'enchilada.'"

There were special moments of tranquillity in the dark, moodily lit Mexican restaurant. They were the times after the lunch rush was over and before the people began arriving for dinner, between 2:30 and 4:30 P.M. I would find a small table in a dark corner with a view. Then I would make some nachos, exactly the way I liked them, with plenty of beef, refried beans and a lot of cheese. I'd get me a mound of guacamole and a large milk.

It had been weeks since the cook had lunged at me with the butcher knife. An older man, in his sixties, walked by the cash register and through the shadows. He had a wide face, small dark eyes and black hair. He glanced at me as a candle on my table flickered. Then he walked over and pulled out one of the dark wood Spanish-style chairs. He had on a white business shirt made of lightweight cotton, blue dress slacks and a tie. I noticed the lower half of the man's face was heavy and wider than his forehead. His smallish eyes were bottomless; his eyebrows, strong and black.

"You been working here long?" the man asked.

"Not long."

"How do you like this type of work?"

"It's not bad." Could he be a cop investigating the knifing attempt? Could something be going on here that I didn't know about?

"Do you know who I am?" the short man wondered as he motioned to Lupe, who was watching him the way a Secret Service agent watches the President.

"No, I don't."

"My name's Mack Cuellar." Lupe stood at attention. "Lupe, my friend, bring me a large Dr Pepper and some soft tortillas."

"I'm Peter Jenkins." He reached out his hand, but my hand was dirty with nachos. I wiped it off. Maybe he was some kind of big shot in the Mexican Mafia.

"Do you know who owns El Chico?"

"No, I don't." I had assumed that this place and the other El Chicos were owned by some Harvard-educated Texans who'd hit it big with some oil wells and needed to invest their money somewhere.

"My family owns El Chico," he said, taking a long gulp of Dr Pepper. "We started in 1926 selling tamales at the Kaufman County Fair. Every month or so I just drive to one of our places in Dallas and look around. Say hello to our people. Hello," he said. He bit down on a soft tortilla.

Mack finished his corn tortillas and I finished my nachos long before he finished telling me his stories. The afternoon melted away faster than cheese. Since I was talking to the vice-chairman of the board of El Chico, I didn't worry about jumping up to wait tables.

He was sixty-nine. He said that in the past thirty-six weeks the El Chico Corporation had net sales over $30 million.

Lupe kept the Dr Pepper glasses full as Mack talked. He loved to talk and I loved to listen. He told me stories from a Texas of long ago. "Our MAMA and father, they came to Texas in 1892." When he said MAMA, which was a lot, it was always in capital letters. "They left Nuevo Laredo, Mexico, right after they were married." Father, his name was Macario, was twenty-three. MAMA, Adelaida, she was twenty. They had not one peso, could not speak any English. But they could see that they were born peons, and if they stayed, they'd die that way.

"Some way the parents ended up in Kaufman. By 1915 MAMA was forty-four, and there were twelve of us Cuellar kids runnin' barefoot through the dusty farm fields of East Texas.

"We were sharecroppers, miles out of town. Father farmed cotton, corn, wheat and oats. We were happy on the farm." Mack hesitated. "When it rained, then we kids could play music. We got to keep three-quarters of what we grew and our rent was one-quarter.

"The white man who owned the land we farmed, his name was Mr. Jack Nash. All of us Cuellar brothers would watch for the dust risin' on the dirt road up to our house. When we saw it, we knew his car was coming. There were few cars back then in East Texas. We would try to sneak to the gate and open it for Mr. Jack Nash. He would throw us a nickel or dime. You know what I promised myself every time I saw Mr. Jack Nash?"

"No, what?" I blinked at Richard Estrello, my fellow waiter, when he shook his head as if to say, "Good deal, pal." Mack talked as fast as a Spanish guitarist's fingers.

"I loved to watch Mr. Jack Nash's gold cuff links reflect the sun. Everything around our farm was covered with dry, gritty dirt. We took a bath just once a week. I promised myself that someday I'd be clean like Mr. Jack Nash. I'd wear soft white shirts, have a gold watch and chain, and drive a big black car. There had to be an easier way to make a living than plowing the rows in a field with a dumb mule who couldn't even understand Spanish.

"What made it possible was *not* selling marbles. I tried that. It didn't work. But MAMA decided that she would open a tiny wooden stand at the county fair and sell some of her tamales. All us boys that were old enough gathered around her with our guitars and sang our *ranchero* songs. In three days MAMA had made a lot of greenbacks. It would have taken months to make that kind of money planting crops. The next year we did it all over again."

"We Cuellars came to the U.S.A. a long time ago, and we've worked hard to make it. This country has been good to us and we're proud citizens, proud Mexican Americans. But we're Americans first."

He shook his head. "Chicanos say they're beat down, but that's just an excuse to hold themselves back. Look at us, we could never have done what we have done in Mexico. We were not born rich. Today I live in a beautiful big house, and best of all, Peter, I have my wife and four daughters. Every one of them went to the finest private schools in Dallas. They all graduated from the best university in Texas, SMU. We have all traveled in Europe, South America and Mexico. And you know, we Cuellars would live nowhere except here, in Texas.

"And now I even have an Anglo son-in-law. But me, I don't look at a man's face. I look at his heart. Rodney married my *oldest* daughter!"

"How many El Chicos are there, Mack?"

"We have over eighty in nine different states. After selling those tamales, my brother Frank, he's chairman of the board now, he decided there had to be a way to keep it going all year.

"In 1940, me and my brother Gilbert opened a place here named El Chico. We hit it big, and MAMA and Frank moved here. Soon the Cuellars opened places in Fort Worth, Austin and Waco. MAMA, she lived till she was ninety-eight. She and Father lived long enough to see their 1892 border crossing come to something."

16

Rattlesnakes, Scorpions and Amarillo Slim

Spring in Texas would soon be here. I had almost enough money saved to continue on with the walk. It took longer than I thought, saving up the twenty-five-cent, thirty-five-cent tips. I had gotten fat and lazy after a thousand plates of beef and bean nachos, a thousand ultra-deluxe "gringo especialie" tacos. It was time for some training.

Lately everyone in Dallas had some advice for us. Most of them made everything west of Fort Worth sound like a great wilderness. They acted as if it were still a territory.

Ron told me he didn't like driving across Texas. Kathy said there were no more big cities after Dallas.

"Don't step on them rattlers and scorpions, Mr. Peter," said five-year-old Douglas Stevens. "There's nothin' out there on the way to Muleshoe, where my grandpa lives," he said.

Shelley Mayfield looked at me with his winter-sky blue eyes and said, "Pete, about the only shade you're going to find walking from Dallas to the Rockies is by a silo, and they're scarce. You aren't thin enough to rest in the shade of a clothesline, I can see that." Shelley studied our predicament for weeks, the way he would a 2-iron shot around a bag dogleg to the ninth green. He studied things till he figured them out. "Peter, I think I've got it figured. You and Barbara need something that will provide you with shade, something that you can take with you. Even better would be a device that you could attach to your backpacks to shade you through the worst part of the day, from twelve to five. If we don't figure this out, on the hottest days this summer, you'll have to quit walkin'. Maybe walk at night." Shelley brought out a long blue and white umbrella. He opened it. I knew what he had in mind. We would attach them to our packs with seventy-five-cent hose clamps. Shelley got us two of the largest golfing umbrellas made, from his friend Ben Hogan. We had our circle of shade that would follow us throughout the West.

Skeeter Hagler and Vivian Castleberry, a photographer and a writer who worked for the Dallas *Times Herald,* told us about the spring tornado season. "There are dust and dirt storms where you're headed, so bad they blind cattle, stop cars. These winds are so wicked they might blow you over. Wait till the summer."

Don Stevens, who could have passed for a Texas Ranger

Barbara and Sarah Stevens: "Saying good-bye is always the hardest part"

with the right black cowboy hat, was worried we'd not be able to get enough water. As a boy he'd worked in the fields in July and August and knew what it could do to a man. He knew water weighed eight pounds a gallon. Before now I'd never worried about getting enough water to drink and had never carried any. Don's warning rang in my ears: "Out west of here you can look further than any place in the world and see the least." He said we might get so thirsty we'd drink from cattle watering holes filled by windmills.

Another friend told me to watch out for Amarillo Slim.

"Who is Amarillo Slim?" I asked Jay Dickman.

"He's T. A. Preston, Jr., the best poker player in Texas. Don't play poker with Slim."

With all the good advice about tornado season, the rattlesnakes, scorpions, blinding dirt storms, thirst and poker players, we decided we'd wait until early summer to leave Dallas.

I was heavier than ever before in my life. My body had adjusted with a lot more muscle to the three and a half years of walking across America with fifty, sixty, seventy pounds on my back. I'd even gained an inch in height. My thighs and calf muscles were so big I had trouble getting pants to fit around them. My chest muscles had expanded, as had my lower back muscles and arms. I weighed 189 pounds. Barbara weighed 143.

I continued waiting tables and improving my pronunciation. I started keeping a record of our training. There was a road that left Ron's house and went about a seventh of a mile, then turned, went another seventh, and eventually made a square. We would use that at first. It shocked me how fast we could get out of shape.

On March 8 we ran and walked the 2.8 miles in forty minutes and fifteen seconds. On April 8 we had improved to thirty-four minutes and twenty seconds. Some days I'd do the first 2.8 with B.J., then do another 2.8 with Bevo, Ron and Kathy's German shepherd. By June 1, it was beginning to get Texas scorching. We'd upped our mileage and were walking fast. Both of us had lost five pounds, so far. I had quit work.

It was 97 degrees and from 10:00 A.M. to 12:25 P.M. we did 7 miles. Later we did another 5. That took from 5:30 till 7:05.

On June 3 we covered 8.7 miles (10:10 A.M. till 1:05 P.M.). It was 99 degrees. We were learning about a kind of heat and sun we'd not known till Texas. Before the sun set we walked 6 more. That took us ninety-five minutes. On June 23 we did 10 miles. We left while the roosters crowed. It took from 6:45 A.M. till 9:05 A.M. We jogged some in amongst the smells of evaporating dew and growing hay. Later that afternoon we did another 5. It was at least 99 degrees in the shade, and I noticed that in this part of Texas, once it got over 97, it was much more stressful, more draining. After all our training I was down to 176. B.J. weighed 136. We would be taking on the "frontier" and leaving "Big D" on June 29.

"Howdee," the Texas waitress said as she pulled the note pad out of her hip pocket, fast and like a six-shooter. Her blue jeans were tight and narrow at the bottoms where her pointed cowboy boots stuck out. "What ya want to eat?" she said without moving her lips much. She was an old cowgirl.

"How's your barbeque?" I asked.

"The best. It's three-toothpick BBQ."

"What's that?"

"Takes three toothpicks to get your teeth clean."

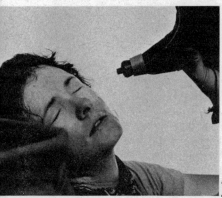

Barbara waters her sun-scorched face

We ordered the barbeque sandwiches and listened to Mel Tillis on the jukebox. Our waitress clicked back and forth in her boots, passed the cow horns, antelope and deer antlers that hung on the walls and all the booths full of dusty cowboys. Dozens of pickups passed the café's drive-up window and got its mesquite-smoked beef.

"Barbara," I said as I thought aloud, "this is where the West begins."

The temperature was still 103 degrees in Jacksboro, Texas, as we left the Pit Bar-B-Q and Dairyland and walked past the town square, where Camaros and Mustangs cruised the main street. I squinted my eyes as I looked west, out of town, where there was nothing for many miles in any direction.

I had sixteen pounds of water on my back, plus the usual weight of my pack. Barbara had about six extra pounds of "life." When we would finally get to dampen our lips with it, it would be close to 100 degrees hot.

The sign when we'd left Jacksboro had said: 39 MILES TO OLNEY. So far this would be our longest stretch. There was nothing but "miles and miles of cow piles" and dead mesquite trees. Could we make it? With this heat it would take at least three days. The sun sapped our strength as if our blood were being drained drop by drop.

As the July sky got more orange and less white-blue, I could look around some. Even with our golfing umbrellas attached to our packs, and mountain climber's sunglasses that were mirrored and had leather blinders, and baseball caps pulled way down, it was hard to look around much in the light of the day.

Brick-red lava rock jutted out from the cracked earth. Behind the barbed-wire fence, which was our only companion much of the time, was a deformed bunch of mesquite trees. The black of the withered, arthritic-looking branches made for a kind of depressing end to the day. It was time to make camp, and we would set up the tent in the dead mesquite.

On the grass was something white, a scorched white skeleton of a dead cow. The bone-white skull, the twisted back and ribs still exactly as they'd been when it breathed for the

Nothing made Barbara run like those rattlesnakes!

last time. There was something, a snake, lying comfortably stretched out along the rib cage. It was a brown-tan, and if it was a rattler, I wasn't going to find out.

I kept looking for a campsite where we would have some camouflage. We needed some live mesquites.

We found our green leaves not far off Highway 281. It was slow cooling off; the land felt like an iron that had been left plugged in. I pitched the tent and Barbara fell asleep in her usual twenty-five seconds. I lay on the cracked ground on my hot sheet and listened for some music to play me to sleep. I heard little, except some digging armadillos.

The next thing I knew it was lighter, but not full daylight. There were loud breathing noises, muffled. I looked; Barbara was lying in the same position that she'd been in when she fell asleep. She almost never moved in her sleep. I lifted my head. Maybe I was having a bad dream about a crazed breather. The breather was no dream; it *was* outside the tent.

Quietly, in the stingiest light, I put on my jeans and unzipped the mosquito netting. Whatever was breathing, it was not in front of the tent. I eased my head out and looked to the left. Nothing. The breathing had stopped. I looked to the right. Standing not ten feet from my head was the most muscle-bound, nose-running white bull I'd ever seen. His head dropped low, trying to figure out what this green nylon tent was doing in its kingdom.

The bull was very white and very big. He snorted. If he ran over this tent, he would certainly break some of our bones. Barbara breathed smoothly and was still asleep. What could I do? I knew he would not just go away. I waited maybe five minutes. He walked a step or two closer. He was scared of this green thing that smelled of people. I knew that if I didn't do something, he might continue coming and finally gore the tent, stampede us or worse. I looked on the ground for rocks. There were none. I saw a six-inch-thick chunk of tree about six feet from the tent.

If he saw me, would he charge? If I moved slowly enough, he might not. He kept breathing loud, maybe louder. Drool flowed from his open mouth and pink lips. Inch by inch I moved in slow motion toward that small log. I got to it and grabbed it with my right hand. I stood facing him; he squared off, looking at me. I waved my arms, hoping to scare him. I yelled, "HAH... Get... GET!" He started pawing the dusty-dry ground. Was he going to charge? I looked for a tree to climb, a way to run away from the tent. The mesquite trees looked like so many twigs compared to this white, muscle-necked bull. OK, Peter. You are going to have to throw that log and hit that thing right in the head. You'd better hope that he runs away. There was no other way out. I moved my free hand slowly, back and forth, hoping that he'd watch it. He did. I moved my feet slowly toward him. I got closer, too close for comfort, and heaved that log. I hit him right on his white head. He shook, then turned and whirled faster than I thought any bull could move and crashed through the live mesquite. If I had known he could have moved that fast, I would have never gone out of the tent. He broke a few small trees down.

Barbara, who was slow to wake up, spoke softly from inside.

"Honey, what was that noise?"

"Nothing, just a couple of cows feeding."

"Oh," she whispered as she fell back to sleep.

17

Asa Pease

We walked down Main Street; the Brazos River was south of
here. We'd made it to Olney, Texas (pop. 3,624). It had taken
us three days. Nothing else had moved much except us. Thirteen miles a day in the West Texas sun in July was like twenty-
five miles a day somewhere else.

There was no county courthouse or square in this town.
The main part of town was about four blocks long. It was so
dry, so sunny, so sapping that my mind had all but retired. I
looked at Barbara. I saw a wet blood-red spot on her left arm.
It was near her bicep and about the size of a golf ball. Barbara
had been putting vitamin E on it, but the sun kept it from
healing.

"B.J., does that burn on your arm hurt?"

"Yes," she answered after a delay. Maybe she was sun-
dreaming, too.

"Are you worried that it's not healing?"

"Kind of." I couldn't see her eyes; they were behind
mirrored glasses.

"Well, we're going to stop here, if there's a motel, and
find a doctor and have it checked out." I didn't say, but a lot
of people had warned me about skin cancer.

"Barbara," I said, "I love you."

A trailer truck full of hay chugged by, loud. With her floppy hat pulled over her beautiful hair, she hadn't heard me. Small pieces of straw blew everywhere.

"What did you say?" She didn't like talking when it was this hot.

"I said, I LOVE YOU." I caught her by surprise. She stopped in the middle of Olney, reached out and kissed me. Our sunglasses scrunched together, and she tried to reach around me, but my pack made me too wide.

She whispered, "And I love you." Cool shivers came up my back, and a couple of young guys beeped their horns.

At the western edge of town we found Pat's Motel. "We have only one room left, room eight, twelve dollars," a brown-haired young lady said. I took it. I had to return to the office when I found there was no plastic bowl for ice. When I reentered the office, I didn't ring the electric buzzer; I just looked around. The walls were painted white. There were no motel paintings. Everything blared white.

On the whitest wall in this small office hung some handsome belts. I had never seen anything quite like them. I took one off the wall while the clerk got me my ice bucket.

There was white leather stitching threaded around the whole belt as a border. The thick leather was carved away to make cactus, horses, saddles and western designs. In the middle of the belt was a blank where the owner's name went. Whoever made these was good, the best I had ever seen.

"Who made these belts?" I asked the clerk. She was a farm girl, shy, and talked softly with her head tilted to the side.

"Those are made by Asa, my husband. He has a shop in town, the Silver Spur. It's about a mile back, near the new bank. Right on Main."

"Is he there now?" I asked.

"Reckon so," she answered.

Barbara had taken a hot shower and was asleep on the clean white sheets. She had the air conditioner turned on High. I left a note on the mirror saying, "Not tired. Went to wander around town."

The Silver Spur Leather Shop and Western Store had a light on, so I opened the door. I heard a mallet tapping from the back of the workshop.

"Hello. Anyone here? May I come back there?"

"Sur-nough," said a voice.

Sitting at a bench covered with leather scraps and all kinds of tools was a teenager just barely in high school. He had on faded jeans, white T-shirt and baseball cap. This couldn't be Asa.

"Are you Asa Pease?" I asked.

"Oh, no, sir. No, sir. M'name's James. I work for Asa. We call him Ace."

"Where is he, son?" I asked. Everyone in these parts called anyone under thirty-five son.

"He's out for a minute. He'll be back right quick." The boy was now sweeping up piles of leather dust and scraps.

"What's this Asa like?" I was curious. Maybe I could find out before he got back.

"Asa. I've been workin' for 'im for a few years now. He's a great man, mister. One of the best I ever known about. Ya know he's teachin' me how to work this here leather."

"Really."

"Yep. Mister, his leather work's so good people come from all over Texas. Why, he even made a bunch of belts and stuff for some country music stars." He named off a few groups that were important to him.

"Ace, he's made belts for Mr. Bill Clayton, the speaker of the House of TEXAS, and loads of millionaires and rodeo stars. Heck, he's the best, in mah opinion." The young boy looked like a young version of Bum Phillips, the coach of the Houston Oilers.

"Did he ever make a belt for you?"

James pulled up his white T-shirt, which was untucked, and showed me a very worn belt. It looked as if he never took it off, even to go to sleep.

"What does Asa look like?" I asked to pass the time. An old radio, coated with some spider webs, played country music. The metallic twangs of the steel guitar never sounded so right.

"Well, sir, he's one of the strongest men I ever known.

Asa Pease

He always wears some kindy cowboy hat, and he's real hard-workin'. Ya know, him and his wife manage the motel and run this place." The bells on the door rang. "Ya know, he used to break horses. Me, I just ride bulls."

The front half of the store was dark. I heard a voice. It was a low, resonant man's voice. "Come on, honey."

Maybe it was Asa. I looked for a long, lanky silhouette.

"Howdy, James," the man said. He leaned hard on wood crutches. His yellow-white straw hat sat square. "Ya got them boots done, buddy?" His legs hung between the crutches.

"Yep, they're over there, Ace."

"Can I help you, mister?" Ace asked me, leaning on one crutch and extending his hand. "My name's Asa Pease, and yours?"

We shook. It was obvious those powerful hands had been supporting that massive upper body, big, satisfied stomach and powerless legs for a long time. "I'm Peter Jenkins. Saw some of your belts out at the motel. You made those, right?"

"That's me." He was reading my mind, and that of every-one who met him. He wasn't shy or sorry about his crutches.

"My legs ain't worth a damn, but when it comes to leather, I got one of the best pair of hands in Texas."

From what I'd seen of Asa's work, he had reason to be proud of his craft, his art. I stuck around for a few more hours as he finished up a couple of belts for an oilman who was taking them to Saudi Arabia with him.

I asked Ace if it would be all right if I stuck around for a few days and watched him work. He said, "Awright. See ya in the mornin'."

Before we did anything else, we saw a doctor. All he said to B.J. was: "Honey, if you want to keep walkin' 'cross America, you better wear nothin' but long-sleeve cotton shirts. You ain't seen nothin' yet, children."

We both hung around Asa's shop on Main Street all day and for the rest of the week. On Asa's Western Wear Calendar, it said today was July 18, 1977. Asa was thirty-four; ten days ago I'd turned twenty-six. It'd been my fourth birthday on the road. It had turned out to be a long walk for me. Asa had never known what it was to walk. All he knew was how to climb.

"Polio hit me when I was four months old. Seems like ever since then people been tellin' me I can't do this, I can't do that," Asa said while sketching a design on a belt. "I ain't listened to 'em ever.

"When I was a kid growin' up in California, they told me I couldn't fight like the other kids. They told me I couldn't be around the stock, to leave the horses alone. Everyone wanted to make a fuss over me. I told 'em I'd do whatever I wanted." He pulled a freshly tanned cowhide from a storage room and cut out some more belts.

"See, I grew up 'roun' the dairy and farm country of California. Everyone thinks that California's full of 'fruits and nuts,' the human kind, I mean. Them days a lot of the milkin' was done by hand. They told me I couldn't get a job, do nothin'. Why didn't I just sit still and collect my money from the government? After all, I was one of the few who really deserved them welfare checks. I told 'em to give them checks to some ol' person who couldn't work. I was gonna get me a job some way. No one would give me a job 'cept this dairy farm. Milkin', twice a day. Ya know I milked more than their milkers that could walk, and they only paid me about half of what them other people made. I didn't let it get me down. I milked harder. Ya know there are almost as many rednecks in California as there are in Texas."

The door opened, and a lady strolled in with brown Levi's and a turquoise necklace on. Ace called her by name. She said she needed some new shirts; she was going to Los Angeles; her daughter got some job on some TV show.

Ace walked up to her on his crutches. "How can you tell when you meet a level-headed redneck?" he asked her.

"I don't know."

"Well, 'cause the ol' boy's got tabacco juice runnin' down *both* sides of his mouth."

She bought four Dickson-Jenkins western shirts.

"When I got aroun' to noticin' girls, they told me I should look for a nice girl like me, maybe in a wheelchair. We'd have a lot in common. I told 'em I'd find me the best good-lookin' woman I could. If she was Miss California, fine. If she was born in a wheelchair, fine. If she hated crutches, all right."

Ace stopped to change blades in his X-Acto knife, so that he could make some intricate cuts in the thick leather. Hands any less massive and powerful would have had a hard time cutting through.

"Asa." Barbara wanted to know something. "Where did you find your wife? In California?"

"Nope. Found her right here in Olney. I roped her one afternoon at a Fourth of July picnic."

"You did?" I said.

"I got tired of California, always wanted to be a cowboy, so I picked up and moved out here. Thought I'd get me a job breakin' horses, some ranchwork. Back before I left California, some therapy lady had gotten me into some leatherwork. Said it was good for my nerves. I needed a hobby, something to keep me from gettin' bored. I found out I could really make that leather do what I wanted it to. So when I saw that a lot of these people needed leatherwork done, their ol' boots fixed, saddles repaired, I decided to open me a store. People told me I was crazy. I didn't even know nobody in Olney. I'd go broke, spend all my savings before the first few months passed. Well, here I am. I got more work than I could ever do. I got a lot of my family working with me now, I got so much custom work."

He opened a drawer. And with silent reverence pulled out a couple of rolled up belts. He unrolled one, like it was a Dead Sea scroll, and showed it to us. A detailed scene was etched and carved and painted into the cowhide, this Texan's stretched canvas.

"I miss this here kind of work. I used to be able to spend a lot more hours, sometimes weeks, on my work." He pointed to a horse, in stretched-out gallop, outrunning a tornado. I knew from the cowboy's expression that the tornado was close. The cactus was not designer cactus, but botanically correct. The cattle lying in the shade of mesquite were as real as the leather.

"This here's one of the thangs that bothers me about bein' successful. I ain't got as much time to do belts like these here." He unrolled another and just looked at it. "You want me to make you each a belt?" he said out of his reflections.

At first thought I wanted to say yes. But then I thought of all that Ace had to do. All the belts to be made, the rows of tired boots to be resoled. The saddles to be reworked.

"I appreciate it, Ace, but you don't seem to have the time."

"I'll make 'em at night. That way we can tawk some more." Anything he said.

"Hey, Pete, you know who invented the Frisbee?" Ace asked.

"A Texan, right? Some NASA scientist in Houston."

He had his bulky arms across his bulkier chest. He had a red western shirt on. He shook his head.

"Of course, it was a Texan. But it happened long bafore any moon landing. One day ol' M. L. McQuinton, he was running to catch a fly ball in a softball game. The sun blinded him and he missed the catch. But he picked it up and tried to throw the runner out. The onliest thang was that M.L. missed the ball and flung a dry cow chip. That's how the Frisbee was invented. Do you believe it?"

"You sure it happened in Texas, Ace?"

"Some of the cowboys treated their boots better 'n their women"

"Yep."

"You think that ol' M.L. might of invented the spaceship that day, too?"

Ace reared back in his seat, made from an old tractor seat, and flung a round scrap of leather at me.

"Some told us not to have any kids. They said I'd not be able to keep up with 'em. Support 'em. Well, I'm doin' better than a lot of people that have all their things workin'." A couple of pretty school girls came in. They said they were just looking.

"I guess I'm funny, I make it sound like everyone tells me I can't do things. But that ain't true. Really, a lot of people have told me I *could* do anything I set my mind to. Now maybe I couldn't dance in front of Lawrence Welk's orchestra or outtwirl that boy in *Saturday Night Fever*, but besides that . . . You know, for some stupid reason, I don't remember the people that said I could as much as I remember the people that told me I couldn't do things. Them people that say I can't, they made me mad, made me want to do it even if I shouldn't be able to." He grabbed another sharp knife and rounded off the end of one of his C&W belts. "I reckon that's why I broke horses for a while. Now *that* is hard cruel work. Someone said I could never do nothin' like that. I showed 'em. A lot of them horses didn't act out with me like they did with some of them fulltime cowboys. I tawked gentle to them wild horses, just like I do to my wife."

Ace was working on Barbara's belt. In the middle, where the name was to go, he quickly, with keen coordination, penciled in her name, then cut out the leather in between. He would use a white material as backing and the "BARBARA" would really stand out. That was the deluxe way of doing it, Ace said. A lot of leatherworkers just stamped your name into the leather. The brass bells on the door rang again. Ace looked out and motioned for a classic-looking Texan to come on back. He was blond, had a ranch tan and was in his twenties, and hadn't shaved today. He was one of the sons of a wealthy rancher and farmer. They had some oil wells on the ranch, too. The thin-legged man's jeans looked like antiques from a Levi Strauss museum. He had on a green plaid short-sleeved shirt. Ace said that all the women around here ran around with him when they could. He ran fast, Ace said. After the blond man left with two pairs of resoled boots, Ace said, "I seen that ol' boy with a lot of women. You know, I think he treats them boots a his better than any of them women. Well"—Ace thought a moment—"it might just be that ol' Willie ain't found the right woman yet. He knows he can't do no better than those Nocona boots."

The ten days we spent with Ace and his family and the "niiiice" people of Olney were much more than a siesta. We went to Little League all-star baseball games between Olney and Graham. Olney lost 2-1, bottom of the tenth inning. We went to a picnic, put on by the bank, where we bobbed for apples, sped across the grass in three-legged races, listened to C&W, and ate BBQ. Ace said he'd like to bob for french fries.

18

In the Mirror

Barbara

The land ahead was sterile-looking and parched. These endless
sagebrush plateaus were not fit for anything except tarantulas,
lizards, horny toads and rattlesnakes that hugged the gray dirt,
looking for shade under the neddlegrass. This was a land for
thickheaded cows with heavy hides—not people. Not me.

I put one foot in front of the other and kept pushing my
body forward. It was too hot to talk. It was too hot to move,
but we had no refuge from the burning sun, no place to rest.
There was only openness with knotty fence posts and rusty
barbed wire to break the monotony. A mad whirlwind of hot
red dust spinned beside me and slapped me in the face like a
sandblaster. Big Texas might have been something to brag
about from a horse, car, plane or oil deck, but it felt like hell
to me on foot.

Twenty-three miles to the little West Texas town of Seymour didn't seem like much, but it was twelve hours of sweating and fighting flies and gnats that landed on my face and
legs, looking for a drop of moisture. It was drinking hot water
as long as we had it, not cold Cokes and iced tea. It was

walking with my face down to keep the blaring light out of my eyes, looking at the ground that was cracked brown, like eggshells, dry and bitter and crying out. In fact, in this 110-degree furnace, it seemed like the whole West cried out and groaned from deep inside the way Willie Nelson did when he sang. A lean land it was. A woman had to get tough and leathery to survive because it sucked the strength and life and water out of every living thing.

Peter was far ahead of me but still within yelling distance. I was all give-out as I lagged behind in my exhaustion and solitude. We had eight miles left to walk, which was another three hours of walking. I wished the Marlboro man would ride by and loan me his horse. Maybe a cowpuncher would come by and have an extra horse I could ride into the yellow sunset. These new cowboys came by, all right, inside their air-conditioned pickups, pulling their saddled horses in trailers behind them. Nothing but mad dogs and scavenger coyotes would get out in this heat. Cattlemen drove by us slowly on this back road, giving us their steely gaze, letting us know they thought we were insane.

I was beyond caring what anybody thought. My mind was too busy pushing back the pain I felt from the quarter-sized blisters on my heels and toes and the sunburns on my legs and arms. Although I kept myself coated in lotion and Vaseline, my fair skin was toasted and dry. The ointments seemed to draw more flies, and it was disgusting because I had no energy left to swat them. They feasted on me. It was only when a gnat got in my mouth or nose that I would raise my swollen hands to slap it away.

In order to survive and keep going, I kept my mind in another world, dreaming about a deep cool bubble bath with streams of running cold water. My body needed a bath in the worst way. I was grimy and smelled sour and earthy. In my mind's eye I could see a real bathroom, cool and inviting, with a tub, shower and commode. There would be a basin to brush my teeth in, a stool to sit on instead of finding spots in the bushes, and there would be rivers and rivers of fresh, sparkling, clear, wonderful water. Then, after I was scrubbed clean, perfumed and oiled, I would slip under crisp white sheets and slip into oblivion for fifteen hours of sleep. Sleep. Sweet sleep, oh, how my overwalked body needed it.

That kind of thinking was only good for a while because the heat gladly reminded me, constantly, of the truth. It was a battle in my brain to keep from getting irritable and mean in this heat, but I had learned that any extra emotion took energy that I didn't have. Miles pass slowly, and I had to conserve what strength I had, which was none. Time was forever in this desert land, where nothing passed between me and the next town but barbed wire. The sun pounded down and bounced off the blacktop, making thick heat waves that quivered. Those heat waves looked like tongues of invisible fire looking for fuel to burn.

Mother and Daddy popped into my head. I grabbed them in my mind and wondered what they were doing up in Missouri. It must be cooler there. Mother's birthday was right around the corner and I had forgotten to send her a card. I would get one in the next town. Boy, if they could see me now, what would they think? The first question everybody asked me was: "What did your parents say about you walking across America like this?"

It was awkward to tell people, but I never told Mother and Daddy the truth about Peter and me. Before we married, I told them Peter was a writer and photographer doing stories about America. I assumed they would think we would travel around America in a comfortable van. That's what I wanted them to think. I could not tell them that Peter was penniless, did not have a job, was a wanderer walking across America and that I was going to join him.

Marrying Peter was a total risk for me. Nothing about him was secure. His future was as wild and open as all of Texas. I reasoned it was not fair to burden my parents with my fears and worries that I had agonized over for months. I had been through enough worry for them, too, and I couldn't handle anyone else's doubts. Even though my parents were sincere in their faith, they would not buy the idea that "God" had called me to go with Peter. They had an aversion to religious fanatics who were all talk and didn't follow through with their revelations, so I knew that I had to prove to myself that God had called me before I could prove it to anyone else. Especially Mother and Daddy.

My parents were hill people from the Ozarks, from the Show Me State. They were planted in the earth like their yearly gardens and both took what came their way. I was sure they would take my decision to marry Peter with the same style, but it was just that I didn't want them to worry about me. In my whole life I had never seen them react drastically or passionately over anything. They carried their joys and tears inside. When it rained, they were glad. When it was hot, they waited patiently for it to cool off. When a flood came, they picked up the pieces and kept going. The only time I ever saw my mother cry was at Grandad's funeral. It wasn't that she never cried; it was that she preferred to shed her tears and sorrows behind closed doors. It was because she felt so deeply and strongly that she guarded her tender heart from open display, fearing she would make a fool out of herself if she let go. It was with this same reserved passion that they reacted to my decision to marry Peter. Instinctively they knew something was different but did not ask.

They were cautiously pleased with Peter and seemed to take to him better than they had to other men I had brought home for them to meet. This was more serious, however. They eyed him and studied him in their quiet ways, and I could tell Peter was passing their inspection with flying colors. Maybe it was because I didn't try to hard-sell him or push him on them. Maybe it was because it wasn't Peter's nature to put on airs. They liked that, especially since Peter was a Yankee. Maybe it was because they sensed Peter's heart was right toward me and he would "do me right," as they say in the Missouri hills. Or maybe it was because my parents knew me too well and that I would marry Peter no matter what they thought or said. I had been on my own for a lot of years, as a headstrong career woman, unafraid of launching out and making my own way, determined to challenge the world, and they knew I would do my own thing regardless. They had not interfered with me since I left from under their roof to go away to college at age seventeen.

"You have to live with Peter, I don't," Mother said to me matter-of-factly. "He's your choice and you have to live your own life." This attitude came from their farming roots that said, "You reap what you sow." It also came from a country shrewdness I still don't understand. Mother and Daddy knew this was a life-changing decision for me and the smartest thing they could do was let me go, let me make my own decisions and mistakes, and in the end they would keep me. They hoped and prayed, beyond my ears and eyes, this was right for both Peter and me.

Now more than a year later they knew the truth, but it had not come from me. They had found out before we reached Dallas on foot, but I didn't know they knew. They never said a word to me about it. The nearest they came to confronting me about walking across America with Peter was in a timely letter that came before we left Dallas to get back on the road:

Dear Barbara and Peter,

Hope this finds you both in fine fettle, we're fine but not in fettle. Daddy fell last week and broke his left wrist, has it in a cast and I've had such a cough can't sleep at night.

Barbara, the first time you ever were in Texas, Daddy said, "Here's Texas," when we crossed the state line and you jumped up from the back seat of the car and said, "Where's the cowboys?"

I've been piecing quilts again. I get in the biggest messes. I don't need to do that at all, but it's so pretty and fascinating. I get started and can't stop. I made a beautiful flower arrangement for Granny and Grandad's grave, must take it down there this week.

Jim and Elaine were down last weekend, fixed a big pan of cornbread, opened some of my home-canned green beans, made some herb potatoes, slaw, stewed apples, fried chicken and had a big peach cobbler for dessert. Wish you were here to eat with us. Jim's laid off from the plant again. Vicky is fine, still working on her paintings.

We've been short on natural gas this winter so

*we've mostly heat with the wood stoves. It's just bad
with Daddy's arm in a cast, keeping the fires going,
getting in wood and all, but both of us together get it
done. The neighbors have been good to help out.*

*One night Daddy's arm hurt him so he couldn't
sleep and I coughed all night. I told the neighbor lady,
Millie, there sure wasn't much hugging and kissing going
on.*

*I'd better close and get the dishes washed and
things put together.*

*I guess you'll be getting ready to get back on the
road again soon.*

We love and miss you.

Mother and Daddy

The sun turned iridescent. It dropped down like a big
yellow-orange ball on top of the horizon, softening its rays and
apologizing for being so hatefully hot all day long. Seymour
was one more mile, one more wide curve through the breaks
that had turned into painted arenas like those famous pictures
of the Grand Canyon with strips of pink, gold, red and brown
throughout. My body was numb from the twenty-three western
miles. All I knew was this day was about over. Getting my
bubble-bath dreams fulfilled was no longer an incentive because my weakened body was past the pain, past the desire to
see my fantasies come true.

Seymour, Texas, was a little dusty American town about
the length of one city block in New York. After what I had
been through today, it was more appealing to me than all the
culture and intelligence and art that New York had to offer.
This little oasis meant people. It meant life and water. It meant
I could stop. It meant help.

I staggered down the street into town behind Peter, who
led the way, checking every building and street and looking
for a motel and place to eat. He didn't have to search very
hard because there weren't many buildings or streets. We had
not eaten all day, but food was meaningless to me now. There
she was. The prettiest sight I had ever seen. Two blocks ahead

sat a long one-story white stucco building with a motel sign overhead. I was too tired to notice much, but I remember the town felt quiet. Only two pickup trucks passed by. The cowboys must have been going out to their ranches for supper. I didn't see any fast-food joints, supermarkets, bustling businesses. It was still. I felt I had stepped back into history when the hot evening wind blew a tumbleweed in front of me.

Peter checked in while I stood fixed in a drained trance, waiting for him outside the motel office. The next thing I knew, he was unlocking the door when I heard the click of the key. I turned around like a robot and ordered my heavy hiking boots to step inside. A cold gush of air conditioning pushed me back and caught my breath. It was the first excited move I had made all day, and it was not voluntary on my part. My cooked body was reacting to the drastic temperature change as goose bumps covered my sunburns.

Peter and I were silent as we unstrapped our gear and dropped everything on the floor like letting a ton of weight off our shoulders. I sank slowly onto the bed, too tired to groan or even close my eyes. I slumped over onto my elbows while Peter walked around the room, checking everything out. He was as tired as I but knew I couldn't make it to a café so he went to get some food and bring it back to the room. He always tried to make things easier for me when I was this exhausted. Whatever I wanted to eat, he would find. He pulled the door shut behind him and locked it.

Peter had turned on the television before he left, and it sounded very loud to me after hearing only the wind and some bawling cattle today. The commercials were gaudy and seemed ridiculous as I was reminded this was still 1977. The world and its ways seemed strange to me now. I sat stooped over on the edge of the bed, trying to get enough strength to get up and take a bath. Nothing seemed alive to me except my brain. It told me to turn on the lamp because it was getting dark. When I did, the dull yellow light showed all around. The motel room was dingy and cheap with blond cardboard-light furniture from the 1950's, and the carpet was full of cigarette burns. The one chair was Danish modern with vinyl cushions, ripped at the corners. There was a chest of drawers, blond too, with a large mirror behind it. When my eyes spanned up the dresser, I saw my reflection in the mirror as I sat on the edge of the bed and I gasped. Oh, dear merciful God! Was that really me?

The person I saw in the mirror staring back didn't look anything like me. That was a haggard, withered-looking woman. Her face was sunken and her eyes were blank. Her skin was burned red and peeling; her body, dirty and slumped over. She looked woolly and worn-out. Her dark hair was greasy and full of tangles as it hung out from under her flop hat. Her squinted eyes were fixed in a narrow slit from warding off the glaring sun. Her bare legs were puffy and muscular, but worst of all, her spunk was gone. The woman in the mirror was an empty frame with blistered skin pulled tight over her bones. That couldn't be me.

"And now for the ten finalists," came the hyped-up voice on the television. Music, trumpets and a full orchestra rang out as the ten most beautiful women in the world walked down the ramp in front of the judges for one final look. This was the Miss World Beauty Contest.

One gorgeous girl after another strutted in front of the camera with their rouge-red cheeks, glittery gowns, painted lips and eyelids every color of the rainbow, and their straight white teeth. Their smiles were full and forced; their movements, practiced and perfect. They were young, beautiful, tempting, and some of the fairest women in all the world.

I sat alone in a state of numbness as I looked away from the mirror to the television screen.

Here I was, stripped of everything. That woman in the mirror had once been a beauty queen herself. She had been in homecoming contests, yearbook contests, best-dressed contests and had won more than once. She had been one of the prettiest girls on her college campus, and now here she sat in the middle of nowhere, sapless, dirty and looking worse than a Stone Age cavewoman.

Alone in this shabby room, I watched the full-bodied beauties before me and experienced a moment of truth like none other in my life.

My body was too tired to take any more jolts because I

had walked 1,000 miles so far and 23 Texas tough miles today. But the truth was stabbing. There was no mask, no beautiful face or body to hide behind anymore. A supernatural knife had cut away my flesh, the layers of vanity, the conceit and pride I had always taken in myself.

There was nothing left. I was seeing the naked Barbara, who looked back at me. I was seeing beyond my skin and into my spirit as I studied the person in the mirror. I stared. Then I stared at the TV and the girls who were decorated and like ripe berries.

I had no energy left to cry or feel sad. After I slowly eased up onto my punctured feet, I made my way to the TV and snapped it off. A keen awareness hit me.

I limped into the tiled bathroom and turned on the shower. There was no bathtub, as I had imagined in my dreams on the long road. I sighed. In my weariness and ugly outward condition, all I could do was accept the shower just the way I was accepting my looks. I reasoned there was a time for all things, a time to be pretty and a time to be ugly. I stepped under the stream of water and let if flush my face. The tiny bar of motel soap slipped through my fingers as I worked up a good lather and gently stroked my parched skin. In a way, I felt free.

We sat eating in Mitchell's restaurant. This was a small café and the first one we had come to on our way out of Seymour. We could see our backpacks through the big picture window as we ate our breakfast.

Peter read the middle section while I read the front page of the *Baylor County Banner,* the weekly town newspaper. There was an article about blood donors and the good rain Seymour had last week: a total of 1.97 inches. In the upper left-hand corner was an American flag, and in the right-hand corner was a slogan "Keep Smiling." Seymour had made me smile again because my body was rested and I felt like a new person. I was in love with everything once more, even Texas and its sagebrush.

Outside, Peter hoisted my pack up and onto my shoulders while I wiggled and twisted to get the arm straps just right.

I noticed the sun was directly overhead because there

were no shadows. This was going to be a scorcher, but I was ready. Today was July 25, 1977, as we headed west out of town, into the wild country. I moo-o-ed at the brown rivers of cattle that walked alongside us behind their barbed-wire fences. Everything felt fine today. We were walking briskly toward Benjamin, a smaller town than Seymour, and it was easy to keep a fast pace after plenty of sleep and food. The hot wind blew against my umbrella and pushed me from side to side.

All of a sudden I heard Peter yell. He was up ahead when I heard him holler something about that stupid driver. A white motor home-camper had pulled off the highway and was on the shoulder of the road, headed straight for Peter. He threw up his arms. The camper was coming to a stop.

"Barbara!" Peter screamed at me. "It's your parents."

"Oh, my Lord," I shouted back, hurrying as fast as I could to catch up.

This was unbelievable. What were they doing here? How had they found us? Was it really them? They had no way of knowing where we were. I had sent them a postcard from 100 miles back, but they didn't know our route or how long it took us to get from place to place. I quickly thought how glad I was they were seeing us today instead of yesterday, when I was so wiped out.

Mother and Daddy were staring at us through the tinted windshield, smiling and examining us from head to toe. I could feel their thoughts as they checked us out to see that we were all in one piece. It occurred to me that my parents had never seen me in hiking boots or carrying a backpack before.

Without telling us in advance or giving us a clue to their plans, they had driven all the way from Missouri to West Texas, looking for us and to surprise us. This trip was Mother's birthday present. They had been searching for several days, stopping at stores, gas stations and even the highway patrol, asking if anyone had seen us. They knew we were in a range of 200 miles from the last town where a postcard from us had been postmarked, and they never doubted they would find us. It was a wonderful moment for me because I had not seen them for many months and now we could talk till the sun went down.

Barbara's parents try on our packs

Early the next morning Mother cooked me and Peter a hiker's breakfast of fried potatoes, eggs, bacon, toast and coffee. Daddy served us some of his "well-water highballs." That was pure underground water from his well back home. Daddy believed water purified your body, so he drank lots of it, even carried water with them when they went on trips in their camper.

We sat under the pavilion of their camper in lawn chairs they brought and talked on and on about the walk, the family, the hot weather, our camping equipment, the future and religion. All this talking was unusual for them, but I guessed that my country-shy parents were so relieved to find us alive and in good shape that they talked out their happy emotions.

They left the next day, disappearing in their camper as quickly as they had appeared. It had been a short, hot and sweet time together, a reward for all the rugged desert we had crossed. That was Mother and Daddy's way of saying they were behind us, and we were in their hearts so much they had to find us on the road. Their actions usually spoke more than they did.

It was several weeks later when this letter caught up to us on the road:

August 1, 1977

Dear Ones,

I guess you are still plodding along under that hot Texas sun. I looked at that beautiful full moon last night and thought about you sleeping under it. We got home about 11 P.M. Thursday. Everything was fine at home. Our garden was awful dry, we had to water it.

The trip did me good, mentally. I know you're not fainting by the roadside from lack of water and food. So good to see you both in such fine fettle. I wished we had waited awhile on driving out to see you, waited till you got somewhere a little cooler. We didn't realize it would be that hot.

Don't know any news. Am cooking a pot of taters and meat, wish you were here to help eat it.

Take care. Be good to each other and keep your umbrellas high. We love you lots.

Mother and Daddy

19

Lightning and a West Texas Lullaby

We lay in large pools of water, so frigid with fear we could do nothing but hold onto each other. The dazing light came again. My body jerked.

"Get out there and get—" Another explosion. The light and explosion had disintegrated another fence post. Pieces of it landed on the tent.

"Peter," Barbara screamed, her face wrapped in her soaked sheet, "why didn't—" CRASH! The sky sounded as if it were tearing itself in two. She shivered and held on till her fingers hurt me.

"Barbara, what can we do if that—" The petrifying light, the booms, CRASH, hit together. Winds attacked us from behind, till they knocked down half the tent.

Rainwater poured into the tent and all over our shaking bodies. We fumbled, jerking, ripping at any metal near our bodies. We must take off our wedding rings. Lying in this water, if one of the jagged bolts of lightning found us, we'd be fried. LIGHT! That bluish light! It penetrated the tent and, like a spastic strobe light, froze the fear of death on our faces.

We lay there in the fetal position, our bodies waiting for another explosion. The ONE. And I mean explosion, as loud as any war. This was no high-altitude rambling. These thunder shouts were attacking the earth, trying to *make* fault lines. The savage bolts and thunder were on "search and destroy" missions. Now they were directly over us. BABOOM. SMACK. LIGHT. Ears shivered; my brain waited for death.

Earlier in the evening the sky was as clear as the truth. We'd fought the sun and won for another day, but when it came time to pitch the tent, I'd gone against my better judgment and had not put up the rain fly, a nylon sheet that went on top of the breathable fabric of the inner tent. Without it the tent was not waterproof, about as protective as sleeping under a screen. From the looks of heaven there was no way it could rain. Much less *this.*

The storm, the worst temper tantrum Texas had ever thrown at us, had blown in from the north, across what they called the breaks. I'd fallen into such a deep sleep that I didn't feel a thing till we were part soaked and the lightning was all around. It was too late now to put up the rain fly. There was nothing to do but lie there, in the water that lightning loved, and wait to either live or die. I'd never been so close. So shaky. CRASH.

Another blast. More light. Even with my eyes shut tight, I could still see the cutting lightning bursts. They hit together, almost. BOOM, LIGHT, FLASH. It was like holding your ear next to an artillery cannon. Our time was coming, that moment when the lightning would seek out our cringing bodies, in the cold puddles.

EXPLODE. Another chunk of earth was killed dead. There were no high trees to draw the sky's violence. I'd pitched the tent on the highest ridge around, so we could look out over the breaks, which were deeply eroded, wild scrubland fit for roadrunners, horned toads and a few thirsty cows.

I could not bring myself to open my eyes. It was as close to playing Russian roulette as I'd ever come. Every bolt was like pulling the trigger. Would this bolt be it? Except that we weren't pulling the trigger.

We just lay in contorted fetal curves, our faces buried in each other's bodies, our hands pressed against our ears so tight my arms shook from pushing so hard. *It hit together.*

Were we hit? *"Barbara, are you all right?"* All she could do was shake in response.

I was so crazed by now that I wished some truck or car would drive by. I had no idea what time it was. It could be 11:30 P.M. It could be 4:00 A.M. If I saw headlights, I thought of running through the onslaught, like a fanatic marine trying to rescue his buddy in the height of battle, and flagging down the car, the truck. We were in the middle of nowhere between Seymour and Benjamin, Texas. We could *die* here as easy as any other spot. EXPLOSION! I wondered how long I could take this before I went completely crazy. Could we be thunder-shocked?

Barbara lay there; her body never stopped shaking. I opened my eyes to wait for the next flash. BANG. It lit up a hundred square miles. Barbara's lips were moving incessantly. I knew she was praying. I was.

There was more time now between LIGHT and EXPLO-SION, LIGHT . . . EXPLOSION, LIGHT . . . EXPLOSION. I had maybe a minute to think. These kinds of violent outbreaks of Texas temper drove the native ranchers into their storm cellars. They touched off plenty of tornadoes. They'd warned, "We done lost plenty a cattle in 'em. Fires, bad fires, get started."

Would it hook on back? Had it passed over us? Was that just the first wave of attack? Could there be more? I couldn't keep thinking of more. We both lay in the wet, our eyes afraid to open, our ears scared to hear any more. We'd never held each other with such need. If we died, we'd be gone together. We huddled and entangled ourselves till we couldn't be closer.

I would not have thought it possible, but we both woke up, close to dawn, still entangled. I guess our nervous systems had taken all they could and overamped. The storm had cooled off the giant oven that was West Texas. I could hardly stand, I was so weak from the all-out assault of thunder and lightning.

We had to hang out our soaked sheets and tent and clothes on some of the endless barbed wire. They would have been too heavy to carry wet. Waiting for them to dry was like sitting in front of a hundred open dryers in a Laundromat. There was never any letup out here. Weakened by all that we'd been through, we had to make it to Benjamin (pop. 308). As sick as we both felt, we needed to hole up and recover. If I had to, I would walk up to a ranch house. We set out.

Two cutting horses, one with an Appaloosa's spots but no white in its face, the other an oak brown with yellow mane, crossed in front of us. The road, Highway 82. On their backs, in saddles that were tools, sat two young Texans. They were fourteen, they could have been younger, but they were doing the work of men. When they saw us, the one on the Appaloosa stopped.

"How far is it into Benjamin?" I asked. They both had rifles.

"'Bout six, eight miles."

"What you boys doin'?"

"Ridin'." The boy on the brown horse was opening a barbed-wire gate.

"You live around here?"

"Yep." Their shirts were rolled up as high as they'd go. Their thin arms controlled the reins without thinking. "We're ridin' this range; it's our family's ranch. We think some rustlin's been goin' on."

Benjamin wasn't much more than a crossroads (82 and 6), a courthouse and café, then a store or two. The sign heading west said, GUTHRIE 32 MILES.

"What's between here and Guthrie?" I asked one of the few fat men I'd seen in West Texas.

"Nothin' 'cept a couple windmills."

We had planned to walk straight west to Lubbock, climb up on the Cap Rock, but now we looked north, to more than windmills. We were finally into *big* ranch country, where there were more cattle than people. In some places there may have been more pumping oil wells than people. This land was so void of people, towns and buildings that the only things listed on U.S. Geological Survey maps were *windmills,* and they were often ten miles apart. Water was "life," and a cowboy could find his way around a ranch by knowing where the windmills were. One was called Devil's Playground Windmill. Other landmarks in "this here area" were called Polecat Windmill, Hanna Draw, Little Getaway Canyon, Ignorant Ridge and Panther Canyon. A tree taller than a Hereford bull could be found only by the "home place."

Those thirty-two miles between Benjamin and Guthrie would have been spent crossing just one or two ranches. They said the 6666 ranch was where the Marlboro man had been a hand. They filmed all the cigarette commercials "out there" till one day the red-mustached cowboy was "ridin' his horse and crossed a tank, and he drowned." (A tank is a ranch pond.) "It ain't easy to learn how to swim 'roun' here in these parts."

Texas has 169,356,107 acres of ground, give or take. The Three D ranch, not far from here, had "500,000 of them acres." One dry-land cotton and wheat farmer told us that that place, "a country in its own right," has one wheat field that takes all day to make just one trip around. "That ain't one day to plow the whole field, on a $75,000 Massey-Ferguson tractor; that's all day just to go around the outside of the field." The Three D, most folks call it the Waggoner ranch, is the biggest ranch in Texas, in one chunk. "The King ranch, down in South Texas, heck, it's got close to a million, I believe 'roun' eight hundred fifty thousand acres, but it ain't in one piece. It spreads 'round a bunch a counties. We got the biggest ranches right 'roun' here, son. Now that original Waggoner man who started the place. He was as smart as a coyote, as tough as iron. They got them a brand that's almost impossible to alter. A reverse triple D.

"The Waggoner ranch was begun in 1851 by a strivin' cowboy, Daniel Waggoner. Once it roamed over more'n a million acres! Today them descendants, there're only four of 'em, three of 'em women, own the place. They don't live 'roun' here. They travel plenty, go to Ha-Wa-Ya a lot." They said a man could drive for fifty miles and still be on the Three D.

We found a place to stay with a guy who didn't own one square inch "out there" or anyplace else. "Wyman Meinzer grew up 'roun' here, his daddy's the foreman at the League ranch. He went to ol' Texas Tech, but he came back here. Spends all his time takin' pictures a roadrunners, rattlesnakes, wild turkey and coyotes. That boy's got a degree, but he says

Heading out of Fort Worth toward West Texas, rattlesnakes,
and Amarillo Slim

Dawn on the Bayous

Right: Glen Hebert heads
for home with his catch

Everybody comes to the rodeo

This bull rider is
about to land hard

Betty Bee Gafford, a West Texas rancher, shows us her favorite Indian jewelry

Western still life, inside a hardware store at Olney, Texas

We fell in love with the golden grasslands and endless skies
of the prairie

Homer and Ruby
in their cotton field

Ruby locks the gate on an ornery bull

A Rocky Mountain bobcat, a rare sight

Left: Tornado's coming!

Sundown in Snake River Canyon, Idaho

Right: "No one stays a stranger around Perk Vickers long"

One Step Below Heaven

Aspen leaves color the
river gold at the
headwaters of the
Rio Grande

Barbara and I are inside our cabin while a winter storm blows up

The Book Cliffs of Eastern Utah

Joe Davidson, the one-eyed gaswell worker,
part-time preacher, who's worked the oil fields
since a young boy

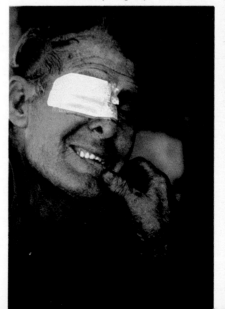

Fall roundup at the Williams' ranch

near the land he
first homesteaded

Rodney re-rides the range down by the
Nevada-Idaho border

An Idaho sunset

Winter on the high plains of central Oregon

The walk ends!

he ain't gonna move to them big cities for a job. He makes his money trappin' coyotes in the fall and winter. Sells his pictures to them that loves this beautiful country. I'll say this for the boy, he's doin' exactly like he wants. He's one of the best trappers this area ever seen. He loves them coyotes, knows 'em better 'n he knows hisself."

We'd been told these West Texans would be the friendliest people we would meet. They were. Their faces were as open as the land they lived on, their hands extended to shake a stranger's hand. Especially if that stranger was beginning to see their countryside as more than desolate, boring, parched and forsaken. They felt it was as "purty" as any other land in the world.

Wyman, who had a dark brown beard and hair, was tied deep to these vast spaces and ranch country. He put us up in his parents' house in town that night.

Wyman had a lot of the poet in him, a desert poet who would rather watch a jackrabbit kick up dust, being chased by a golden eagle at sunset, than slurp Lone Star beer. Around here, Wyman told me while sitting in the shade of a windmill, were black vultures, wild turkeys, Cooper's hawks, eagles, red-tailed hawks, rough-legged hawks, bobcats, owls, all kinds of snakes, big deer, wild pigs and thousands of other living things, including coyotes. Trapping coyotes was the only way that Wyman could support himself and live in this freedom, in the midst of his love for "out there."

We headed north into the breaks. The breaks were land that looked as if it had been broken apart, sucked into the earth. The land for thousands of acres could be as flat as plywood, then without reason just drop off abruptly into eroded, shallow canyons where the dirt was reddish brown, sprinkled with off-white and bluish rock. These breaks could be thirty miles wide and hundreds of miles long. The wildlife Wyman knew so much about had a sanctuary in these breaks. Some scraggly mesquite grew. A drop of water in this jagged land would evaporate before it hit this forlorn ground. Even the measureless barbed wire looked lonely.

Topping a slight ridge, we saw our first stretch of breaks.

Ahead we could see two days of walking. Before sunset we made it to the Wichita River, if you could call it that. It was an important river for this part of Texas, but was an ankle-deep muddy brown stream. We took off our boots and socks and waded about a quarter mile up it till we came to a sandbar. I pitched our tent.

The coyotes tried to outdo each other, reaching notes that demanded answers from their friends. A dim light covered everything, a warm gray-purple. I could see Barbara's outline against dark golden reflections from the river. She had her boots off and had straightened out her legs into the running water. She had collected some of the muddy water in her plastic canteen and strained it through some rag so that she could bathe. In her hand was her favorite green washcloth.

How she kept her black hair curly and soft walking through West Texas in the heat of summer, I did not know. Now it rested on her cloud-white shoulders. Barbara had removed her damp T-shirt and was slowly washing her neck and arms. I got some soap and gently cleaned her back. The moon showed me where to wash.

Hot, dry winds dried our bodies and soothed the night. I got our sleeping mats from inside the tent and we just lay there on the still-warm sand. We listened as all the animals and night birds tried to sing us their normal lullaby, but we weren't ready for sleep. Every time a star blinked, it was like they were blowing billion-mile kisses to us. The kisses landed on our clean, sun-colored bodies like a shower of love.

I didn't zip shut the door of the tent that night.

Sundown on the west branch of the Wichita

20

Homer and Ruby

"It ain't too smart, goin' up through Quanah, mister, when you can take a couple ranch roads and cut you off over twenty-five miles." The man giving instructions stood under the shade of the porch by the Truscott post office.

"Which way do we go?" I was always ready to cut off a mile, much less twenty-five.

"You head straight west, cross over into King County, then work your way up to Grow, then north to Childress." The middle-aged man turned his back to spit. "You wanna' pinch?" He held out some Skoal's.

We headed toward King County. A silver Dodge pickup drove up.

"Excuse me, my name's Homer Martin." He had half-gray hair, a white shirt, sunglasses and a quick, excited way about his talk.

"I heard those boys were givin' you instructions on how to walk to Childress. I don't aim to be nosy or nothin', but they done steered you wrong."

I was somewhat confused. Never before had I been given wrong directions, but then again, these stone-faced West Texans could tell anything straight-faced.

"Listen, me and Ruby, that's my wife, we just live five

miles east a here, in Gilliland. I'm headed home for lunch; you both come on home with me if you want. I'll tell you the right way to get to Childress." There was no gun rack in his pickup.

I looked at Barbara and she nodded. We ended up at Homer and Ruby's for lunch. They call it dinner.

Homer and Ruby's house was a half mile from the cotton gin, a mile from J. T. Cook's. J.T. sold gas, diesel and cold "sodies." Their small house, with its gray shingles and silver-gray roof, sat alone, like a boat on the ocean. The ocean that surrounded Homer and Ruby was made of flat dirt. In these parts they did dry-land farming.

Their ocean was plowed up and planted within five feet of the house, and a dead skunk lay in the yard. It had been shot while rading their chickens. It was so hot the insects wouldn't even fly. It was so hot that wild rabbits wouldn't move from underneath an old 1949 Ford tractor. It was so hot birds fell dead to the ground. There were four trees for shade and a big Case tractor parked as proud as any Cadillac.

Clothes that Ruby had hung out flapped like breaking waves and dried in minutes, even heavy overalls. There was no backyard; it was mostly scratched bare dirt. Their chickens kept it bare, the ones that survived marauding coyotes, skunks and snakes. Even the front yard was plowed except for a small chunk for grass. Water was too precious for a lot of lawn. Homer said that he always hoped to see tarantulas crossing the road. That meant rain.

Bunches of white onions hung from the back porch. There were three grain silos—one was a Butler—and all kinds of old plow blades were stacked up; old pitchforks lay rusting. Guinea hens clucked and squawked. There were hundreds of places for rattlesnakes to hide, and Ruby had killed more than hundreds since she and Homer had built this small gray house. As we walked to the front door, Homer saw a whirlwind. It was brown, eerily silent and a mile high. Homer said it was a sign of dry weather.

Ruby had turnip greens with bacon ends, speckled butter beans, cornbread and homemade rolls, hot pepper sauce, beef tips and corn. The tea was some of Texas's best. Barbara and

Homer steals a kiss from Ruby

Ruby hit it off, I mean, immediately. After we finished eating and Homer was ready to go back to work, Barbara asked me to come outside.

"When I was helping Ruby wash the dishes, she asked us if we'd like to stay with them a few days. I'd love to do that!"

So we became part of Homer and Ruby's family. They'd never had any children of their own, but they had a huge family. Not so many blood relatives, but they seemed to know everyone within fifty miles.

This lonely land had broken a lot of people, "made 'em move off to the big city for a job, a wife or somethin' ta do. Sometimes they had to run from something they done."

Homer took me out to the front of the house to show me the baby cotton plants.

"Don't you ever get bored living this far out in the country?" I surprised myself by asking Homer.

"Cain't say that we ever get bored, son; we know worlds of people. My brother, W.B., he lives in Houston. Now he makes big money. But them people down there, they're lucky to know their neighbor two doors down. They get up early, fight traffic, work and strain, and then they fight home. They ain't in the mood to see no one after that. It surely is a fight in them big cities."

"Homer, of all the people that live around here, how many of them do you know?" Homer opened the windows in his pickup. The heat could build up and shatter the windshield.

"We know everyone in this here town, Gilliland. I'd say we know ninety-eight percent of the folks that live in Benjamin, sixty percent of them that live in Crowell, one hundred percent of the people in Thalia, maybe thirty percent of the folks in Vernon. Me and Ruby, we don't know as many in Quanah, say twenty-five percent. We know ninety-eight percent of them that lives over the fields in Truscott, say, eighty percent of them in Medicine Mound, Texas. Over these many years drivin' grain trucks, farmin' cotton and workin' for Santa Rosa, I guess you'd say we got to know plenty of good people. Some have died, but then a lot have been born. Some of the kids done moved off, got married, went into the service. But then some are moving back. Some been put in jail and a few are big shots in Washington."

Homer continued. It was hard for me to imagine knowing so many people. They knew thirty percent of Knox City, twenty-five percent of Childress, and twenty-five percent of Seymour. He mentioned them knowin' fifty percent of Devol, Oklahoma, just across the Red River; fifty percent of Randlett, Oklahoma, fifty percent of Elmer, Oklahoma. Then he included seventy-five percent of Oklaunion, Texas, sixty percent of Goodlett and Kirkland, and seventy-five percent of Tell. Homer rubbed his chin after all that. "You know, son, I never thought of it quite like that bafore. We sure enough do know worlds of people. No wonder we ain't never got enough time to do what we want to do."

Barbara

"Git over thar," Ruby hollered in a tough and high voice as she stood behind the black bull. He must have weighed over 2,000 pounds, and with one charge Ruby would have been smashed in pieces. It was late in the afternoon and we were making a daily check on the small herd that she and Homer kept in addition to their wheat farm. Ruby had been steering her cows in from the back fields on foot when the bull decided he wasn't going any farther and hedged her against the fence. She raised her knotty switch and slapped his broad rear, snapping her wrist so the switch would sting through all of his muscle. The bull snorted and raised his head, daring her to hit him again. He looked mean.

"I told you to move," she hollered. "When I say to move, I mean for you to move." She locked her jaw and waited.

The massive animal swished his tail defiantly and stepped toward her. He stopped with his legs apart and lowered his head like he was going to charge. Ruby braced herself, and without warning, she popped that switch so hard I could hear it crack all the way over to the gate where I stood. She was five feet seven inches, 150 pounds, and Ruby Lee Martin held her ground. I couldn't believe this gray-haired sixty-five-year-old woman. She wasn't afraid of anything that walked. To my total surprise, the bull backed up and moved inside the corral where Ruby wanted him to go.

The mother cows headed for the water bin and Ruby was close behind. She dipped her hand in the slimy water to see how hot it was. A mesquite tree hung over the bin and shaded the water being pumped out of the ground through a small pipe from the windmill that towered overhead. The wooden blades on the windmill only turned once in a while when a slight breeze would give some relief from the Texas heat. It stayed over 100 degrees every day in the summer and the only mercy offered to the parched land and cattle was the thorny mesquite trees and their airy shade. Occasionally a good thunderstorm would bless the land and animals with a bath and fresh drink.

Finally the sun was going down and the temperature was beginning to drop. Ruby pulled out her ever-ready handkerchief, laced all around, and wiped the sweat off her brow. I felt almost cool, leaning against the fence in my gym shorts and T-shirt, watching Ruby inside the corral. The sun became like a bright orange as it started to fade behind the breaks and the canyons, squirting out red-pink streaks across the sky. It would be dark soon.

Everything was quiet except for the slurping noises of the cattle drinking and an unexpected bawl from one of the young ones. A crow was cawing far off in the distance, and I thought I caught one or two yips of a coyote. Here in West Texas their yelps were as common as pond frogs croaking back east. I liked it here even if it was hellish hot and I ended up eating as much dust as I did food. And I enjoyed watching Ruby handle her cows, almost like a mother with her brood.

"Sure love those animals, don't you?" I called across the sagebrush and dirt pasture. My voice broke the evening stillness and seemed out of place.

Ruby wasn't much of a talker, but she enjoyed it when I would ask her questions and would listen. She had so much to tell and no one to tell it to, no children of her own anyway. She told me she wasn't like most women who like to "chew the rag" so she kept her thoughts and comments to herself unless asked, and then watch out. She always said exactly what she thought when asked.

"You bet," she answered. "Only kind of animals I don't take to is rattlesnakes, corals and cottonmouths." She raised her hand to shield her eyes from the setting sun as she walked toward me, holding onto her broken switch just in case the black bull needed it. Her homemade red print bonnet had a wide brim and shaded her face except when she was facing directly into the sun.

"Animals is my babies." She chuckled softly.

With a childlike skip she reached for the heavy iron gate and pulled it shut. She braced her right shoulder against the gate and pushed it hard to force it next to the fence post. I could see a strain on her seasoned face, yet it was graceful. Her body had stubbornly fought the hazards of Texas for more than a half century, herding cattle, chopping and picking cotton, and plowing wheat in everything from dry-hot to boiling-wet weather, not to mention the winter blizzards and spring floods and tornadoes. Ruby was Texas-tough on the outside, but on the inside I would learn that she was as soft as the cotton that grew in their fields.

She pulled the wire loop down and caught the gate, locking it shut before I could fumble my way around to help her. I felt awkward and clumsy next to her skillful western ways.

"We better git on to the house or the boys will have that roast done eat up and we're liable to get slighted on some of the food," Ruby said as she walked past me toward the old 1954 black pickup truck they used for corralling and hauling hay. She slapped the seat of her green coverall pants and pulled out her handkerchief to wipe off her face and neck. Dust and sweat covered her.

As she climbed into the truck, she mumbled something about a rugged cloud north of us, but she pushed the gas pedal and we left a rise of dust before I had time to ask her anything. She was in a hurry. I had not noticed the black and brown clouds bunching together in the sky. They seemed to come out of nowhere, but I had learned that is how storms appear in Texas, fast, big and suddenly. We were only four miles from Gilliland, where Ruby and Homer had lived since 1934, but Ruby turned and took one last look at her cows behind us as we rounded the curve and out of sight.

We bounced down the blacktop road in the old truck and my mind was jumbled at seeing such a beautiful sunset in the west and a terrible storm brewing in the north. A roadrunner on the side of the road reminded her of a story. During a storm, a nest of birds had fallen down from a tree in her yard and they were cold and wet from the rain. She wiped the corners of her mouth with her ever-present handkerchief and grinned as if I wouldn't believe her. I asked her what she did with them.

"I did what anybody would do. I dried the little things with a towel and put thar nest in my oven to dry good," Ruby said.

Leaning forward, she looked across in front of me, then back behind us through the rounder rear window of the old truck. I could see her clear gray eyes sparkle and dance across the horizon like a radar needle. She was looking at the darkening sky and the shapes of the clouds. She had the kind of eyes that picked up everything, saw everything and weren't fooled by anything or anyone.

Ruby told me those baby birds fell out of their tree again the next day, so she took them inside, dried them and put their nest back in her oven a second time. To make sure they wouldn't fall down again, she put the nest inside a plastic milk bottle cut in half, with the spout hanging toward the bottom. Then, when it rained again, the water went on through and the little birds were safe. She wired the plastic jug to the tree so the wind couldn't blow it down again.

"It was the cutest thang. I watched that mother bird learn all five of those little fellers to fly. She took 'em one at a time, jumped on top that old jug, and when she'd fly, a little bird would fly with her. I saw the whole thang out my kitchen window."

The sun slipped behind the jagged vista, leaving just enough light to see a long, dark, tube-shaped cloud to the north. I was sure it was a funnel, but I had never seen a tornado so plain and close before. Ruby had seen it before I did but didn't want to scare me. We bumped down the road past the one filling station and turned left on the gravel road. We passed the cotton gin and sped home.

Ruby sensed I was getting scared. She said she had worked twenty years in civil defense and even taught classes and trained people for natural disasters and wars. In most disasters she told people to stock the trunk of their cars with supplies, draw up and store plenty of water, and listen to official reports. But all the training in the world won't help if people refuse to listen, she said. There was a young woman driving to Vernon with two small children in the car with her who wouldn't listen to the highway patrol when they told her to turn around. Homer was in his truck behind her car. The woman drove right into the path of the tornado, and the next time they heard, the car was found upside down, blown off the road, and the woman was dead.

"We knew that girl and she always was a stubborn one.

Not a scratch on them children, though. The Good Lord must have been takin' care of 'em. You gotta respect nature in these parts," Ruby said.

Peter and Homer were sitting on the porch, waiting for us and watching the funnel cloud, about thirty miles away, they estimated. We jumped out of the truck and made it to the porch before it started a heavy rain. Streaks of lightning fingered across the sky and the drumming sounds of thunder and rushes of wind kept getting louder and louder.

Ruby untied her flowered bonnet and tiptoed inside the house. The screen door barely screeched behind her as she shut it. For such an outdoorswoman, Ruby was exacting and agile. She hung her bonnet neatly on a nail and stepped lightly across the linoleum into the kitchen to check on supper. Her steps were small and dancing as though she had an unconscious reverence for their home. She and Homer had built this three-room frame house back in the 1940's with their own hands and had added two more rooms since. It had withstood all the dust storms, thunderstorms, tornadoes and was like a symbol of their marriage, which had held together for forty-five years. They had survived it all—the Great Depression, living in tents and a one-room shack, and eating water gravy because they had been so poor.

"It was hard times back then, but people thinks they got hard times now and you haven't lived till you've picked cotton fer twenty-five cents a hunderd."

Ruby didn't seem the least bit frightened as she took bowls out of the cupboards, grabbed plates and silverware, and stirred up a pan of cornbread. She said we had plenty of time to run for the underground cellar in their backyard. Besides, Homer would holler at the first sign of the funnel turning toward us. Even though she seemed unconcerned, I knew her every nerve was in tune and she would act in a split second if necessary. It was important not to overreact. I wondered how many times she had been through these vigils in her sixty-five years.

Most towns in West Texas were remembered by the last time a tornado wiped them out. But Gilliland had sort of died on its own. Ruby said the original name of Gilliland was

Coyote, Texas. She supposed it was called that because of all the coyotes in the area. Ranchers had always had a battle with them preying on newborn calves, and trappers could make a handsome fee off their hide because there were so many of them. Back in the early days the town was a lot bigger. It had two grocery stores, one blacksmith, three filling stations, two barbershops and, of course, the cotton gin.

"Even had a pitcher show," Ruby said.

Ruby remembered all the community suppers they held on the lawn at the cotton gin and how she loved the dinners at her house after church on Sundays. Since she and Homer had been married in June 1933, they made a tradition of having friends and relatives to their house to eat after church. They would have as many as thirteen people at once and it was hard to fit them all inside the one-room shack they lived in, mostly because they only had sitting room for four and that was on apple crates.

Ruby stuck her thumb out at me and said the holes in the shack were as big as her finger. They heated it with wood and had to poke old newspapers and rags in the walls to keep out the cold air in the winter. She pointed to the east and said that old shack was still standing. It was within walking distance of where we were now. She didn't have any trouble remembering where she and Homer had started from because she could see that shack every day from her backyard.

"Most folks want to ferget their hard years, but I like seein' how far we've come," Ruby said.

I liked hearing how far they had come, too. Her stories made me feel better about living in a tent and doing without food on days when we wouldn't make it into the next town or find a store. I had nothing to complain about compared to Ruby's life. She had grown up very poor in a family of thirteen children and had come to Texas in a covered wagon when she was only four years old. It was 1915 and her daddy had a chance to oversee some land, so he packed up his wife and children and left Oklahoma for Texas. They came in three wagons with their stock. Ruby could still see her mother washing clothes in the river while her dad watered the animals. It took almost two weeks to cover the 300 miles to Foard City on the wagon train. Most travelers at that time went by mule and wagon because only a few people could afford the first automobiles. Only a limited number of cars were on the roads, and good roads were mostly around large cities in the East. So Ruby and her family migrated to Texas and lived in large tents for over six months until Ruby's father could get them a place to live. Her childhood was spent working in the fields and helping her mother with all the younger children. When she was twenty-one, she married Homer, who was three years younger than she.

"I was boss till he turned twenty-one," Ruby said. There was a twinkle in her eye as she smiled over at Homer.

Making a living after the Depression wasn't easy for the newlyweds, so she and Homer worked at whatever they could find. Homer did a lot of work "grubbin'," digging up mesquite trees with an ax by hand. It took him an entire week to clear one-fourth acre, working from dawn to dark. His week's salary was $1.50.

"I told Ruby that if we was gonna starve to death anyway, we wasn't gonna starve to death workin' so hard." Homer drawled, his voice thick with a Texas accent.

Ruby raised chickens to help out. Her very first batch cost her six cents apiece and she ordered them from Montgomery Ward. She had to put all 100 baby chicks in a cardboard box with a coal-oil lamp next to them to keep them alive through the winter in that old shack. She boasted that 88 of those first chicks lived to become fryers. When she needed meat for her Sunday dinners, she would kill several chickens on Saturday, dress them and then fry them on Sunday. Because she didn't have a refrigerator, she had to wait until the day before she needed them to kill them. She had an old ice hutch, but fresh meat wouldn't keep very long in it.

Homer peddled ice all over the county and took old tools or hens for payment when people didn't have the cash money to pay him. He shocked wheat—that means stacking it into bundles—and then they really struck it rich when they ran their café in Crowell from 1935 to 1937. That was a town about twenty miles from them. She said they made as much as $200 a week, but they were too foolhardy to invest it or think ahead. It was more money than she and Homer had ever seen in their lives, so they blew it and had themselves a big ol' time.

"We called ar café Centennial, and I'll never ferget this feller who worked fer us called Sleepy Francis. His real name was Lloyd, but we called him Sleepy Francis cause he slept near half the time," Ruby said.

Besides shooting rattlesnakes and occasionally trapping coyotes, Homer got a good price when he was a bounty hunter. He made five cents for each jack rabbit ear, and some days he would kill a dozen or more. In the last twenty years Homer had worked for a regional telephone company and he and Ruby raised cattle and wheat on the side.

A loud crack of lightning sounded as if it had hit the house as I stood over the sink, scrubbing pots and helping Ruby. She and I ran to the door and looked outside. Peter and Homer pointed to the funnel which blackened the horizon. We were getting a blowing rain and lightning storm as a backlash from the tornado that was probably hitting Vernon, the next town northeast of us. The sky looked furious and mean. It was twisting and throwing out violent gushes of rain and claps of thunder.

The curtains over the open windows were flapping in the wind. A pair of Homer's cowboy boots bounced up and down in the corner of the living room. They were black leather with white stitching that had turned brown from the Texas dust. The lamp on top of the TV swayed too. I looked around as the lights flickered and noticed how simple and western their home really was. Even the lampshade had a picture on it of a cowboy riding a horse. Their brown vinyl sofa had a big emblem of a covered wagon on the back and the sofa arms were curved wood with spokes like a wagon wheel. A few rattlesnake tails, some with as many as ten rattlers, were resting on a nearby table and there were a couple of Texas ashtrays for people who smoked. Farm journals and livestock magazines were stacked on the floor. Spread across one of the reclining chairs was a bright yellow and brown afghan Ruby had crocheted. It had an Indian design, bright and angular. Before we would walk on, Ruby would give us that afghan and another pure white one she had made. She said she would keep them for us until we settled down somewhere. Her needlework was one of her favorite hobbies. She loved it almost as much as she did her cows.

The light from the cowboy lamp caught the shine in Ruby's silver gray hair as she opened the screen door to go sit on the porch with the boys. She kept her hair waved the way women wore their hair back in the 1920's and even wore a hairnet. Her hair was naturally curly. In fact, everything about Ruby was naturally something. Homer stood up when she came outside and he sat on the edge of the porch, a concrete slab. The rain had eased up, but the wind was still gusting as if trying to hold on to its strength. The sky lit up with lightning and we could see the funnel cloud was getting farther away. I sensed the tornado did not want to go away. It seemed to want to bully its way back toward us, but a force greater than the tornado was slowly dissolving it.

Ruby threw me one of her handmade goose-down feather pillows to sit on. She had grown up making pillows like these. Goose picking was supposed to be as easy as shearing a sheep. Both animals looked naked when you finished. "Just put a sock over that head and hold 'em down and start pickin'," Ruby said.

More than an hour had passed since the storm began. What a wonderful moment this was, sitting on the open porch with Peter, Homer and Ruby! The night air was wet and cool. The storm had been like a giant dishwasher cleaning the whole countryside, and not destroying it, I hoped. The crickets were starting to come out again and there was a sweet smell of sagebrush in the air. The sky was turning from an upset rumble to a still blue-black, and the stars that had been hidden by all the rain began to shine down at us. Everything was quiet. Nothing in our fast and electronic 1970's would ever replace the peace that comes from sitting on a country porch, listening to the quiet after a storm. I wondered how many people in our busy and crowded world knew what I meant.

Ruby pointed toward the one church in town and to the graveyard nearby, just to the right of the gas station. There was a single light bulb shining through the darkness at the station a quarter mile down the road. It was easy to see for miles around because the land was open and pancake-flat. Ruby said that until two years ago the town residents dug all their graves because the town couldn't afford a gravedigger.

"When thar was a body to bury, they'd put a sign and maybe as high as ten men would show up early the next mornin' and I might only have to git down in the hole onct," Homer added.

He had dug so many graves he couldn't remember how many. Ruby and Homer said that in a small place like Gilliland, people didn't rely on anything except each other. Several times neighbors would get sick and call the ambulance, but most of the town would show up at the sick person's house before the ambulance arrived.

"You even look after people walking across America," I said to Ruby and Homer, just teasing.

"Aw, the first time we laid eyes on you and Peter, we knew you two was all right. We can just tell about people," Ruby sang. She was so convincing I felt proud and was sure Peter did too.

We moved from the quiet outdoors to the kitchen table full of food. I felt light-headed and my stomach had started to growl. The clatter of plates and silverware filled the room and it was good to be getting back to ordinary things. Peter and I were piling food on our plates as fast as we could without being rude. The conversation had turned mellow and rosy as we began to forget the tense hour we had spent watching and hoping the tornado would not come toward us. In spite of the violent weather, Homer talked with fervor about Texas, its bluebonnets in the spring, the golden wheat fields in the fall, and his attachment to their home place. He spoke with passion for his Ruby and their ranch. Ruby talked about her cattle, the quails, the scissortails and her deep affection for all of nature. Texas wasn't a bad land to her—it was jut a little cantankerous at times, but that made life here more interesting.

Ruby stepped into the kitchen for more of her rich iced tea while Peter and Homer got into a big talk about rattlesnakes. I cut another chunk of roast beef and poured some hot gravy over it. I liked everything about this meal, this ranch, the danger of the storm, and Homer and Ruby. I mused over the stories Ruby had been telling me about her life and marveled at them all, especially about her coming to Texas in a covered wagon. My grandmother had traveled to Missouri in a covered wagon, but her trip was back in 1890, when she was a little girl. It didn't seem possible that Ruby could have been a pioneer, too. She seemed too young. I was thrilled to be learning from this real pioneer, but I felt sad that women like Ruby and my grandmother (who had died years ago) were overlooked and forgotten. Sad that their stories and adventures were overshadowed by the tales of wild cowboys, gold miners, fast-drawing sheriffs, outlaws and cattle rustlers.

Like my grandmother's stories of crossing the Mississippi River on a ferry with the wagons and oxen, hanging her stocking on the bow of the covered wagon the Christmas she was on the road, and hunting for wild game for food along the way, the stories Ruby had told me about her life would lodge in my memory forever, too. Sitting here at their table, in this little West Texas town where coyotes made more noise than anything else, I saw myself for the first time as another pioneer, another link in history. Ruby didn't know that she had helped me understand my walk across America in a new way.

I forced my thoughts back to the meal and listened to Ruby tell about killing a rattlesnake last week in their garage with her garden hoe. She said that snake had been in there all summer and she had been waiting to find it. I happened to notice one piece of cornbread was left on the platter at the other end of the table near Peter. Back in Missouri I had been raised on cornbread and it was one of my favorites, so I asked Ruby to pass the bread. But just as I did, Peter reached for the last piece without hearing me. His fingers were already around it when Ruby slapped his hand and pulled the bread from his reach.

"You bet," she said as she passed the platter and kept on with her story.

21

Watch Your Curves Eat More Beef

We were headed for the northwest corner of the Panhandle. The only living, moving life we saw at midday was horned toads. They looked like armored lizards to me with a yellow stripe more vivid than the center line. Our umbrellas still offered our moving circle of shade. Some days I felt like a trail boss, pushing the herd, forever north, eternally dusty, wanting to lie down and die, but there was no piece of shade big enough to lie in.

I questioned if we could have kept our spirits up if the people hadn't kept reaching out to us. These Texans almost overdosed us with kindness, In Crowell (pop. 1,399), a local high school teacher heard about us from an article in the newspaper, the *Foard County News*. He drove out to find us and gave Barbara a turquoise-studded bracelet.

We were walking one evening south of Quanah. As we walked by a darkened white frame house on a hill, a voice from the shadows said, "Excuse me." It was Leroy Gibson, a rancher, farmer, rural route-postman, and a life-time member of the Southern Baptist Church.

We drank iced tea under a mimosa tree in the backyard as we sat in lawn chairs and answered questions about what we were doing. Leroy's wife, Iva Mae, smiled at us through

227

An old-timey baptism near Quanah, Texas

the dark, starlit night and invited us to stay with them for a few days. "You bet," Leroy chimed in. "The eighth annual Quanah Rodeo is about to kick off." He told us there would be bareback riding, calf roping, barrel racing, saddle bronc, steer roping, a wild mare race and bull riding.

Leroy was very persuasive in that patient rancher's way. I ended up riding a bull, one named Tan. They said they wouldn't feel right if I walked across Texas and never sat on one of their bulls. It'd be a downright shame. My body thought it was a shame after I tried it. After a few attempts by Tan to jump into a moon orbit, then spin out of control, I ended in the dirt and more. I almost had to ride Pet, "'cept the ol' boys thought again' it." Seems sweet Pet liked to try to gore people; once he tried to break them in two by throwing them to the ground. Like I said, these people wanted to make everything easier on us. I was so glad they decided on Tan instead of Pet!

Then there was the long-haul truck driver from Hereford, who stopped and told us we had to try the pie at the next café. Said it was the best west of the Mississippi. Get the lemon icebox or the apple crumb. He gave us two dollars to buy it. It was the best I ever inhaled. The driver said look for the waitress with his name on her arm. She wore skintight faded Levi's, a pretty smile and "RAY" on her arm. She served us one of the best pies we ever ate.

When it seemed that the walk could get no worse, when we felt like so many dead grasshoppers splatted on the road, someone would bless us with a cup of cold water or a lemon pie.

On August 24, I felt especially down. It seemed Texas would never end. It was Barbara's birthday and there was nothing I could do but try to get to Pampa. We were sitting under the first tree we'd seen for ten miles. Oil wells pumped everywhere. A man stopped in a truck marked "Phillips 66" and gave us an orange soda. It was better than if he'd given us an oil well. I got around to telling him it was Barbara's birthday and he said, "Oh," and asked if we'd be walking the rest of the way into town. Asked if we'd take a birthday ride. He said his name was Bill Salsberry. We said thanks, but we couldn't. About an hour later he came driving back. He stopped and pulled something out his tinted windows. Inside two bags were four large Cokes, about a quart each, six huge Dairy Queen burgers and about six orders of fries. He just said, "Happy birthday." It was back in Virginia, thousands of miles ago, in the Appalachian Mountains, where a stranger drove up to me, rolled down his window and handed me five red apples. He had come out of nowhere and at a time when I was hungry and down. Now, out here in the flat sagebrush plains of Texas, another stranger had appeared with his hands full of food. He drove away, and we never saw him again, but he gave Barbara a birthday present she'd remember for the rest of her life.

"Will you stop draggin' your behind? You're as slow as an old lady." Being in this furnace that was the Panhandle had finally got to me. I felt mean. There was no one to take it out on but Barbara.

The more I hassled her to walk faster, the slower she walked. She tightened her lips and boiled.

"Barbara, if you don't speed it up, I'm going to just leave you behind. If someone hassles you, then *tough luck,*" I shouted above the mirages the sun made.

She'd taken all of my meanness that she could or would. I pulled her, with a bit too much force, out of the way of a semi coming over the hill. She punched my arm and took her pack off. When I tried to help her, she slapped my hand away. As the trailer truck, filled with cows going to market, sped up and got closer, she said, "Well, if you don't think I can walk fast enough, you just take this walk and this pack and shove it." She threw her pack right into the middle of the road. The semi would crush it flat in seconds. I hesitated. Would the truck hit me if I tried to save the pack? Yes . . . No . . . Yes . . . I dashed for it, the truck blasted its air horn, and the pack just missed getting disintegrated.

We sat in the hot sand and burned grass like two Indian chiefs, mad at each other, but trying to talk treaty. After a half hour or so we stood up and continued down our empty road. For a long time I stayed about a half mile ahead, glancing back every once in a while.

A huge sign was just ahead. It was the only thing that stood higher than a sagebrush and could be seen for miles. There was a patch of shade behind the sign where I could stop and rest and wait for Barbara to catch up. The sign said: WATCH YOUR CURVES. EAT MORE BEEF. Maybe Barbara would think it was funny, too, and we could start talking again.

When I sat down to wait for her, a man in a white Chevy pulled off the road onto a gravel driveway near me and sat there, facing me. He was somewhere between fifty and sixty years old and had on a dusted cap that had the name of a golf course on it. He had a half grin on his face. I was already aggravated with Barbara and life in general. I wasn't in the mood for some stranger to stop his car and stare at me.

"What do you want?" I grumbled, tight-lipped.

"Nothin' really," he said. He had a strange blend of accents as he smoked a cigarette.

"I'm not from around here, so if you're lost, don't ask me for directions."

"Who's that walkin' back there?" He squinted through sunglasses and heat waves.

"None of your business."

He lit another cigarette and fumbled with his right hand for something on the seat. He pulled out a letter and handed it to me.

"Where'd you get this?" It was a letter from my mother, postmarked Greenwich, Connecticut.

"Let's just say, I have my ways." Barbara was getting closer to the man's car.

"Come on, mister. I don't have time to play with you."

"Just read the letter."

This was the last thing I needed. A strange man, a mysterious letter from my mother, and Barbara still mad at me. I kept one eye on him, the other on the letter.

> *Dearest Son, Peter,*
>
> *We're all working hard up here and thinking about you and Barbara. Freddy is getting into selling Real Estate, your Dad's working a lot of overtime at Pitney Bowes. Winky's getting her Master's at Penn State. Betsi and Abbi are working after school and by the way, be sure to look up your uncle Bud when you go through TEXAS.*

I put the letter down. "I still don't know who you are, mister." Barbara was only a hundred yards away.

"I'm your uncle Bud."

"No, you're not." I hadn't seen Uncle Bud since I was eight years old and he didn't look like the picture of the Robie family reunion, my mother's side of the family.

"Are you really Uncle Bud? No, you can't be."

"Your mother's been callin' us since you two left Dallas. I knew you were headed here when your mother said that you sent a postcard from Clarendon, and you said you were walking north. Welcome to the Panhandle." He had a cooler of water in his hand.

Just then Barbara walked up and I introduced them. I still could hardly believe it. Uncle Bud wound up the windows and we sat in the cool and comfort like two rescued from a plane crash in the Sahara. Barbara was so spent it took her a half hour before it sank in that this was our relative.

A couple of days later, when we walked into Phillips, Texas, where Uncle Bud lived, we decided we'd spend a few days with the relatives. A person doesn't walk 3,000 miles and just spend the night. Uncle Bud and Aunt Chaine had the same black and white picture of that family reunion hanging in their small tidy house. My three cousins were grown and married; two lived away from home, and their youngest, Patti, was living in town with her husband, Danny.

Aunt Chaine washed all our clothes, Uncle Bud took us around the oil fields, we ate more meaty barbeque ribs, and the days passed further into the fall of the year. The Rockies beckoned us to hibernate with them for the winter and we would have to count our days here very carefully, mostly in money. When I checked how much money we had from my El Chico savings, it hit me that we might not have enough to make it through a long, snowed-in winter. Patti's husband, Danny, got me a job at Diamond Well Service.

Joe was the driller; I was his tool dresser. We used what was called a cable tool rig, and we sent different tools down through that roaring, escaping gas to clean out this well. We cleaned away mud, sand, water, carbon and all kinds of crud. We began each day with our hard hats on and our coveralls clean and blue. Our faces smelled from our early-morning showers. We came home with every square inch of our exposed bodies black except our eyes and teeth. Zach, Bruce and Eric would have been proud. I was darker than they were. I was unable to stop thinking about the fact that one spark could blow us all up. Someone said a million cubic feet of gas escaped from some of these wells a day.

Usually at lunch Joe and I would sit in the little shade of our rig and eat our sandwiches. Our hands were soot-black and oily, against the sandwiches made with white bread.

"Never thought I'd still be alive, workin' this type a job so long." Some days Joe moved so slowly, every joint, bone

In the gas fields of the Panhandle

and muscle drained from the forty-five years he'd put in. Even if it was 110 degrees in the shade, Joe drank cup after cup of black coffee. "When I was eleven, I chopped cotton for fifty cents a day. When I was twelve, I ran a team of mules, diggin' a slush pit. I was rich, got forty cents an hour. I been in the oil and gas fields ever since." Joe took the patch off his empty eye and cleaned off some of the soot. "You know, when I was a boy, people had to go wherever the job was. Today they don't want to go nowhere. If they can't get a job, they just sit down and hold out their lazy hands. You know, today I gross about five hundred a week, but after them leeches in Washington get through with me, I got just barely over three hundred. In a way I'm no better off now than when I was makin' fifty cents an hour." It was time to go back to work. Joe moved as slowly as a stalled cloud. I think he'd given about all the work he had in him, but I doubt he would ever stop workin'.

In one area southeast of Borger, where Joe and I had cleaned out two wells, there were some sixty-six gas wells in seventy-five square miles. Almost one every mile. This Panhandle discovery *had* been the largest gas field in the world. No more. It'd been just about pumped out. As the prices of oil and gas were decontrolled, more and more wells were cleaned out by the Diamond Well Service, rigs operated by men like one-eyed Joe and younger men, coming along to take his place someday.

On our last day working together, Joe made a small speech. We sat on the rig's fender, tired as marathon runners, our faces black as night.

"I've got to keep workin', Pete," Joe said. "I done put my life in this oil and gas work. I'm proud of what it done for this here country. I seen the days when almost no one had cars, everyone heated with coal or worse. I done had to heat with cow chips bafore. Well, this oil and gas made all this comfort we got possible. Just think, boy, what would happen if it was all shut off."

If you had the Panhandle in your blood, you felt closed in even driving through some trees. You felt like you'd suffocate in a big city with skyscrapers. Jack Gross was one of those Panhandle lovers. He was a longtime friend of Uncle Bud's, a successful wildcat oilman, in his late forties or early fifties, and a man who dared the Panhandle to produce oil. One day Jack Gross asked me where we were headed in Colorado. He had just the place for us to go to, a place called Lake City, Colorado.

"We'll consider it," I said to appease him.

"There's nothing to consider," Jack ordered. "I've been all over the world. Switzerland. All over Europe, seen all the beautiful mountains of Idaho, California, and back east. Ain't no place that can compare to Lake City."

I stood at attention. Jack's face got redder as he wrote down something on a piece of paper.

"You miss this place and you've missed it all," he commanded. I read his writing. "The Vickers Ranch, Perk Vickers."

No one could ever blame a Texan for not speaking his mind. I told him thanks, stuck the paper in my pocket and forgot about Lake City.

22

Windmills on the Prairie

Texas went on and on and on, and on, and on and on. We had left Uncle Bud and Aunt Chaine's five days ago, waving good-bye as they stood on their front porch and we walked away.

Now we were in Dalhart (pop. 5,708) in a Laundromat, washing out sweaty clothes. Inside, doing barrels of wash, were two rodeo riders. They traveled the Southwest from one rodeo to the next and had a transistor radio turned onto KXIT, the local radio station.

"Afternoon, everybody, this is KXIT, Dalhart, Texas," the radio weatherman said. "Moderate to severe hailstorms can be expected between Dumas and Dalhart, this afternoon. Highs near a hundred degrees, lows in the high sixties due to cooling by storms." Here in the Panhandle there could be a three-act sky drama going on all at once. To the north a black thundercloud; to the south a blinding blue; to the east, jet trails racing the darkness; and to the west, deep red and orange silhouetting a great horned owl on a fence post. The sky was your eyes' delight, and you never knew what would come next.

"Also, there's a winter storm watch in the mountains of Utah. It's expected to bring snow to Colorado by late tomorrow."

Barbara pulled our clothes out of the dryer and gave me a worried look when the radio announcer told about the winter storm.

"Honey, do you think we can make it to Colorado before winter?" she asked. She laid her folded T-shirts neatly inside her backpack.

The rodeo cowboys had been watching us out of their well-traveled cowboy eyes. One rider dropped an armload of dried jeans on the table and said, "I cain't help but hearin' what ya-all are tawkin' 'bout." He gave me a hard look. "I'd rather be crushed by a mad rodeo bull than get caught in one of them storms that blows 'cross these plains. Fact of the matter, I'd rather be stuck in a blizzard in the Rockies than on the prairie."

The other rodeo guy, who had a beard, spoke up. "You ever heard of a town in Colarado called Lake City?" I flashed back to West Virginia, when farmers in three different pickups told me I just had to go see a mountain man named Homer Davenport. That was back in the Appalachians.

"Yes, I've heard of Lake City."

"If you would like to see a Colorado unspoiled, the way it was a hundred years ago, I'd head for there. If you can't make it, there are other towns before it. If I were you, I'd try to make it, though." What was it about this place Lake City? I could barely find it on the map.

Right before we left, a woman shyly stopped Barbara. She asked if it was possible that she'd seen me somewhere before. Barbara said she didn't know. She asked if I could possibly be the one who had an article in the *National Geographic* about walking across America. Hadn't my dog, Cooper, died on the trip?

Barbara said, yes, that was me. The bull rider overheard.

"Yeah, I done read about that in the dentist's office in Colorado Springs. Had a few teeth kicked out." It was the first and last time we'd ever be recognized on the walk.

We had a countdown going to Texline (pop. 100 or so). That was the town where we would cross into New Mexico. Then something happened that made Barbara almost run the last six miles. I hadn't seen her run since we trained back in Dallas.

One of the hard facts of the walk was that we could not drag a bathroom on wheels behind us. Therefore, much of the time the great out-of-doors became our outhouse. Around woods it was no problem. But in the Panhandle, where the tallest thing to hide behind was no taller than a coyote's back, well, it could get downright embarrassing.

This particular broiling afternoon Barbara was roaming around in the sagebrush and flour-dry dirt for a spot. I collapsed in my tiny circle of shade made by my golfing umbrella. I wasn't there minutes before I heard a scream and turned around. Barbara was running like a shot deer. Then she jerked to a halt and screamed again. She ran a few feet, screamed and stopped.

"Peter, *help*." Could she be having heat stroke, going crazy, seeing things?

I ran over to her, and when I got close, I heard rattling. Not one rattler's tail, but a bunch of 'em. Barbara had tried to turn a rattlesnake's den into a "Port-a-Potty." For some reason I wanted to laugh, but I could see one crawling for shade that looked more than five feet. She seemed to be cornered by another. I heard still more.

"Peter, do something. Please...please..."

I looked for something to throw at them. Nothing. This was one time I wished I had a gun. I ran back and took my umbrella off the pack and rolled it up. I'd kill 'em with this if I had to. I threw some dirt on the fat one that had Barbara cornered. It was curled and ready to strike. It uncurled and turned. I tried to pick it up with my umbrella by the middle of its poisonous body. It struck my umbrella. I struck at its head. It moved faster than I could see.

Barbara ran, sprinted back to her pack. She breathed and sweated hard for more than fifteen minutes before she calmed down enough to hit the road. I sure was glad that I didn't have to use my snakebite kit on Barbara. Especially when I thought of where she would have been bitten!

We walked by West Rita Blanca Creek. This was the high plains, our elevation over 4,600 feet. I could see a sign, a yellow and orange sign that said, WELCOME TO NEW MEXICO,

THE LAND OF ENCHANTMENT. There was no champagne, just us and some warm canteen water. I yanked mine open and poured it all over Barbara. She did the same with my canteen; then I grabbed her and we danced. Cars and pickups passed; some drivers lifted their arms and waved, some honked, some stared, some thought we were wacko. We sure had come a long way since Barbara first doused me with that pitcher of water in New Orleans. Her skin then had been white as a magnolia petal; now it had become the vibrant colors of the West.

We walked past the border line, turned and looked back at some hot high plains and heat waves off the blacktop road. Texas had come to mean a lot to us as we looked back. There was so much to Texas.

Hello, New Mexico. Soon we left Highway 56 and camped by Antelope Well, on Trabajo Creek. We were circled by golden grasslands. The prairie was so big it seemed to spread all the way to northern Canada. I saw a prairie falcon dive into a flock of mourning doves. Gray feathers fluttered to the grassland as one of the doves stayed in the talons of the falcon. Then I saw dark brown shapes, a whole herd of shapes, by the rim of Apache Canyon. I figured the shapes were cattle. It hadn't been that long ago that they would have been buffalo. The Cimarron Cutoff, which crossed this road soon, had been a shortcut for the settlers, off the Sante Fe Trail. The cutoff was shorter but deadly. Then there were no windmills, and Apaches and Comanches watched for dust and cooking fires. Most pioneers didn't take the shortcut, but stayed in the mountains and went over Raton Pass.

At sunrise we moved down our trail. I had been in a rush to get to the Rockies; now I wanted to fall in love with the prairie, and so did Barbara.

To the south, toward the old Mexico, I saw a cloud of dust. It seemed close, but the eyes have special power on the plains. I thought it was a stampede of cattle until the dust stopped at a fence and went under it. *Under it*. Cows don't go under fences.

Inside the dust were pronged-horn antelope and they ran as beautifully as the falcon flew. That day we saw more antelope than we saw cars, maybe five times more. I'd never seen antelope before, except in pictures and my dreams. What a day it was on the plains!

On the third day we made our first friends in New Mexico. They were very shy and had trusting round brown eyes. They had babies that could run forty miles an hour after being born. They were a pair of antelope, a male and female. I didn't know if this was mating season, but they did seem to like each other a lot. When we first saw them, they were chasing each other around. One would run a bit, then slam on the hooves. The other would run the other way. We stopped, knowing this was a once-in-a-lifetime chance. They must not have seen us. The wind was blowing away from them, surely.

After sitting and watching them play, just 150 yards from us and the road, we got up and walked away. I wished I could run through the grass as smoothly as they could. I'd chase Barbara more. When we left, they followed. They just happened to be moving our way, coincidentally.

I stopped; they stopped. We walked faster; they walked faster. We talked to them. They looked back as if they understood. We walked for an hour, about three incredible miles. They strolled right next to us, only the thinnest fence of wire between us. They must have known we had no gun. Maybe they were in love, they knew we were in love, and they liked that, just wanted to hang out with another couple.

Then Barbara crossed the fence, her pack off, and walked toward the antelope. They ran to her, and at the last second, almost a blur of yellow-tan and white, they stopped and looked B.J. in the eye. They were no more than thirty feet from her. The three of them played for about a half hour; then it began getting hot. The antelope followed another mile or so, stopped, turned toward Apache Canyon and ran full speed, till they were dots, then blended into the golden grass. Maybe the prairie had given us a gift for giving it a chance. Maybe the antelope were young and foolish. Maybe we'll never live long enough to forget what happened.

We had been climbing higher, yet imperceptibly, since

we'd left Clayton (el. 4,970). Now we were close to 6,200 feet above sea level. If we went 500 feet more, we'd be higher than any point east of the Mississippi. A lonesome windmill had company because standing near it was a mother cow. She had a black body, a white face, and was acting nervous. I scanned the seemingly barren grass to see why she seemed jittery. There had to be a reason for her to be alone like this. Then I saw why she was here. A small white patch was struggling in the short golden grass. Less than a half hour ago she'd given birth to a calf. It had not taken its first steps yet. To the north the Don Carlos Hills were turning dark blue; the sun was leaving. What a way to be born, out in the middle of this grass. At first I thought of it as cruel and desolate, then as I thought it through, it seemed like a wonderful way to come into being. No barn, no blaring light.

As we walked up the slightest grade, I heard a coyote call. Then another answered across the road. I saw nothing. The animals, birds and reptiles that lived here absorbed themselves into the wavy flatness. Then I saw a vulture on the ground, black shape against gold. I heard the coyote to the north again. There it was sitting on its haunches, knowing a baby had been born, waiting for darkness. The mother heard its hunger and howls and walked over and nudged her baby till it stood. It was wobbly and cute, its shinny black legs like rubber sticks. She pushed it with her nose over to the windmill. There was a wood pen there where the baby calf would be safe.

We continued moving up the incline. I wanted to make every mile we could. It was September 26 and the air was getting crisp at night. We were to pick up our sleeping bags at the post office in Springer, General Delivery. It was getting too cold for sheets, and the past two nights Barbara had tried to use me as a blanket. I was warm, but nothing like our purple Camp 7 down bags rated for sleeping comfort down to 10 below zero.

I saw a yellow-pink tint to the sky in front of us but could see no land except the ridge a half mile ahead. The sky above darkened, but I did not want to stop until we topped the crest.

When we topped it, my mouth fell open. My eyes could look only west. There. Way out there. The Rockies. Mountains jagged, exploding from the flatness at right angles. The sky behind them was blood red, fizzling orange, streaks of purple-pink, holes of remaining blue. I could barely stand up. My emotions surged, caught by surprise. The intense joy started at my feet and went to my head and back and forth and back and forth.

Could that really be the Rockies? I knew it was still seventy miles before we'd be in their midst. Just two hours before, I'd studied our map. How could we see so far? They had to be the Rockies. I just sat down.

It had taken me four years less a few days to walk to these Rockies. I knew how every pioneer, wobbling along in a covered wagon must have felt, when he saw them for the first time.

Barbara jumped up, without warning, stretched her arms up into the sky, her hands opened to God, and said, "Thank you, Lord, hallelujah." She kept standing and began to cry. I cried, too. What an indescribable relief to see these mountains, finally, after upper New York State, the farmland of Pennsylvania, Washington, D.C., and all the marble pillars, the Blue Ridge Mountains and their fog-comforted valleys. Then came the Smokies, coated by white winter and warmed by quilts, the wild flowers in the hollows, the moonshiners' shacks of northern Georgia, and the hounds with their lazy tongues hanging out during July in Alabama. Then there was long and green Tennessee, the live oaks that still cried over rebel graves, and the Gulf that soothed Dixie. "Noo Awlins" didn't care as long as the slurpy brown Mississippi kept movin', even if it was as slow as a jazz funeral. The Cajuns ate crawfish and floated in the hypnotic greens of their beloved swamps. Then there was TEXAS! Pine-scented air east of Big D, three-tooth-pick BBQ, roadrunners dashing for rattler food, and sky that wrapped around us. First the Texas sky overwhelmed; then it became our friend. The oil pumping in the Panhandle, a 500,000-acre ranch and the cotton fields that came within fifty feet of Homer and Ruby's front door. Then the antelope that turned us onto the freedom-making prairie. What a country! If it had

We got our water at the windmills just like the cattle did

taken me my whole life to walk this far, it would have been worth this sunset moment.

This section of the Rockies was named the Sangre de Cristo Mountains by the Spanish long before any other white pioneer ever saw them. In English that meant "Blood of Christ." The sky was now nothing but blood red. I opened our map as we sat close to each other. The mountains stretched for about 100 miles from the Colorado-New Mexico border toward old Mexico. We were still sixty miles away. I felt I could jump and land in their midst. There was Elk Mountain, Wheeler Peak (el. 13,161), Ute Mountain (el. 11,093), Agua Fria Peak (el. 11,086), Trampas Peak (el. 12,175), and hundreds more unnamed and named.

No sooner did we pitch our tent, and the first owl flew silently over, than I began to think like a pioneer again. What would it feel like to get to those massive mountains that rose from the open plains? How could you ever get a wagon through the trees, over the cliffs, up the rock? What if they got there at the wrong time of the year, like now? What if they got trapped in those view-enclosing mountains for an entire winter of blizzards, ten feet of snow and 30-below-zero weather. What if *we* did? I thought so many things during our last night lying down on the high plains.

23

Three Outlaws

The mountains stayed before us, always getting closer. The closer they got, the less of them we could see. Never again would we see such a sweeping vision of them. We walked and wove our way up historic Cimarron Pass. The cottonwood trees, and they were giants, caught the glaring blue sky afire with punching orange and yellow. Almost through the pass, in a patch of blue, I saw a golden eagle swoop down and grab a squirrel. We walked through Eagle Nest (pop. 164) and Red River (pop. 185). Then into Questa (pop. 1,095).

A lot of the people lived in adobe homes, that were a soft orange-red, with parts faded to a dark pink. Strings of hot red peppers hung from rusted nails and flocks of black crows picked around in small, rocky fields of cut corn.

Young barefoot Mexican children ran down dirt side streets; others rode fast ponies. A few sun-dulled cars as loud as a crazed pep rally peeled out. A thick-walled Catholic church was surrounded by some old graves marked by weathered wooden crosses. After school the young Spanish beauties went home to hang out the wash.

We stopped at a little adobe café and got into a talk with a man named Virgil Martinez, sitting in some skin-drying shade on a bench in front of the building. He owned a business or two here.

"Mr. Martinez," I asked, "are all the people in this town Mexican?"

He was a middle-aged man with flat black hair, a rectangular face and skin whiter than mine. I could see the rising emotion in his eyes. "I'm glad you asked me that." He spoke, collecting himself, coolly and in deliberate English.

"If you asked the wrong person, you might not make it out of Questa alive. You see, here in New Mexico the natives, like myself do not consider themselves Mexican. We are descendants of the Spanish conquistadors. Mexicans are mixed bloods, with some Spanish, but mostly Indian. We have no Indian blood. You see we were in New Mexico long before any of the Anglos came."

He went on to tell us that the young warriors of Questa were neither Chicanos nor Mexicans. They called themselves SPAM's. Spanish Americans. Before we left, Virgil warned us, "You are in dangerous country, my friends. Be watchful. Gringos are at the bottom of the list around here." The list went: the Pope, SPAMs, Mexicans, Navajos, Jicarilla Apaches, Utes, blacks, gringos, Texans and the devil. The last three were interchangeable, depending on the beholder. Virgil spoke seriously. I laughed nervously. He said, "This, I tell you is no laughing matter."

It was twenty miles to Costilla, New Mexico; then another hour of walking and we would be in Colorado. I wished we could have spent more time in this beautiful state. I believed what Mr. Martinez said about where we were on the list, but I knew if we had had time to stay, we could have changed that. The weather reports and snow reminded me we had to move on.

For some reason I'd expected that as soon as we set one foot into Colorado, things would change. The Rockies would rise, studded with dark green pines and orange aspen leaves that glowed in the dark. The high-country meadows would be there with glass-pure spring-supplied ponds where beaver and trout jumped for the fun of living in paradise.

But when we crossed the border, we were still in land so arid that only sagebrush grew there.

The sun was setting. After four years on the road I'd become a connoisseur of sunsets. Tonight it was a yellow-white circle, sending out a honey yellow shaft. It made the cottony-soft seeds of the sagebrush glow. They looked like hundreds of heads sticking out of the flatness. The Piñon Hills were more than ten miles away, stark and black. Fence posts, crooked and eroded from years of blowing, cast long shadows. Every shade of orange and red was shining on something. I was pointing my camera everywhere; everything in my frame was worth a picture, a memory. I was engrossed and focused on this moment.

A roll of film was gone, thirty-six pictures. I looked in my pack for another roll, to catch the deep reds and maybe some purples that I knew came last. Where was Barbara? I looked for her; she hadn't stopped. She was almost a mile ahead. I saw a car. We'd seen few all day as this road, Highway 159, became our private trail.

It slowed more, then stopped by Barbara. Seemed to be asking her something. It was an old car, kind of round. It moved past her and I saw Barbara begin to walk back toward me. Maybe she'd noticed I was taking pictures and she wanted to see what was so interesting.

The car was sunburned and gray-blue. It was jacked up, had small rust spots, and ran rough. It drove by me at about 10 mph. The window opened and a brown beer bottle flew out and broke near me. Glass hit my leg. There were two or three people in the car; I couldn't tell, they were all sitting down low. They shouted something at me in Spanish. One of my best friends in high school, Alvaro Manriquez, had moved to the United States from Chile with his folks. The first Spanish he'd taught me were all the swear words. In amongst what these men were screaming at us were all the foulest words Alvaro had taught me, mixed in with "gringo." There was much I didn't understand. If you can judge a man's voice from its tone, these men hated us.

They ground some gears and backed up the car toward Barbara, swerving wildly, almost flipping. Maybe they had at first thought she was a SPAM, with her black hair and tan legs. They might not have recognized that she was a woman, as covered as she was by her pack. Barbara was smart enough to try to disguise herself with baggy T-shirts and always kept her hair back. Halter tops and sleeveless skin tight T-shirts were for models and places where there were plenty of police.

I slung on my pack and began running toward Barbara, who was walking fast in my direction.

There were three men, and they all had black hair. One hung out of the car, obviously high on something other than this sunset, swearing at Barbara. He made signs with both of his hands that needed no interpreter. On roads like this we might not see a car or truck for an hour. All I could think was: How can I protect Barbara from these men? It'll be me against the three of them. I have no gun. My knife won't help. I fought back thoughts of what they could do to her if they could get rid of me. The only way they could would be to kill me. I'd kill them first, all three of them. What if they had guns and knives? I was sure they did. Most people who lived around here did. Their car had a green and white Colorado license plate.

They drove alongside Barbara as she walked toward me. We were still a quarter mile apart. I took my umbrella off my back. I'd use it, if I had to, to knock them out, stab them in the face. Anything. I thought of nothing but how I could take them all out before they got to Barbara. I'd try to talk to them if they had guns, to get close enough to make a lunge at the gun. The fact that they were as drunk or drugged as they were would help me. They sped up again, coming at me.

I stood waiting. I could not give ground or run into the sagebrush. They sped up, ground some more gears, and tried to run me over. I jumped out of the way. The car's brakes smoked as the driver stopped. The passenger door opened and the biggest of the three got out. His face was flat and greasy, and he looked younger than twenty-five. He could hardly walk and swore at me like he'd rather kill me than anything. He pawed in both pockets and pulled out a knife. I was almost twice his size. I would use my long umbrella, my bare hands, a boulder, my feet. Anything. I'd get the knife out of his hands.

He said more in Spanish. I never would have thought I could kill someone. I knew now I could. If I killed him, I'd have to do the same to the other two.

I spoke, doubting he could understand what I was saying. "If you touch me or her, I'll kill you with my bare hands." Even as high as he was, he could feel what I said. He made a drunken slash with his knife. I smashed his scarred hand with my umbrella. It knocked the knife from his hand. I wanted to puncture the metal tip of the umbrella into his stomach like a bayonet, but I just stood my ground. I felt alert, ready to do whatever I had to to protect Barbara. He bent over, almost fell down, picked up the knife, and staggered back to the car. All the men slurred and swore constantly.

Barbara was now standing next to me. I never said a word. All I could do was think of what I might have to do. They got back into the car and backed up again. They swerved so out of control that they went off the road. The driver slammed the car violently back into forward and floored it out of the sagebrush. Dirt and dry grass flew from the bushes where they might throw us, bleeding, to die.

Once they had backed up about seventy-five yards past us, they came at us again. They tried to run us over again. The car made no attempt to get back on the road but went out through the low-lying brush, trying to turn around. It came after us again. "Barbara, when they come near us, you run for that fence. I'll try to get them to chase me." They came, driving crazily through the sagebrush, trying to run us over, screaming, laughing wickedly. The one who'd come after me hung out the window, slashing his knife through the air.

I motioned with my hand for them to come for me. They were, as Barbara slowly walked away. When they were obviously aiming for me, she began running to the fence. I never saw if she made it because I jumped and landed on the ground again. I rolled, came to my feet, and ran for the fence. They struggled to turn around in some soft dirt. Their tires spun. We leaped through the barbed wire. I cut my leg.

A pickup truck, a new brown one, was coming. I hoped it wasn't friends of theirs, maybe more sober than they were. Maybe they had a CB and had called for help. The pickup stopped and asked them if they needed help and they swore at them. The pickup seemed to recognize the three men and floored it.

The car decided to chase the pickup, or maybe they were worried about getting caught. Maybe they just wanted us to think they'd left so we'd get back on the road; then they'd finish the job in the dark.

As soon as their car was out of sight, I lifted Barbara to her feet, and we half ran through the brush, away from the spot they might return to. When we got to a spot where the sagebrush was higher than most, I told Barbara to get down. I began scooping out places in the dry dirt for us, so we could lie down and hide from view. There would be no tent tonight. It would stick up over the bushes.

After we got into our sleeping bags, we whispered to each other. Occasional headlights, some driving by too slowly, hushed us.

"Barbara, were you afraid we were going to die back there?" I was half surprised she hadn't cried. Maybe she was in shock. Maybe I was, too.

"No, I wasn't afraid. I was going to try to get the smallest one." I couldn't see her face, but I had never heard such a cold, dead-serious tone in her voice.

The first thing I saw was a white cross, atop the Catholic church, surrounded by blue sky. This was no everyday blue. Blue sky like this would blind people east of the Mississippi. Raucous brown birds landed all over the cross, almost covering the white, peeling paint. We'd made it to San Luis, Colorado (Pop. 781).

The fear of what had almost happened to us didn't really take hold until late the next morning. At least twenty people had offered to give me a gun, and I'm afraid if I had taken one, I would have used it. How easily I could have pulled the trigger. A sigh of relief passed through my lips as I told Barbara how thankful I was that I turned down the guns.

"Can you remember what they looked like?" the deputy

asked. We were at the courthouse, in the police station, in San Luis.

"There were three of them. They all had black hair, not much taller than five-seven. They drove an old Plymouth."

"What color was the car?" the short man asked with a tempered Spanish accent. He felt the worn wood on the butt of his pistol. It hung comfortable and ready.

"It was a gray-blue and was faded by the sun," Barbara answered. "They pulled a knife on Peter, you know."

"Yes, I know. You're lucky they didn't have their guns or were too high to use them. They might have plans for you two, later down the road." He had a black mustache, with a couple of gray hairs. His eyes were capable of love and killing.

"Did these men speak any English to you?" he wanted to know.

"No," I said.

"Did you notice if there were Colorado plates on the car?"

"Yes, there were."

"I'm afraid these boys were part of a bad gang that lives east of here, up in the hills. There are some mean people livin' up there. They'd kill me if they could get me away from my guns. They kill for the fun of it. It ain't much different around here than during the Wild West. Might even be meaner now." He told us he'd read all the westerns ever written, the true ones.

"Fact is, that gang tried to kill me a few weeks ago. Now them outlaws, they live up in the Culebra Mountains." He said Culebra in growling Spanish. The name sounded wicked. "Some live up on San Pedro Mesa. Around Chama. They're inbred, half of 'em. Anyway, the gang caught me out patrolling one Saturday night, out towards Fort Garland. They got to chasin' me. I wasn't chasin' them, mind you. They were chasin' me. I'm supposed to be the law. Well, hell, them outlaws don't give a damn for the law. If they get high enough on drugs and booze, they'll do anything. They had about four cars chasin' me. They passed me, cut me off, and ran me off the road, You think that was enough?" He pulled a long-bladed fold-up skinning knife from his pocket. It was well worn, too. "Hell, no. They're crazy when they smoke that dope they grow up on the mesa."

"What did they do then?"

"They yelled at me to get out of the patrol car. I did. Then they said they were going to kill me. I had eased out with my sawed-off shotgun partway up my sleeve. I didn't think they were really serious, even though some of them had shot at my car when I patrolled up in the mountains where they live. But when they began closing in on me, I shoved the shotgun into the chest of their leader. I told them I'd blow his heart out. If I hadn't had my sawed-off shotgun, I'd be buried by now. That's all these animals respect." This short Spanish deputy, with cutting eyes, did his job and planned to live to retire.

He said he used to work over in Trinidad, east of here. He'd been in law enforcement all his life, since he finished the marines. The stories he told us that night made Billy the Kid's adventures sound tame. He told us that if the jail didn't fill up, we could sleep in there tonight. We did not want to sleep anyplace that the three could find us. The jail did get a few drunks, so he let us pitch our tent outside the back door of the courthouse.

"You ever see the movie *Walking Tall*?" he asked, holding up his tightened chest. He had a tan uniform on.

"Yeah. I thought it was great."

"You know what they call me around here?" he asked.

"No, what?" Barbara asked.

"They call me Walking Short."

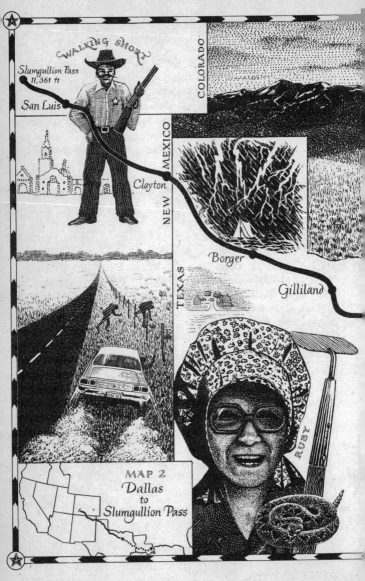

WALKING SHORT

Slumgullion Pass
11,361 ft

San Luis

COLORADO

NEW MEXICO

Clayton

TEXAS

Borger

Gilliland

RUBY

MAP 2
Dallas
to
Slumgullion Pass

Olney

Dallas

ASA

Paul M. Breeden

24

One Step Below Heaven

To our east was almost half the state. There were no mountains out there, only land that could make a Comanche look for company. To the west, mountains often rose to over 14,000 feet. Lake City was 150 miles away.

In the silent, drowsy town of Blanca a thin Spanish man walked up to us, looking very serious. He had an old, but clean, white T-shirt on and a turquoise cross that hung from his long tan neck.

"Why are you walking in this wind? Winter will soon be with us," he said.

"We're headed for the mountains."

"Those packs look so heavy. Don't they hurt your backs?"

"No, they feel good," I said. They felt like friends.

"Are you and the *señora* doing penance?" the Spanish man asked.

"What's that?"

"Are you repenting by walking and carrying those heavy burdens?" He looked so sorry for us. "Are you being punished?"

"No, we are not being punished," I said. "We are being blessed."

The snowstorms didn't come that first week, but there was a snow shower when we were almost into Del Norte (el. 7,882). The fall sun warmed our faces from the bluest skies I'd ever seen. It sent shafts of light through the falling snow in the foothills to the south. People in Del Norte had heard of Lake City but warned against trying to make it. About 1,500 people lived here in Del Norte through the winter. Stores, even a café, were open year-round. "I ain't even sure twenty-five people spend the winter in Lake City. You get caught in a blizzard between South Fork, west a here, and Lake City, and they might never find ya. Coyotes'll eat you before the spring thaw."

Now the mountains showed themselves to us. They had intense powers of attraction. A kind of suction pulled us deeper into their hidden forests, their unnamed river gorges and their thinning air that made a person feel invincible, light-headed, high.

They drew us on as the nights dropped below freezing and the cottonwoods shed their yellow leaves into a shallow blue Rio Grande. The leaves that stayed on the cottonwoods reflected in the river and turned whole stretches of it gold. Water-rounded white rocks stuck out of the blue and gold water. We were very close to the headwaters of the Rio Grande, born from the melting snows and rocky springs of the mountains.

The Rio Grande rushed by some big trout and carried fallen aspen leaves till it drained this part of the Rockies. It picked up speed and eventually wove south through New Mexico till it formed the curved border of South Texas and Mexico. Mexicans swam across it, and it didn't stop till it mingled with the Gulf of Mexico. I'd never seen the headwaters of a river before.

I couldn't get my mind off Lake City. We both felt drawn to this supposed ghost town. Heading for Lake City, Colorado, reminded me of heading for Homer Davenport's cabin on top of his mountain in Appalachia.

My map said it was fifty-four miles of no towns but ghost towns. If we could make it over Spring Creek Pass, we would

Barbara finds a cool sping

cross the Continental Divide. We were going to spend the winter on the western side of the continent.

Two elk broke and ran from some willow thickets by the Rio Grande. Because the river narrowed here and rushed loudly over a smooth rock bottom, I at first did not hear them. When they ran across the river and clattered over the loose rocks, I looked up just in time to see them run toward a mountainside of deep green pine.

Then I saw it. First my eye caught some white. The sun shone through it. It was a fanned-out white tail. I saw a white head. Because of the dark background of the trees, the eagle's dark brown body was not visible. All I could see was a flying white head and a white tail. It was a bald eagle diving toward the river, splashing in a deep round pool. It flew out with wet, empty claws.

The eagle flew over the river, landing in a bone-white aspen tree. A few remaining aspen leaves shook in the down-mountain breeze and circled the eagle in yellow. When we walked closer, the eagle lifted from its perch and flapped slowly up the Rio Grande. We were close enough that I could see its beautiful white head bobbing, tilting, concentrating on another deep blue pool. Where was that trout? I couldn't see its strong, X-ray-vision eyes, but I knew they were a fierce, freeing yellow. It dove again. Its yellow feet held a squirming rainbow trout.

The eagle flew farther up the river with its catch, settled in a tree and began to eat. We sat on a bare warm rock and watched. This was the bald eagle of the U.S.A. We ate some Cheddar cheese and a couple of apples and the bald eagle ate its trout. It flew south, down the river toward Goose Creek. We walked north toward Spring Creek Pass (el. 10,901) and the Continental Divide.

It was 4:20 P.M. when we crossed that invisible barrier, the divide, October 27, 1977. Four years and twelve days ago I'd taken my first step toward this. One more step and I was on the western side of our huge continent.

A mile before crossing the divide, we came upon a porcupine. It plodded along in some dried grass headed for a stand of yellowish, wind-deformed aspens. At first it seemed so goofy, too slow, as if it were wandering aimlessly. But it was in no hurry. Above, in the almost navy blue skies of late fall, a jet left tracks of white lines, headed somewhere.

In a jet we could be to the Pacific in not much more than an hour. . . . We thought of the jet. . . . We thought of the porcupine. We had chosen the pace of the porcupine.

Being in the midst of these mountains was different from

anything we'd ever known. Inside the Rockies even the colors of things were different. Instead of the orange and red skies that seemed to cover the earth on the plains and in West Texas, the sky was so blue you had to wear sunglasses to look into it.

The scraggly gray sagebrush of Texas and the red clays, brown prairie grass, and windmills of New Mexico were replaced by building-sized boulders of faded grays. Slashes of white rock cut upward into the blue sky that dared you to try to look to the end of it. The sky seemed to be so deep and clear here in Colorado it had to stretch till it blended to black in the outer galaxy.

When we walked over Slumgullion Pass (el. 11,361), one of the highest in the Rockies, we were higher than we'd ever been before. Since we'd left Dallas, early in the summer, we'd been climbing, sometimes slightly, lately dramatically, always higher. Our backs, our legs, our lungs and our hearts had adjusted slowly to less oxygen. These mountain roads seemed to go up for days. They climbed enough that they ate up car transmissions and burned up brakes. These mountains also killed people who lacked respect for them. Some came and thought they could run up a Rocky Mountain the way they could a base path in a softball game. Too often their hearts burst.

We began an equally dramatic climb down. We rounded a sharp, dangerous curve in the road, and before us was a string of mountain peaks. They made everything that we'd seen before practically forgettable. Strung along a line were five Rocky Mountains. They looked as jagged and sharp as shark's teeth, stuck up from the mammoth rock below. They were gleaming white and all of them were over 14,000 feet tall.

In all of Colorado there were fifty-three mountains taller than 14,000 feet. These five formed the castle walls for Lake City. Uncompahgre Peak, the most dramatically shaped of them, was the sixth tallest in the state at 14,309 feet. Adjoining it were Wetterhorn, Red Cloud, Handies and Sunshine peaks. I'd heard the word "breathtaking" before, but this was the first time in *my* life that I ever had my breath taken away by a turn in the road. Our hearts beat harder; we actually had to gasp deeper for air to keep up with the overwhelming mountains before us. Lake City must be at the bottom of them somewhere.

We came to the sharpest curve, as hard to the right as any road could turn. Many thousand feet below us was a river. It was so far down in the steep-sided valley that it looked like a thin silver trickle. To its left were some miniature-looking green fields, a couple of buildings, just specks. A couple of dirt roads, as thin as a pencil line, went across the river. It was the Lake Fork of the Gunnison River.

The road curved like a snake. Soon we lost sight of the view and the river. It had taken almost all day to walk down this mountain of rock and storm-withered pine.

The road hugged the river on one side and a mountain climbed on the other. By the river there was a small pasture where horses grazed. I saw a weathered wood sign, hanging from a forked aspen log. VICKERS RANCH, it said. Above it on a rocky knoll were two houses with hand-cut wood shingles, and I saw an orange glow in one of the windows.

"Hello." A man's voice echoed from the gray shadows. I hadn't seen anyone.

"Who is it?" I asked.

"I'm Perk Vickers. Welcome to God's country."

"Mr. Vickers," I said as I faced him with my hand stretched out to his. He clasped mine and took the big cigar out of his mouth with his free hand. Even though it was dusk, I could see that Perk Vickers was a man about sixty years old with a pair of laughing eyes that were excited to meet us. They were very blue and bounced from me to Barbara and back to me.

"Don't call me Mr. Vickers. My name's Perk."

"All right, Perk it is. I'm Peter and this is Barbara."

"And this is Emma Jean, my wife," Perk said as he introduced the petite lady who stood to his side, with folded arms and a shy smile on her face. She reached out and we all shook hands again.

"How do you do," she said very properly.

"We've been hearing about the Vickers ranch and Lake City for a long time. Does anyone live in town in the winter?" Sounds of a river moving were the only noises around.

"There's been more the past five years than for many years. Maybe ninety to a hundred people live in town," Perk said as he worked his cigar around and around. Then he pointed up to a large meadow on top of a rounded mountain. "I've seen more elk feeding there last winter than there are people living through the winter 'round here.

"Come on, Emma Jean's got a cabin all fixed up for you. By God, I know you're tired. Your friends down in Texas called and said that if we didn't take good care of you, they'd buy up even more of Colorado." Perk chuckled as we all walked down the dirt driveway, across an old wooden bridge over the rushing river, and toward a log cabin. Perk told us that Texans are drawn to the Rockies like kids to ice cream, and when a Texan loves something, he tries to buy it.

"You plan on stayin' the winter with us, don't you?" Perk asked.

"I'm not sure...."

Things were happening too fast. We had decided that we'd check things out in this enchanting mountain valley before we decided where to live. We wanted to make friends with the mountains, the snow and the eagles. Never till now had there

*Emma Jean Vickers, at
ease after a busy day
on the ranch*

been the chance to stop, huddle, maybe cuddle around a fire-place in a log cabin and just *be*. The winter was here. It would force us to stop walking for at least six months. Many had told us that in May, even June, these Rockies could get two feet of snow.

Also, this could be the right place for me to write a book about the first half of the walk, about all that had happened to Cooper and me as we walked together and what the walk had come to mean to me. The more I thought about all there was to tell, the more I hoped that the winters were as long and snowbound as these mountain people said. There was so much to think about.

Perk pointed up into the sky. It had turned ash gray with clouds sailing over the peaks. "From the looks of those clouds we'll be having our first good snow before morning." While his arm was still raised, he pointed toward the mountains and said that most of the Vickers ranch was on this side of the river, "up there."

Emma Jean showed us around the cabin, where the dishes were, towels, and blankets, while Perk kept talking. "Me and my brothers, Joe and Bob, we built this cabin out of hand-cut, hand-peeled aspen." The logs couldn't keep out the north winds that carried cold sometimes 50 below zero, so they'd covered it with rough-cut boards. The windows were small. There were red shingles on the roof and a mountain behind us. Perk pointed to a riverside meadow and said that if it was a bad winter, the elk would come down. They'd paw through the deep snow and eat the grass.

One of the first things we noticed inside the cabin was the large fireplace. "We built that, me, Joe and Bob, with rock from the river and from the upper ranch." Some of the rocks were rounded from thousands of years of stroking by the water; others had crystals in them; some, fool's gold.

"Where do your brothers live?"

Perk turned toward a window and said, "Both my brothers died in the past year." He stood there silently, as though overwhelmed by the thoughts of his brothers and all they'd done together. No one stays a stranger around Perk Vickers long.

"By God," he said with a long sigh, "these mountains can give a lot and take a lot, and they've given us Vickers plenty, but this year they've taken a lot." Perk roused himself; the light danced back into his eyes. "Well, you goin' to stay the winter with us?"

I glanced over at Barbara. She nodded. "We'd like that." It snowed all night. That next morning, on October 28, everything was covered with six inches of white.

There was a so-called road, but only a mountain goat or a person born in this vertical land would consider it that. Perk talked about it as if it were an interstate, as if with a little smoothing you could drive a Lincoln Mark V up it. It was a dirt-and-rock pathway that was deeply rutted in places, thin enough that a "downstream" horse might get nervous going up it. The Vickers drove up and down it as casually as they breathed.

It would become my road to the Rockies. I headed up it almost every day, usually in the morning. Our cabin sat at about 8,850 feet and the "road" led to what the Vickers called their upper ranch. Climbing up it the first few times was hard and humbling. I had to stop more than once to catch my breath. The air was stingy, and the road steeper than it looked.

Perk said that if I wanted to see the wildlife that lived around here, all I had to do was explore the upper ranch. The road went through a rock-strewn field behind our cabin. Before it forked off to the left, it passed rusting antique tractors, some old haying rakes, and other things retired from "upland" ranching. They only grew some hay "up there" for their cattle and horses.

Entering between some ten-year-old pines and perfectly formed blue spruces, the road curved to the left. Here it was cut out of a shaggy rock cliff and dropped off into a gulch where many cottontail rabbits lived. The road wove in between some rock outcroppings and turned hard to the right, climbing. Then it went through some bigger squat-shaped pines. When a fresh snow fell the night before, the mornings were like the first day of the world. All kinds of tracks crossed the road, followed it, and leaped across it. I had no idea what track belonged to what animal.

I decided that I'd learn as much as I could about the animals in these mountains. Perk said I could see bobcats, golden eagles, bighorn sheep, mountain lions, beavers, magpies, bull elk, muskrats, snowshoe rabbits as white as a snowdrift, coyotes, ermines and possibly wolves. There were also packs of wild dogs. Only during the winter do animals show themselves.

Many mornings, when the blinding blue sky met the glaring white of everything else, my snowshoes would make strange-looking tracks and a blast of the cleanest, coldest air would blow snow back over the trail and I would remember Cooper. I thought of him sprinting through the powder, his tail bouncing with fun, then turning around and running back at me, knocking me down. Cooper would have loved these mountains. This was a Malamute's heaven, and I missed him. After all these years without Coops the pain of his being gone persisted. I guessed it always would.

The road continued up past a muskrat's pond, surrounded by thousands of silver aspens. The first time I went up the road, the aspens still had a few yellow leaves. They were small

A herd of elk seen from our cabin window

and as bright as 100-watt lights. Our first snow had knocked most of them down and I'll never forget the beauty of fluffy snow sprinkled with those yellow aspen leaves.

The road climbed again between a thick grove of straight aspens and a cliff. To my left were an expanse of sloping meadow and, farther up, a treeless, smooth mountain called Station Eleven. Then it turned back to the right by an old log cattle pen. The road opened into what was called Horse Park, an open meadow about a mile long. The first time I walked through this meadow, I felt light-footed, free like a child, and wanted to run and never stop.

Following the road to its end, I passed the remains of some old pioneers' cabins. It ended at Water Dog Lake, which was encircled by a thick stand of evergreens, the kind that elk and owls spend their days in.

On the second day I climbed the road to the upper ranch again, and at the halfway point, through the largest aspen grove, there came an opening where I could see a large part of the huge meadow above. I saw an enormous animal outlined against the snow, its head bent and grazing. It lifted its ebony brown head, supported by a massive neck, a mane of dense fur attached to a body of soft tan, with legs long, fast and as shapely as a thoroughbred's. The sky-combing antlers were what gave the king away. He threw his head and antlers back as regally as any living thing and looked in my direction.

Maybe my feet had crunched the snow and made a noise that he was not used to. His presence, even a half mile off, jolted every sense I had. No animal could be that magnificent. He looked five feet broad at the shoulders and made a whitetail deer seem scrawny. I hurried around a rock outcropping. When I came into the clearing, by the horse pen, the elk was gone. How could anything so perfectly huge disappear in a mile-long field?

Then, as I stared into the snow, the massive outline appeared again, and I saw a mature bull elk. He seemed to look back and dare me to follow. I ran through the deep snow, breathing hard and fast, huffing and straining to catch him. He led me through one stand of trees, into another clearing, then through some dark evergreens, where I lost his tracks. I felt I'd lose my lungs. No two-legged man runs down an elk.

I told Perk about seeing the elk. He had come over to our cabin to show us how to burn aspen wood and coal in our fire to get more warmth. Nights, when winds funneled up the canyon from our north, it often got to 10 to 15 below, not counting the wind-chill factor. The three of us sat around our fire.

Perk Vickers had spent over sixty winters on this high-altitude ranch and he had seen as much as the elk.

"You can never *plan* to meet the elk, a pack of coyotes, a bobcat," Perk said in a chipper tone. He sparkled like the dry aspen wood in the fire. Perk was like his name, peppy, chipper and perky.

"You learn their ways, then spend as much time in these mountains as you can. You'll see as much as anywhere else by walking that road to the upper ranch. You may not see anything for a week, then see that bull elk again. Don't give up. You have to work for what you get in these mountains." He flipped the ashes from his cigar into the fire.

For ten days I'd looked for the elk and seen only snow-filled tracks. Today I would take the road past the upper ranch meadows, past the gate that led to Water Dog Lake, toward the pines where the light that filtered amongst them was black-green.

A bunch of brown caught my eye through some aspens. When I walked to it, through snow that was halfway up my thighs, I saw it was a herd of mule deer. There were ten, maybe more, mule deer does and one buck. They were all fat from the lush meadow grass of summer, but that fat wouldn't last all winter if it was a hard one. Some would die or fall to a pack of coyotes. I'd already seen bloodstained sites with some deerhide and hairs on top of the snow. Coyotes knew precisely in which direction to chase the panicked deer, so that they would get bogged down in the deepest snow.

The buck, their main man, circled around the outside of the does and yearling fawns and came toward me. Mule deer weren't tawny brown like flatland whitetail deer but were more a rock gray with black tips on their dense hair. Their color helped them blend into the rock cliffs and dark green pine. The buck had no fear of me and acted as if he were getting ready for my challenge. His neck was bulgy thick, and the base of his antlers was as wide as a man's wrist. He weighed close to 400 pounds and kept easing toward me till there was less than thirty feet between us.

I'd never seen a buck deer, or any deer, act so bold. He stared in my eyes without looking up or down, as if he were considering taking me on. He breathed hot air out of his black nose. I stood still. He waved his antlers to one side, to show me their size and how he'd sharpened their points, rubbing them against trees. Their tips were white and sharp as a spear. Deer that I'd seen before were scared of me. This mule deer buck was scaring me. I took one short step in the snow. He grunted a weird sound, then turned and led his does off through the deep snow, jumping over fallen down trees, deeper in the grove.

I was still obsessed by finding the elk. I wanted to make sure that I hadn't imagined him. The road went into the pines and narrowed. Suddenly three female elk emerged from the trees, so big that their bodies took up the whole road. They were surprised when they caught my smell and charged through the woods.

I remembered what Perk had told me about the elk. They were secretive, easily panicked and stayed as far away from the humans' riverside valleys as they could. Perk had said that sometimes when you see female elk come into a meadow or clearing, the bull may not be far behind. The bulls usually send the she-elk out first to test for danger.

I listened, heard nothing. Then I saw him. It all took place so quietly; could anything so big be this silent? He materialized before me, just melted into the opening. He looked larger than the first time and even more imposing. Now that I was closer, away from the glare of an open snowfield, I could see his head, which he held high. He seemed to look at me with his wild brown eyes; then he walked fast down the trail, disappearing into a dark chunk of forest. I followed.

At first I thought I had him. Surely those huge antlers would slow him down among the trees. But the elk, with six points on each antler, simply turned his head from side to side, curled it around this tree, bent it around that one. He moved through the trees with the ease and grace of the best downhill skier in fresh powder.

I kept going, trying to keep him in sight. I flushed some blue grouse. We came out into a clearing with tracks everywhere, then began going down the mountain, till he led me to some rock cliffs. I knew he wasn't trying to lose me, or he could have disappeared in an instant. Everywhere he went, whether crossing a clearing of cold winds or breaking through a series of snowdrifts, I followed, watching this elk's magnificent power and grace.

He took a rough trail, barely as wide as his chest, down the mountain cliff. I was afraid to follow, the path was so narrow, iced over, unstable. His hooves broke rock loose and I heard them clatter far down into the gulch. I lay on the edge of a rock, watching the elk weave back and forth across the path till he was down. When he got down, he looked up at me, his antlers so long they touched the middle of his back.

The light was fading into the evening and I wondered if I could find my way back through the meadows and forest to my "road." A lot of my trail was still there, but chunks of it weren't. I cut around the dense part of the pines and found the upper ranch road. Half of the way home I was guided by blue moonlight.

Barbara had the windows of the cabin glowing orange against the surrounding night. The fire's warmth invaded my chilled, drained body like a body massage. We sat close and I told her about the elk. That night the air was brittle, and we kissed, happy to know that we'd be in our log cabin for the entire winter.

I heard the crunch of stiff, cold tires on the snow outside. It was a way-below-zero night. Headlights. A knock on the hollow core door. Barbara said, "I wish I was hearing things." I had just warmed enough so that I was comfortable.

"It's Perk," came the voice outside the door. "Just came over to make sure everything's going all right." He walked in and sat down in front of the seductive fire. Perk told us that if we wanted to, we could come to the grocery store with them tomorrow. He said there was one open in Lake City, but the prices could be real high. And besides, for most of their life there had been no stores open in the winter. I asked him how far it was to the store. He said fifty-seven miles. I asked if that was fifty-seven miles round trip. Maybe they liked to drive that far to get good bargains. No, Perk said, that was fifty-seven miles, one way, to Gunnison. A hundred fourteen miles to get groceries.

I told Perk about seeing the bull elk. It reminded him of the first time his son, Larry, had gone hunting with him. These Vickers, native to Colorado since the land first opened to settlers, had been hunting to put meat on the table for many decades. Every young mountain man and young mountain woman must learn to hunt elk and deer.

Perk would begin a story, his sharply intelligent eyes softened by the fire, and three hours later we would want to hear even more. Winter nights in the Rockies could sparkle like fresh snow if the stories and the teller were good.

*Perk Vickers, the way
he looks when he's
about to tell one of his
great stories*

"We were up on top of Station Eleven. I looked right down, right straight down under us, I did, and there was a nice big buck. I said to Larry, he was nine or ten at the time. 'Boy, look, you got to shoot at that deer, it's your only chance.'" Perk whispered as he had to Larry.

"No, I can't, Dad. I'm afraid to pull the trigger."

"He had my thirty-five Winchester Special. And I said, 'No, you've got to do it.' I finally talked him into laying down on his stomach, in the snow. By gosh, the boy had never shot a gun before in his life 'cept a BB gun. So he pulled that trigger, I'm telling ya." Perk was reliving the excitement. He made stories come to life right before us, like watching a good movie. "So he pulled the trigger and the deer fell deader than a doornail." He raised his voice; his smile was contagious. "And I remember exactly what he said. He said, 'Golly, Dad, that's fun!' It took us thirty minutes to walk back down that cliff where the deer had fallen. It's very steep there. He shot, probably, a hundred fifty to two hundred yards. But we couldn't go straight down to get it; we had to circle around and climb back to it. The boy had never shot a rifle. I made sure when we got there, I had Larry get some blood on him, help me dress it. I've got the head of that deer in the house to this day."

That story reminded Perk of the first time he took his grandson, Paul, Larry's son, hunting. "Paul's been beggin' me to take him huntin' so this fall we did. Larry was out on packhorses, guiding some other men. We got up to the upper ranch over where the old barn was, and we looked over by the west gate and saw these elk grazing by the edge of the timber. I said to Paul, 'Look at the elk over there.' He said, 'Oh, my, Pop, let's go get 'em.' But I didn't want to stop the truck because I knew if I did, they'd take off. So we kept on a-goin' like we was goin' up towards Water Dog. There was one bull and four or five cows." Perk said that Paul was seven at the time. Paul was built like his grandfather, short and stout, with cheeks as red as a rainbow trout's spots. "We drove to where we got out of sight of those elk. I parked the truck and said to him, 'You stay right behind me now.' So we walked in and around on the other side of those elk. When we got over there, within five hundred yards of the elk, they walked into the timber. So we kept right on a-goin', climbed through the fence, climbed over a ridge there. Mind you, here's a grandfather, almost sixty-five, and a grandson, seven, walking through snow above my knees. Poor ol' Paul, the snow was at times over his waist. But he kept up. We got up on a little ridge there and those elk, they got to a-runnin' towards the San Juan ranch. I kept saying, 'Let's get around them, see if we can turn 'em back.' We got to the bottom of that hill, and the snow was too deep. I said, 'Well, let's go back to the truck.' I didn't think I could make it there a few times." What Perk didn't say was that many men, half his age, have heart attacks walking a few hundred yards in this altitude.

"Paul, he was about one hundred feet behind me, climbing back up that mountain. He was up to his waist all the time on that snow. I kept saying, 'How you a-doin', Paul? You gonna make it?' 'Yep, I'm gonna make it, Pop,' he'd say.

"When we got to the top of the hill I told Paul, 'You go right out 'crosst here, follow that fence down and you'll come to that haystack.' 'OK, I'll go,' the boy said.'" To Perk it was natural as a whiteout to let a boy go find his way through a wilderness by following a fence line. I guess that's because to them, this wasn't a wilderness; it was home.

Paul Vickers

"I got up to where I'd seen those elk, and they were gone. In the meantime, Paul walked down the top of the mountain. He's still a little young to shoot a thirty-ought-six rifle. Another year or two. Now Faith can start shooting a high-powered rifle." Faith was Larry and Paulette's daughter, Perk's ten-year-old granddaughter.

Growing up on the Vickers ranch was nothing like growing up in the city. Kids had to learn how to ride like an Indian, herd cattle and fish for trout before first grade. They had to learn how to shoot a high-powered rifle accurately enough to bring down deer and elk before seventh grade.

Perk got up to leave. "Well, I don't want to take up any more of your time." What time? Winter in the heart of the Colorado Rockies had nothing to do with clocks or hours. It had everything to do with winds and snowfalls. With dreamy-warm nights in your cabin and cold-blue days when your cheeks turned red as cranberries. Winter was searching for the bull elk. It was looking for eagles and listening to the rages of blizzards. It was more stories by Perk. His voice was a combination of warmth, a pure flow of emotion and compassion. There was always something funny ready to appear and an edge of toughness. Perk would laugh at himself and we'd laugh, often uncontrollably, with him. Perk always chose humor over toughness and meanness because without laughing in the Rockies, a person was broken fast. There were times when a man had to be tough. Perk could be as tough as a storm-abused pine on the side of a barren rock cliff.

Perk sat down again. It was so cold out tonight that cracks in logs around the windows and below the doors let in below-zero drafts. I made coffee. We warmed up our hands with the hot cups.

Someone else drove up. It was Emma Jean, wondering where Perk had been. "Well, Mom," Perk said, "I've been tellin' Pete and Barb stories 'bout the kids and how they learned to hunt." Emma Jean spoke only occasionally. Usually it was something short and it sparked Perk to yet another story, taking in another direction.

Emma Jean spoke up. "You remember when Peggy was with you by herself? That was a glorious time."

"Oh, I forgot about that." These were stories of their family history. "One time me and Peg were comin' down from Water Dog, just above the upper ranch, and we saw a herd of elk comin' across the flats in our direction. Boy, we had a lot of snow that fall. I got within about three hundred yards and I had to start shootin'. I picked up that gun and the telescope fell right off that gun into the deep snow. I didn't have a sight on the gun at all. Fell right off. I said to Peg, 'We're blowed up now.' So I started shootin'." Hunting to this Rocky Mountain family was one of the reasons they still lived in these hard-rock-hearted mountains. "I got three elk there. I was shootin' from the hip. I was just shootin', that's all there was to it." Perk's voice was edged with the excitement of that day with his daughter. "I shot one elk through the jaw, one through the shoulder and one through the neck. I was after somethin' to eat and I hadn't gotten a good shot all that year till then.

"You know, I've told guys that story and they didn't believe me. But I'm convinced that if your eye's on a certain spot, your trigger finger will permit your eye to guide the rifle. If I hadn't a done it myself, I wouldn't believe it." Perk figured anyone who shot from the hip like that could do it. He didn't realize that could only happen to a man like him who'd spent his whole life in the mountains depending on his eyes and rifle.

"Perk, would you say hunting is your favorite thing in these Rockies?" I asked.

"Yeah, I love to hunt. I love to be out in the hills and hunt. But I don't care if I don't get a shot." Now that Larry, their son, was back living on the ranch fulltime, Perk didn't have the pressure to kill something. It wasn't till we heard a whole winter full of Perk stories that we learned that hunting was just a small part of the Vickers family's history. I was beginning to realize that their history, now into its fifth generation in Lake City, was much the same as Colorado's history. After all, Colorado had only celebrated its hundredth birthday on July 4, 1976.

"Boy, I want to tell you, ol' Peg, she never has gotten over that hunt." Perk got up to go.

Emma Jean stayed seated, soaking up that last bit of warmth before going out. "Peggy still talks about that day her dad shot those three elk from the hip." Peggy and her husband, Bill, lived in Austin, Texas. Winter in the Rockies made distance from family seem much farther. Emma Jean missed Peggy, a lot, in the winter.

25

In a Log Cabin

Barbara

Emma Jean pulled another cigarette from her leather case, then propped her right leg up underneath her on the straight-backed kitchen chair. She flipped the lighter, inhaled deeply and blew a long stream into the air, filling our tiny log cabin with smoke. I had not smoked since my college days, but on winter days like today the smoky smell was warm and nostalgic. Emma Jean and I had been sitting at the pinewood table for the past hour, drinking coffee and making small talk to pass the time together. Perk had gone into Gunnison on business and Peter was up in the mountains, checking his traps. Peter would be back soon, but Emma Jean didn't expect Perk home until late tonight.

"I've got to get going," she said as she blew another puff of smoke. She hesitated. "Soon." I think she was afraid she might hurt my feelings because she had to leave. Emma Jean was careful not to offend people, so I figured that explained why she chose her words cautiously. Sometimes she would stutter them. Living in such a small mountain town where everybody knew everybody else's business must have been one of the reasons she guarded her words.

"I have a hot bridge game coming up in a few minutes," she said. Bridge games were the social event of the winter for Emma Jean, who had not always lived in these isolated and snow-blocked mountains that rose 14,000 feet into the sky. She missed the fun and activity that came with normal towns, but Lake City was not like most towns. She had not always lived fifty-seven miles from a supermarket or from a town that had high schools, department stores and hospitals. Gunnison was the nearest city but it had only about 6,000 people. Lake City was more like a village with its 100 year-round residents who held out through the long winters, and Emma Jean had been one of them for the last thirty-five years. She was originally from the hot plains of Texas.

This woman was old enough to be my mother, but neither of us cared about any age difference on this lonely cave-gray day. It had been snowing since morning. These February days were short and it would be dark again before 4:00 P.M. The sky was full of low-hanging clouds and whirlwinds of snow, making it impossible to see a stone's throw away. This was the kind of day to hibernate beside the fireplace and read a good book, but I was learning that every day was like that here. The days were running together and all alike. They were inward, gloomy and immobile. Most people here said these kinds of unending days caused cabin fever and would drive you crazy if you didn't get out, but there was nothing to make a person want to go anywhere.

Everything was moody and Emma Jean seemed like that, too. I didn't know if that was her real personality or just the effects of these sullen winters here in the San Juans. I preferred to think it was the weather because every once in a while Emma Jean would burst out in husky laughter and fling her head around, letting her short auburn curls fly back and forth, almost like a schoolgirl. She was pert. There was something playful about this woman in her late fifties, a streak of sassiness I couldn't understand. That must have been what hooked Perk so many years ago, along with her candid beauty. These fickle mountains, where Perk had brought her after they married, had been both hard and good to her. Their goodness had preserved her beauty to this day.

The flat white light that came through the kitchen window and trails of smoke made a silhouette of Emma Jean's face, making her look dreamy and in deep thought. There were so many stories behind her pensive blue eyes. Her face was etched with experience, with untold stories that made me hunger to hear them. I wondered if she missed her daughter, Peggy, who was married and lived down in Austin, Texas. Or if she was thinking about her only son, Larry, who left a job he loved in California to come back and help Perk with the ranch. Would Larry be satisfied and would his wife, Paulette, and children be happy here? Maybe she was thinking about her other daughter, Patsy, hoping her recent marriage would be a good one. Maybe she was thinking about Perk getting home from Gunnison, traveling those dangerous mountain miles alone through blinding ice and snow. Or maybe she was working on her strategy for bridge. Then maybe it was all my imagination and she wasn't thinking about anything as she sat silent, absorbed in her own world.

Whatever, she didn't want to talk about anything or anyone in particular. Being with another human being seemed enough for her, but I jabbered nervously about my Missouri roots, school, my job as a social worker, seminary in New Orleans. I was talking too much, too fast. Her faraway eyes understood that I was ill at ease. She didn't tell me much. She met Perk while he was in a training school in Texas; they married and moved back to his ranch in these mountains. She had been here ever since. I so much wanted to dig out the details of her life, the way miners dig precious nuggets of gold and silver out of these rich hills. I was in the presence of a special woman and my every instinct told me to press her to tell me more.

Emma Jean was unique. Any woman who loved social functions, had a rare talent for classical music and piano and an astute eye for fashion had to be unique to carve a life out of these mountains. Emma Jean had married a bachelor gold miner-rancher, come back to a hand-hewn log cabin before telephones, before paved roads, even electricity. For her to live through avalanches, help construct and maintain guest cabins, then to live entire school years in Gunnison away from

Perk so they could send their kids to high school had to take guts and fortitude.

Emma Jean was fascinating and didn't know it. When I started asking too many questions, her full and experienced eyes told me not to. Just sitting here together, sharing this winter's day, passing time and drinking coffee, watching the snow pour out of the darkening sky, then breaking into occasional laughter were enough for her. I wasn't supposed to probe. Her secrets were her own.

"Whoopee . . . yah . . . hoo-o-o-o." We heard Peter's yells coming down off the mountain behind our cabin. He was coming home and was hollering, happy about something.

"Whoop-e-e-e-e!" came Peter's jubilant voice again. Emma Jean threw on her coat and was out the door before I could stop her. Peter's hollering was her cue to leave. Her car crunched down the freshly fallen snow as she backed up and drove slowly down the road, across the highway, and up the hill to her cabin, which overlooked the ranch and faced ours.

I stood shivering on the tiny side porch of our cabin, looking past the wire clothesline full of iron traps. They were hanging down, fastened to the line by clothespins. Peter had soaked the traps in some foul-smelling potion to destroy the human scent and hung them on the line to dry and remain sterile. It was too hard to see him through the white-gray storm, but I sensed he was close to home. I could only see as far as the giant Douglas fir that was weighed down with globs of snow, more beautiful than any Christmas tree.

I wanted to run out and see what Peter was yelling about, but it was better to wait here. I smiled to myself, wondering what it was this time. Those excited outbursts were not unusual for my red-bearded Welsh-descended husband. I often wondered if the Welsh blood had any effect on his personality. Nothing was predictable about Peter, yet everything was predictable.

Flurries started to blow through the open door, robbing our little house of its heat. I pushed the cabin door shut behind me and hurried over to the fireplace and poked the fire to get the flames higher. I threw another big chunk of black coal on top of the aspen logs to keep the fire blazing hot. Peter would be freezing. I wished I could have waited outside. I wanted to see Peter stalking through the knee-deep powder with whatever was making him whoop it up, but it was too dark and cold. He would be here any minute. I wondered what kind of surprise he had.

Peter had a poet's heart and was a romantic man who took pleasure in bringing me surprises. He would bring me flowers from the hills, quartz rocks, cactus and other natural treasures. He also wrote me love notes, poems, and always brought me a gift when he had to leave me, even if it was a candy bar. He was like a year-round Santa Claus to me, preferring to give me presents than receive them. Sometimes he would get so excited he would make me guess what he had for me or slip up and tell me himself. But I didn't dare find out in some other way because he would be hurt.

Peter's heavy boots stomped on the side porch; then he threw open the cabin door and stood like a white bulldozer. He held a big coyote upside down. At this second, in his excited stillness, he looked like a man from 100 years ago, like a real mountain legend. He had finally trapped his first coyote! Peter had been working for months, setting traps and checking them daily, but had never caught anything. Now he was recklessly happy. He wasn't cold; he wasn't hungry; he wasn't worried about the snow blowing through the open door.

Peter's face was a brilliant red, redder than his ice-covered beard and mustache. His moon-round blue eyes flickered with the call of the wild. I had never seen him so proud. He was beaming, smiling with his mouth open, as if this coyote were a college diploma. He held it up high, dripping with melting snow and pushed its thick gray-black fur into my face. It smelled hairy and gamey.

"Can you believe this beauty?" he boasted, about to pop the snaps on his purple down jacket.

"Oh, Peter! He's gorgeous!" I quickly pulled Peter's frozen red face down and planted a warm kiss on his cheek, the only place that wasn't covered with snow or ice. "I've never seen such beautiful fur before in my whole life." I felt elated, seeing one of Peter's dreams come true before my eyes.

Before more dripping water and cold air filled the kitchen, Peter draped the big coyote over his shoulder and strutted back in the dark storm. He was going to hang the coyote from a nail on the back of the cabin to freeze overnight and stay preserved. That would keep the fur in perfect condition until Peter could skin it tomorrow.

We had never been so free. We sped across the open snowfields that glistened in the bright sun. It looked like a trillion sparkling diamonds. Peter and I were snowmobiling on the upper ranch at about 11,000 feet. There was nothing in sight except clean white mountaintops that touched the clear blue sky, nothing but the natural delights of being as close to heaven as we could get on this earth. The engines of our snowmobiles roared and spit like motorcycles as we zoomed up one rolling field and down another. The upper ranch was beautiful. It was gentle, serene, wide open but hidden and protected from all the people of the world.

Peter and I laughed and yelled at each other from our snowmobiles as trails of white powder sprayed behind us. We were making our own roads up here on top of the world. We were going all the way up to Water Dog Lake and then back down. We had planned to do some ice fishing, but it was more fun to speed through these high pastures like the elk than sit and fish. Besides, it was too cold. The wind was blustery. We wound our way through a stand of barren aspen trees and saw a wild turkey prance through the brush. He fanned his colorful feathers at us. We sputtered on up, higher and higher up the side of a mountain and were blessed with a herd of deer. There was one bull. What a sight they were! The bull threw back his head full of antlers and ran powerfully through the trees, thrashing his head back and forth, up and down, weaving in and out with elegance and ease. He was out of sight before we could stop our machines.

"Did you see that?" Peter shouted over the engine of his snowmobile. He wanted to follow the bull and take pictures, but these wild creatures were too quick, even for our sliding cars. Peter loved the deer that roamed the crests of these mountains, but he loved the elk, the eagles and the bobcats more.

Their world challenged him. The animals' brilliance and un-
tamed ways called him.

Peter looked as wild as they were with his scraggly red
beard, uncombed hair that stuck out under a dirty baseball cap,
torn purple jacket and blue jeans. Neatness was last on his list.

We rounded a curve and saw some fresh bobcat tracks
right in front of us. Peter stopped and jumped off his snowmobile. He squatted down and examined the tracks closely,
reading every detail, how old they were, where they were
going, if it was a young or old cat, etc. He began wading
through the banks of snow that came above his knees. With
his camera around his neck, he was off to find the cat and get
some pictures. I sat waiting and watching, hoping he wouldn't
get out of my sight or get lost. The precious and exciting
moments of life never slipped by Peter unnoticed. He always
caught them.

26

Lake City, Colorado

It was time for our first weekly expedition for winter supplies. Perk and Emma Jean would pick us up around 8:30 A.M. in their Oldsmobile.

In Lake City we had to stop twice because dogs lay in the middle of the white streets. Perk tried not to bother their lounging. He honked and they refused to move. He eased close to them and they moved just enough, before flopping down again. Perk said that often when they returned late in the afternoon, they'd have to slow down to miss four or five deer walking down Main Street.

Lake City was so small that it only had one and one-quarter pages in the phone book. There was a weekly newspaper, the *Silver World*. In the winter it sometimes shrank to two pages, while in the summer it bulged to eight.

One week the *Silver World* reported some late-breaking item: "A young elk wandered into the northern part of town Monday evening." Grant Houston, a guy in his twenties, was editor and publisher. Frontpage headlines said, LOCAL DOGS: YOU BETTER WATCH OUT; CHAMBER MEETING: MUCH DISCUSSION, SOME DECISIONS; and HARTMANS JOIN RANKS AS PARENTS.

Lake City has hardly changed since the mining booms of the nineteenth century

Sometimes the *Silver World* printed corrections: "Seems the Sheriff's Office got some lines crossed, which in turn we tangled even worse. In other words, Tuffy the dog was not asleep, nor was Ralph Martinez's tool box stolen from the VC Ranch in the dead of night. Rather, it was Mayor Bud Mc-Donald who had a tool box stolen, as well as two sets of tire chains."

Most of Lake City, its tiny downtown area, was built during a building boom that lasted from 1876 till 1881. It still looked like the classic gold mining town that it had been. There were even a few log cabins left from the first days of town, 1874. The grammar school, the same one that Perk and his brothers and sisters had gone to, would have the smallest graduating class in the history of the world that year. One guy, Shawn McConnell, would graduate from the eighth grade. Someone said that one year, long ago, half the births in the county were illegitimate. Two babies were born that year.

In 1960 Hinsdale County was the least populated in the lower forty-eight states. That year the census said there were 208 folks in the county, 106 in Lake City. "That's less people in this county than on one floor of a big apartment building in New York." As Perk thought about 1960, he said that maybe there were closer to 175 living in town this winter.

The fifty-seven miles into Gunnison were on the most dangerous road I'd been down. It snaked through steep canyons where with just a touch of the brakes we'd have been bumper-first in the frigid river. It was cut atop high stone canyons that fell hundreds of feet. There were no guardrails. At times the road was like driving on an ice skating rink.

Perk, as always, was filled with imagination-inciting stories that made the slow motion of wintertime pass unnoticed. He told of a young man driving home after some hard partying. He lost control of his pickup and dropped 200 feet, maybe 300, down a hard-rock canyon into Henson Creek. It was past midnight. Somehow the booze and whatever kept him loose and the freezing water of the creek sobered him up or numbed him, Emma Jean said. He crawled up the canyon on his hands and knees and walked miles into town. He knocked on some stranger's door around 3:00 A.M. and was covered with blood.

Lake City's Lower Graveyard, where they buried outlaws, gamblers and loose ladies of the evening

That boy was one of the lucky ones, Perk had to say as our car slid on some ice.

When we got close to frozen-solid Blue Mesa Reservoir, Perk slowed down and pointed toward Big Mesa. There was a group of bare and big cottonwood trees. I didn't see anything. "Look again." The trees stood cold and lonely, surrounded by miles of ice-topped snow. In the trees were four adult bald eagles.

Coming to town reminded Perk of when he was young and he and his brother Joe made a trip into Montrose. Montrose was over 100 miles one way, and in the old days of the Vickers ranch they went to town only twice a year. They were to pick up all the groceries for the Vickers family for six months. "To go into town [Montrose], in them days was like me goin' to China today. It was my biggest thrill of the year."

We weren't huddled around a fire for this story, but Perk had the heat in the car turned up. Another story began:

"We brothers used to take turns getting to go to town. That year it was me and Joe's turn. We couldn't sleep for the week before thinkin' 'bout it." I tried to imagine what it would be like living on a ranch so far back in the mountains that I could go to town only once a year—if it was my turn. The Vickers family had a lot of brothers.

"By God, we got the ol' truck ready. Half of the thing was held together with baling wire. Our dad told us to stop at a ranch, by the Gunnison river valley, and pick up a Hereford bull he'd bought. So we did. I'm a-tellin' ya, the roads today are like four-lane interstates compared to what they were then. So we picked up that ol' bull, pushed up into the front of the truck, and put some boards across so we had room for the year's groceries."

Perk slowed down, to look at an old bull elk that was sitting within a hundred yards of the road. His head was sagging; he looked sickly-thin. Perk said that he probably had been shot during hunting season and the hunters couldn't find him. The wildlife guys would be out soon, Perk was sure, and put him out of his misery. Happened every year; otherwise, you'd never see a bull that size anywhere near the road.

"Anyway," Perk continued, beginning to smile to him-

self, "we bought a truckful of groceries, hundreds of cans of
beans, corn, beets and anything else that came in cans. Hundred-
pound sacks of flour, metal cans full of lard, salt, sugar, cornmeal, et cetera. Six months' worth of food. Me and Joe were
just motoring along in that old truck when someone drove by
and said, 'Hey, boys, you're a-losin' your groceries. That
bull's had his foot in a bucket of lard!' I looked back; we
almost got in a wreck. Flour bags were ripped open; the bull
had knocked down the wood partition and stomped through
every bucket of lard. Flour flew out of the truck in a big cloud.
That bull had let loose all over everything." We filled the car
with our laughing, trying to picture the groceries with bull's
feet all over them.

"What did you do? Weren't you afraid of what your father
would do?" Barbara asked.

"Yep, but what could me and Joe do? We drove home,
with the bull covered with cornmeal and flour, everything but
the cans ruined. We drove in the river and washed off the cans.
All their wrappers washed off. All that winter my mother had
no idea what we were eating till she opened the can."

We shopped at Safeway, buying enough for a week. I
didn't feel so isolated anymore. It was 10 degrees colder here
in the valley than up in our mountains. The revolving clock
said —19° F.

Perk had more heater-side stories for the way home. He
was a man who always bubbled with an unquenchable opti-
mism. He'd inherited that from his dad, he said. It was the
way he'd made it through sixty-five winters. When Perk got
a serious edge to his voice, we knew it was serious.

"Let me tell you one thing. Everyone that lives in Lake
City knows this. They never drive this stretch between Gunnison and Lake City at night. I mean *never*. Too many people
have died on these roads at night. You can hit deer and elk in
the road at any moment, and if you go off the road, there
probably won't be a car come by till the snowplow in the
morning." I didn't think there was anywhere in the U.S.A.
left where the winters, the elements had such an effect on life
routines.

Later that winter a Lake City native for more than sixty

years, Mr. Joe Wells, went into Gunnison to visit his wife in a nursing home. He had driven these roads thousand of times in his pickup. He was a mountain man, no wide-eyed, suburban pioneer in his twenties. He decided to dare the stretch on a black, frostbite-producing night. He knew better. Maybe he didn't care anymore. He left Gunnison about 8:00 P.M. His truck ran off the road into a soft snowbank about halfway home. He let the truck run and the heater till the gas ran out. Then he got out and tried to walk. No headlights found him walking that night. That morning the first snowplow saw a mound of snow in the middle of the road, right after dawn. It looked strange, so the driver stopped. It was Joe Wells, frozen to death. No one would say if he'd had to fight off hungry coyotes that night or not.

The news of Joe Well's death had a forceful effect on all who made "the drive" every week. It swept into every coffee cup conversation like an avalanche. Around every glowing-hot wood stove and rock fireplace people were reminded that we were just an ice patch away from death. Perk had experienced much tragedy and knew traumatic stories to fill a 1,000-page book, but he knew more stories of human triumph. Of snowflake-small inspirations and mountain-sized victories. He never let a "heavy" story just lie there to fester in a winter where the loudest noise was the falling snow.

We were back at the Vickers' place now, and Perk was cooking Emma Jean, Barbara and me a meal called the Prospectors' Dinner. It included fresh elk steaks smothered in his homemade gravy of bacon grease, flour and plenty of onions. He also had homemade biscuits and fried potatoes. I never did see Perk drink a Coors, but then drinking beer when it's below zero doesn't seem to make a lot of sense.

Four people came in: Larry, Paulette, his wife, and Faith and Paul. When Perk's brothers died unexpectedly and left Perk the ranch to run, Larry returned from the big city for good. That was the way Larry and everyone wanted it. You can take a Vickers away from the mountains, but you can't take the mountains away from a Vickers.

The plates of smothered elk steak steamed and Perk remembered another story. It was our dessert. Every Vickers had at one time or the other left these Rockies, the 14,000-foot walls of stone, for the plains where the cities and dollars were. Sometimes they were called away. Joe and Bob fought "like hell" in World War II. Larry had gone off to college and got a job as a coach, teacher and guidance counselor near Denver. He was making good money, had built him and his family a nice house, even had a far-off view of the Rockies.

Even Perk chased after dreams of becoming a millionaire and left for Texas. He had met a millionaire oilman who promised Perk that if he'd come to East Texas (Tyler) and go to business college, he'd help him get plenty of his own oil wells. When he was in his early twenties, he got together what little he had left with visions of gushing oil and gushing greenbacks.

"And I'll tell ya. I'd been in there, I guess, oh, six weeks. One day I had a note on my desk. 'Please come into Mr. Robert's office.' He was the head of the school." Even grandchildren sat spellbound by his stories. "So I walked in there. He said, 'Mr. Vickers?' I said, 'Yeah.' 'You must not be observing what's goin' on around here too much.' I said, 'What's the problem?' He said, 'Haven't you noticed that everybody in the classroom's got a necktie on except you?' I'm sure my face got as red as that table mat." Emma Jean poured more coffee. "I had never recognized it. I was the only guy who didn't have one on, but then we never wore neckties livin' in the mountains. Then he said, 'We've got something we'd like to have you do. Your English is very bad. You've got to take a class in grammar.' It's kind of embarrassing for a guy as old as I was. I was old enough to be a man. I was a man, but I was an unlearned man."

"I never noticed that your English had anything wrong with it." Emma Jean spoke softly.

"Well, that's what they told me," Perk said. After all, these were city folks telling Perk what he needed to become a millionaire.

Barbara asked, "Didn't you miss the cool mountain air, Perk?"

"Oh, yeah. Yeah, I asked myself every day how did I ever get myself into this. I even had to take typing. Now you should have seen me when they gave me a speed test." Larry, who was at least a head taller than his dad, smiled to himself. He was a young man of deep feelings and had a personality like the good county judge he was soon to become.

"I'll tell you what finally got me away from trying to become a millionaire. One day I was takin' a test for some kind of accounting course. There were hundreds and hundreds of little squares on that paper and numbers and numbers. Finally all those numbers just blurred together. You know what happened?"

"What, Pop?" Paul asked. Nobody thought he was listening.

"Well, Paul, I thought for a minute there I was losin' my mind. I didn't see those numbers on the page anymore. All I could see were beaver ponds. Round and clean with those blue, blue skies behind 'em. The beavers were swimming right across that accounting test, slappin' their tails. I knew it was time to get back."

27

Hollywood Jed

All the Vickers cattle had their brand on them, the reverse J lazy V-I. If we were going to stay on the ranch for the winter, which lasted for half the year, I wanted to help out. Get a job. Do some work. There was no way I could spend half a year inside a cabin, no matter how cozy. Perk said the only thing to do in the winter was feed the cattle. That's how I met Hollywood Jed.

Hollywood Jed wore mirrored sunglasses and had curly blond hair. He loved rock and roll, beer, Jimmy Buffet songs about sailing on the Caribbean, and playing Space Invaders at the Pine Cone Saloon. He also liked the Silver Street Saloon. Jed and his mother, Beverly, lived near our cabin. Hollywood was first and foremost the son of Joe Vickers. We were sorry that we hadn't gotten here in time to meet Joe. Everyone said that he was a great man of the mountains, the ultimate hunter and cowboy and thin as an aspen. Perk showed us some pictures.

Jed was twenty that winter, and for all the fast licks he could play on his electric guitar, he wouldn't leave the mountains either. Almost every morning Jed would come by our cabin and we'd head for the upper ranch with the back of the pickup filled with bales of hay. The horses and cows spent the winter "up there." Some mornings Jed might not have made it back from skiing over in Crested Butte, seventy-five miles north. They said he could ski like Robert Redford in the movie *Downhill Racer*. He reminded me more of the character the movie portrayed than Redford did. Jed had a performer's flair. That's why I called him Hollywood. But his blood flowed too thick with these Rocky Mountains to leave. Hunting on horseback down stone trails above the timberline was a high unmatched in the city. For someone in his early twenties and single, these winters must have been long. But then Hollywood Jed had twenty years of his own memories of summers past and twenty falls of blinding blue and aspen yellow. Winter was a time when the hard core did any job they could so they'd be here for spring and beyond. Jed and I dished out bales of breakfast to a lot of hungry cows and horses seven mornings a week. If this was work, the view from the upper ranch was our pay. These mountaintop views could make a man forget that you had to eat, keep the fires going and the gas tank full. If you could tie yourself to a lone aspen, forced to stare at the same view of peaks, gulches and clouds, it would never look the same.

Jed didn't talk a lot, but then after Perk, no Vickers did. I noticed that Jed never stopped moving his handsome face and blue eyes here and there. Always looking. You'd think he'd be bored after spending almost every day of his life on this thin-air ranch. He remembered stories, adventures, too. His were brief, often one sentence. They left a lot of holes for my imagination to fill in.

Like his father before him, Jed was in charge of the horses. The Vickers had a whole herd of the surefooted, elk-tough, mountain-mean type. These were no bluegrass-munching high-strung horses. Jed guided a lot of hunters in the fall.

First we'd throw out all the bales onto the snow; then we'd walk together, stripping them of the wire that held them together. Getting the wire off was a western art learned slowly.

If we looked behind us, to the west, we could see one of the most dramatic views in all the Rockies: the five peaks over 14,000 feet that always reminded me of shark's teeth. There were unnamed "hills" over there over 13,000 feet. That

*Hollywood Jed
feeding the horses*

view reminded Jed of some of their best hunts. He'd been hunting since he was old enough to follow his dad. Knowing Jed, I figured he could probably have ridden around the ranch and kept up before he was three. A horse took the place of a bicycle on these mountain trails.

After we finished spreading out the hay, we'd sit on the back of the pickup and Jed would point "over there."

"We've hunted all that." He was talking about the gulches and forests that only the big elk knew well. Beneath Wetterhorn Peak, at the edge of treeline and tundra, there was a ghost town called Capitol City. Perk remembered when people lived there. Up Big Casino Gulch was the Pride of America Mine.

"We've had to go up in the dark and rescue men at the

base of Red Cloud Peak." Hollywood took for granted riding
on loose rock in the night when even the moon was clouded
over. Many flatlanders wouldn't even walk some of the paths
they rode, in the bright sunlight. There were all kinds of deserted mines in between the cloud-cutting peaks: the Yellow
Medicine Mine and the Silver Jack. "Up the Henson Creek
Canyon," Jed said one morning, "are some beautiful waterfalls." Another time, after we'd seen a golden eagle catch a
white jackrabbit, Jed said, "You know I could live right here
for a hundred years and never see half of what there is. There's
places on this ranch that none of us ever set foot on." Perk
said many times if there were only more good-lookin' women
in Lake City, then Jed would be happy. Winter in Lake City
meant that women were as scarce as royal elk in huntin' season.
Now Denver had loads of good-lookin' women. But that was
the big city. Jed put up with a lot to stay on the ranch. But he
was smart enough to know what he'd miss if he left.

The Vickers didn't come to these mountains in search of
good ranching. Perk's dad, John, came in search of gold. He
left the dreary coal mines of Nova Scotia as a fourteen-year-
old, traveling with his uncles. John got to Lake City in 1891
and married Miss Vera Madison on September 24, 1899. They
had ten children. Bob was the sixth, Perk the seventh and Joe
the eighth. Now Perk was the only child of John and Vera
Vickers left in Lake City.

Of all the pioneer families that had settled in these parts,
there were few left. Like Jed once said, "You know a lot of
these people come to Colorado in the summer from somewhere
else. All they can do is walk around and say, 'Oh, *Wow*, oh,
Wow.' Well, it takes more than 'Oh, *Wow*' to hold on." Perk
said that it seemed that all he'd done his whole life was keep
the wolf away from the door.

That evening at Perk's house the fire colored the hand-
peeled aspen logs of the living room a warm orange. The news
was on Channel 9, coming from Denver. There had not been
TV here until the 1950's. Perk was talking.

"Before I was born, my dad was in the mining business.

When he first got here, that's what he did, was mine. Then he got into the saloon business and the gambling business.

"My dad opened the Silver Street Saloon. He was a professional gambler. He liked to play poker. Fact of the matter, his main game was draw poker. That's how he made his money. He won mines in poker games. Daimond rings, anything a man would bet. I've got a diamond ring that he won. He won the Cleveland Mine up Henson Creek in a game of poker. He bought the Independence Mine from money he won gambling. Now that Independence Mine, we still have that. That mine shipped the first carload of ore, lead-zinc-silver and copper ore, that went out on the D&RG Railroad, a narrow-gauge, from Lake City to Leadville. And in 1934, when they were abandoning the railroad, we were all down there. The last carload of ore on that railroad went out from the Independence Mine." Perk told us that soon his son-in-law, Clay, and one of the twins, Patsy, were going to be opening their own saloon. It would be called the Silver Street Saloon, too.

The teapot whistled, and it reminded Perk of the year their water froze off for an entire winter. That was the first year of the twins' life; they had been immature and very delicate. Perk had to carry all their water from the river, almost a half mile from the house. The nearest doctor was about sixty miles on dirt roads. "I'm the pessimist of the family," Emma Jean said. "If it hadn't been for Perk that winter, I don't think I would have made it."

Perk chimed in. "If it hadn't been for me, you wouldn't of had the twins in the first place."

"Perk, how did the Vickers get from the Silver Street Saloon, and their home in downtown Lake City, to this ranch?"

"I guess it was two things. In those days men would call everyone to the bar for a drink. There was a pitcher of cold water and bottles of whiskey. They'd pass out the glasses, pour the whiskey and then put in however much water they needed. Well, by God, this prominent lawyer called everyone to the bar for a free drink. The first man that drank his down dropped dead, fell flatter than a pancake." Perk loved to say "flatter than a pancake." My dad yelled for everyone to stop. He took a drink of that water. It had been poisoned by that lawyer with arsenic. It ate holes in the lining of his throat and stomach. They say that he was never quite the same after that. It weakened him. Then what really shut him down was Prohibition. The saloons all closed; so did the gambling. That's when the family moved up to the ranch."

Perk's dad lived until he was ninety, arsenic and all.

It was the night before Christmas and all through our cabin everything was stirring. In the next half hour the moon would be rising above the mountain behind us. The moon first showed itself by glowing light rays of ice blue. Looking up for long could give a person a neckache. As it got closer to showing its round self, it lit up more of the black sky. I could see the ridge and the thick stand of bare aspen it came through. Then it was halfway visible, then huge, white and round. The moon sent shafts of light through the shimmering trees. The colder it was, the brighter the moon. When it finally cleared the ridge and the trees, it was as if a cold blue light were turned on.

We had got up earlier than usual that morning. Since the end of the first couple of weeks we'd been sleeping in the living room instead of the cabin's bedroom. The bedroom faced the north, and when the arctic winds kicked up, there seemed to be no walls. The cold made it impossible to sleep in there. So we shut off that north room for the rest of the winter and slept on an old foldout couch as close to the fire as we could. We stuffed towels under the bottom of the door. I'd quit burning wood, even if it was supposedly romantic. I could put a forty-pound chunk of coal on the fire and it would still be warming us at sunrise. After I got over thinking coal was dirty, which it wasn't, it was more dreamy than wood. It glowed and flamed romantically like wood. It lit Barbara's soft, smooth skin a warm orange. The good thing about coal was that I didn't have to be jumping up every half hour to put more on the fire. Having to go outside in the cold to get more wood could be a real interruption, especially if I was giving Barbara one of her Christmas presents, like a one-hour head rub.

Barbara put on her red down jacket. I had on my purple

one. We had borrowed an ax from Larry and were going to
walk up the road to the upper ranch till we found it. I'd always
wanted to go out and cut down my own Christmas tree. So
had Barbara. We took a fork to the left before walking halfway
up the mountain. We could see a monument of rock called
Crystal Peak across the river. Then Barbara saw our tree. I
would chop for a while, then Barbara. We dragged it home,
our footprints covered by the tree sliding over fresh snow.

Barbara made bags of popcorn and we spent the day
stringing it. Many of our friends from the walk and our families
had sent us cards and we hung them in the tree. Barbara made
some dough and we sculpted little figures to hang up. I made
an elk. Barbara made a mother, a father and a baby. She said
that someday soon these figures would be us with our child.
I didn't say anything, but children seemed a far-off thought,
at best. We both made a Baby Jesus for the top of the tree.
We had no lights or store-bought decorations until Perk came
over with a box of tinsel. He said they had some extra.

I don't think there was a store in Lake City that was open
that had anything to buy for Christmas presents. Even if there
were, we didn't have enough money to buy each other much.
I bought Barbara some pajamas with yellow feet and little bears
on them. There were about four presents under the tree, and
we liked it that way. This was the kind of Christmas I'd always
wanted to spend. In a high-mountain log cabin, covered with
snow and guarded by rows of icicles, where smoke eased out
of the chimney while we watched a bald eagle fly over the
frozen trout ponds. All the hype of Christmas was far-off. Our
TV, the fireplace, didn't run any commercials.

Christmas morning I got up first, made coffee and just
looked out the window. A blizzard was whipping snow in large
flakes toward the Continental Divide. I had gone over to wake
Barbara when I saw something moving in the field by the side
door. It was a herd of twenty elk, no more than fifty yards
away. They heard me call Barbara as I ran outside to get a
closer look. They kicked up inches of fresh snow and ran like
gods. Watching them lope off toward the mountain of the
moonrise was a cherished Christmas present that I remember
more vividly today than most of the presents I've ever received.

Barbara pulled a flat present out of an unused closet. She had painted, with watercolors, a picture of our cabin, with the orange glow of fire in the windows and the Continental Divide in the background.

We got her Bible and read some verses and stories to each other. Barbara read from the Book of Isaiah:

> For unto us a child is born, unto us a son is given: and the government shall be upon his shoulder: and his name shall be called Wonderful, Counselor, The mighty God, The everlasting Father, the Prince of Peace.

I turned to Luke, Chapter 1, and read it:

> And thou, child, shalt be called the prophet of the Highest: for thou shalt go before the face of the Lord to prepare his ways.
>
> To give knowledge of salvation unto his people by the remission of their sins.
>
> Through the tender mercy of our God; whereby the dayspring from on high hath visited us,
>
> To give light to them that sit in darkness and in the shadow of death, to guide our feet into the way of peace.

God had gifted us, guiding "our feet into the way of peace." Our fire was alive for another day.

28

"An All-Night, All-Day, Stay-Inside-and-Hold-Your-Woman Storm"

We had no ticking clock hanging in our log cabin. Our way of telling time was not accurate, but then we didn't need to be accurate. We were staying here, on the ranch, till we could walk west, over the wall of pointed stone. "Way up there," Perk said, "there could be more than twenty feet of snow in May."

Our way of telling time was with icicles. When we first arrived, there were no icicles. After a few weeks of icicles forming, then melting, then forming again, some took hold for the winter. By Thanksgiving a few of our "clocks" were half-way to the ground. They were very clear and thin as a broom handle. By Christmas they'd reached the ground. New Year's saw no change.

By midwinter the icicles were as thick as a small tree. It was after midwinter that I met Tom Ortenburger. I had already been up with Hollywood and fed the cattle and horses. The horses' fur was longer than a mountain gorilla's to protect them from the cold winter.

I'd come back for some breakfast. It was hard getting used to eating anytime I was hungry or having a cup of coffee

Tom Ortenburger

anytime I wanted. Barbara made some stomach-excitin' biscuits. All winter she'd been painting, reading, and helping me with the book. I took off for my road to the upper ranch.

About three-quarters of the way up I heard a noise. It was a wiry guy, in faded jeans, on a snowmobile. He rode the thing fast, straddling it like a horse. Snowmobiles had taken the place of horses during the winter here. Perk said that they used to ride their horses in the winter's snow with special horsehoes that had cork on the bottom.

"Howdy," the guy said. He looked about my age, with chestnut brown hair. "Who are you?" I think he was surprised to see any human up here.

"I'm Peter Jenkins. Been living on the Vickers ranch since the beginning of winter."

"I've heard about you from Emma Jean. People in town been wondering what you're doing here."

He had on a red and black checked wool shirt, the kind lumberjacks wore, and laced leather boots. His brown eyes were penetrating.

"Why you walking around up here?"

"I've been looking for the animals that live up here. I've never seen country like this. I can't get enough of it."

He turned off the snowmobile. It had begun to snow.

"You want me to show you some of the places they live?"

"Sure."

"Well, get on." No sooner had I thrown my leg over the back of the seat than Tom gunned the throttle. There was more of an art to riding one of these snowmobiles than I thought. Especially when we went through the deep powder of the meadows. Tom would yell, "Lean to the right."

He'd go down "trails" covered by two feet of snow. Tom knew they were trails; he'd been coming to this ranch since he was three. The snowmobile would come to an abrupt stop.

"You see that?"

"What?" All I could see was an expanse of snow and some bushes.

"Those tracks going around there." He jumped off and headed off into the deep snow. It was above our knees. There was a single line of tracks that circled around a clump of underbrush. He said they were coyote tracks. There was a frozen pond near. He followed the coyote's signature in the snow to a white mound. He explained that the snow-covered mound was where a family of beavers were spending the winter. The coyote was just checking. We followed farther. The elegant white line through the whiter snow ended. The wind had erased it.

We swished across another sea of snow to Water Dog Lake. Tom showed me where there was a hole in the ice because a spring kept it from freezing over. There were indentations in the middle of the snow, not connecting to each other. Tom said that bald eagles caught trout from the opening in the ice and then flew down to the snow to eat. There were a few scattered fish bones and some fresh bloodstains in the snow.

We moved on. Every few hundred yards Tom would stop. There was a well-worn trail, leaving one forest of pine and entering another. Tom said that was elk. He pointed out droppings. There were tracks that hopped with a lot of distance

between them. He said that was an autograph of a marten. He
saw snowshoe rabbit tracks, pine squirrel dashes from one tree
to another. We were by some rock cliffs. He saw something
that excited him. A line of tracks followed a space between
some boulders, then went down the narrowest trail at the base
of rock cliffs, by a pine that grew from the cracks in the rock.
The pine was twisted like a bonsai, and its green needles were
frosted with snow. Tom got down on one knee. "That's a big
bobcat. See how these tracks are rounder than the coyote's."
I could see that. "See how sure the paw placement is on the
rock." Sort of. He read them and interpreted what they said
like this line of tracks was a short story in a foreign language.

Tom knew the upper ranch as well as he understood the
animals up here. He took me straight up mountainsides on
trails that were just wide enough for our snowmobile. Higher
and deeper we moved into seldom-seen views. There was an
excellent possibility that the land we were exploring was not
touched by any human the whole winter. Few made it this high
up even in the summer.

We rode for hours, the feathery powder blowing over
the windshield and into our faces. My beard was coated with
ice. Our light changed; it seemed to be dimming into night. It
couldn't be. When we came back from the fork in the trails
that led to the Golden Wonder Mine, we turned back to the
right. Ash gray clouds were coming over the peaks like tidal
waves in slow motion. The clouds would clear the mountain's
top and roll down into the skinny valley. Some would get
caught by stronger winds, blowing in from Utah, and never
come down. What was bright blue became creamy gray over-
cast. The hard white lines of the horizon were dissolved by
millions of snowflakes.

We'd be in a whiteout soon and Tom said it felt like this
would be "an all-night, all-day, stay-inside-and-hold-your-
woman" storm. What we saw now was just the "hello" part,
a warning to the natives. Shafts of daffodil-yellow sunlight cut
through the snow and spotlighted stands of aspens, dead trees,
everything. The snow abruptly stopped. The hello was over;
the shrieks and anger of the cutting winds were next.

Tom said that we should stay around because the animals

that we looked for also knew when a day-and-night-dissolving storm was coming and they often came out right before to feed and hunt. Crossing under Station Eleven, Tom gave me a shot with his right elbow in the chest and stopped. He pointed down. There were two coyotes, jumping up in the air. Their front feet would land together in the snow. Both of them had beautiful tan fur, which was rare.

"There are two yearling coyotes. They're hunting mice. They'll jump up and push their front paws into the snow and grass and then listen for a mouse. You can tell they're young by the fact that their tails aren't as bushy as full-grown. Their chests aren't as full. See what I mean?"

"Yes."

The young pair sprinted away. They ran swiftly through the snow.

"Look, they're chasing a jackrabbit."

I looked hard. The coyotes had spread out, and there was a flash of white fur bounding for its life. The coyote on the left made a grab at the long, fast rabbit, knocking them both into the snow, rolling, powder covering up the death scene. But when the snow cleared, the rabbit jumped off into a bunch of bushes. The other coyote spotted us, as the wind blew our scent to it, and yipped once to its brother or sister, and they loped off. Tom had reached around instinctively when he'd first seen them. He said he almost always carried a .270 rifle. Perk wanted him to keep the coyotes thinned out so they wouldn't kill too many of his calves come spring.

"I'm comin' up in the morning to set some traps for those young ones. You ever done any trappin'?"

"Nope. I'm not sure I'd want to."

"You do know that it was the trappers that opened up the West? You don't think it was John Denver. They explored these Rockies, looking for beaver mostly."

Tom aimed for a wind-piled snowbank. We cut it in half. He then headed for a clifflike dropoff and stopped inches before going off, then gunned it, and we went straight down. I thought it was the end of my life. It was worse than the hairiest roller coaster drop. Tom floored it home, skidding around the tight turns of these snow-covered trails. Pulling up to the side door

Dogsled races on San Cristobel, the height of winter excitement in Lake City

of my cabin, he said, "You know who's going to be on *Saturday Night Live* this week?"

"Who?"

"It's going to be Steve Martin or maybe Richard Pryor and you gotta watch it!" He left in a spray of snow. Tom lived in a restored home in town, alone. If this were going to be the kind of storm he said, he'd be looking for something to hold. Tom was one wild guy. I could tell we had a lot in common.

The next morning right after the first bitter cold light, I heard a snowmobile pull up. It was Tom. We had been up till past 2:30 A.M., working on the book. On nights when it snowed it was always warmer. Also, on ice-clear nights when you could look farther than you ever thought your eyes could, it was too cold, even in the cabin, to write. The only place warm enough was by the fire, under a down sleeping bag, close together.

Tom banged on the door with a gloved hand. I asked him if he could come back. He said that he'd go scout out tracks in the fresh slate of snow and be back in a few hours. He was back in exactly two hours. He wore a Russian-looking hat with four fur-covered flaps.

I made coffee and we all sat around and talked and ate venison sausage and Barbara's bran and raisin muffins. Tom knew a lot about Perk and Emma Jean, Larry and Paulette, and the whole family. When he was about three years old, his father and mother discovered the Vickers ranch while touring Colorado on a family vacation. That was close to thirty years ago, he said. In those days the Vickers had built a few log cabins on the river and rented them in the summer. They did anything they could to make money to keep "the wolf from the door." They loved the Rockies and their riverside ranch, cloud-slicing ranchlands, trout ponds, and they learned that they could share that love with vacationing flatlanders like the Ortenburgers.

Tom's father was a bank president in Tulsa when they began coming to the Vickers ranch. Tom and his two brothers attended Tulsa's private schools. Tom said that he was never happier than when the family came to Lake City on their annual vacations. They came back to the same log cabin for many years. Tom said there were many families that had never missed a year for thirty years.

It seemed that Tom had experienced it all. He appreciated Porsches and he played pinball. He sold Mercedes in Tulsa and knew the difference between $100-a-bottle wine and a Coors, but he preferred mountain spring water, right where it was created. He knew when he ate five-star food and loved cowboy bars. He pronounced cowboy "ka-boy."

He read the *Wall Street Journal* and was passionate about historic preservation in Colorado and everywhere else. Tom understood corporate depreciation and had lived in South America. He could shoot any kind of gun and raised and pampered flowers and plants all winter for his flower boxes. Tom could track, trap and skin coyotes and bobcats like an Indian in the day and curl up in front of his wood stove and read *Smithsonian* magazine cover to cover. Many women liked him and he liked many women.

Tom and I spent the rest of the winter getting to know each other. He taught me to trap and skin, and he told me why he'd decided to live in Lake City full time. That decision was no easy one, for he knew that if he wanted to, he could become a very wealthy man. He also knew that to do that, he'd have to live in a big city, and it was Vietnam that helped him make the decision not to. Tom's dad had fought in World War II as an officer in the Navy. The Ortenburgers are a fiercely proud family, even military in their bearing. But Vietnam was no World War II. Tom followed his dad into the Navy and became a young officer on a ship that fired crater-producing shells many miles. They were aimed by lifeless numbers that were coordinates called in by ground troops or reconnaissance aircraft. They couldn't see their enemy; only at night could they see the fireball blasts of death. Tom never did say exactly, but knowing him, I think it got to him that they were shelling people he couldn't see, an "enemy" that might not have been an enemy. He knew there could be villagers taking the brunt of their shelling. When Tom returned from "Nam," he didn't say much. He had decided that he'd return to the place where he had the happiest memories. He didn't want to be hassled

A Colorado winter is hard on everybody!

by people; he just wanted to feel the thin air, see the bare rock peaks, and get high above the treeline to watch a baby elk nurse in the yellow fog of morning. He got a tent and moved up with the golden eagles to sort out what he wanted to do with his life.

All that summer and fall he worked in a gold mine and sorted ore and his feelings. He decided to live in the way that made the best memories. He stayed in Lake City. He would do whatever he could to make enough money to get by. A lot of people who tried that didn't last beyond the first winter, but Tom settled in and made a life for himself in the place that he loved.

We spent a lot of the winter exploring the white magic of the hills. We tracked coyotes and set traps. Tom would tell me what to do and let me make a hundred mistakes. Trapping in the snow is the hardest kind of trapping. Traps freeze, tracks marked our coming and going, and the ground was frozen.

The coyotes made me look like the fool I was. One time,

unknowingly, I dropped a pair of pliers from my back pocket.
It must have fallen into the foot-deep snow. When we came
back to check the trap, the coyote had come over, pawed
through the deep snow and picked up the pliers in its mouth.
Then it dropped them right into the jaws of the trap, springing
it. Tom said he'd seen coyotes do things a lot smarter than
this. Tom told me I'd have to learn how to think like a coyote.
He said, "You know, Peter, that could be a major improve-
ment."

Bobcats didn't have the intellect that coyotes had, but
they were scarcer and didn't roam as much. Cata, as Tom
called them, stuck around cliffs, rock canyons and rimrock.
Tom led me down many miles of cliffs and canyons, looking
for signatures of their nighttime prowls. We'd find where they'd
been, rarely, and make sets, using rabbits hanging in trees as
bait. Cats used their eyes more than their noses.

The bobcats and coyotes made a constant fool of me till
I learned my lessons. Before the winter was over, I'd learned
the art of the first Rocky Mountain pioneers. I learned to think
like a coyote and a bobcat and, in turn, learned to appreciate
them as I never could have otherwise.

I hadn't had a friend like Tom since junior high. Maybe
it was because we had the time that winter to really be together.
To explore, to dare each other, to run down cliffs in snowshoes.
Spring to Tom meant that he had to get ready for summer.
Summer was the time of the year when most people in Lake
City made the money they'd live on through the half-year-long
winters.

Perk told us stories about how the Vickers held tight to
their Rocky Mountain valley and their upper ranch, which was
friendly with the sky. Tom took me to his mountains and
introduced me to the high snow-covered meadows that he and
the elk loved so much. He led me along secret rock trails that
wound so high I could hardly breathe. Tom and I got along
great.

29

Perk

Winter was leaving. The icicles said so. In town and in our secret valley, cabin fever was at its worst. For six months people had been more or less attached to their warm fires. No one wandered far in winter, except maybe in their dreams. It was almost the end of April.

A few patches of ground were melting back to brown. I'd been exploring the mountains all winter, always walking on top of a foot of snow, usually more. On my feet were either snowshoes or heavy boots, and I was used to feeling the pull of deep snow as I broke my trails through it. Today I'd set foot on the first solid ground in six months. It felt hard and secure. I felt something crunch under my right foot. There were round patches of green with bright pink stars of color, cactus, hugging the ground, as ecstatic to be free of their cover of snow as I was.

All week everyone on the ranch and in town seemed to be breaking loose from the dark mornings and early nights of winter. Tom had said that toward the end of winter many folks had "the inside cabin blues" so bad that if you didn't wave to them when you drove by on Main Street, they'd be upset for weeks. Small aggravations could fester. There were so few cars that everyone knew everyone's license number. Colo-

307

rado's license plates had two letters before the numbers. I guessed the biggest county, around Denver, was AA. We were ZN, dead last.

I'd assumed that after hearing twenty or thirty of Perk's stories, we'd heard it all. No one could have any more tales from a lifetime. Perk gave the impression that every story was the last. He told all, never held back.

Then one night, at their kitchen table, over three pots of coffee, Perk cut loose. Perk was ordered to sit still for a few weeks and maybe that was the reason he told so much that night. Three days earlier Jed, Perk and Larry had been on the upper ranch, cutting down dead timber. Perk was slinging his chain saw when he slipped on an icy stump. He fell on the blade of the whirling chain and about cut his leg in two. Perk was only aggravated that he had to sit still for so long.

Before Perk's main tale he told a short one. Sort of a primer. I'd learned by now that living with these Rockies was no "neck-bending stare into the high country." The challenge was how to make enough money to stay around long enough to call this place home. Long before anyone thought of coming to the mountains for the view, there was little to do. First there was trapping. The mountain men rarely stayed. Then came mining. The Vickers did a lot of that. After all, when you've got a dad who can win mines in poker games at his saloon, you've got a mine. Perk told about how they made it through the Depression and the real tough times, like before World War II, by working a mine they owned on the upper ranch called the Golden Wonder.

"My oldest brother, Ivan, and our brother Jack lived at the mine. We had a little cabin there alongside the mine." Perk took a drink of whiskey; his leg was hurting, I could see it in his face. "We worked there all week, and most of the time we'd come back down to the lower ranch on Friday night and take a bath. Mother'd cook a big Sunday dinner, and after we had the Sunday dinner, we'd ride the horses back to the mine."

"What was it like working the Golden Wonder?" I asked. Mining was something I knew nothing about.

"We got up right at sunrise, which came a lot earlier that high up in the mountains. That mine is over ten thousand feet.

There wasn't a watch in the camp, by God. It was a small two-room cabin and we had a wood cookstove. We stuffed the cracks in the logs with newspapers, if we had any. Ivan, bein' the oldest, would holler, 'Get out of bed, Perk... out of bed, Jack,' and if neither one of us got out of bed there'd be a frying pan coming in our direction. Generally me or Jack would cook breakfast. We had home-cured bacon and fried potatoes. If the chickens were laying at the ranch, we had eggs. If they weren't, we didn't. We had lots of coffee. Right after breakfast we got down into the tunnel." That was when the Vickers boys left the hypnotic views. A person can look down on the lower ranch and the river and know exactly what views eagles live with. They'd spend most of the day in the darkness of the narrow tunnel. With each charge of dynamite and each chop of their pick they'd come another chunk of gold ore closer to staying.

"My older brother Ivan, he was the ore sorter. We'd dump the ore over what we called a grizzly, which was like a heavy wire mesh. The heavy rocks would run down into the bins and the fine stuff would fall into the grizzly. Ivan had to sort that ore and cob it. Cobbin' means breakin' that piece of rock with a hammer to get the best pieces. The extremely rich ore you'd put in a sack. The second grade we'd just throw into an ore bin. We'd ship that ore about twice a year, sometimes three times." The Vickers blasted for gold into the hard-rock soul of the mountains. Perk told us his final story.

"It was along about 1929 or '30. One day my brothers and I were down to the courthouse and Bud Vernon said," he told us, "'We better take a look at your title to the lower ranch.' (The upper ranch had been a land grant in 1914.) 'The patent has never been issued and your dad is payin' taxes on the improvements only.' We found out that was true. The title had never been issued. The people who he'd bought it from didn't have a title either." If the mountains couldn't get rid of the Vickers, the U.S. government would try. "We had a lawyer file a homestead entry for us. They kicked that out immediately under the grounds that the land wasn't open for entry because it had come under a government power withdrawal site. The government, in the early days, came out to the West and withdrew certain tracts of land for power development. And our ranch came under that. So we started talking to the Federal Power Organization to get our ranch set aside. After all, we'd lived on it all those years, knowing we owned it. Having bought and paid for it. We had all kinds of meetings and hearings and lots of correspondence with them until finally they did cancel their withdrawal of our ranch.

"Then, after they got off our backs, we made an application called color of title. A color of title means that if you had peaceful and quiet possession of a piece of land for a period of twenty years, mind you, thinking that you owned it, you could qualify for the title, and they'd issue you a patent to the land. They *kicked* that out immediately." So far it didn't seem like that much of a story, but from the look on Perk's face I knew it had to be. His face was flushed and his voice was high and fast. "The grounds for that were that we couldn't qualify because we automatically admitted we didn't own it when we made the homestead entry. We then exhausted every means of appeal with every state organization there was. They said they would be taking the ranch. That was as far as we'd ever go. But we knew a lawyer named Eddie Pringle. He helped prepare our appeal to Washington, and I went back to Washington to present our case. This whole thing had been goin' on for years by now. I was with our lawyer and I knew our congressman, Wayne Aspinall, and Senator Gordon Allott. They were close friends of ours and they knew the problem that we had. They loved the family and they wanted to help us." (Perk has been chairman of the Republican Party in Hinsdale County for many years. Of course, with a total of 200 to 300 humans in the entire county, it isn't the biggest organization.)

"So we appealed our case to the secretary of the interior. I even wore a tie and suit. Now that Washington was the biggest city I ever seen. At that time the secretary was a man named Fred Seaton. He was a western man, supposed to be favorable to the western people. But they're not always that way. You get 'em back in Washington and they go haywire.

"Anyway, after we got our case presented, this man Seaton had a little lawyer about this high [he motioned that the man was about as high as the chair]. The lawyer said, 'Folks, we've reviewed the Vickers case and we want to be very fair with the Vickers family.' Right then I started beaming. I thought sure, we got the thing won. He said, 'We're going to be fair with 'em. We're going to give them a reasonable time to move all their possessions and their improvements from the land and put the land back in its natural state, and *pay*'— Perk's voice went through the ceiling—'trespass for all the years you Vickers have used it!' If I'd had a gun, I'd have killed that man. I mean, my father had paid his hard-earned money for this land. Now they said they were taking it. This thing had already been goin' on for over fifteen years. I'm a-tellin' ya I was emotionally shook up. I had to say something." (For Perk to be shook up took more than an avalanche).

"So I'll tell you what I said. 'I've got my two brothers as partners on this land we've worked our whole lives. Now,' I said, 'I never was in the service myself, and I'm not feelin' bad about it, but my brother Joe was in the service, drafted in about 1941. He fought all through Africa, through Sicily, Italy and France. Finally he was captured up there in Germany. My brother Bob, my partner, he fought his way through the Japanese war. Now, when you notify those boys to move off that land, with their families, you better go pretty damn well prepared because, I tell ya, they won't go!'" Perk tensed strangely.

"My friends told me that they thought sure I was going to drop dead right there in the room when they told me we'd have to move off that land. I went down to my hotel on Pennsylvania Avenue and I got up in the room, and I'm not a-kiddin' ya, I tried to go to sleep and I'd see little bubbles start about the size of a pinhead, and they'd get bigger and bigger and bigger, and just before they'd bust, I'd kinda come to. I called my brother Ivan and told him what happened. I told him I didn't know if I could stand it. But I *did* stand it. I caught a plane to Denver, thinkin' how we could hold the government off from takin' our ranch."

Perk got up for about fifteen minutes so Emma Jean could change some of the bandage. I threw some wood on their fire.

Perk hobbled back, his eyes popping with anger, thinking about all that they'd had to go through. "Peter, now here's the thing. You move onto a piece of land and you live here, and you build here, on land that you thought you owned, that you thought you paid for, and in comes some government sharpie and says, 'You gotta get out of here.' You'll go to war before you'll move out and take your family with ya."

"So anyway, Aspinall, our congressman, he said, 'Now that's fine, Perk, we've exhausted every means available to us. Now we'll present a special bill.' And our senator said, 'That's fine, I'll carry it through the Senate.' They wrote the bill directing the Interior Department to convey title to this land, about a hundred forty acres. Now mind you if a congressman wants to present a bill, he must read that bill on the floor of the House of Representatives. Then the speaker of the House assigns that bill to a particular committee. To show you how lucky we were, he assigned it to the Interior Affairs Committee, and our congressman was chairman of that. Then the same thing took place in the Senate. Then what did we do?" The teapot whistled. Perk got up; he was making hot chocolate.

"We knew we'd have to have a lot of political influence because if you get up in front of four hundred congressmen saying you have a bill that you want the government to convey title to an individual, they'll say we don't have time for that kind of baloney. We started calling all our friends that we'd made over the years. People that had stayed with us during summers in the cabins, and I'll tell ya, I know the value of friends better than anyone in the world, I guess. A true friend, there's no way you can ever repay a *true* friend. So we had a doctor friend in Shreveport that's dead now, God bless 'im, Dr. G. A. Creel. Doc Creel was a lifetime friend of Russell Long. So he immediately started talking to that Russell, saying, 'Now look here, when that bill comes up in the Senate, you've got to be on your toes and help these Vickers.'

"And Raymond Whittington, another old friend of ours. Now remember I told you about that family that drove through here in the twenties in that Pierce-Arrow car, and Bob and I sold them worms." (Since Perk almost never left the ranch, all their friends, and they were thousands, had become friends by staying with the Vickers for some part of a summer.) "Raymond's dad was one of the founders of the city of Amarillo.

A very wealthy family. Raymond was a fraternity brother of Lyndon Johnson, and boy, you ought to see the letters he wrote to ol' Lyndon.

"You see, we weren't tryin' to get nothin' from the government that wasn't ours. They give away a million times this farm every day. All we wanted was what was ours. And our friends knew that without them we'd already lost the place. And they loved us. As that bill progressed through the Senate and Congress, we'd get telegrams saying, 'We read the bill to so-and-so committee.' Finally, after a whole year of those telegrams, the bill came up. One day I got a telegram saying, 'The bill has passed and it's in front of the President,' who was John Kennedy. Then I got the last telegram, letters saying, 'THE PRESIDENT SIGNED YOUR BILL.'" Perk said that this was only the second time in the history of the U.S.A. that the government had been forced to convey title over to a family. The only other time, Perk thought, had to do with the Rockefellers.

Perk remembered back to that last telegram. "By God, I've been Republican all my life, and you know what Kennedy was. I could have kissed the man that day." Even though the Vickers got back their ranch, by an act of Congress, signed by the President, they still had to pay for it again, thirty years after their dad had paid the first time. They also had to pay for the surveying of the land. At least a small war was avoided.

There was even green grass outside the cabin now. We knew it would soon be time to leave. Staying in one place this long was exactly what we'd needed. Now the road called us again. We got out our dusty packs and stood them against a log wall.

That afternoon the hot sunlight dimmed and it snowed. It was one of those heavy spring snows that come to the Rockies. It stuck to everything like white cotton candy.

Perk pulled up. He was in the mood to talk, but he seemed to be kind of sad. "When you two leaving?" It was the second week of June. Perk had said that there was still ten feet of snow on the pass that we planned to cross.

"As soon as we can cross Engineer Pass," I said.

Heading for the snowfields of Engineer Pass at the end of June

"I called down to the road crew; they doubted they'd be able to clear off that trail over Engineer Pass till after the fourth." The Fourth of July.

"You think that we can walk over the pass with the road uncleared?"

Perk lifted an unlit cigar to his mouth and smelled it. He loved the smell of a good cigar. "I kind of doubt it. You don't know that road, those high mountain conditions, and with the road under ten feet of snow you'll have no idea where you're going. You should wait till they clear the road."

"How high is that pass, Perk?" Barbara asked.

"It's around thirteen thousand feet. That's mighty far up for a pass. Even jeeps have a hard time makin' it."

Perk lit his cigar. "Pete, Barb, we sure are sad you're gonna be leavin' us. Emma Jean and me, we were talking about it last night.

"You know, if I was a few years younger, I'd like nothing better than coming along with you and Barb. There sure is a lot more to this country than a person might think. Really and truly, I've about spent my whole life within sight of these mountains. I never have wanted to leave, really." He stopped to think. "Barb, get your jacket on and come on. I want to show you two something." Perk threw his hay-handling gloves into the back, and we all drove up the road.

At the first fork, instead of staying left as I usually did, Perk turned right. Even the truck seemed to be happy driving on dirt and rock again. Some black crows sat in a blue spruce hung with springtime snow. We drove alongside a cliff where Tom and I had tracked many bobcats and coyotes, onto a cliff that overlooked the whole lower ranch. It had a rock face that went straight into the river. Many beavers were up and repairing their dams.

Perk's voice and face poured out a lot of emotion as we stood on the tabletop flat rock, looking down on the ranch and river that Perk had spent his life working on, loving, and fighting for. Jed had brought the horses down from the upper ranch and they pawed around in the grass of the fields below. Faith and Paul, Perk's grandchildren, were down by the barn, jumping off a mountain of hay bales. They held sheets in their hands to see if they could fly. Way down there, across the road, we saw Emma Jean drive home from a bridge game. We could hear nails being pounded by Larry. He was building his family's house right next to Perk's. I looked thousands of feet up to the top of the mountains that rose behind the Vickerses' house. A few black dots drifted in the winds. Perk said they were a pair of golden eagles hunting.

It was one of Perk's favorite views. He could sit up here like an eagle and look down on his life.

"Besides my family, you know I love these mountains and all of this more than anything. Have you and Barb ever thought of where you're going to settle down once you finish this walk of yours?"

At first I thought Perk was just talking out loud about his love for Colorado and the mountains. He did that a lot, as if even after sixty-five years he still couldn't get over the magnificence of it all. Then I heard his question.

"No, Perk. We haven't really thought about it much. We won't know till we see what's left of the country. We may never know, we've come to love the country so much." Spring was an emotional time in the Rockies anyway. We were all at the edge of crying. All winter our feelings had been kind of frozen. Now, emotions were loose, popping forth like the wild flowers.

"Well, there are a certain few people that the family has come to know over the years. They've become as close to us as our family. The Ortenburgers, the Pools, the Drabeks and some others you've not met. They all own a few acres of our ranch. They love it as much as we do and will pass it down from one generation to the next, protect it like we do. This land we're standing on, I've been saving it for years. Once or twice even thought of building Emma Jean and me a place here. If you and Barb ever want a piece of this ranch, this piece, it's yours."

The warmth of our mountain spring day cooled with the coming of night. The kids had gone home after hours of jumping from the mountain of hay. Larry had quit hammering and was probably watching the news on Channel 9, while Paulette cooked dinner. The horses still ate some fresh sprigs of grass.

I think Perk had been thinking about this for a long time. We felt like part of the Vickers family and we'd fight arm in arm with them to preserve this land as long as we lived. When we had children, we'd see to it that they came to feel the same way. It was a great security to Perk, knowing that he had many adults who would fight with him for this beloved land. Even a greater security was the love for this land he saw in their children. Perk was thinking of them now. There were the Pools' grandchildren, the Tycers' kids, there was Jake Golbitz, the Drabeks' two, and the Ortenburger boys.

We got back in the pickup and Barbara gave Perk a kiss on the cheek. Perk knew we were leaving in a week or so and never got serious and emotional again. He just kept trying to get me to smoke one of his cigars with him.

30

From Tundra to Desert

The wind clubbed our tent like invisible hammers, trying to drive us off the top of the mountains. I had staked down our new dome tent on the flattest piece of ground I could find, trying not to crush too many wild flowers that grew on this tundra, in rainbow colors that lit up the snowfields.

It was night now, and the winds seemed to strike in pinpoint blasts. I'd thought the winds down in the valley were intense, but they were like a baby's breath compared to here. The blast of wind never let up all night, and it pushed and bent our flexible tent almost flat, till it touched our bodies. We had a hard time getting to sleep because it felt as if we would be blown off the tops of these Rocky Mountains, back to the valley where the people lived. It was our second night since leaving Lake City.

The morning of June 23, 1978, Barbara got up while it was still dark. She was packed and ready to be on the road. Many of our friends in town and from the ranch had decided to walk with us that first day, and they met us at the center of town.

Tom and Jed were there. Perk, Emma Jean and Larry and his family and some friends of the Vickers had planned to meet us at the end of our first day with steaks and other goodies. I'd promised Perk I'd smoke a cigar with him if his steaks were as good as he said. They were. And I did.

Gary Wysocki, the senior deputy in town, and his wife, Jean, hiked with us that first day. Many of the kids from town, sons and daughters of store owners and teachers and ranchers, had their packs on ready to walk with us. There were more than fifty people there that morning, and about twenty walked with Barbara and me. That first day we made it to a ghost town called Capitol City.

Dawn came to our tent bedroom where tundra was our bottom sheet. The 360-degree view made me want to sit and stare for a month as the rising sun lit rocks, snow, mountain peaks and wild flowers.

We would be crossing these mountaintops, some of the highest in the country, by way of Engineer Pass. From here on out there would be no more road. The trail was now covered by a wall of snow twice my height.

Ahead was something of a bowl, the size of ten football fields, surrounded by a semicircle of mountaintops. We were looking at the peaks we'd seen when we walked down Slumgullion Pass. The problem was that the bowl was covered by snow. Some places it looked twenty feet deep. It looked as if we were blocked by the sheer stone wall that had guarded us through the winter. Could we go around? I looked to the south, the north. No. The ground fell away. Could I have missed some fork in this supposed road? Could we make it over the wall? It didn't look like it.

There was no choice but to go over the wall. We dug our boots into the snowfields and gritted our teeth. I just hoped we were going in the right direction. Heave. Heave. Up. Up. Each step was an all-out effort and took all the breath we had since the air at this altitude was thin and had very little oxygen. Barbara was right at my heels. We both wore our mirrored sunglasses to keep from being blinded by the brilliant white all around. We made it across and up the wall, to the very top where the wind swooshed and sang so loud we had to yell at each other. We thought we could see clear into Nevada.

As we wound our way down the other side of the peak, clutching onto rocks and guarding each step, Barbara slipped and had to dig her pack into the slanting snowfield to stop her fall. This was the place where she almost met her death, where we almost lost each other. We could see far below where the trees and spring flowers were popping out. We would keep moving down, slowly, until we were on clear ground again. Although we did not have a compass or anyone to guide us, we hoped we were headed in the right direction. The sun and our walking senses told us we were.

A day later we were on what they call the Million Dollar Highway, which connects Durango, Silverton and Ouray. We spent our fourth night in the St. Elmo Hotel, built during the days of the gold rush, where the gold miners stayed and the ladies of pleasure burned a red light in their window. Our room had old washbasins, and mountain winds blew back the lace curtains. There were many more people here than in Lake City. Some had never heard of Lake City, so forbidding was the wall of stone, ice and snow that separated these mountain villages.

As we walked northwest toward Utah, the mountains disappeared as fast as they'd burst from the earth back in New Mexico. All that remained of them, since we left the paradise of last winter, was a view on a clear day. Here in western Colorado, the land was cracked, burned and barren. Grand Mesa was the only thing for our eyes to look up at. It had never been hotter than 75 degrees in Lake City; now it was way over 100. Mirages melted the roads ahead, and some days we staggerd like lost Arabs in the Sahara. How could the land change like this, so abruptly? It wasn't fair. We wanted to withdraw from the Rocky Mountains gradually, but little about the West was subtle. East of the Mississippi no change in the land was so sharp, so hard on the senses. Everything melted together. The seasons eased up on you. The land was curved in gentle ways.

We'd walked through this change in less than a week. I had gotten a thermometer to measure temperatures for our walk through the deserts and I put it on the pavement between Delta and Whitewater. It read 118 degrees. Both of us came very close to heat stroke between these two towns. An irrigation ditch, full of melted snow runoff, coated with floating sticks and leaves, saved us from the hospital.

Out here it was important to walk close together because I'd felt myself swaying, almost falling, from heat that sucked us dry. I had trouble keeping my eyes open, it was so hot. Barbara's steps were faltering, too.

We had to rest, so we set out packs down and curled our bodies so that they lay in the circle of shade that our umbrellas made. The only other shade for miles was made by unending stands of barbed wire.

My head throbbed and the heat felt as if it were building up so that my brains would boil. The part of my leg that would not fit into our shade seemed to blister before my eyes. I could feel my heart beating in my eyes. Heat-crazy thoughts of snow falling on my face and snakes sinking their poison fangs in my legs fought each other.

"Let's go," Barbara said. "I can see a clump of trees just a little way ahead."

"I can't," I thought I answered. If I stood up now, I would pass out.

"Peter, come on, let's go," Barbara said.

I didn't say anything. She bent down. "Are you feeling

all right?" She put her sand-dry hand on my limp face. "Peter, what's wrong with you?

"Peter. Get up." There was anxiety in her voice. She'd never seen me like this. She slapped me in the face. Instead of being mad, I didn't notice.

"We're less than a half mile from Whitewater. Come on. You'll die lying here without water." We'd run out of water long ago.

"Peter. *You're going crazy.* Now come on." She slapped me as hard as she could on my sunburned thigh. She grabbed my arm and with all her strength she tried to lift me to my feet. She couldn't. My weight was unmoving like a dead man.

Cars with tinted windows and air conditioners straining had been speeding by all day. Then a Colorado state trooper stopped. "Is there anything wrong?" It must have been obvious. Seeing him snapped me back. I wasn't going to quit now. I could make it to Whitewater in spite of the trooper's offer to drive us anywhere we wanted to go.

Why they called the couple of stores, whose paint peeled before our very eyes, and a few homes Whitewater, I'll never know. It was dry as dust. There was an old, funky motel and we both collapsed on the swaybacked bed in our room. Barbara put cool washcloths on my forehead and soothed my body, which shivered with sunburn. My mind cleared up, but not till morning.

Our map told me that after walking through Grand Junction, Colorado, we were headed for Utah and 100-mile stretches of dehydrating lizards and little else. There was no way we could walk through that without some help. Someone to bring us water. This would be the first time we'd ever need someone to bring us supplies, water. But we knew no one. Would we have to call Perk? No. They lived too far away. Maybe I'd have to call Tom and have him follow us for a week. No. He was busy.

We bought a Grand Junction newspaper. There was the usual world and national news that changed little no matter where we were, and there were some ads for some local churches. We could call them, tell of our problem and hope that there was someone who would offer to help us. The first church we called was the First Assembly of God. The pastor said to come to their services Sunday. There we met a young couple named Ron and Kitty Maupin. No one seemed to notice our Sunday clothes were hiking boots and shorts.

Ron was red-headed and from table-flat eastern Colorado. He was in his late twenties or early thirties and worked in construction. At one time he'd been a fine bronc rider, with hopes of getting to the big-time rodeo circuit. But that was before the dry day he got thrown off this ornery bucking horse. Getting thrown was not unusual, but Ron was thrown off the back of the horse, and before he hit the ground, his head was kicked. The hoof connected with such force it broke his skull. A cowboy any less rough would have died. Ron ended up living with a metal plate protecting his brain. He was sad when he was told he could no longer ride bucking horses.

Ron and Kitty knew what the sun could do, so every day for a week Ron would come out in his pickup with coolers of iced-down springwater, iced-down fruit, iced-down sandwiches, iced-down potato chips, iced-down peanuts. Everything that could be iced down was.

The sign on the road that scared me the most said: NO SERVICES FOR NEXT 107 MILES. That sign made people going 65 mph nervous. It would take us at least a week to walk it. Many experts said that we should drink two gallons of water a day, considering the exertion involved and the high temperatures. We would be lucky to get a gallon between us. At best we were at half strength all week.

Loma, Colorado, was the last place that had anything like a store. The next day we came to the Colorado-Utah border, where a sun-blistered sign announced the changing of the states. The land said little. Most of the life had been baked and burned from it long before. There were cliffs to our north that they called the Book Cliffs and they bubbled from the flatland that felt hotter than a sizzling frying pan. The steep red cliffs were spotted only occasionally with stunted juniper. The face of the cliffs was the color of an Apache's skin dotted with scrubby sagebrush.

We lived for the moment of the day when we'd see Ron's

pickup. It was always late in the afternoon, after he'd put in a day's work. Every day was spent on the teetering edge of heat stroke. The mornings were too hot. We didn't want to get up and leave the shade of our dome tent, but the heat found its way inside. By the time we got our faded blue packs repacked, and our tent stuffed into its attached sack, it was too hot to move. But we had to move. Even the rattlesnakes would boil if they stayed out in this. Too seldom we came upon a bridge that gave some hot shade. We wanted to stay there till night, but here in Utah, in July, even shade could be too hot. We had nothing left to do but walk. Our mouths got as dry as the fine orange dirt that flaked and slid down from the tops of the cliffs. When we finally got the iced-down water in our hands, we had to be very careful. We wanted to drink too much, too quickly. I guess our insides were so overheated that too much cold water made us feel we'd pass out. We had to let that first water warm up a little. We'd drink and eat all we could possibly hold, then fill up our flexible plastic canteens. Since water weighed eight pounds per gallon, we couldn't carry what we would have liked to. On this stretch of Utah desert, my pack weighed more than any time of the walk, more than eighty-five pounds.

Day 1 was barely OK. Day 2 was tough. We camped by some nameless patch of nowhere. At sunset the colors of the cliffs and canyons and other-worldly landscapes were rich with black shadows and brick red rock. The ground turned tan-yellow. These Book Cliffs had nothing to do with the hard-rock grays and pointed peaks, so close, in the center of the Rockies. Back there was planet Earth; this was more like Mars. The cliffs were eroded, their tops like crumbling turrets of the oldest English castle. Day 3 was brutal. Ron showed up late, almost at dark, and we were afraid he'd run into something that would keep him from delivering our "life," our water. Day 4: Desolation Canyon and Tavaputs Canyon were to our north. Devils Garden. Fiery Furnace. Dead Horse Point and the Arches National Park were to our south. Day 5 made a place like Devils Garden sound as soothing-cool as a beaver pond. Then Ron didn't show up when we expected him. A

Even the town looks lonely in Green River, Utah. The next nearest town is over a hundred miles away

long camper pulled up. Out stepped Ron and Kitty and another family, the Easters.

They had been cooking all day, had their water tanks filled. We could take a *shower* in their camper. That fifth day of "no services" was twelve hours of a barely controlled stagger and three minutes of blissful shower. They'd made me a birthday cake.

Day 6 was hell. Ron brought our last shipment of "life" before noon. They had to go somewhere that afternoon. We told him he'd never know how we appreciated his giving of himself.

Day 7 was as close as we'd ever come to losing our sanity. We were beyond temper. Crying. Even giving up. There was no place to give up to. We were walking a razor ridge between reality and hallucination. Heat waves burned away rational thought. We'd drunk our last sips of water that night as the winds evaporated us. I felt like a slice of apple laid in the sun. Barbara's lips cracked open. She couldn't keep her contact lenses in; they felt gritty. We stumbled, knowing that Green River, Utah, was supposed to be in front of us soon.

We did make it, and our first relief came from a small store by a campground. A thin, sun-dried lady was at the counter, and when we burst in, a look of fear came over her face. I guess we looked like wild-eyed crazies as we headed straight for the coolers filled with soda, juice and a chain of unending cold drinks. She might have thought we'd leave without paying but we couldn't pay till we got back to the world. It took more than a half hour till we were recovered enough to pay up and walk into town.

My parents and two youngest sisters, Betsi and Abbi, were going to be meeting us here in Green River. They were driving out from Connecticut and would spend their vacation with us. We waited the day that they were supposed to have arrived in Green River. They never did. I was glad that they didn't because we were far from recovered after our 107 miles of no services. I didn't want them to see us this drained.

We waited all the next day and they didn't show. Had they had an accident? Had they left when they said? Had their car broken down? It was a long drive from Greenwich, Connecticut, to Green River, Utah. I thought back on growing up in suburban Connecticut and I thought about the last seven days. This walk had taken me far.

I was really excited about seeing my folks. Not only had I discovered a country that inspired me, but for the next few weeks I would be able to share it with my parents and my two youngest sisters. My mother and sisters had never been anywhere west of the Mississippi and I hadn't seen them since Barbara and I had been married on February 6, 1976. Today was July 18, 1979. It had been too long. My sisters were just growing up when I'd left New York on my walk. Now, my mother said, they were young ladies taller than she was. Before leaving on my walk, I was no more than a boy who thought he was a man.

Right before dark they drove into town in their rent-a-car with Connecticut plates. They'd been delayed because Betsi had a horrible toothache and had to have a filling in Nebraska.

Dad had always wanted to see what was called the Four Corners area, where the borders of New Mexico, Colorado, Arizona and Utah came together in one point. My folks certainly couldn't walk there, so we piled into their car and drove south. We saw the Arches National Park, where stone had been eroded into arches the size of huge bridges. We drove through the Navajo Nation, where their reservation stretches as far north as southern Utah and well into Arizona. Dad said that he wanted to drive around the way we walked. Whenever we saw a turn in the road or a mountain that interested us, we'd just head for it. We'd stay as far from the areas busy with tourists as we could. The family just couldn't get over how far apart everything was in the West. How few people there were. How could we possibly walk all of this? Where did we get our water and food? Did the snakes try to crawl in our tent at night? My sisters had to know.

It was one thing for me or Barbara to tell them on the phone about what we were going through on our walk west. It was another thing to see some of it. Watching my mother's eyes and expression as we drove through Monument Valley and saw an old Navajo woman herding sheep on a tired horse, fifty miles from "nothing," was thrilling to me. This was as different from Connecticut as England was different from Saudi Arabia.

Before they dropped us off, at the same spot where they'd picked us up, my mother and sisters just had to walk at least half a day with us. Dad was not too excited about it, but he was outnumbered. He said he'd drive ahead and come back around lunch. As I watched my father's concern for my mother, my sisters and his daughter-in-law, I was glad that I hadn't been a girl and tried to get his blessing to walk across America. If Barbara and I ever had a daughter, I could only imagine what would happen on the day when she announced that she was following her father and mother's example and was going

Campfire

exploring. Maybe she'd want to orbit Saturn. My folks drove home through Texas. They had seen a piece of the West and would take it home with them. Every time Dad and I had a chance to be alone before they left, he'd tell me how proud he was of what I'd done. When he'd say how proud he was, the strongest swirls of emotion would rise within me. All I could say was: "Thanks, Dad."

31

"I Never Refuse to Marry Any Respectable Woman Who Asks Me"

Barbara and I crossed mountains called the Wasatch Range and saw the valley that was the Mormons' Promised Land. It was a thin strip of land almost 350 miles long that began at the northern border of Utah and went all the way south to the Arizona border. The whole state was so void of the kind of land or forest or water that drew original pioneers to settle that I wondered why anyone would have ever settled here in the first place. The Mormon settlers huddled up to the Rocky Mountains, where they were able to get fresh water from the spring runoff.

The first city was Logan. Then came Brigham City, Ogden, Bountiful, and Salt Lake City.

From Bountiful, through Salt Lake City, and down to Provo lay the heart of the great Mormon kingdom. Next came Nephi, Richfield, Cedar City, through Zion National Park to St. George. In St. George, less than ten miles from the Arizona border, Brigham Young, the grandaddy of the Mormon faith, had made his home. It is still standing, a large house, looking like a motel. Not a creak in the floors can be heard. Brigham had twenty-seven wives, and each wife had her own room. Brigham Young once said, "I never refuse to marry any respectable woman who asks me."

While walking through the nation of Utah, which was once called the kingdom of Deseret, we were told, and overheard, many stories. One day we were eating lunch at an old-fashioned counter at a drugstore in a small, sleepy town in Utah. Everything and everyone looked so straight and proper, 1950's proper. The immaculate streets were lined with trees and flower gardens. All the houses seemed to be white, with shutters; many sprinklers watered the lush green lawns.

Three older ladies worked at this drugstore. They looked and talked like grandmothers from Anyplace, U.S.A. Until they started talking about their boss. The year was 1978.

The thinnest one said, "Well, they're at it again."

"You don't mean," said the one who had waited on us. "Which one is acting up this time?"

"They say it's the fifth one. She says the others are picking on her and that you know who is not giving her enough"—(pause)—"attention."

"Did you hear that he is thinking of marrying another one? Some girl that just graduated from Brigham Young U." The thin one refilled our water glasses.

"Maybe that's why he's been so mean lately. He's worried he'll need more money for this new wife."

Turned out, their boss, who walked in before they were finished talking, still believed in polygamy. Most Mormons could find some relative who was a descendant from a polygamist family. The owner was very thin and in his early forties. He had Utah tan skin, brown hair cut short, and looked very wholesome. He looked like the owner of a family drugstore in any small town in the U.S.A., except maybe he had a bit more on his mind.

As we walked through one tidy town after the other, I couldn't stop thinking about what it must have been like for the first Mormon pioneers. They'd arrived in this valley of the Great Salt Lake in July 1847. Some of them wanted to keep going to California, where people were rushing to find gold, but Brigham Young knew this was the place. They had been driven out of Ohio, Illinois and Missouri, and they found this place where they could build the perfect society without interference. They needed an isolated land, hard to reach. What guts that must have taken, I thought as I looked out at the massive stretches to the West, the salt flats and the mirages coming up from the desert. I thought that if the Mormons hadn't settled this state, there might not be anyone here today. Hundreds of miles of people-killing desolation lay to the west of the Mormon strip. So did Nevada.

I'd always heard the people of Utah were clever and hardworking. One story we heard about a large Mormon pioneer family stuck with me. This farming family settled down on the Utah-Arizona border, and the head man had a lot of wives with sixty children. He always kept one of his small sons on the lookout for the law riding by. They lived within yards of both state borders and when the law from Arizona kicked up some dust about polygamy, the whole family would run across the border to a house they had in Utah. If the law rode in from Utah, they'd run back to Arizona.

The Mormons and this state got started because of one man, Joseph Smith. He was the founder of the Mormon faith. Joseph became so important to the religion that when Brigham Young was on his deathbed, his last words were: "Joseph, Joseph, Joseph." When Joseph Smith was fourteen years old in 1820, the lad went into some woods by his family's house to pray. It was there that he had the first vision that would lead to the founding of Mormonism. Today these woods are called the Sacred Grove. This grove is as important to Mormons as Mount Sinai is to Jews and Christians.

Joseph said that God and Jesus came down to visit him in the grove. Joseph was confused and asked to know the truth. Which church was right? Were Baptists right? What about Presbyterians and Catholics? Joseph said that God had chosen him to restore the true church because it had strayed too far since the time of Jesus. Joseph Smith would become the founder of a new faith called Latter-Day Saints.

A giant billboard in Salt Lake City advertising the Mormon's Temple

Late one evening in Provo, Utah, my oldest sister, Winky, showed up. Both my brothers Scott and Freddy had joined me on the first part of the walk and walked along with Cooper and me. Winky, short for Winifred, was sixteen months younger than I was and had some of the most beautiful red hair I'd ever seen and a smile like spring sunshine. After graduating from Wilson College in Pennsylvania, she got her master's at Penn State. She was a gifted teacher of preschool children and was on her summer vacation. Two of her friends were to drop her off on their way to California.

The first day walking we all spent getting reacquainted. Barbara and Winky had not had the chance to talk much before this, so they shared a lot about life on the road and Wink's life living on a farm in Pennsylvania and teaching in a Montessori school.

The end of the third day we were eating our dinner in a Pizza Hut. This area of Utah was not heavily populated, but then it wasn't "out there" either. One thing I had noticed was that everywhere I looked, it seemed that every woman under forty was pregnant, with three or four blond children all holding hands, following her. I would later learn that having lots of babies was another part of Mormonism, so that there would be physical bodies to house all the preexisting spirits in the universe.

As I put a couple of quarters in the jukebox, I noticed a middle-aged couple staring at us in a less than subtle way. Barbara and I were used to stares, but they were really bearing down. How did they know Winky was my sister? Maybe they thought I was a Mormon zealot out on a pilgrimage, looking for more wives. Maybe they thought Winky and Barbara were my wives. I was feeling a bit feisty; a cool wind had blown off the Rockies that afternoon. I would sit by Barbara for a minute, kissing her on the cheek, whispering to her, then go over to Winky's side of the booth and kiss her on the cheek, etc. After the music quit playing, the people in the Pizza Hut hushed their busy whispering. Every eye was on us. I guessed they'd been reading about one of the militant polygamists in the Salt Lake City *Tribune* and thought I was one of them. They probably figured I was on a protest march across Utah.

The middle-aged man walked over to us. His hair was dark as Utah coal and short as the first haircut of boot camp. He asked where we were going. Then asked if we were Mormon. When I said that we were walking across America and that we were not Mormon, he seemed relieved. He walked back over and sat down with his wife. They talked intently to each other. He came back.

"How would you three like to spend the night over at our house? We live near here." We were somewhere between Pleasant Grove and American Fork.

I thought how great. Winky was getting the chance to see how we met people on the walk. I looked at them. They both nodded as if that sounded like a fine idea. "Sure, we'd like that," I answered.

It turned out that Mr. Paul was one of the leaders of their local church, called a ward. Every man over twelve in the Mormon Church was a priest. Instead of a paid minister, like in the Protestant churches, the head was called a bishop. He was unpaid. Each ward consisted of 300 to 500 people. Mr. Paul was also a foreman at the huge steel mill near here and talked to us all night about why we should become Mormons.

He pulled out a big chart, showing us his family tree. We found out that Mormons baptize the dead, and that's why they are into genealogy. They must search back in their family for four generations, and when they find a relative who was not a Mormon, they go to the temple and make the person one through this baptism of the dead. I asked if we could go to their temple for a worship service. There was a temple in Provo and the main one in Salt Lake City. He said, in a reverent voice, that nonconverted people (Gentiles) were not allowed into the sanctuary of any Mormon Temple. It sounded so secretive.

Like a kid who was told, "No," I wanted to get in one of those temples to see what went on behind closed doors. We never could.

Mr. Paul had to get up real early to go to work at the steel mill. Both Mr. and Mrs. Paul seemed sorry that we had stayed with them and had not become Mormons.

Wasatch Mountain was to our right and Salt Lake City was to the north, a few more hours of walking. Earlier that morning a blond couple with three blond babies had stopped next to us on the road and wound down their window. I figured they were going to ask us if we wanted a ride. That happened constantly.

"Hello. It's a beautiful morning," I heard the young father say to Barbara and Winky. I was walking a little behind them.

"Good morning," Winky said. There were two bumper stickers on the back of their car. One said, "Have you hugged your kids today?" The other said, "Discover America. Read The Book of Mormon." Someone had written in the dust on the trunk, "Have you hugged your aardvark today?"

"Are you Mormons?" the thin man asked. His wife's head glanced nervously back and forth first at me, then at Barbara and Winky.

"No, we're not," Barbara answered.

"Oh." He was surprised that we weren't. "Well, have a nice day." They drove off.

32

The Accident

The sign said: "Sandy, Utah—City Limits."

"Peter," Barbara said, "Let's cross the road. There are trees over there and we can walk in the shade." It was late morning and we'd been looking for a café to have some breakfast since dawn. Barbara knew that one of the rules of the walk was we always walked facing traffic. But she and Winky had been enjoying each other's company and conversation so much that I forgot the dangers of walking with our backs to traffic and crossed the road. Nowhere had the sun tried to cook the life from us any more than here in Utah and the shade would feel good. It was too hot for a morning.

For a while we all walked close together, by the side of the four-lane road. It was obvious by the energy of the traffic that we were nearing a big metropolis, Salt Lake City. Winky and Barbara were having a talk about children and what it would be like when they became mothers and what they were going to do.

They went on for almost an hour as I listened and thought about having children. When I'd begun the walk, there was no way that I would even consider having children. How could I bring them into the kind of world that I thought existed? Would the earth even last long enough for them to grow up? Now I had some dramatically different ideas about it. As strange as it seemed, even though Barbara and I had married each other, to have a child was a major decision that we both had not made yet. Deciding to have a child seemed the ultimate in a man-woman relationship and I hoped that someday I would not be afraid of all it meant. I felt I was getting there. Maybe someday soon we could throw away the birth control pills for good.

I walked ahead of them, wanting to get alone with my thoughts. Just having the freedom to think through so many thoughts made the walk worthwhile to me.

The traffic was slacking off; everyone had already commuted into Salt Lake, parked and was hard at work. The shade trees were thinning out. We were walking by a graveyard that had a duck pond with three or four fat white ducks paddling around amongst some pale lily pads. Looking at the water made me feel cooler. I thought how strange that none of the grave markers had crosses on them.

A sign said: 55 MPH. I heard a vague sound of metal glancing against metal. That sound shouldn't be behind me, my mind registered in some millisecond of time. I heard a louder sound of metal on metal. Had something dropped from a truck going in the other direction? My mind reacted too fast to keep up with. There was a partial screech of tires. WERE THE TIRES COMING TOWARD ME? SHOULD I RUN? Turn around and see, my brain ordered at the speed of light.

I whirled to see a long deep blue car skidding sideways. It may have been happening at fifty miles an hour, but from here on out, everything went into slow motion. Then it slowed down to single pictures, frozen before me, one at a time. Some of the pictures were in color; others were in black and white.

That first picture was of Barbara and Winky. They still talked. TURN AROUND, I thought I should yell. RUN. No, don't say that. There is no time. They will be hit from the front. NO. NO. THEY ARE GOING TO BE HIT.

The next picture was a blurred but frozen picture of a pickup truck, out in the outside lane, forcing this skidding blue car farther off the road and right into them. THE CAR MUST STOP. Yes, it has to stop. STOP, BEFORE IT HITS THEM. It was skidding too fast.

Winky Jenkins

The most horrible picture was the expression on their faces. I saw them both, but mostly I saw Barbara's face. Their faces went from the warm glow that comes from a conversation with a friend to the terror of death thoughts. NO. NO. THIS CAN'T BE HAPPENING. The look on Barbara's face was ripped by fright.

My next thought was: Please don't let that look be the last look I ever see on her face. PLEASE, DEAR GOD. SHE CAN'T DIE LIKE COOPER DID . . . LIKE COOPER . . .

I'd never let myself think that I could lose Barbara like I'd lost Cooper. No. This couldn't be happening. NOT BARBARA, NOT WINKY. BEING KILLED BY A CRASHING CAR. NO . . . NO . . . NO . . .

Then the killer car, out of control of its thousands of pounds of steel and tires and chrome, came onto the dusty grass where we were. I was standing frozen to the sunburned lawn of the Desert Mortuary. IT HIT THEM. IT WAS COMING FOR ME. I DIDN'T CARE. IF IT WAS GOING TO TAKE BARBARA, LET IT

TAKE ME. The blur of blue and glass ripped up dirt and dust and kept skidding till it hit Barbara and then Winky.

Would Barbara be dragged under the back wheels and crushed dead? Winky was hit by the front fender, rolled over onto the windshield and smashed it. Then she was thrown through the air, landing in a human heap. Was that heap lifeless? I couldn't stand this slow-motion terror. PLEASE RUN ME OVER. Kill me so I won't have to see Barbara die.

THE CAR HIT BARBARA. Would the driver panic even more and step on the gas, after pulling her under the car, drag her back down the road? Tearing, crushing. She was thrown through the air, 50 to 100 feet. She landed on the hot, dry grass of the funeral home in a still heap.

The car didn't hit me. The next thing I knew I was running around, screaming. WHO DID THIS? WHAT, ARE YOU PEOPLE CRAZY? CALL THE POLICE. CALL AN AMBULANCE. I'd been surprised by death once. I couldn't stand it again.

Barbara

The ambulance siren whirled and screamed while a man dressed in white leaned over me and lifted my eyelids, making it harder for me to focus my eyes. The siren sounded shrill and nervous. The smell of medicine was on the medic's hands, but the smell of dirt and fresh grass was stronger on me. I could taste gravel and dirt between my teeth while the medic wiped my face with a wet cloth.

My legs were shaking and jerking uncontrollably, and when I tried to stop the shaking, I realized I couldn't move them or stop the jerking. Even the weight of my heavy hiking boots didn't stop the spasms. The medic tried to feel for broken bones and then gave some orders to the driver as we wove back and forth, going very fast. A loud static and voice came over the radio while the driver talked back. We were rushing to a hospital outside Salt Lake City.

But where were Winky and Peter? I remember Winky walking beside me when it happened, but everything was mixed up as my head kept going in circles. What had happened? Were they all right? Was I all right? Then the thought hit me I might be seriously injured, even paralyzed, and a big knot lodged in my throat. It was all I could do to keep myself from screaming. Tears rolled down my face and onto the stretcher. I didn't want to cry in front of the medic, but I couldn't stop myself since I didn't know what was wrong or where Peter and Winky were. It had happened too fast. One second I was walking next to Winky, and then a loud crash hit my body and I was spinning through the air, rolling head over heels, ripping through grass and landing facedown in the dirt. It felt like being in a time machine, twirling through space and wondering if this was the end for me; maybe I was dying.

"You all right, Barb?" Winky's voice was faint. Before I could get my sense of place, her hand was reaching for mine across the ambulance, where she was lying on the other stretcher. I looked over through my wet eyes and saw her beautiful red hair matted with blood, grass and rocks. Her face and legs were scraped, bleeding and scuffed with dirt. Her round blue eyes, which reminded me of Peter's, were uneasy, but she had a smile on her lips. I flinched when I noticed the temporary brace around her neck.

"Barb, you all right?" she asked again.

"Yes, I think I'm OK," I said, trying to sound reassuring. "What about you? Are you hurting anywhere?"

"The first time I come out to walk with you and Pete and look what a welcome I get—nothing like being hit by a car. Thank God for big buns," she said dryly.

Her Yankee humor caught me off guard. "Thank God for what?"

"For our big rears."

"O-o-oh, Winky!" I laughed, and when my stomach bounced, something hurt and reminded me this was serious. We clasped each other's hands and fought off fears about our condition as the ambulance sped to the hospital. When I closed my eyes, everything was going in funnel-like circles as I made myself rethink what had happened.

The three of us left Draper, Utah, early on the morning

of August 25, 1978, and were only twelve miles out of Salt
Lake City. We hoped to reach the city before the burning sun
did. This was Winky's second day on the road with us, and
she was eager to make miles, not realizing the importance of
pacing. After two years on the road Peter and I learned that it
takes discipline and good pacing to keep going mile after mile,
day after day. But Winky was caught up in the thrill of being
with us, experiencing what a long hike was like. It had been
a long time since she had spent any time with her oldest brother,
Peter, and she also wanted to get to know me better since I
was her only sister-in-law.

The temperature climbed into the nineties within an hour
after we hit the road, joined by a hot breeze that blew into our
faces, making us dry and thirsty. It was a nagging thirst, the
kind that forced our thoughts to cold water and soft drinks.
Winky was keeping an easy pace beside me while Peter stayed
fifty yards ahead. She and I were caught up in a conversation
about breakfast since we had not eaten anything all morning.
Winky was hungry for scrambled eggs and I wanted pancakes,
but we both craved a tall glass of squeezed orange juice, so
ice-cold it would have frost on the outside of the glass.

I liked Winky without trying. She was mellow and able
to adjust to the aches, the hardships and sore muscles of walking all day in the hot sun without complaining. This kind of
hiking wasn't romantic or exciting, like the backpacking catalogs showed in their advertisements. This kind of trekking
made a woman irritable and impatient with people who com-
plained about little things. So I was really glad to have Winky
along, especially when I saw that she could hold up under the
strain. She had a toughness about her.

As the sun got brighter and hotter, I noticed a row of
shade trees across the busy four-lane street and yelled ahead
at Peter. When we caught up, I persuaded him that we should
cross over and walk where it was cooler. He didn't like the
idea because our backs would be to the traffic, but he reluc-
tantly agreed, feeling outnumbered with both Winky and me
wanting to cross over. I assured him it would only be until the
shade ended or until we found a café.

It was 11:15 A.M. and we still had not eaten and nothing

was in sight as we approached Sandy, Utah, a growing suburb of Salt Lake City with new construction, homes and hot concrete everywhere. For all of its streets, there were no sidewalks, so we stayed far off the shoulder of the four-lane street and walked in the grass. Peter had crested a rolling hill and was out of sight as Winky and I moved upward in our easy pace. When we leveled the hill, I could see Peter ahead. And off to my right was a huge green lawn and an impressive building which looked like a modern monument, long and sleek. It wasn't like any traditional office building I had ever seen. When we reached the driveway, which was paved and winding up to the building, we saw the sign that told us it was a Mormon mortuary.

Skidding tires and a loud screech came out of nowhere and I had grabbed for Winky when a thunderous crash and thud hit me from behind, plowing into me with a heavy force so cruel and powerful it could have been the end of the world. The slamming screeches blocked out everything except my thought: Dear Jesus, help. There had been no time to turn around and see what was aimed at me in cold blood.

It was in the ambulance with Winky that I learned a 1974 Chevrolet had skidded off the shoulder of the busy four-lane and slid into both of us like a bulldozer without brakes. It hit us as the car skidded sideways at 50 mph. Winky was hit and thrown straight up in the air like a ball, landed on the windshield so hard she broke it, and then was flung through the air, landing about thirty feet away.

I was hit at the back door on the driver's side. The door slammed into my lower back and shot me into the air about twenty feet. The impact caved in the door and threw my body, rolling and spinning and then scooting across the ground, where I landed in a pile next to Winky. We were on the huge green lawn of the Mormon mortuary.

People came running from every direction. I could hear a boy crying and Peter shouting, "Who did this? Who did this?" People were huddled over us, talking in hushed tones while a man from the mortuary came running with a silk pillow to put under Winky's head because someone said she was going into shock. Someone was holding an umbrella over us to keep off the glaring sun. I faded in and out, groaning and trying to move. I could hear myself whimpering like a dog that had been run over. An older man told me to be still, he was a chiropractor. He was touching my lower back, spine and legs and I overheard him tell Peter that my hips and back might be broken. His voice was frightened.

Peter immediately screamed at the man to get away from me and to keep his mouth shut since I was conscious. My face was buried in the dirt, but I could still hear bits and pieces of everything through the sirens and ringing in my ears. At this point I could only moan. Some men walked up to the circle of people hovering over us and told Peter they saw the whole accident. A driver in a pickup truck had cut off the driver in a blue Chevy, forcing it off the road and into us.

Peter raced from me to Winky, then back to me like a frantic animal who had lost his family to a predator. Peter was yelling, he was ordering people away, he was loud and angry, but Peter was mostly scared. No one knew how badly Winky and I were hurt and Peter could do nothing to help. His voice was shaking as he assured me everything was all right, he would stay by my side. He petted my head and planted a kiss on my bruised face.

The next thing I knew, men in white picked me up and I was on a stretcher inside the ambulance next to Winky. When the medics unloaded us at the emergency room, one of them said if we had turned around to see the car headed toward us, our faces and chests would have been crushed, or if the car had skidded into us ten feet sooner, it would have hit an above-ground gas line and we would have all been blown apart.

What a freaky accident! This was the first time Peter and I had walked with our backs to traffic since we left New Orleans, the only time Winky had ever been with us, and then to be hit onto the front lawn of a Mormon mortuary, a few feet from a gas line, was too incredible to believe.

The hospital was sterile and white as the doctors and nurses brooded over us; then Winky was whisked off to another room. I was rolled off the stretcher onto a hospital bed, then pushed into a tiny cubicle in the emergency room. The doctor on duty stood over me, poking, pushing, examining and not saying anything. I feared the worst as my hips and legs turned a bluish black. My body still shook in nervous spasms and I was hurting somewhere but couldn't decide where.

X-rays were taken of my pelvic area and back. Urine was taken to test for internal bleeding and all I could do was lie still, staring at the cold ceiling, hoping my body was all right. My teeth were chattering from fright. In a way I wished I had been tied to the table so I wouldn't have to worry about the jerking. Minutes turned into gut-wrenching agony. Where was Peter anyway?

I thought I would go into hysterics before the nurse finally pulled back the curtain that separated me from the truth. Peter walked in behind her, and the doctor followed.

Here it comes, I told myself. I just knew the doctor was going to tell me that my hips were cracked, I needed surgery, there was internal bleeding, and I'd have to be in the hospital for at least a month.

"The X-rays show no broken bones and there is no internal bleeding," the doctor said flatly, very businesslike. With that message he politely turned and was gone.

The nurse shook her head, but her face showed all the feelings the doctor didn't have time for in the emergency room. There was a half smile on her face. "I've seen lots of people come in here after being hit by a car, but I've never seen anyone hit at that speed and walk away from it."

The nurse handed me my torn walking shorts and boots, motioning for me to put them on. "It really was a miracle," she said to me. My body was trembling so hard I couldn't sit up without help or dress myself and I was beginning to feel very sick to my stomach. She said my body was reacting to the shock and I would have the jitters for several hours. The nurse held me up while I pulled on my shorts and boots.

Peter was bubbling from my room to Winky's, practically shouting his thanks to God for our safety.

"Praise the Lord," I heard him say down the hall.

Before I could get my boots on, Peter and Winky were standing in the doorway, both smiling that special Jenkins grin. Winky got the same report as I did, no broken bones or internal bleeding, but she did have a pulled neck muscle and had to wear a temporary brace for a few days. Their blue eyes sparkled together, brightening the whole emergency room. Winky and I had not known each other before, but now I felt bonded to her as *my* sister, not just Peter's sister.

We had been in the hospital about two hours when I finished getting dressed and hobbled over to Peter and Winky as they waited to leave. With Peter in the middle to help, Winky and I braced ourselves against him and limped down the hall past the nurses' station. The nurse who had helped me get dressed stood in the doorway and waved. I looked back to wave good-bye. She was staring at us curiously as we hobbled out into the Utah sun.

Barbara limped over to Winky. They both got quiet and whispered some things to each other. They'd been through something that cemented a lasting bond.

In a few minutes Winks would be loading her semi-crushed backpack into her friends' Volkswagen convertible to head back east to green Pennsylvania.

"You know, Barb, it's good that the car didn't hit Petey. That was a pretty good-looking car. If it had hit him, the thing would have been a total wreck."

Barbara gave Winks a big kiss on her face. Winks sat down in the car, but first she put a pillow on her seat. I leaned over and kissed my sister; then they drove off, the convertible roof down and Winky's long red hair streaming in the wind.

We had no choice but to hole up in a room in Salt Lake. This sacred city was fortified by walls of stone, a part of the Rockies. The mountains protected the city on its east side. The desert fizzled and fried for hundreds of miles to the west, south and northwest. I never said a word to Barbara, but I knew there was a definite chance that the walk would end in Utah. I didn't know if she was in some sort of melancholy shock or if she was considering stopping the walk. I wouldn't blame her if she wanted to. After all, getting run down by a car at over fifty miles an hour, from behind, could traumatize anyone. She might never be able to get back on the road.

When she felt like she could walk a little (the doctor had

Exuberant graffiti in Ogden, Utah

recommended it), I thought it would be good to take a stroll to a restaurant where I had been getting her food.

At the table I asked her how she was feeling. I was ready for whatever she might say. The waitress set the plates of food in front of us as Barbara looked all around.

"Just give me another few days and I'll be feeling good enough to get back on the road," she said.

I swallowed a large bite of lunch I hadn't chewed. "Don't you think it's a bit too soon?"

"I'll be ready in a week." She had that determined look.

We left in six days. The frame of the pack hurt some at first, but Barbara wasn't going to miss the rest of the country just because she was hit by a car. Like the pioneers before us, we decided there was no way we could make it across the deserts of the rest of Utah and Nevada into California. Like the pioneer pathfinders, we decided to head straight north through Brigham City and Tremonton toward Idaho. Once we got into Idaho, we'd continue north till we came upon the Snake River. We'd follow the river and the Snake River Canyon west into Oregon. The first white settlers through this part of the massive West walked and rode this route and called it the Oregon Trail.

As we got closer and closer to Idaho, there were fewer and fewer people. Barbara was walking slowly but did not seem jittery about anything. The rushes of freedom that came when we were walking down unknown roads had become a part of her now. Walking with pain was worth it, and the unknowns that were Idaho added to our anticipation.

Idaho might be a discovery, like Louisiana. I knew Louisiana had New Orleans. I knew Idaho had potatoes.

I was astounded by how quickly Barbara had recovered from her accident. The soothing winds danced in fast from the west. The first night in Idaho I pitched the tent with its door facing Cache Peak and the wind. It would stroke us to sleep and make us dry-mouth thirsty by the dark red light of morning. Barbara was asleep on her side, on the sandy ground, before I saw my first falling star.

Most nights I sat or lay on my sleeping mat in front of the tent like a farmer on his front porch, watching the crops grow. Often I thought how special it was to be able to go to sleep when the sun took away the light, when you were tired enough to appreciate the gentle touch of the ground. The smells of crushed wild herbs and sagebrush hanging on the cooler night air spiced this, the most rewarding part of our day. I even liked the smell of my skin as it dried from a day's sweat.

This night I stayed longer than usual, trying to listen to the coyotes talk. I'd come to listen to the coyotes as I had at one time listened to Johnny and Ed and Tom Snyder. My thin foam sleeping pad felt extra-nice, as I lay on my back and stared into the eternal black above me. There was little or no moonlight to turn things blue-purple. When I was growing up, I remember wishing I could see the night sky, but there was too much interference from streetlights and cars and houses. Tonight nothing interfered with my view. I wanted to keep my eyes open and look up into the stars and planets and whatever else was up there. The air was a special kind of dry. It made me feel as though I were suspended in space, instead of lying on my back.

A glaring white blur of melting energy streaked and then was gone. I saw falling stars till I tired of them. I tried to look farther into space than I could. I wanted to see something I'd never seen before. I saw something moving. A jet going to some big city on the coast? Maybe Seattle. No, it was a satellite.

I tracked it until it was no more. It made me think. Is there anything or anyone up there? Millions believed there had to be, what with the billions of stars and millions of possibilities of life. Maybe some of them were more advanced than Earth. I'd read about men near the Gulf Coast, in Pascagoula, Mississippi, who had been taken up in the spaceship and asked all kinds of questions, tested on operating-room tables. Many farmers had met UFOs and alien beings, at least, that's what they said.

I concentrated. I focused my eyes harder than I had before. All right, I said to myself, if there are some intelligent, mind-reading beings out there, I am going to dare them to come down here by the tent and take me into their ship or vehicle of interspace travel. After all, why pick up some country boy who has never been out of Mississippi? Here I am! Certainly, if they can beam each other through space, they can read my thoughts. I would be a perfect subject. I wouldn't be afraid. I'd seen a lot of this country that I could tell them about. They could take me up with them and drop me off before Barbara woke up.

"Come on. If you're up there, I dare you. Come on down here. Ya-all come see me, ya hear. Prove you're so intelligent." I got no answer. All I heard was a calf calling for its mother. Maybe it scented some hungry coyotes.

"OK, excuse me for daring you. Please come down here. I know you can travel faster than light and sound. I'll be glad to be friends. I'll even take your picture so that once and for all people will know you are for real." I heard a noise. A machine sound. It was only a couple of semi-trailer trucks far off in the distance.

"OK, I understand. You're worried I'll tell the wrong people about you. Look, if you'll come down here and take

me with you for a while, I promise that I will not give the
story to the *National Enquirer*. If that's what's holding you
back, forget it." The stars popped, jiggled and glowed in subtle
colors always close to white. I stayed on my back and never
before had I looked so deep into the uncountable stars. It made
me feel insecure, looking for too long. I must have fallen asleep
because hours later I woke up cold. The next morning I checked
for weird footprints, burn marks, anything. Even a note. There
was nothing. I decided not to tell Barbara what I had tried to
do, daring those outer spacers like that. There's no telling what
she would have thought.

We both woke up feeling strong. It may have been that
we could sense that fall would soon cool our days and comfort
our sleep with crisp nights. After living with the trees and
mountains and snow and sun for so many years, we could feel
the delicate moves of the seasons. Like a beaver that stores an
extra abundance of wood or a muskrat that grows extra hair,
we could feel it all coming.

I'd opened my eyes earlier this morning than Barbara
and looked at her face and her graceful and shy body covered
by a white sheet. There was not one piece of her that I had
not memorized, that I didn't love. She looked so at peace while
she slept.

There was something moving in between us on the floor
of the tent. It was a light golden brown, and in no hurry. It
was some kind of bug maybe. No. It was a scorpion! Seeing
it woke me faster than the strongest coffee. Of course, we
never woke up to coffee anyway. I unzipped the door of the
tent and flicked the scorpion out onto the ground.

"Is it time to get up?" Barbara asked.

"Yeah, let's hit the road." I don't know how it all came
to pass. Maybe it was seeing her so close to death a few weeks
before. It certainly had to do with all we had shared, having
made it this far together. Maybe I'd been afraid to think about
all the responsibilities of it before now. I had always known
that to make the decision I was thinking about making would
cement our relationship like nothing else could. I just felt I

had to say it and say it now. Maybe I should wait till the walk was over. No, it needed to be said now.

"Barbara, I've been thinking. You know for the first time since we got married, I think I'm ready to be a father."

Normally she woke up slowly. This morning she just got out of the tent, wrapped in that sheet, her long, curly hair falling onto the stark whiteness of it.

"Oh, Peter, that's beautiful. I was beginning to wonder."

She stood close to me and buried her sleepy eyes into my chest.

"Barbara, where are your pills?"

"There in my pack, in the second side pocket. Why?"

"Because I think we should throw them away." I said it, almost testing myself to see if I really meant what I'd just said.

She never hesitated. She went straight for her birth control pills, about four months' worth, and we both stood there popping each one out till there were more than 100 tiny white pills on the ground. For me it was a ceremony as moving as our wedding had been.

33

Cattle Drive up Cottonwood Canyon

My horse spooked a buff-colored jackrabbit. It leaped about twenty feet, then zigzagged through the open field. Two more started running. The dust the sprinting jackrabbits kicked into the air turned the color of sunrise. It was early even for a cowboy.

Just a week before, we'd been walking fast through Idaho. There was no reason to stop and go to work. The weather was great. But when we discovered the Williams ranch, I had to stop. It was a chance to fulfill a lifetime dream. I'd always wanted to be a cowboy. So had Barbara and W. T. Williams said that we could help out with the fall roundup. Before we knew it, we were coated with dust and sore from hours in the saddle.

Three nights ago it had been a typical late-summer night, dry, slightly cool with fat, full clouds shaped like potatoes. Two nights ago the sky was filled with purple-gray clouds. They passed overhead with a cold front blowing in from the Pacific. That night it snowed about six inches up in the mountains. These mountains could be seen from the back porch of the Williams ranch, and that early snow was bad for the ranchers. There was no doubt, one of the cowboys said, that their cattle would leave the mountains now and come on home. But it was too soon to come home. There was still plenty of time to leave the cattle and their calves up there in the hidden spring-watered valleys where the grass grew green.

Sure enough, maybe 900 cows got through some barbed wire and came down Cottonwood Canyon. They were all spread out, east of Hub Butte. One of the cowboys, called Billy, rode next to me as we moved through the flat sagebrush. We were on our way to a roundup.

Billy wore a hat that looked as if it had been trampled by a herd of longhorns. It used to be a light brown, but it had absorbed enough sweat to irrigate a small field. Billy was lean and wore glasses.

"When I was a young boy, wild stallions used to come close to these here ranches." We were, give or take, about nine miles south of Twin Falls, Idaho (pop. 24,512). It was about ten miles farther south to Idavada, Shoshone Creek and the Nevada border. By the end of the day Billy said we'd be a lot closer to Nevada if we could drive the cows back up the canyon.

He pointed to the west. "See that butte. That's Hub Butte." It was a kind of scrubby mound that rose about 100 feet from the middle of some very flat fields. "Well, I've heard tell that not too many years ago wild horses, especially some of the more daring stallions, would round up people's mares right from their pastures. Maybe even right by their ranch headquarters." That meant the main house of the ranch, which was usually lived in by the elders or the founders of the ranch. There were no small ranches round here.

I saw a cloud of dust rising and moving fast through the sage-studded prairie before us. Billy said that was probably some of the cowboys bringing their horses from home in a horse trailer, pulled behind their pickups. "Those stallions, now I admit they're something awful beautiful. But when they steal a mare from a rancher, well, darn. That's about as bad as stealin' the man's wife. They'd romance them mares and run 'em back up into the hills before anybody knew what happened." A red-tailed hawk circled above us, hoping we'd scare up something to eat.

There were ten people on horseback. Our trail boss for this day's drive was Davy Crockett. Davy was on a jittery,

W.T. Williams and his banker, Jack Ramsey

prancing cutting horse that was dappled and gray. A cutting horse can react to every move an escaping cow can make. They call that cow sense. Davy sat, more like floated, just above his saddle, as if the saddle were only there so that he'd have a horn to tie his rope to.

"All right, we all know why we're here. We've got to drive them cattle up the canyon till we get 'em back around Elk Butte. At the very least, somewheres near Grand View Peak. It might get hot today, so let's be as easy as we can with them mama cows and them calves. There's a lot of beef on them from all that mountain grass. We don't want to drive the meat off 'em." Everyone looked reverently at the cows and their chubby calves. They had been driven into the Sawtooth National Forest last spring and many of these ranchers had not seen their cows since. They'd been watched over, all 3,200 pairs, by three cowboys who lived with them from spring through summer till fall. A pair is a mama cow and her calf, which was born last spring. They eyed 'em hard, looking for their brand or earmarks to see which was theirs. They all tried to claim the fattest cows and calves, even if they couldn't see the brand.

Davy told us to fan out into a semicircle and start easing out through the sagebrush. "Some of you check out the cottonwoods by the creek bottom. Make sure you look careful around them willows." At first glance the land looked as open as these ranchers' faces, but there were a lot of places to hide. Some of the smarter and older mama cows knew what lay ahead: that they were to be driven back up into the Sawtooth, and they could hide their big selves in the smallest patch of cover.

As the riders moved out, Davy told me and Jeff, Billy's tall twenty-three-year-old son, to ride the old road. They'd be trying to get most of the herd moving up it till we got to the canyon. The road looked as if it had been rolled over by thousands of pioneer wagon trains.

I was on a tan horse, and Barbara was on a slick brown quarter horse. She was riding out to our left through some ornery ground that was dry as ashes and rough. Her riding partner was a widow rancher named Charlotte Crockett. She ran her own ranch and was in her late fifties. This lady, Charlotte, her short hair threaded with dignified gray, was *born* ready for anything. The first thing she said to Barbara was: "I was liberated before women wanted to be." Charlotte was one of the rare ranchers we'd met who talked and liked to. Most of them talked about as much as it rained in this arid land, "'bout never."

One day a few winters ago, Charlotte said, she was coming out of the bathroom after taking a bath. She'd been up all night with a couple of her hired hands, watching some young cows about to give birth. It was around first sun, she said. She glanced out into her back pasture, as she often did. She never knew what she might see out there, a fawn, some butterflies, maybe the sunrise highlighting her wild flowers just so. Anyway, this morning she saw something crouching down in the middle of that pasture, the one where she kept her favorite cattle-working horses. It was a mountain lion, waiting on her chickens. The chickens were scratching their way through the grass, picking up bugs.

Her hair was still wet and she was in her bathrobe as she grabbed her 25-35 rifle. Charlotte slipped out onto the porch and shot. She didn't say if she was shooting to kill or scare. Everyone knows Charlotte Crockett is a master marksman. That old mountain lion shot straight up into the air, ten feet. "That thing hit the ground scratchin' and runnin'," she said.

Charlotte took off after that ol' lion all the way through the pasture, then into the trees and down a half-dry creek. She was still barefooted and in her bathrobe. She never did see the mountain lion again. She did say that she figured it might have been an old she-lion, too old to hunt wild animals anymore.

The cowboys, which meant everyone except Barbara and me, had their ropes off the saddle, swinging them through the air, whistling and shouting, "Ha...Come on...Let's go...Back up them mountains, Mama...COME ON!" We got right into it all. I was living a lifetime dream. I thought to myself, Boy, I'm taking to this cattle drive stuff like I was born in the saddle! I even gave my quick-footed horse a kick when one of the mother cows tried to break out of the herd.

She ambled back, but her calf bolted. Jeff brought it back after chasing it a quarter mile. I could see the land was slanting up, barren of trees for the most part, to the mountains. These mountains were nothing like the slashing rock kings of the Colorado Rockies. The highest of the four named peaks ahead was Monument Peak (8,060 feet). The other three were Trout Creek Mountain, Trapper Peak and Grand View, which is where we hoped to make it by this afternoon. So far driving a herd of 600 cattle seemed like a piece of cake.

The closer we got to the canyon, the more cows we

picked up. They were half Herefords, half Hereford-Angus crosses. They called the crosses Black-White Faces, and this cross seemed to be what most ranchers had in this part of the West. It had to do with the crossbred vigor, at least that's what Billy said. Billy knew an awful lot about cattle.

A horned toad scrambled out of the way of my horse's hooves. The wild bunchgrass was vivid yellow-gold, but Jeff said that right near the roots there still might be some tender green leaves. About five miles away I could see a craggy reddish black rock rising from the land we now rode.

"Jeff, where does that canyon begin?"

"You see where them rocks are stickin' up, well, right around that bend."

Around that bend the canyon did begin. A gully splattered with medium-sized rocks was running some water from that rare snow the night before. About the only time water was abundant in this country was when the snows of winter melted and ran off, and that only lasted till about late April, maybe May, if it was a hard winter. A hard winter killed plenty of calves and old cattle, and a warm winter gave little snow, which meant little water, which meant drought. Drought meant not much green grass in the hidden valleys of the Sawtooth and thin, maybe sickly cattle. Sickly cattle or dying calves meant no money and maybe bankruptcy.

At first the straight rock walls were set wide apart, so we all had to string out wide, to the east and west, to make sure none of the cows got through the line. Our job was to ride up the middle of the stream or to stay on both sides of it. In some places it was dry, with a snake or two sunning on top of a dead log. They moved their dark green bodies fast as a canyon gust into the shadows of a thicket. Sometimes there was a trace of a trail, worn deep by years and years of cattle. Occasionally we'd splash through shallow pools and some few minnows would zip out of our way. Most of the cattle stayed higher up on the gentle sloping sides of the canyon. The going was easier. Soon it would be different.

Davy bolted away from his position after one thick-headed cow, then another. Their big calves, grown fat and strong since early last spring, would always try to follow. The bulls, which

I thought would be harder to handle, stayed in the herd like
good bulls. It was a cow that was in the lead and cows that
made all the trouble for us. Davy rode by, his nimble-footed
cutting horse flying after a cow trying to run straight up the
canyon wall, as if it thought it was a big-horned ram. It made
it farther than I thought it could. So did Davy and his horse.
They cut her off before she could really get her wind back,
after that first charge. How did they keep from falling, rolling
off that canyon? How did Davy keep in the saddle while moving, cutting, jerking? They defied gravity.

After a half mile the canyon walls closed in on us. For
a mile we'd be closed in, maybe only 100 yards across, gagging
on clouds of dust and bugs kicked up by the 1,000 head of
cattle in front of us. We'd been in the saddle now for three,
maybe four hours and herded in another 400 head. Cowboys
don't punch a clock; they work till the job's done. Barbara,
Charlotte, Bill Brockman and his daughter, Carol, had split
off from our main herd, before we got tight into Cottonwood
Canyon. They'd ride up by Sugarloaf, then ride up another
canyon where the West Fork of Rock Creek ran. I had no idea
when I'd see B.J. again. She looked like she was born to ride
the range, though. One of the cowboys had given her one of
his extra cowboy hats.

Keeping our herd moving was Davy Crockett, Rodney
Hopwood (one of the cowboys who lived up in the range camp
with these cattle), Billy Williams, Jeff, his son, Gene (the
other cowboy who lived up in these mountains), and Jim, the
Williamses' hired man. There may have been others. The dust
blocked out my view most of the day.

It was hotter than noon when the cows decided that they'd
had enough. The cows thought these cowboys who were yelling
their fool lungs out, trying to drive them back where they didn't
want to go, had gone crazy. The lead cow decided that she
was going no further. She stopped in a tangled mass of bushes.
The signal must have gone out because all the calves began
bawling. It echoed off the canyon walls. The bulls just acted
confused. The massive Hereford bulls hung their massive necks
down, their tongues drooled out of their mouths, and their
bulky muscles quivered and twitched from the oppressive heat.

"Jeff," I shouted over the thousands of complaining moos and bawls, "how far we got to go before we get to the end of this canyon?"

"Well, it's about fifteen miles, maybe more, from the beginning of the canyon. I reckon we got 'bout ten miles, probably more. There's a lot more cattle come down with this snow than we figured."

Davy and Rodney rode down by us. They had posted Gene, Billy and Jim behind the herd so that they wouldn't bolt, trample us and head back for Magic Valley. That's what they called the valley where all these ranchers lived. They began shouting, as loud as their strained voices would allow.

"Come on, you fool thangs. Move. Get goin'. Ho! Ya!" The lead cow just moved deeper into the thicket, as if to say, "I ain't goin' nowhere, boys."

The cattle were now grouped tightly, too tight for my comfort. I could feel their confusion, their indecision. They were getting hotter by the second; the winds of morning had died to weak breezes. They were thirsty, and there was water behind us. I'd never felt what I was feeling now, the imminence of stampede. Tens of thousands of pounds of panicked cows, bulls and calves that could crush all of us and our horses on the rocks of the canyon floor. The herd shifted like one mass of muscle and hot hide and dazed eyes.

Rodney and Davy could tell that what they were doing was not going to budge the lead cow. They got down off their horses, and with one hand on the reins, they worked their way into the thickets. They threw rocks at the cow's rump, broke off willow branches and switched them as hard as they could. "Come on, cow, move. Get up that canyon." The cattle grew increasingly edgy. Maybe just one more YA! or rock on their backsides and they'd stampede. I hoped that Barbara hadn't gotten herself into this kind of rock-walled cattle jam.

I got off my horse. I was beginning to feel I'd been dropped rear end first onto a concrete sidewalk, from three stories high. And we still had ten miles left till the canyon opened into high-altitude pastures. I picked up the biggest rocks I could find. I broke dead branches on the cows' backs. Some moved; others turned their heads in defiance. Then a bunch, off closer to the far canyon wall, broke through the thickets and headed back down to the valley. They sounded like five tanks at full speed.

The cutting horses behind, along with a couple of Australian shepherd dogs that Gene and Davy brought along, were thrilled by this rebellion. They stood their ground and stopped most of the cows. It was a crucial moment. If the cows had broken loose, the whole herd might have followed. Then we'd all be stomped and maybe worse.

Rodney sent Gene's dog after the lead cow. He nipped at her back legs and pulled on her tail with a possessed vengeance till she turned, lowered her head and tried to do battle. While the dog kept her busy, we worked our way deeper in the tangle, hoping to get them moving. I felt the hot, steaming bodies of cows and nervy calves pressed against mine. My horse was jerking its head back nervously. Once or twice it almost pulled my arm out of its socket. If it could, it would jerk loose and run home.

Finally we got the front cows moving again after a lot of prodding with rocks and dead branches. The canyon got narrower, then it opened into a wide, flat place with some nice pools of springwater. Davy said it was time for lunch. My rear felt like a mass of bruises, my knees as if they'd been beaten on with sledgehammers and stretched till they were going to snap like a rotten rubber band. I began to notice the cowboys' builds. Every one of them had thin, wiry legs that bowed. There was little in the way of rear ends. I guessed they had been beaten off, bounced to the bone, after all the years in the saddle. Their facial expressions, every part of their bodies, wasted not one gram of energy. They even held their eyes about three-quarters closed. Since none of them wore sunglasses, they had no choice. Before they touched their lunches, which were stored in their leather saddlebags, they took the saddles off their lathered-up, panting horses. They beat back some of the cows to get them to the water. None of us had anything to drink and we couldn't drink from the stream because it was filled with mud and other things from the cattle. We couldn't get ahead of them to the clear water because they blocked us, filling up the canyon from rock wall to rock wall.

The horses didn't care and they drank for many minutes, their graceful arched necks bent low to suck up the water.

Rodney sat by me. He had two bologna sandwiches with mustard on white bread. He gave me one. It was hot from the heating it took in his saddlebag, and I didn't like mustard usually, but it tasted great. A golden eagle circled at the top of the canyon in the blue Idaho sky. Its wingspread was almost seven feet across, and brown feathers went all the way down to its huge, clawed feet. It landed on a rust-colored boulder, circled by some patches of wild grass, to watch us. It called, with rapid chirps. Another eagle glided over the top of the canyon. "Time to move on," Davy said, his mouth still filled with food. There could be no real rest; we had too far to go. It seemed we'd stopped only to rest the horses and dogs. None of these cowboys would ever admit to being tired, at least not out loud.

After being in the saddle for more than eight hours, I began to wonder if I could stand much more of this. Sure I could walk twenty, thirty miles with seventy pounds on my back, but that was on my feet. Certain parts of my body were not prepared for hard work. Rodney and his horse, a long-faced Appaloosa, took off. One of the black cows bolted from the fringe of the herd. She had been slyly working her way to an escape. All day she had been one of the main troublemakers. It was as if she knew exactly where we were and she had the whole thing planned. Maybe she thought we were all too tired to give chase. Really, we could have let her go, we had pushed them high enough into the mountains now, but the cowboys were keeping the herd together out of pride, meanness, or some reason only a cutting horse would understand. Rodney, Davy and Gene had incredible horses. The rest were OK; maybe they spent too much time in the corral.

Rodney could point or just move the muscles on the inside of his bowed legs, ever so slightly, in a certain way, like a special language between him and his horse, and she would know what to do. It wasn't always the same. Unless a cow took off through the roughest ground, Rodney would not have to hold on, and his horse would take care of business. "She loves to do this kind of work," he said. "She acts like them cattle challenge her some. She ain't the greatest for fence riding or pleasure riding. Course, we don't do no pleasure riding like you think of. All riding gives me pleasure. At least most of the time, it does anyway."

This daring cow walked slowly till she was almost out of touch with the herd; then she sprinted, kicking up her heels in rebellion. Rodney's horse saw her before Rodney did. The horse went after the cow with such suddenness that a rider who didn't live half his life in the saddle would have landed on the ground. She had a thing about a cow getting by her. It was more than a game. No horse would get so stained in sweat and breathe so hard just playing.

The cow went over a mound of loose rock; the horse stumbled, fell, her front feet crumbling under her. Rodney lurched forward but stayed on. The long-legged horse kept on, over the mound and around it. Then the cow splashed into a wide pool. The horse leaped the pool and hit a step ahead of the black cow. Rodney had pulled his rope out in midair and lassoed the cow. Both Rodney and the horse were aggravated. They were going to make sure that they got her back, so they dragged her till she walked along like a good cow, into the center of the herd.

Davy told me that I had ridden long enough in the center of the herd. He'd been watching me, and I seemed to be doing pretty fair. "Why don't ya try ridin' up on the canyon? Keep 'em turned into the middle. You know what to do, right?"

"Yeah, right." I had been watching them all day.

Right away cows began breaking out on me. They must have known who I was. Breathing dust and shouting at them to move on were as easy as sleeping on a water bed, compared to this. If one would try getting away, I could handle that. Well, only if it wasn't real stubborn. Then twenty came right for me. Gene and Jeff had to go after them.

Cottonwood Canyon began curving to the right, like a bend in a river. Cool, almost cold winds blew down over the hot rock. The canyon ended, and before us was a grass-coated mountaintop pasture. Now we had to open a barbed-wire gate and drive the herd through it. I wasn't sure they could take any more pushing. It took a long time, but we got them through.

There were fields of grass, with an occasional leafless bush. We were up high enough to come across some clumps of aspen trees. Their leaves were turning a stunning yellow. The hills far off had turned a bluish green with the coming of night, and against them the glowing leaves of the aspens reminded me of stained glass windows. The men had closed the gate and were sitting on their horses, talking about the heat and the toughness of the day's drive. A couple of the men still had blood on their hands. All day, whenever they spotted a calf that had not been castrated or marked by having its ears cut, they'd rope it and do what had to be done. Rodney's leather chaps had long scratches where the thickets had ripped at his legs. His shirt was stiff with dried sweat.

It had been just another day for these cow people. Tomorrow could be worse; it might be better. The cows walked off with their calves, two by two, to bed down for the night. I hadn't thought about it till now, but how was I going to find Barbara and get back to Magic Valley? I rode over to Billy Williams. His white horse was coated with dust. His glasses were, too.

"Billy, how we gettin' back to the ranch?"

"I reckon someone from the association is going to be waiting for us by the windmill, up there."

"Where?" I didn't see any windmill.

"'Bout a mile from here." Oh, no. I didn't know if I could stay in this saddle for another mile. Every time the horse set down a tired hoof, it would shoot pain into me. Every step and my knees couldn't take another one. We rode to the windmill. No one was there. We could see tire tracks. Davy figured they'd been here long before. We would have to ride our horses home. I wanted to sleep here; I'd never make it another fifteen miles.

Rodney and Gene kept going higher into the mountains, through some aspen, by an ancient log cabin. They lived in the cow camp, somewhere up there. Davy said he'd gallop back and hope he'd run into the person with the horse trailer who was supposed to pick us up. A cloud of dust and the sound of hooves on a hard dirt road and he was gone. How could his body take more? I rode for a while; then I had to get off and walk or, rather, limp.

A couple of hours later we ran into Barbara, Charlotte, Mr. Brockman and his daughter. They'd found about 200 head and driven them back in the Sawtooth. Barbara was walking, too.

A lot more time passed. It got dark. We could see the lights of ranch houses off in the valley below. Billy stayed with us and so did the others. I think they felt kind of bad for us. Back at the windmill I drank like a cow. Even dunked my whole head in. The air was so dry my hair was brittle in less than a half hour.

Then we saw the pickup, just as we were beginning our final climb down in the valley. Davy said, "Listen, you two did good. In a few weeks we'll be coming up here again. It'll be OK if you want to help out." It was too dark to see if he was smiling as he closed the gate on the trailer. I couldn't sit down, so I stood in the back of his pickup. I wasn't sure if I ever wanted to see a saddle again.

34

The Double Cross Brand

W. T. Williams was seventy-seven and as unforgettable as a soaring mountain. I'll never forget what W.T. did when we were standing around one of their corrals.

He grabbed my right hand. "You feel this," he said as he pushed it onto his chest, against something that felt strange.

"They say I came pretty close to dyin' not too long back. Well, I had this ol' heart attack. My chest hurt and they took me to the hospital in Twin Falls." A farm truck filled with corn silage drove in from the corn fields to the south. Fine-grained dust cut off our view. I coughed and W.T. breathed as deep as ever. Breathing dust was almost patriotic around this part of Idaho.

"The nurses, they said they massaged my chest first, whatever that means. They said I was lyin' there dead. Well, then they said they started poundin' on me. Still, my ol' heart wouldn't start up, so they gave me a jump start. They 'bout jumped up and down on me. Beat so hard they broke a rib. My ol' ribs sure have been sore since. I guess they did get me goin'." Another truck dumped a load of leaf-green silage on what was becoming a hill of feed for winter. It took a lot to feed as big a herd of cattle as the Williamses' through winter, till they were driven back into the Sawtooth Forest next spring.

"This here thing you been feelin', that's my pacemaker. I stayed at the hospital 'bout six weeks. While I was there, they opened up my chest and put it in. Lately I've been feelin' a bit tired. Maybe my batteries are runnin' down."

We moved over by a corral the boys had made themselves. There were eight horses picking at hay. W.T. told me to hold out my hand again. This time he reached in his pocket and dropped something into it. It was a three-ounce nugget of gold. It had been in his pocket for twenty years of overalls and Levi's. Three cock pheasant rocketed from the corn field; they'd been flushed by one of the Williamses' many dogs. W.T. said they inherited stray dogs " 'bout as fast as them ASPCA people.

"Them six weeks in that hospital, well, I ain't never been down for more than a day or two in my whole life. They were feedin' me through my veins, taking my blood every day. I was never so hungry. You know some of them people told me that meat was bad for me and my heart. Can you imagine that! Pete"—W.T. motioned toward their house—"let's go have us a big steak." We got inside and Mrs. Williams, as small as W.T. was big, was building her own mountain of food on the table. In a minute there would be six or seven men around this table. I don't know how they knew the food was on. This meal was the highlight of their day and they just sensed the table was piled high as if they had extrasensory powers when it came to T-bones, cornbread, coleslaw, macaroni and chocolate cakes.

Tommy was the last one to sit down. Mrs. Williams said, "Now, we don't worry about big-city manners here. Everybody just puts their head down and eyes this here food. Then no one sees how everyone else is eatin'." Tommy was their youngest son and a devout Mormon. Right then I became a devout T-bone eater. The Williamses ate steaks almost as big as a pony's saddle.

After lunch everyone went back to cutting corn. Billy and Tommy were the Williamses' two children. Billy was forty-two and he had two sons, Rex and Jeff, and one daughter, Anna. Rex was married and had given Mrs. Williams her first great-granddaughter. Rex and Karla lived in a trailer five miles or so down the road toward Twin. Twin is what everyone called Twin Falls for short. Their trailer was on the north end of the ranch. Rex was a few years younger than I was and was growing a dark red beard and had a wide-toothed grin. Every one of the grandsons wore jeans. If you stood a thousand cowboys up side by side in Idaho, you'd have a rainbow of blues. Rex was built like W.T., Tommy and Billy were on the thin side, "like they ain't never seen a full table." They could polish off two full tables a meal, though, Mrs. Williams said. They were both deceptively strong and had the stamina of long-haul sled dogs.

Billy's other son, Jeff, twenty-three, was the tallest of the five grandsons, darkly handsome, and a good roper. He, like all the other grandsons, had grown up right here on the ranch.

Billy's marriage had not worked out, we heard somewhere. Ranchers don't talk much about anything, much less about things that have to do with feelings. It's even hard to get them to talk about the government. Like W.T. said one time, "This country's been great as long as I can remember. Some years we get Presidents, and them in the Senate, that mess things up for us farmers and cowmen more than usual, but then they might be helpin' some other people. Like them in the cities. Then other times we get Presidents, maybe they been reared on the farm. Then they might be good to us. It comes and it goes. Good times. Bad times. We ain't got time to worry about what they're doing in Washington. All we can do is keep our cows healthy, pray for the weather, and keep the family full of good steaks. The main thing, Pete. We're free." Just being around W.T. made me feel secure.

Life on ranches whose boundaries can strain your eyes, where your neighbor might be ten miles away, is hard on anyone. Like it said on a pickup bumper sticker, "Only Cowgirls Are Brave Enough to Marry Cowboys."

A lot of girls marry cowboys before they know what they're getting into. Most cowboys I knew enjoyed being coated with straw from a day's haying or covered with grease from fixing a broken-down combine. They got all of the culture they needed by watching a mama golden eagle teach her young one how to fly, going to church or listening to Merle Haggard sing. They were dressed up if they had a clean shirt, jeans and their best cowboy boots, with the deluxe stitching. A tie and a suit were for funerals or the bicentennial.

Barbara

Mrs. Williams and I sat on the edge of the gray, weathered fence, watching her favorite mare trot around the corral. This mare was Mrs. Williams's pet. As we watched the muscular animal parade, Mrs. Williams asked me to call her Viola, but I couldn't bring myself to do that. It was deeply ingrained in me to respect my elders, and calling her by her first name was not a sign of respect where I came from. After all, she was seventy-two years old. She had been married fifty years. She said that she and Bill started out their married life as sheepherders, living in a log cabin with a newspaper for wall covering, orange crates for cabinets, and sagebrush as heating fuel.

She pointed to the south, to a mountain range in the distant horizon, and said they had bought up all the land from here at the ranch house to there. "Folks said we was lucky." She laughed. "It was plain hard work that got us all this land." She reached for a handful of corn silage to feed the mare. "I've spent the last fifty years takin' care of my boys, cookin' three square meals a day so they could put in a good day's work." I couldn't tell if she was complaining or bragging.

"Have you ever thought about hiring someone like a housekeeper or cook?" I asked innocently because I thought she needed help at her age. As soon as the words were out of my mouth, I realized I had said the wrong thing. I had insulted her. I would soon learn that a real ranching woman took to her kitchen, housekeeping, and meals like a mother bear to her cubs. That was her territory. No other woman, especially an outsider, was welcome. Mrs. Williams was happiest when she could stand over steaming pots on the stove and at the telephone. I had seen her in action as she would put a ten-course meal on their giant round laminated table (their pride and joy since someone had offered them $1,500 for it), all the while answering the phone, telling one ranch hand who came through the door where the boys were rounding up cattle, and directing another dust-covered man to the field where a few hands were harvesting corn. She was like the dispatcher, giving out assignments and keeping tabs on everything that happened with the Williams outfit.

And I would soon learn that she had a reputation for miles around as the best cook in Magic Valley. Her laminated table was always set and anyone who came through the door was welcome to put his feet under it. Even the milkman tried to deliver milk around noon so he could join the daily feast. And I would soon learn that Mrs. Williams felt she had done her job when a man and woman ate hearty, filling their plate two or three times. That was the best way to say thank you, to tell her how much you liked the meal. Peter pleased her and put away her food like a real cowboy.

"See that corn field over there, in front of the house?" She pointed north. "I griped all last year about that corn field and told the boys not to plant there again. I felt like I was in jail, couldn't see a thing."

I noticed the field was harvested and now she was able to look across the flatlands and see for miles.

Mrs. Williams slapped some dust off her jeans and looked me in the eye. "You call the Ramseys by their first names, Jack and Lucy, and they're old enough to be your parents. So why don't you call me Viola?" She scolded me in her high, quivery voice that sounded sweet even when she was trying to be tough. "Why, you and Peter make me feel old."

I didn't know what to say. She was dead serious. How could I tell her she reminded me of my grandma, even had the same first name as my grandma, was a little like her, and had that same high voice. But to me, Mrs. Williams was the youngest old woman I had ever known. She didn't seem seventy-two and didn't look it either. She kept her dark brown hair styled in a French roll, piled on the top of her head by her hairdresser every week. She had very few wrinkles, healthy-

looking skin, and round, adventurous eyes. She was a small
woman, not even five feet tall. Yet she had the spirit of the
frisky mare that pranced around us.

"Come here, baby," Mrs. Williams cooed, calling the
mare in a sing-song way. The mare poked her head between
Mrs. Williams and me, nudging for more corn silage.

It was late afternoon and a golden glow surrounded everything in sight, the haystacks, the barn, the corrals, the corn
and bean fields, the Sawtooth Mountains seventeen miles away,
and Mrs. Williams and her mare. It was a tender, soft moment
at the end of the day. Most of the hands had quit work and a
truck was leaving a trail of dust behind it, far off to our left.

Peter and Tommy Williams were strolling toward us,
talking in low, relaxed tones. They had been looking at the
mountain of corn silage that would be used to feed the Williamses' cattle through the coming winter. Mrs. Williams held
out her hand toward the mare, with an offering of grain. Peter
was stopping every so often, snapping pictures of the mellow
sunset and trying to catch Mrs. Williams and me unawares, as
we talked and she fed the horse.

Mrs. Williams let out a soft moan. "Oh-o-o-o-o," she
groaned. I couldn't imagine what was wrong.

"She's got my finger."

I could see her struggling with the mare.

"Oh-o-o-o-o. I can't get my finger out."

"Tom-m-m-my," she cried. Tommy and Peter heard her
cry and came running as fast as they could. Tommy grabbed
the mare's head, and with cowboy quickness and guts he grabbed
the horse's fat lips, pushed them back, clutched at the mare's
big teeth and began prying them open with all his strength. I
could see the mare resist as she slid her teeth back and forth,
obviously trying to keep on chewing. Tommy didn't cuss like
most cowboys, but he had the same hard edge to his voice as
he ordered that stubborn horse to open her mouth.

When Mrs. Williams finally pulled her tiny hand out of
the mare's jaws, the horse had bitten her little finger, exposing
it to the bone.

"You kids keep taking your pictures, I'll be back in a

minute." Mrs. Williams was smiling, though the finger must have hurt badly. She jumped down off the fence.

Tommy grabbed his handkerchief and wrapped her finger as he rushed her to his pickup and they sped off for the hospital in Twin Falls. I watched as they drove away, thinking what an incredible woman she was. She had not shed one tear. I sat stunned for several minutes, until the mare brushed at my arm and I nervously hopped off the fence.

A few hours later Tommy pulled the pickup into the dust-covered driveway and stopped. When he helped his mother out of the truck, she had her hand wrapped from her wrist to the tip of her little finger, which was stuck out on a plastic support.

"The doc fixed it where I can still use my hand to cook. Have to feed my boys," she said. It was clear that she was in a lot of pain, but she never let on. "Took over twenty stitches, and the doc said I was lucky to have a finger left."

After seeing her go through this, I would never again think of her as a grandmother-type or as Mrs. Williams. Now I saw her for who she was. She was Viola.

One night, while Barbara was helping Viola clear the table, Billy and I went outside. I asked him what was the most beautiful thing he could think of in the world. "You know them environmentalists think the land's beautiful with nothing on it. Well to me, the most beautiful thang is to see some fields that used to be choked by sagebrush, and dry as a desert, growing tall with green grass. The cattle, they're happy and fat and the aspens quake and are yella." A sky-filling bunch of rain clouds flew through the sky.

Billy thought a moment and said, "There's nothin' more pretty than when our cattle come home from out of them hills. I jus' love to see my favorite cows and find out how much weight their calves have put on. Ya know, see how much they grew while they were up in the hills."

Tommy, who was forty and Billy's brother, had a wife who was one "fine girl," W.T. said. They had three sons and

*Tommy holds the
trophies won by the
Williams' cattle at
many county fairs*

they lived in the finest home of any of the Williamses. It was
no mansion, or anything like that, but it was nice, bricked and
ranch style. It was also the newest home on the ranch. W.T.
and Viola talked of a new home for them, but they were used
to the one they lived in, and besides, they had five grandsons
that were all within marrying age. This ranch supported four
generations. Tommy and his family lived at the southern
boundary of the ranch, at the edge of the mountains. Wade
was their oldest. He was in college at Brigham Young University. Wyatt was the middle boy, feisty and blond. He loved
to trap coyotes and had graduated from high school in Filer.
Aaron was the youngest and still in high school. Their mama's
name was Elsie. She enjoyed living on the ranch and she
worked at one of the fine jewelry stores on Main Street in
Twin. She left the roping, branding and combining to her boys.
The few times we saw her she was dressed carefully and fash-
ionably. She was pretty, friendly and a devoted Mormon. I
always thought that Wyatt looked most like his mother, Elsie.
She had a sparkling smile.

One thing about the Williamses was obvious. Everyone
was allowed to be himself. And everyone was. Some places
I'd been where generations of family lived together, they all

dressed alike, talked alike and acted alike. The Williamses enjoyed the special and quirky qualities that made each of them different. One day, while Viola was hand-feeding a motherless calf, she got to talking about how it wasn't the easiest thing for four generations of any family to get along. All these stout, stubborn sons and grandsons and W.T. Then there were all the Williams women. "There ain't no ranch that runs and supports such a big family that can stay together with all kinds a family fightin' and orneriness. You just can't have that on a family ranch. You know that's one of the main reasons so many farms and ranches break up. People can't get along."

I heard the CB base station inside the house calling Mrs. Williams. Her call name was Double Cross Base. That's because the Williams brand was the double cross.

We went inside and there sat Alvin. He would sit in this one chair all day and into the night, never getting up, his head tilted down, his light blue work shirt buttoned right up to the top button. Alvin was sixty-three and Mrs. Williams's first cousin. His daddy, Mr. Greene, was her daddy's brother and they all grew up on homestead ranches in the area they called Soldier Creek. Viola's dad used to rope wild horses and tame them for her so she had something to ride to the neighbors on.

If someone tried to talk to Alvin, he might say a word or two; then again, he probably wouldn't. You might ask him a question, and he'd answer it three hours later. His voice had no fight; it just barely made it out of his mouth. Everyone tried to make sure that Alvin was included in all the work and conversation around the Williams ranch, but he rarely entered in. No one gave up on the fact that maybe someday he would. Before Billy or Tommy slammed the screen door, they always asked Alvin if he wanted to come. Alvin wouldn't even nod his head sometimes.

"Now that Alvin," W.T. told me later, "he might act some strange, but he's as smart as a genius. He can take apart and put together anything on this ranch, if he would. He always was kinda quiet, but since his mother died, then his father, well he ain't said or done much since." Alvin's chair was up against a wall, by some elk antlers and an old painting of snowcapped mountains.

Billy cutting the cattle toward home

At first I thought Alvin had something wrong with him. Maybe he was slow-witted. The way he hung his head and sad eyes down all day and all night, just sitting there, expressionless, regardless of how active or quiet things were around him. Then one day, after Alvin had been seeing me around for some weeks, he spoke. I'd been trying to talk with him since I first came through the door.

His head hung straight down and his eyes never looked anywhere near me, but he said, "I guess it's a far piece to be walkin' crosst Oregon. I never been there." His voice was almost like silence and had no inflection, like singing the same note for a whole song. Even when Alvin ate, he held his eyes down, fixed on the food. "He sure enough eats good," Viola would say more than she realized. She worried over Alvin and maybe she was worried about how we'd react to him.

His eyes were always bloodshot and watering. Billy said that was from that dry-land ranch he grew up on. So much dust had blown into his eyes through fifty years on tractors, plowing behind mules and living through the dust storms. His eyes seemed to be always crying. For an average-sized man, he had the big, dry hands of a man born on a working ranch. He rubbed his eyes all day long.

Alvin had been the Greenes' only child and he'd never

married. Someone said that he never even went on a date and that his parents would not let him leave the ranch. They needed him to work around the place, was what they'd say to Alvin. Viola told me one time, as we sat down to one of her mountains of food, that Alvin's parents were so poor and so tight with their money that they would use water on their cornflakes, instead of milk. The Williamses must have spent thousands a month keeping all their boys fed properly. Alvin's daddy was so tight with his money that they'd only leave that dust-blanketed ranch maybe two, three times a year.

When Mr. Greene died, well into his eighties, it had been just him and Alvin on the ranch for many years. Alvin's mama died long before. He'd inherited the ranch, but there was no way he could live by himself at Soldier Creek and run the place. Especially if he just sat in one chair all day. Someone told us that silent Alvin had a fortune in the bank. The Williamses took good care of Alvin. He loved to pile gravy all over his juicy steaks. It wasn't till I got to know Alvin and this man-busting land that I could understand the way he was. The land could break a man's back. It could snap your mind, if you were trying to survive on its stingy, dry surface. It could disintegrate your desire to fight back, and back, and back after droughts, death, rustling, floods, meanness, and water on your cornflakes. A man and woman had to fight so hard to get their hands on anything, it made them afraid to let it go. This land made people and it broke people. Idaho made W.T.

We got into W.T.'s blue pickup. He wanted to show me a dam he had made up by Cottonwood Creek. Water was everything in this part of the West. Never before had I ever heard people talk about water the way they did around here. From central Texas through New Mexico, Colorado, Utah and now Idaho, water was talked about as much as they talked about the Civil War in the South, football in Ohio and fine food in New York. W.T. loved water. He made me want to be happy when it rained.

W.T. took me on a ride down miles of dirt roads to a place called Goat Springs. He said that once Billy saw a black panther there. A cloud of dust rose behind us as we sped south.

"W.T., where does the Williams ranch begin and end?" I asked him. He had on his straw cowboy hat. His head always seemed to tilt to the right and his eyes had the piercing qualities of a prophet.

"You see them mountains?"

"Where?" I could see something far off.

"Them." He pointed far off.

"Yeah. How far are they?"

"'Bout fifteen miles, maybe more, maybe less. I ain't sure how far we've driven," W.T. said.

"Well, what about those mountains?"

"The ranch ends at those mountains and begins way north a here, down by where Rex lives."

I was staggered, thinking of it all. Just think of standing on the back porch of a modest ranch house, like the one that W.T., Viola and Alvin lived in, and looking at some mountains fifteen, twenty miles south and knowing you owned all that.

"How many acres do you have, W.T.?" Then I remembered a man we'd met in West Texas, Don Jackson. He'd told me once that asking a farmer or rancher how much land he owns is like asking a man how much he has in the bank. I couldn't retract my question fast enough.

"Let's just say it's more than the hundred sixty acres I homesteaded fifty-six years ago in 1922. You know, this whole thing started with only a horse and a dog."

A coyote was running through a field almost 200 acres big that was a giant green circle in the middle of the desert. It was watered by a revolving sprinkler system that cost close to $100,000, just for the sprinkler. That's where they grew some of their hay for their cattle, W.T. said.

"Were you born here in Idaho?" I asked.

"No, sir, I wasn't. I was born near Bethlehem, Pennsylvania, in 1901. 'Round the steel mills. There weren't much of a future back there in them days. Some man visited us around 1908 and told the folks 'bout Idaho. What a beautiful place it was, how a man could get free land if he had a mind to work it. Improve it. So we all moved here to Twin Falls. Came on the train."

We pulled up a rutted desert road that led east to Goat Springs.

"When we first got here, we lived in a tent. That tent blew down the first day and we been trying to win out with the wind ever since. My folks, they took a contract to clear one hundred acres of sagebrush with a team. They got the team of horses as pay, then rented 'em some land and grew hay. But to get back to your question."

He stopped the pickup in the midst of some wild scrubland and got out. I followed.

"I wanted my own land worse than anything. The day I was twenty-one, in 1922, it was, I homesteaded on one hundred sixty acres. All I had in the world was a sheep dog and a horse. Been workin' as a sheepherder till I turned twenty-one. I promised I wasn't gonna work for no one but myself, so I built me a tar-paper shack. It was only ten feet wide and twelve foot long. Made it out of scrounged wood and stuffed the cracks with newspaper."

W.T. walked toward a skeleton of something. "Had an ol' barrel for a wood stove. Used ol' dry sagebrush for heat. Some nights that first winter, it'd go down to thirty below. I had to make my sheep dog sleep on my feet. I was gonna clear that flat, dry ground of sagebrush and go to ranchin', no matter what come at me."

This was hard for me to believe, that I was walking and talking to a still-living pioneer. The kind I'd only heard about or read about. Even at Perk's, the stories came from one or two generations back. This Idaho was so young. To think they were giving chunks of it away just a little more than fifty years ago. To think that this man came with his family as a boy, started with a horse and a dog, and now had a ranch whose southern boundary went all the way to those mountains.

W.T. kicked the skeleton. A gray-colored chipmunk had built her nest under it and ran away. She stood brazenly under the shade of a grandaddy sagebrush and told us in no uncertain terms how mad she was at W.T. The man had a heart that could melt as easily as a late summer snow. W.T. bent down and put the skeleton back just the way it was.

"I remember when Billy used to ride ol' Tybol. That was the boy's favorite horse and he'd ride that old pinto to school. Billy'd turn Tybol loose around the school and it'd graze all day till Billy called for it. He rode that pinto to school every day, from the first grade through the eighth. Never missed a day." Billy never missed a day of work either.

"Now some would say I ain't too good a man 'cause I don't go to church too regular. If I ever did join a church, I should join Tommy's. When I had my heart attack, those good Mormon people, they prayed for me a time or two, and I can't say that it didn't help me 'cause I'm still here."

W.T. pulled a long bronze wire out of his back pocket. It was about as thick as fence wire but very flexible. I was about to find out why he had brought me out here. Not only could he "witch" water with a stick, but he told me he could walk over the ground with this flexible wire in his hands and find streams of water, veins of gold and other metals.

"Here, you try it, Pete." He handed me the wire. With anyone else I would have felt silly, but with W.T. it seemed possible.

"Now most people think this idea of mine is crazy, but then that's what they always said 'bout me. Even when I put in my dams or drilled my deep wells. I think you got what it takes to do this ESPin', Pete." He called it ESPin' for lack of a better word. He had me walk up a dirt road and when I passed over a vein or some metal deep in the earth, the wire was supposed to begin bouncing and pointing down. He said that he had been developing this talent all his life and now he didn't need a wire or anything else. He told me that he could "feel" what was under the ground. Whether it was oil, gas, gold, water or whatever. He said it was something like the gift they talk about in the Bible called prophecy. He just knew things.

"You know, son. One reason why this ol' land ain't never beat me is because I always had dreams bigger than this ranch. If only I could have gotten my hands on a bunch of millions to go prospecting for oil and gold. Now that was my big dream. I probably ain't never gonna get the chance to do it now 'cause I got to hand this ranch down to all the boys and their families."

If anyone had extrasensory perception, W.T. did. By now the chipmunk had darted back to her nest in the skeleton. The CB in W.T.'s pickup was calling him. Viola's high-pitched, high-energy voice told us to get on home. Jack Ramsey, their banker was coming over for lunch.

"Hell, ever since I done had that ol' heart attack, the boys been treatin' me like a silent partner. The boys been running everything. They don't pay much attention to me anymore. Then let 'em make a mistake and I'm a full partner again." W.T. drove these dirt roads looking everywhere but where he was going. I hoped he had memorized them.

"You know, when I started this ranch, all I had was some free land that could barely feed my horse and my hairy sheep dog and a strong back. There was no such thing as money in my pocket then. You know it ain't been much over fifty years that's passed and I still don't have much money in my pocket."

He paused and slowed down as three of their dogs came out to meet W.T.'s pickup. "Now our ranch has to borrow almost a million dollars a year, every year, just to keep things going. Sometimes more. Now that's more money than I ever thought I'd hear tell of in five lifetimes. Today it takes that much every year just to keep things going and to cover expenses."

He got out faster than usual and went straight over to one of their biggest dogs. It looked like ol' Yeller. W.T. shook his head. "That fool dog's been up runnin' in the mountains again. Look-it here. It's got into a porcupine." There were quills in its nose and some were working their way into the dog's eyes. W.T. went inside and got Tommy and Rex. They pulled as many of the quills out of the yellow dog as they could. Jack Ramsey, the banker, who looked like no other banker I'd ever seen, held the dog down. He was dressed in blue splattered jeans, a flannel shirt and a Pendleton Mills vest. His cowboy hat was turned up sharp on the edges and was somewhere between Billy's and W.T.'s as far as vintage.

Of course, no one on the planet Earth wore a hat like Billy. His family joked that Billy's hat looked like it had been eaten by a bunch of mice and glued back together. Or buried in a silage pit for a decade and then unearthed by scientists.

Billy loved his hat. W.T.'s hat was in good shape. This banker's hat had a lot of character, too.

Jack, Billy and Tommy and a pack of dogs went walking through the fields, talking business. W.T. said he had been leaving that up to the boys lately.

"I know for a fact that one of our neighbor ranchers near here borrows three million *every* year." Near here could mean within one hour's drive "And that's a family ranch just like this one. Ten percent interest a year on that kind of money, that's three hundred thousand dollars, just in interest! Now that's a heap of money. You listen to me, Pete." W.T.'s tone was no different from when he talked of digging irrigation trenches with a team of mules. "That's not just one loan; that's *every* year. That don't matter if people quit eatin' meat or if them foreigners bring in all their cheap beef or anything else." I could see the banker walking in between Billy and Tommy, his head down, deep in figuring.

"I never thought I'd see it come to this, but without our bank, Idaho First, there'd be no Williams ranch. Without them bankers givin' us ranchers and farmers these loans, there'd be no food, no cotton, no meat, no nothin'. You know, only four percent of us grow all the food."

The thought of borrowing $3,000 for a car frightened me. The interest on a $3 million loan had to be paid back in one year, and it could amount to $6,000 a week in interest payments alone.

"Every year we got to pay the salaries for all the boys and the hired hands and cowboys. Then there's all the taxes and Social Security. I doubt the younguns will ever see any of that money. There's John Deere tractors. You know some of them things can cost over seventy-five thousand dollars. We have a big bunch of tractors around here. Then we need combines and trucks to haul what we cut. We need sprinklers big enough to water one hundred sixty acres at a time. Should we use Zimmatic or some other kind? We got Ford pickups and Chevies. We got to buy a new John Deere press drill soon; the old one is 'bout wore out." (That was used to plant the wheat.)

"Then we got all kinds of vet bills, and medicine for heel

Viola's down-home cooking was famous throughout southern Idaho
LEFT TO RIGHT: *W.T., Alvin, Billy, Peter, Viola*

fly, and a thousand other things that can go wrong with our cattle. Just the electricity to run our pumps and sprinklers and stuff costs in the thousands every month."

The Williamses had often talked of hiring a cook and getting a big dishwasher. Viola said it would make her feel she was retired and old. Besides, that cost money. "Hell, just fertilizer can cost hundreds for every acre. Nowadays they even have crop insurance. And it never ends. I wonder what the boys will be borrowin' from Jack this year, much less twenty years from now when they'll be talkin' to Jack's son. He's a banker, too. A million a month? A million a week?"

Jack, Billy and Tommy were in the ranch house. This banker usually met Billy in his office in Twin, but he knew where the best steaks in the country were served. At Viola's table.

35

Ridin' Fences

A bright flash caught my attention. I was washing myself awake in a winter-cold spring when one of Rodney's spurs splashed the sunlight in my eyes. This was to be our first full day living with Rodney and Carol Hopwood at the Shoshone Basin cow camp. Rodney and Carol lived here over half of every year, in a log cabin or a small trailer that looked like a sheepherder's outfit.

Their water was running from a pipe stuck into a spring by one of the stands of aspens that shielded this camp. The spring and the lonely rock cliffs that surrounded this camp on three sides were the reason that cowboys had been living here as long as the ranchers in the valley could remember.

It was a cutting, crisp Idaho morning and now that my face was awake from the slaps of springwater, I watched Rodney. He was sitting on the ground, leaning against his favorite saddle.

Rodney had a thick curved needle in his right hand and he was sewing a tear in his leather chaps. These chaps were thick leather leggings worn every day to protect him from the thorn-infested thickets where cattle often headed if Rodney, Carol or Gene tried to rope them. Gene was the other cowboy who rode these ridges, valleys and canyons. Gene always rolled the sleeves of his western shirts up high. His tan hair and darker beard blended in with his western face. When you looked at this quiet cowboy, the only way you could tell that you weren't back seventy-five years in the Old West was that he wore a watch with a stainless steel band. It stood out against his tan forearms, which were coated with sweat, dirt and dust.

I watched the way that Rodney and Carol treated their tools, their gear. I noticed Rodney's saddle, worn from years of horse sweat, fall thunderstorms and winter blizzards. He treated it like a living thing. That same care was shown to their working boots, dulled by exposure, cut by barbed wire. They treated their stiff lassos and their cast-iron frying pans the same way.

Carol came out of the trailer. Her hair was pulled back in a brown ponytail. She and Rodney were both in their early twenties. Two cats ran up to her. One was black and white; that was Sylvester. The other was yellow and white and its name was Puddin. Carol stopped and put her strong arms on her hips. The cats rolled on top of her boots. Maybe they could smell the sick Hereford bull they had to rope and drag out of the roadless area where they'd found him. He was worth all kinds of money, that bull. Carol said the bull was real weak. Rodney said Carol was a lot of help.

"Yep, she's as good at this cowboyin' as any man."

Their two dogs, which were as important to them as their saddles and horses, were Australian shepherds. Shorty and Shadow crawled out from under the cabin. It was cozy and warm under there and they had run hard yesterday. Carol had told us last night, while Rodney cooked T-bones bigger than a big plate could hold, that Gene had had to shoot his two dogs last week.

"Gene, he really loved them dogs, too. Sure was a sad thing, but they went and killed our goat, Josephine. If they start killin' stock, they might kill a calf next."

Carol Hopwood used to be Carol Brockman, the oldest daughter of one of the ranchers in the valley. Rodney's folks were working people from Buhl, a farming and ranching town up the road a good piece. That day, while we rode toward

Carol Hopwood,
cowboy

Mahogany Butte, Carol did most of the talking. Carol was straightforward pretty. She wore glasses with tortoiseshell rims that were sort of round and in fashion and turned dark in the sunlight. She wore a blue and white baseball cap. She was trim and had thin lips and alert blue eyes. She wore jeans as if she were born in them and a hand-cut belt with a leather buckle.

"It was spring, and I was ridin' with my dad pushin' our cows onto the forest. Rodney was the head cowboy like he is now. I was on my horse Toby." (Toby was a gelding and a bay with a slick, shiny coat. Carol said he was a mutt.)

"I don't know, I might have seen Rodney ride before, but that day the air smelled special, and it was cool. First I just noticed the way he rode. He looks so good on a horse." She looked over to see if Rodney heard that. He had.

"Of course, he doesn't look so good on his feet." Rodney spurred Paint, his horse, pretending he was mad. He jerked the reins back; the horse's front hooves flew into the air.

"I decided that sometime that day I'd talk to him. We'd moved the cows up onto the forest and were just sittin' 'round on our horses, looking over the cows and the newest calves. I just rode over and started talking."

"What did you talk about? The weather?" Barbara asked, reining in her horse, which was always wanting to gallop.

"Probably whose cows looked best. Rodney was the shy, silent-cowboy type. While we waited for all them cattle to mother up, we just talked. We went out awhile later to a Chinese place in Twin Falls called Koto's. That was special 'cause Rodney don't like drivin' a car in all that traffic; big cities get him nervous. But 'bout six months later we were married."

Rodney and Carol loved riding together. It was October 10. Today, all day, we would reride the southernmost end of this 87,000-acre chunk of national forest where Rodney, Carol and Gene watched over about 6,000 head of cows and calves. Many of the calves had been born here since their mamas turned out on April 1. The cattle belonged to the nine ranchers who were members of the Western Stock Growers Association. There were about 200 head of bulls mingled in.

"We get paid for doing what we like to do more than anything else, being up here with these cows, where it's quiet and nobody to bother us. Cowboyin' is the best job in the world," Carol said.

Rodney was teaching me how to wrangle. One horse was kept in the corral all night, while the rest of the horses were allowed to graze in the eaten-down brush. They picked around for occasional blades of bunch-grass, roaming over a couple of hundred acres. I saddled my horse while Rodney watched. I felt like a second grader learning how to spell.

Rodney or Gene normally did this wrangling every morning. "All you do is ride up to the horses kinda slow. Not too slow; they'll get jittery, suspicious-like. Most of 'em will probably be grazin' over there at the base of the butte, by that small bunch of aspen trees. When you get on the other side of 'em, start movin' toward 'em, slow. See if you can get 'em comin' along toward me. I'll open the gate when you get 'em over to the corral. It ain't hard."

The horse I saddled was a bony white one. They usually kept him there because he wasn't much good to ride and they used him just to wrangle. No horse got retired around these ranges. If it couldn't run the canyons, it wrangled. If it couldn't wrangle, it was used to teach the grandchildren how to ride.

They were right where Rodney said they would be. I got around them, then moved the old white horse slowly toward them. They moved closer together. Then a heavy-muscled bay ran toward the stand of trees. I rode around the trees and kicked my horse lightly, so he'd go in after them. They walked and nibbled nervously, till they hit the open ground, then ran. The white horse sprinted after them, then helped turn them toward the deep-cut horse trail that led to the corral. Rodney was sitting in the sun on the far side, as if he weren't expecting to see me again for a long time. He opened the gate, fast, and the horses were in, surrounded by a cloud of dust. It was morning dust, heavy and cool.

"That ain't too bad, Pete. Here, rope you a horse."

Some happy bird sang, perched on top of a fence post. I could understand why it sang on this mellow morning. The sagebrush glowed yellow.

"You get yours first." I handed Rodney back the rope.

I'd seen him, Gene and Carol rope their horses dozens of times, but I'd never paid close attention. He got the horses to walk around the outside edge of the corral in a circle; then he walked inside them and started swinging his stiff rope. It whizzed over his head. It was like a dance. Rodney was getting into the rhythm of the horses' steps. Once they all got going around and around, Rodney picked out the horse he wanted to ride. He placed the rope around its neck as if it were standing still.

I tried to get the horses to go around in that smooth circle. They wouldn't move. I tried to rope the pinto with the long back while they stood still. They each dodged the rope. When I threw the rope, it looked like a shot duck. I finally got them moving. When I threw the rope again, they stopped. How come it looked so easy when Rodney did it? I handed

Nothing like a dust bath after a long day's work

the rope back, but Rodney wouldn't take it. It took awhile, but I roped the pinto I was to ride. That rope landed in a lot of other places first.

I roped Carol's horse, Barbara's and Gene's. It took us longer to get going that morning, but then it was a rare morning that Rodney had the chance to laugh until it hurt.

That day we were going to do what was called reriding. In reriding the cowboys would ride to the far ends of their range, where they had already opened the gates and see if there were any cows that they'd missed the first time through. Almost always they'd missed a couple of head. After all, there was no way they could ride every square inch of the 87,000 acres. Even if they could, the cattle would avoid them. They would just do the best they could reriding and hope that the next snow would not be a blizzard, the kind that could strand cattle.

Today we were headed for the southern border, toward Nevada. I'd always thought Nevada was nothing but gambling and desert, but Rodney told me, as we rode south, down a dirt trail, that the part of Nevada that we were riding toward had some of the best ranches around. He said that the cowboyin' that went on in Nevada was as close to the old-time way as there was. He made it sound as if they were space-age cowboys.

"I know an ol' boy down in that part of Nevada." He pointed south; we were on top of a butte covered with only sage and rabbit brush, and we could see into Nevada. I saw nothing for over 100 miles, no lights, no fences, no roads, no ranch houses, no jet trails, no nothing. It was one of the most beautiful views in the world.

"We used to ride together when I was just learnin'. Now that man, he can ride." We stopped. "There ain't no rodeo cowboy that can come close to Tim Connant." Rodney's voice got passion in it. "Ya know, rodeo ain't the real thing. This is. Rodeo lasts only a few seconds, no longer than a minute. Now I done a lot of team ropin', bronc ridin' and all that. But there ain't no comparison to rodeo and what we do for a livin'. When we rope cattle out in the open range, like we done that day we drove that herd up Cottonwood Canyon, now that's it. There ain't no fence to keep the cows in, and there are no canyon walls for the rodeo steers to run up. We do it all day long."

I saw the slightest puff of dust coming off the brush, miles below us in a wide, scrubby valley. It was Carol and Barbara. Gene was opposite us, five miles away on the other ridge.

"Yep, Tim rides for the Bell Brand ranch. That man can rope anything that moves. He's one of the few cowboys good enough to ride down a coyote and rope it. Now that horse he's got, you ain't gonna see nothin' like it ever. It can run down a coyote in the open range, just so long as there ain't too much cover. And a coyote can run fast and jerk and twist like a whirlwind, but it gets tired pretty fast. If you got a good horse that can cut and stop with that coyote, you can tire 'em down, then rope 'em. You got to be fast and good."

After trying that morning to rope those slow-moving horses in a tiny corral and after seeing how fast a coyote could run, I couldn't imagine roping a coyote from a running, zig-zagging horse.

"Tim, he done told me coyotes are easy to rope. He said he done roped bobcat and even a mountain lion. He said the hard thing was gettin' the mountain lion loose. His buddy had roped its back legs."

To think that a boy from the suburbs could be reriding the range, pushing straggling cattle, wrangling a string of horses and hearing stories about roping coyotes! Sometimes I had to almost fall off the horse to believe this was for real.

The first day I'd met Rodney and Carol, I had tried to call them cow-persons, half a joke, half serious. I figured Carol might be insulted at being called a cow'boy.' Carol was very feminine, intelligent, loved pretty lace curtains and getting dressed up. But she hated being called a cowperson.

"You just call me a cowboy." She wasn't worried about words; she could do everything a cowboy could and that was enough.

Rodney and I rode as fast as our horses would carry us, through the brush, jumping dried stream beds, sidestepping loose rocks. We galloped like this for hours, for miles, on and on, never coming to a fence.

Only three times did we find some stray head. We had no time to drive them, so we just got them moving in the right direction. We rode through dried weeds, almost as high as the horses' bellies. The weeds had pods on them filled with dry seeds. When we brushed against them, they rattled, sounding exactly like a nest of rattlesnakes. I kicked my horse even faster until I caught up with Rodney. What's that noise? I asked.

"Jest some dried weed," Rodney drawled, cowboylike.

They rattled all afternoon as we covered the range, Rodney looking easy and relaxed. I had to concentrate every second. I just knew one trip or jump or cut, and I'd be off. I fell only once.

By lunchtime we'd ridden across the range. We hobbled the horses, took off their saddles, watered them and the dogs. Then we ate. Rodney lay on his back, and Carol laid her head on his stomach for a pillow. I knew that as long as I lived, I would never forget riding through that wide, open range. Barbara sat in sagebrush shade, eating an apple, while Gene watered the horses in an old galvanized tub.

Alvin's old homeplace, the Green ranch

"Ever had cowboy coffee?" Rodney asked as he gathered some dried cow patties and brush to start a fire. He got an old empty coffee can, filled it with water out of the pipe that ran into the horse's watering hole, dumped a handful of coffee grounds into the can and sat it in the middle of the fire.

"Jest let it boil till it gets good and thick. It'll keep a cowboy in the saddle."

The Idaho sun, the broken sagebrush branches, the boiling coffee scenting the air, watching Rodney ride, remembering the dust of Carol and Barbara miles across the horizon and feeling the warmth of my horse radiating up into my sore legs would make me want to be a cowboy the rest of my life. I loved this open land.

Tomorrow we would return to the Williams ranch. I was going to learn how to throw a steer.

Billy was the only one of us on a horse. There were two corrals at Alvin's old home place, the Greene ranch, and we had a couple of hundred head of cattle to work.

There was a big corral and a small one. This ranch and

these corrals had changed very little since the 1930's. The fences were of thin logs or rough-cut boards and some of them were practically falling down.

We had to move this small herd from the big corral through a narrow wood gate into a much smaller one. Once we did that, then we had to look over every one of them. We were looking for calves that were five to six months old that had never been branded, earmarked or vaccinated. If we found one, we'd separate it from its mother and keep it in the far end of the corral.

Everyone was here, even Alvin. Each one of us had a job. The excitement in the dry air made it obvious that all the Williamses couldn't wait to get started. Rex said they got a bigger rush, a bigger thrill, out of branding when the calves were this size than when they were small. These calves had been born up in the mountains and weighed as much as 450 pounds. The biggest ones were the little "baby bulls."

We found about twenty calves and now they were the only ones left in the corral. Some of the calves tried to climb over the fence that kept them from their mothers and they broke some of the old boards on the fence with one kick. On his horse Billy roped the back legs of about a 300-pounder and called: "Get 'em, Rex."

Rex ran up to the frantically kicking, bug-eyed calf and reached over its back, grabbed hold of its front and rear legs, and flipped it down to the dirt. Billy roped another one. "Pete, throw this one."

I ran up to it as it bucked, darted and kicked the air. Then I reached over the way Rex had. Right then the little 350-pound bull jumped up and its protruding backbone hit me right in the stomach and knocked the wind out of me. I fell to the ground, instead of the calf.

"Come on, Pete, this here is only a calf." Billy's horse tightened the slack. There was a hint of a grin in the corners of Billy's mouth.

I grabbed the bull again, but he didn't want to be thrown. I hung on as he dragged me across the corral. Then Wyatt ran over and both of us took hold of that "baby" and threw him down. Once he was down, Rex showed me how to hold him there. It was like trying to hold down the defensive line of a football team alone.

Somehow the calf got up and ran, faster and more carelessly. I leaped up and chased him across the corral, fine dust coating the streams of sweat on my face. He stopped in a corner, then heard his mother bawl, and he burst for the gate. I made a flying jump for him and pulled him down again.

Barbara was helping Tommy build a sagebrush fire to heat the branding irons. Alvin would hand the red hot irons to W.T., who did the branding. Then Tommy would make the bulls into steers.

Alvin did all the vaccinations for blackleg and Aaron filled the needles. Billy roped and caught their hind legs from high up on his horse only because Jeff (the best roper on the ranch) was in California. Rex, Wyatt and I threw the calves. Sometimes they were so strong it took two of us. Jim, the hired hand, did the dehorning.

It took until sunset. The coals of the branding fire dimmed and turned to ash quickly. W.T. had started with a homestead and a horse and a dog. I looked over the corral to see Billy and one of his dogs riding over to the horse trailer so they could load up and go home. The never ending work of throwing calves and branding hadn't changed since W.T. was twenty-one. A million other things had. One thing was certain: Sunrise would start another day on the Williams ranch.

As we drove home in Billy's pickup, right past Tommy's house, Billy stopped in the middle of the road. He pointed up on a barren hill where a mule deer buck stood. When we stopped, the buck bounded off. Billy didn't say anything, but I knew it was seeing things like that buck that kept him looking forward to the next sunrise.

36

Our Oregon Trail

Everything said fall. But this was a western fall, an Idaho fall. There were leaves that fell from the trees, but the trees were almost as far apart as eagles in the sky. In Magic Valley there were fewer trees and a lot more eagles than in most places. Almost all the aspen leaves were gone and Barbara and I were taking our saddles off our horses at the cow camp's corral. Rodney and Carol were doing the same. Soon there would be no more cattle for Rodney and Carol to watch and drive and lasso here in the Sawtooth Mountains. In a few weeks they'd be packing up their red pickup, gathering up their string of horses and moving back into the valley to their trailer.

The falling of the aspen leaves, the driving of the cattle down the canyons and hunting season also meant the coming of blizzards. Blizzards in Colorado were one thing, they said, taking nothing away from their killer qualities, but the blizzards that blew over this ornery ground could not be slowed down by a stubborn mountain. No fence, no butte, no huddled mass of cattle could stop the snow-filled winds. No cowboy, not even cows, could take the winter in this part of the Sawtooths.

I thought of our Colorado cabin and felt a nostalgia for winter, looking forward to the soaking warmth of a fire, being inside while the storm clouds hurled down their snow, wiping the condensed moisture off the window to see that outside, the thermometer was 10 below zero, feeling the winds blow through the cracks of the logs and hearing them wail all the way down the chimney.

All four horses were taking turns rolling in the deep, dusty dirt in their favorite spot in the corral. It was their way of freshening up after a hard day's ride. Rodney and Carol said they'd miss sitting by an ash-covered fire when the moon lit the canyons purple. They'd also miss getting to take their special baths. They had an old-timey bathtub at the camp, set in a grove of aspens and pine. Carol said that she liked nothing better than that bath. She and Rodney would cowboy all day and come home to the grove and Rodney would build a sage-brush fire right next to the tub. Then they would heat up buckets of water until the tub was full. Carol had a picture of Rodney in the tub in the middle of the bony-looking aspens. He had his hat on.

Barbara shook out her horse blanket and put it in the shed with the saddles. She said she wanted to take a walk up the hill before dinner. Rodney always cooked T-bones, and Carol had baked some country-fair-good apple pies in their tiny stove.

"Peter, what do you think we should do this winter?" It was sneaking up on us faster than I thought it should be. Barbara looked worried.

"Well, we have two choices. We can stay around here or we can move on."

"What do you think we should do?" Barbara sat on a rock. We could see far, almost to Nevada.

I had to think about this. If we did keep going, we would have to walk through this coming winter. I knew we could be out of Idaho before the hard part of the season hit. But what about Oregon? I'd never seen the state, but I had an idea that it would be more mild, with ancient moss-covered trees, a lot of bearded joggers, flannel shirts, loggers and heavy fog. I doubted Oregon could have any harsh blizzards or punishing land in it. So many picture books I'd seen seemed to back that up.

If we stopped for the winter, the walk would stretch past six years. I felt it was time to end this journey. I knew Barbara was ready to have a place of her own for a change, and I'd spent five years of my life crossing the country.

We would walk on, toward the Pacific, winter, and whatever Oregon had to offer.

Normally, when I packed my stuff into my backpack, my emotions danced about as joyously as an Irish jig. No matter what I'd been doing, the thought of being back on a road of unending curves and corners always excited me. It made me strong, ready for any challenge, anything the road would lead us to. We were always walking toward a place and a bunch of people that we'd never seen or known. There was always something more, something new to discover.

My Jan Sport pack leaned against a fine antique dresser. The more I stared at it, the more depressed I got. Why? I loved to put that faded blue pack on my back. It had carried everything I'd needed on this journey. I'd rested against it when there was nothing else to lean against. It had almost become a part of my body.

The more I looked at the pack and the neatly divided piles of clothes, and food, and other things, the more I wondered why I felt so down. Then I realized what it was. Instead of heading toward our next adventure, our next mountain range or our next family, we were heading toward the end of this long walk, this pilgrimage. There were many times when I wished that it would never end. I wondered how I would be able to readjust to normal life, what it would be like when there was no more road to hike down, no more discovery. The Bible said that there was a time for all things. A time to be born and a time to die. A time for beginnings and a time for endings. It was that ending time, and each day brought it closer, but that didn't mean that I liked it. Of course, we still had all of Oregon and the winter of 1978 to walk through. The thought cheered me up a little.

There was no way that we could have prepared for this winter. It was the coldest since 1919. We walked by the side of the Snake River and watched waterfalls shaped as thin as icicles. They fell and misted down for hundreds of feet from the top of the canyon walls. We passed near Salmon Falls.

Once we walked through the canyon and got out onto the open plains, we were in for some brittle cold, cold that stung our faces until they were chapped, even cracking. Once we left Mountain Home, Idaho, there was nothing for days but flatlands. We walked for miles and miles, our eyes begging for a break from the rawness of the land that gave us no protection. Everything was some shade of gray. Gray-blue, gray-green, gray-gray. Often the sky seemed to be coated with ash. I was glad we were not walking through here in the summer. The ground between Mountain Home and Boise looked as if the sun had a grudge against it and had tried to burn it to death.

We walked through Boise. Supposedly Idaho had the highest percentage of millionaires of any state. There was no doubt this state was one of the better-kept secrets in the U.S.A. And most of the natives wanted to keep it that way.

Colorado has dramatic green and white mountains on its cars' license plates. New Hampshire has "Live Free or Die." Louisiana has "Sportsman's Paradise." Minnesota has "The Land of 10,000 Lakes." Florida has "The Sunshine State," and Missouri has "The Show-Me State." These kinds of mottoes attract people. Before I got to Idaho, when I'd seen the green and white license plates that read, "Famous for Potatoes," I thought, Is that all Idaho has to offer? Now, as we got ready to cross the Snake River and begin walking through our last state, I wondered if the Idahoans had purposely made their motto about potatoes, so they could keep Idaho all to themselves.

The weatherman on Channel 7 out of Boise predicted the coming winter would be a cold one, harsher than normal. I figured that he was talking about Idaho. Oregon was a coastal state and had to be very different. It was different, but not in the way I thought it would be. It was even less populated than southern Idaho.

We came to a crossroads in Vale, Oregon. We could go to the northwest and head for John Day or head southwest toward Bend, Oregon. It was almost 300 miles to Bend if we took the left fork. The map told us we'd be hitting places like

Oregon's coldest winter since 1919

Stinkingwater Pass, Skull Springs, Buzzard Spring and Blitzen (ghost town). There was so little life here that even the ranches were marked on the state map—Roaring Springs Ranch and Whitehorse Ranch. The map said in little red letters, "Largest of the Few Remaining Herds of Wild Antelope in North America Roam These Plains."

We chose the right fork, like most of the other pioneers before us who lived to the end of their journey. The small town of John Day would be our next town of any size. To get there, we'd have to walk by Baldy Mountain and Looney Spring. We'd have to cut through Eldorado Divide. There were towns ahead called Ironside, Brogan, and Unity. I hoped they had stores and were not ghost towns.

After our first week I began to doubt we'd be able to end the walk this winter. Barbara was determined to try, so I said nothing. A deadly blizzard hit the West sometime in the first week of November. It killed ten people. Near Willowcreek, we slept in a newly plowed field and it got close to zero that night. The next night near Ironside (pop. 37) it began to snow and that next morning the snow weighted down our tent. Waking up when it was below 20 degrees was not easy. The cold here was dry and brittle, and it hurt. Our winter in the Rockies had been protected by the mountain walls of hard rock. We'd snuggled in our log cabin, watching the fire glow until we fell asleep. Here, in the high desert, the winds hurt like freezing knives.

From Unity we walked almost fifty miles, climbing, turning always higher, away from the moaning winds of the winter desert into the white silence of the forest. All that broke the silence were falling clumps of snow from the branches of old pine. At times the snow on the winding road would get slushy. The slush soaked through our boots and our socks and numbed our feet. We kept moving anyway. Once, as we neared the top before Dixie Pass, we heard a groaning sound coming up the other side of the mountain. It was a logging truck, carrying the biggest logs I'd ever seen. When it passed, it splashed slush all over us, sticking to my face, my beard, soaking through to my chest, and drenching the part of my blue jeans that was still dry. The logging trucks wouldn't move out of the way for anything. The roads were treacherously slippery, and one skid and they'd crash over the side of a cliff.

After we were soaked through by many sprays of slush, the temperature dropped and the slush froze. I could not remember any time of the entire walk when I had been so close to the edge of my endurance. Could we take any more of this? How much farther could this John Day, Oregon, be?

It was supposed to be 12 miles away, but in this winter snowstorm it seemed more like 120. We fought the snow, slush and logging trucks all day. Just a mile before we got to town, a small Japanese car drove up and stopped to look at us. I'm sure we looked strange covered with frozen slush on our faces, stiff with the pain of wet cold. The window wound down and a young lady sat there and watched us as we got closer. Who was she? What did she want out here in the middle of this whiteout?

37

Tsuchi Koto

Barbara

Tish Koto sat on the floor, rubbing my bare feet. Her real name was Tsuchi, but everyone called her Tish. For at least a half hour she worked her thumbs into my arches and then squeezed my toes and heels with gentle skill. Tish was a small woman in her fifties with silver gray hair, round face, full lips, flat nose and slanted eyes. Her skin was a richer color than mine. She was a Japanese American.

There was a sparkle in her dark eyes and a steady smile on her Oriental and motherly-looking face. I could tell she was pleased to rub my feet and did not feel self-conscious about it. It seemed she was showing me respect, and something about her bowed position reflected the old ways of her Japanese ancestors. She would rub Peter's feet when he returned.

I leaned back on the sofa and took a deep, relaxed breath. What pleasure! I basked in her healing touch. For some reason I had felt sick the past few days and figured I was coming down with the flu. Tish could tell I wasn't feeling well and her foot rub was making me feel better. I thought how unbelievable it was to be here. Never in a million years would I have dreamed of spending the last Christmas of our walk in

John Day, Oregon, getting my feet rubbed by a tender, softspo-
ken nisei (a second-generation daughter of immigrant Japanese
parents).

I felt dreamy and far away as I heard the fire pop and
could feel its warmth from the sofa. It seemed unreal. Peter
and I would be ending our long journey in twenty-four more
days. There were only a few hundred miles left to walk until
we reached the Pacific. All the thousands of miles were behind
us and the years of walking were almost over. Tish looked
content on the floor. She worked quietly on my feet, like some
women who sew or do needlework.

It had all been worth it, I thought, drifting far away.
Tish stopped for a moment to rest her fingers. She smiled up
at me, satisfied with her good job because I was loose and
sleepy. When I realized Tish was watching me, I jerked awake.
I didn't want to be rude or ungrateful for her massage, so I
began to ask her questions.

She knew I was being polite and obliged me. She told
me about herself like a person removed from her own story.
She simply gave me the facts. She explained how her parents
had been moved by the government after World War II broke
out. All Japanese immigrants in the United States were sent
to relocation centers, mostly inland. She was moved to Idaho.
There was little feeling in her voice. She talked like a woman
who had resolved the injustices of life and had left them behind.

In Shoshone, Idaho, Tish became seriously ill with tu-
berculosis and spent five years in and out of hospitals. During
those frail years, Tish and her husband, Masato Koto, were
able to have only one child. Mike Koto was born in 1949. He
was the sansei, the third generation. New hopes and goals were
wrapped up in this son, their all-American boy who was far
from the past. Time had passed since the war between the
United States and Japan, so Mike was not burdened with old
prejudices Tish had faced.

Nevertheless, Tish warned her son, "You must not get
into trouble or do anything wrong. People will always remember because you look different on the outside. If other people
do wrong, it is forgotten. But if *you* do wrong, it will *not* be
forgotten. My son, you must not bring any shame to your

grandparents or to your family name." Tish's words would be forever printed in Mike's memory.

Mike grew up obeying his mother's words. He became a striking and honorable young man. Mike stood taller than his small-framed parents. He was a muscular six feet tall and very handsome with broad football shoulders. He carried himself like a straight, posture-perfect athlete except he tilted his head slightly forward when he walked, as if he were thinking hard, working out a complex mathematical problem. He had a mechanical mind and was thoughtful about everything.

Mike had his mother's round face and rich-colored skin. His hair was thick, straight and coal black. It matched his mustache. Even though he had an intense air, his voice was mild and gentle. He had a mysterious quietness about him, but it was his crisp black eyes that made him intriguing. They were quick and observant.

Tish was very proud of her intelligent son, who had graduated from Boise State College in 1972, got married in 1975 and was now the head man in the Fire Management Department with the U.S. Forest Service. His office was in John Day. I could feel Tish's delight in her son through her fingertips. Just as Peter and I had come a long way, so had Tish.

A fresh shine came across her face when she changed the subject and began to tell me about Mary Lou, Mike's wife. Before she could get much said, we heard the back door open. Peter and Mike plunged through the kitchen door, carrying wrapped presents and some more wood for the fireplace. Tish lowered her voice, then stopped talking altogether when she heard Mary Lou behind them. Mary Lou was singing "Joy to the World" in her chirping soprano voice as she rushed inside, unbuttoned her snow-sprinkled coat and stuck her head in the living room to see what Tish and I were doing.

Mary Lou flashed us a big smile and danced off down the hallway. She shouted back to us, "What a *j-o-y* to have you here for Christmas!" It rang true. Mary Lou was like a frisky and friendly pup that had never met a stranger. She had big, bouncing blue eyes and long blond hair.

When I glanced over at the blinking lights on the Christmas tree, they reminded me of Mary Lou because she brought the same kind of energy and color to everyone around her. Mary Lou was the reason Peter and I were here.

A cold stream of mud and slush hit me when the semi truck passed. The big logging truck was full of giant timber headed back east. Peter and I were on Highway 26, about eight miles out of John Day, Oregon. We had been walking through a wet snowstorm all day and both of us were soaked. I feared frostbite because my wet fingers and feet were beyond the aching and numb stage. They were turning pale gray. The weather forecasters said this was the worst cold snap Oregon had seen since 1919.

Sometime later the slush turned into a fresh, heavy snowfall that came down out of the sky like big feathers. The flakes spread a new blanket across the deserted highway. There was no traffic, and the last motorist who passed had heavy chains on the rear tires, so I figured there must be travelers' warnings out. The world around me was white and quiet. My breathing was the only noise I could hear.

I walked with my face down. When I looked up through the curtain of snowflakes, I couldn't see Peter. He was out of sight and around the next curve. Panic hit me. I was all alone. I stepped faster, not able to feel my toes any longer. I felt scared and out of control. I could freeze out here or lose my contact lenses in the snow banging my face and not be able to see.

All of a sudden I heard a loud crack, a snap of a limb in front of me. Gray-white flurries blocked my vision. I blinked several times and squinted to keep my eyes dry. Then I froze. There in front of me, within six feet, as still as a statue, was the most angelic fawn I had ever seen. It was delicate and had a cape of snow on its back. The soft brown eyes stared at me. It stood motionless and so did I.

We looked at each other in the midst of the white walls that closed us in and we wondered what the other one was doing here. The fragile deer seemed bewildered to see a human being (or was I a human being with my weird body shape, a wool cap over my head and big hump on my back?). At least sixty exciting seconds passed while we studied each other with nothing to disturb our communication.

The young deer seemed to tell me the town of John Day was not far and everything was going to be all right. "Don't be afraid." It told me I did not have frostbite and a warm room and food would be waiting for me. The fawn skipped away, then stopped and looked back to say good-bye. Into the woods and back into the stillness it went. As I watched the fawn disappear, I was sure I had heard it tell me those things. A sense of warmth buoyed my cold, heavy body.

When I finally rounded the curve, Peter was there. He saw that I was all right, so he turned toward town and kept walking.

About an hour later a compact foreign-made car came toward us very slowly on the empty road. It pulled over across the road from us, and the young woman rolled down the window.

"Are you Peter and Barbara Jenkins?" she yelled.

"Yeah!" Peter hollered back. He was too cold and in no mood to be cordial.

"Would you like some hot coffee?"

We dumped our packs on the cushioned ground and climbed into the back seat of the warm car, crunched up like two big bears. This was the first time we met Mary Lou. She had heard we were headed toward John Day and had been waiting to meet us. She knew a lot about us. It was her parents, the Hagermans, back in Idaho, who had told her about us and that we were headed west on our way to the coast. Mary Lou was fascinated with our walk and our adventurous ways. She became determined to find us. When she heard from a truck driver that we were close to John Day, she made some wheat germ brownies and picked up some A&W coffee and drove out to find us.

Peter and I swallowed the brownies in one gulp. Her broad smile and her happiness over finding us made us feel that we were Mary Lou's long-lost friends.

After our feet and hands had thawed out and we'd drunk the last drop of hot coffee, Peter and I climbed back out into the cold. Mary Lou drove away, leaving us where she'd found us to finish our walk into town but with an invitation to come to her house for dinner.

She was nice and I liked her right away. But something about this milk-pale-skinned young woman caught my interest. She had an unusual last name. I had never heard of Koto before and wondered what nationality it was.

The smell of pine filled the house, making everything seem like Christmas. Mike had cut the tall pine tree from the national forest and Mary Lou had decorated it with her hand-made dough ornaments, red balls, tinsel and several dozen candy canes. She said the red and white stripes were symbolic of the spiritual meaning of Christmas. Pine cones were scattered around, adding a natural touch to the festive house.

Five handmade stockings hung from the paneling behind the wood-burning stove. One stocking was mine. Mary Lou had made it out of blue felt and had sewn white rickrack along the edges. Peter's stocking was like mine except Mary Lou had sewn an American flag on his. The other stockings were for Tish, Mike and Mary Lou.

Red ribbons were dotted around the house, on wreaths, on pine greenery and on candles. Mary Lou had everything looking like Christmas. With her long hands she had made the lovely ruffled kitchen curtains and tablecloth that we would be eating Christmas dinner on. For all of her creative talents, it was her piano playing that really captured the spirit of Christmas. She ran her fingers across the ivory keys as if playing a piano were as easy as using a push-button telephone. She played so beautifully it was no surprise to find out that she was a piano and music teacher.

Tish finished setting the table and we were ready to eat. I could taste the turkey and dressing already, but when we gathered around the table, Tish had a surprise for us. She had made her specialties. There, spread out in front of me, were platters of bright food I had never seen or heard of before. We were having nori sushi, aburage, mazegohan, shrimp tempura and yokan for desert. This was my very first Japanese Christmas dinner.

Mike handed us some chopsticks and told us to dig in. It wasn't the same as digging into the traditional yams, creamed onions, giblet gravy and dressing. It was even more special except we couldn't get enough between the sticks.

Tish explained what each food was as it passed. The nori sushi was a seasoned rice wrapped in seaweed, the aburage was fried bean curd stuffed with seasoned rice, mazegohan was steamed rice with vegetables, shrimp tempura was deep-fried shrimp in a thick egg batter, and the yokan desert was made of gelatin and bean paste. What fun we had. Mike and Mary Lou spent most of the meal laughing at us as we tried to master the chopsticks. We finally scooped the food into our mouths off the plates but were rescued with knives and forks before the meal was over.

When our stomachs couldn't hold any more, we decided it was time to open presents. We grunted into the living room and found a place around the tree. Black-haired Mike played Santa Claus. Tish looked on, like a happy mother over her brood, glad to be with all of us young folks since she had lost Mr. Koto not long before.

Tish had driven the six hours from Twin Falls, Idaho, to be here, while Peter and I had walked over two years to get here. It felt pre-planned. It was right and we all sensed we belonged together as a family on this Christmas Day 1978.

The snow fell outside, making a perfect setting as we opened our gifts to each other. Mike handed us a gift to open first. It was small and hard, but when I saw what was in the ripped paper, my heart leaped inside. It was a plaque in the shape of Oregon with brass on the front. The inscription read:

Peter & Barbara Jenkins
A Walk Across America
Alfred, N.Y. October 15, 1973
Florence, Oregon, January 18, 1979
4,800 miles

It hit me hard that our fantastic adventure was almost over. This was the first time I had seen statistics in black and white. I fought back the tears and at the same instant another wave of nausea crept over me. It was back again. I wondered what could be wrong with me!

Peter and I gave Tish a crystal candy dish we had bought the day before, which she loved. She remarked how she would never buy such a luxury like that for herself. I gave Mary Lou a handpicked bouquet of wild herbs. I arranged them in a basket and put a ribbon around it. Peter gave Mike an electric iron. Of course, Mike probably wouldn't be ironing his own clothes, but the iron was something needed in their home. Tish gave Peter and me some hand warmers, little boxes that burned on the inside and were very useful for people who had to be outside in the cold.

The last present under the tree was for Peter. Mike handed it to him with a sly smile on his face. All the while Peter tore at the paper, there was a sucker in the side of his mouth. He looked as excited as any boy getting his first bicycle. Something blue was inside the crumpled paper.

When Peter lifted the blue cotton T-shirt out from the wrappings, high for all of us to see, everyone started to laugh. Most easterners and Yankees pronounced Oregon incorrectly, calling it "Ory-gone."

The cotton T-shirt had the outline of the state, mountains in the background and a ponderosa tree in the corner. Then, in the very center, were bold letters that read: "O-R-E-G-U-N."

Mike Koto laughed. "That's the way we natives pronounce our state."

38

The Minister in Black

Mary Lou and Mike took us to church with them. It was an Assembly of God, an average-looking little church that sat on the side of a hill on the north side of town. In the lobby was a bulletin drawn by the young kids. About six people mingled around before going inside to sit down on the wooden pews. We had walked by hundreds of churches just like this one. Everything about this church was very typical, so common.

We opened the doors to the sanctuary and walked over to the pew where Mike and Mary Lou always sat. From the moment we sat down, everything changed. It was the last time anything about this day would be normal or common. That's because it was the first time we set our eyes on Milo Franke.

Milo was the minister. A thrill ran through me as soon as I saw him. There was sort of a supernatural aura about the man in the pulpit, about the way the long, almost white sideburns contrasted with his still-dark hair, about the way his angular, muscled body moved in that black suit of his. The suit reminded me of those old-time circuit riding ministers of the Old West. It was the kind of suit a man could ride a horse in, even gallop fast to the next small outpost. Milo was like a minister out of a John Wayne movie. It looked as if he had a lot more of John Wayne than minister in him. I could imagine this man walking into the rowdiest loggers' bar or the fightingest cowboy bar in the West with a Bible in one hand and a sawed-off shotgun in the other. His eyes burned with the fires of the Gospel. Everybody called him Brother Milo.

As they began the service, I just had to find out more about him. I was sitting next to Mary Lou, so all during the service I whispered questions to her about Milo. "He looks more like a rancher than a preacher," I whispered. "How long has he been preaching?"

Mary Lou whispered very quietly back to me, "He's been preaching about all his life, but he was always a rancher and a logger, too. He's been able to preach more since his kids have grown up. There's his wife, Evelyn, over there." Mary Lou pointed inconspicuously toward a lady, maybe sixty, with silver gray hair, round, soft eyes and a peaceful look on her face.

Our whispering caught his attention and he looked my way. Milo had eyes that made a guilty man want to hide, that made a sorrowing man or woman want to spill forth all the pain and secrets never told before. There was no hiding from Milo's eyes. Either you let them turn you inside out or you ran from them. His lamb-chop sideburns ended at the tips of his mouth. He smiled and his eyes told you that there was nothing you could have done that he hadn't heard about or seen. They pierced like laser beams and loved you like family, all at the same time.

Milo opened his black, tattered Bible. His voice rang out, filling the small church. No one could fall asleep to this. When he said the word "Jesus," it would echo and reecho. He moved from one side of the pulpit to the other, stalking like a lion, quoting scripture, and he'd look upward with those eyes and practically shout, "Glory to God, hallelujah." Then he'd take a deep breath and keep going. Most of all, the minister in black exuded *power*. Mary Lou whispered that Milo always wore a cowboy hat and on Sundays it was black.

While Milo was preaching, he kept staring at me. He would take his eyes off me only momentarily to glance at Barbara. He knew we were visitors, but the stare was more than that. Milo stopped right in the middle of his sermon. It was like halting the power of the Mississippi River and re-routing it over us.

"You could say Milo sang us across the Cascades"

"I see a young man has blessed us this day." The entire congregation hushed and started looking around for the one he was talking about. I knew he was talking about me, but I hoped not.

"I've never seen this young man before in my life. I have no idea what he is doing here with us, but I want to find out something about him and why he is here. I think God has got something for him."

Oh, no. Please don't let it be me. This could be embarrassing. He pointed me out. "Please stand, young man." I stood. I could feel everyone looking at me. Certainly this couldn't be the usual way of doing things. "Now tell us what you are doing here, what is your name, and what you need."

"My name's Peter Jenkins. This is my wife, Barbara." I pointed to Barbara, putting my hand on her left shoulder. "This may sound hard to believe, especially this time of year, but we are walking across the country, and we're on our last stretch, headed for the ocean." I started to sit down.

"Don't sit down, Brother Peter. Please come up here on the platform."

No, please. I was not in the mood for any of this stuff. I wanted to remain a stranger. I got the feeling that no one remained a stranger once they got in sight of Milo's blue eyes. I walked down the center aisle to the podium.

"I know there is something you need. God has impressed me about it. I'll be glad to tell you what it is if you are shy."

As I kept walking toward him, I thought to myself, What do we need? I wasn't sure. We knew the Cascade Mountains lay before us, and Mike and others had warned us there would be many blizzards and many long, empty stretches in these mountains, but we had crossed snow-filled peaks before. We had made it over the Rockies after all. What was this preacher talking about? Maybe Milo and God saw a need coming up that we didn't know about yet.

"OK, Brother Peter. I feel that you and your wife have to finish this walk of yours this winter." He looked out across the congregation. "I know this country around here. If you ever got stuck out in one of our blizzards up in the Cascades, they might never find you again." By this time I was up on the platform beside him, and his arm was around my shoulder. I faced the people and they seemed used to this kind of thing. "Congregation," Milo boomed, "do any of you feel impressed with this? I believe God is leading us to help this young couple."

"Amen, Pastor," most of them said, powerfully convinced.

"I think that our church should take it upon ourselves to get Brother Peter and his wife over the mountains. If I could get an amen on this, I would be willing to take some time, as much as necessary, and drive beside them all the way to Santiam Pass, to Three Fingered Jack—just whatever the spirit of the Lord says." He lifted one hand toward heaven and sort of waved it around.

"Amen. Amen." The people agreed.

One woman stood up and testified. "When I first set eyes on these young people, I was impressed that they were doing something special. That there was something we were meant to do to help them. It's no accident that they're here."

"Amen." The voices sounded hearty.

I felt as I had on that fall day back in New Orleans when

Barbara and I had walked out of church, after hearing Mom Beale preach that sermon, "Will You Go with This Man?" Something happened in this little Assembly of God church today. As we left, I said a silent amen, too.

Milo knew this high desert and these mountains and canyons and buttes as well as he knew the Bible. He knew their every mood. He knew what this land could do to a man's will, dissolve it, freeze it, then shatter it. He knew that a stranger had no idea what to expect of Oregon. Only a narrow strip along the coast, Milo explained, was rainy, jungly and the way most people thought all of Oregon was.

Milo sized me up fast. I didn't believe in mind readers. But Milo was a soul reader. He told us what we would do and how we would do it. How many miles to walk a day, when to rest, where to camp. I'd never walked through a winter before. Sure, Cooper and I had walked through parts of North Carolina in the snow, but it didn't last long. Anyway, North Carolina winters were like basking on the beaches of the Gulf compared to these.

All day for more than two weeks Milo would drive alongside us, most of the time his car kicking up clouds of powdery snow. He would creep along at a snail's pace because that was as fast as we could go in this cold. Some days, like the day near the tiny, canyon-walled town of Mitchell, he'd drive in and bring out some warm food and coffee, soup, hamburgers. Anything hot or steaming. Other days, if it was snowing especially hard, or it was real slushy and the logging trucks had coated us with ice and sand from the roads, he would put a tape in his eight-track tape player and sing to us. This man had a smile that could make the moon rise again.

When he sang, the gold cap on his front tooth glittered. He would belt out gospel tunes, sometimes country music, shaking and dancing his shoulders, beating on the outside of his car door in rhythm to the music, his four-wheel drive going two miles an hour. You could say that Milo sang us across the Cascades.

We fell in love with Milo and he fell in love with us.

He was going to get us across these winter mountains no matter what. Somewhere in between Prineville and Bend, even with Milo's singing and food and smiles, we came close to quitting. It was the week when the highest temperature was 2 below zero. The lows were 25 below. It hurt to breathe, it was so cold. Breathing deep was like inhaling glass. We'd subjected ourselves to some of the toughest times that our country's weather could deal out, but this was the worst.

Before we'd walked away from John Day, we'd had a serious talk about the end of the walk. We knew we had two choices. One was to let people know about it. The other was to end it quietly, privately, on a deserted stretch of winter beach, maybe at sunrise, maybe at sunset. Just Barbara and me, making our last footprints in the sand, to be washed away forever by the Pacific. Someone had told us that there was a magnificent stretch of beach west of Eugene, Oregon, that had sand dunes as big as the Sahara. He had assured us that it was very private there, even desolate. I would never think of a beach as desolate. I thought that beaches should be empty, for it was the only way to really soak in the sounds of the waves, the crunchy sands, the mists of morning. Just talking about it, we knew that it was the only way to end our walk.

I glanced down to a table, while my mind was full of thrilling thoughts about the long journey's end. On the table was a letter, forwarded here by my dad from Mary Elizabeth. We had written postcards all the time to our many families every time we stopped on this walk across America. We heard back from them, too.

The gospel-shoutin', happy-sad news from Smokey Hollow, Mary Elizabeth said in her letter, was that Zack finished one year at college and while there, he met a real fine girl from Louisville. Her name was Selma. "I'm a grandma now, and sure miss not having my sons, you and Zack around. The grandson's called little Zack. No one's sleeping on that old couch anymore because Bruce, he married Angie. Remember her, she stayed over by the old school house? You make sure that Barbara don't get pregnant before you finish."

Eric was six-three and all-Cherokee County fullback. He

had rushed for over 1,200 yards. "You should have seen that boy run against Hayesville. He tore 'em up." Mary Elizabeth was happy some, but there was sad news, too. Her phone had been turned off 'cause she talked long distance to Zack so much. From North Carolina to Kentucky to her was like around the world. She'd gotten another job at a restaurant makin' biscuits, beginnin' at five in the morning. Her diabetes were gettin' real bad, her blood pressure was way up, she could hardly see, and Pau Pau had died from the cancer. She said she had had a huge tumor cut out of her stomach. Frank, Jr., was still there and the preacher at the Mount Zion Church always asked for me. Last week she sang a solo and dedicated it to Jesus and Barbara and me. She prayed for us every day and hoped that "none ah that meanness" across the country would ever hurt us. Sometimes she forgot I was white.

In Montgomery, my friend Lanier, the southern belle extraordinaire, had moved to the big city, Birmingham. Birmingham was Alabama's big city. She was driving a forest green MGB and working in an advertising firm. She wasn't married *yet,* her mother, Gloria, wrote.

Stephen had gotten out of jail for the marijuana bust. He had taken the rap for the whole commune. The Farm and everyone who lived there, all 1,200 of them, were close to Nirvana now that their Stephen was back, living with them twenty-four hours a day. God was still everywhere, and fact was, a letter said, when was I going to finally admit that the Farm was what I was looking for? Babies were being delivered by the midwives at a record pace and they'd got a beautiful used combine. Stephen and the Farm band had bought a fine Trailways bus and were planning a nationwide campus-city tour to lure people to their planet within a country. Joel, Jane, Marilyn and Patrick the operator of the mill who'd graduated from Stanford, were all fine. Everything was far-out.

The news from Saltville came via one of the ladies at the post office. Homer couldn't read or write, so when he came to get his mail, she read my postcards and letters to him and then he would answer my questions. She would write me back. A black bear had come and killed three sheep. Homer had to shoot one of his "everything" dawgs after a bunch of porcupine quills got "real bad" infected. Brownie, his favorite dawg, was gettin' old but could still outrun all them young, lazy hounds. "Ain't no tellin' what else is happenin' with Homer," she wrote in the neatest script. "The way Homer lives, almost every day's an adventure." The last thing he said was: "Be careful of them woomen." He had never responded to our wedding invitation.

M. C. Jenkins and a lot of the farmers around the Black Belt of central Alabama were worried that the summer rains were not going to provide enough moisture. They might have to start feeding their cattle hay before the winter comes. Our beautiful green pastures are drying up, M.C. wrote from Orrville. That would be a disaster, Miss Margaret said on the phone. Packy was playing tackle on a midget league football team and attending a fine private school in Selma. It looked as if this year would bring a good cotton crop, Carl Henderson told M.C. The cattle business got so bad there, M.C. said, that he had to take a job in Birmingham working for the government, loaning money to farmers. They were called disaster loans. M.C. never lost a chance to tell me that for a Yankee, I was gettin' there.

Thinking back on all these people made it obvious. There was only one thing we could do. The walk had not been a solitary adventure. The *people* were the walk. They had been my family; now they were *our* family. And it wasn't just Mary Elizabeth, Zack, Eric and Bruce. It wasn't just Homer and M.C. and Miss Margaret, Lanier and the Farm. It now was Grady and all the men on the J. Storm I. It was Preacher Hebert and the rest of the "A-bears." It was Homer and Ruby, Leroy and Iva Mae, the people from the Panhandle. It was all the Vickerses, Perk, Emma Jean, Hollywood Jed, Tom and Larry. It was the Williams ranch and the Ramseys from Filer, Idaho. It was Milo, Mike and Mary Lou and Tish. It was our parents who'd supported us and were proud of what we were doing even when others thought we were crazy. Our walk had been the people. Certainly the land had affected me forever, but then how do you invite a Rocky Mountain to the end of a walk across America? Even inviting an alligator would be hard.

We made up our minds. We would end the walk on

January 18, 1979. We looked at maps and chose a place. It was near Florence, Oregon, at the great sand dunes we'd heard so much about. We would write up a simple and quick invitation to all our families and friends, saying that we would like them to join us on the last mile of our walk. They had meant everything to us on the road; now we wanted them to know that on the great day when our long journey came to an end, we wanted to share it with them. Of course, we knew that it was unlikely that anyone would come. Oregon was at the other end of the country for most of them. At least they'd know we were thinking of them.

Besides the fact that it was the coldest winter since 1919, there was still something wrong. Seriously wrong. For all the below-zero brittleness of the air, there was beauty everywhere. Sagebrush lightly coated with big flakes of snow barely hung onto the stingy walls of Picture Gorge. It was the same around Crooked River Canyon, I'm sure, but there was no time for exploring anymore.

Before, even when the weather had made brutal demands, Barbara had been able to see the beauty all around. It seemed strange that usually the most stunning geographical beauty inflicted the most pain, like the mountain passes, the deserts, the plains. Now, however, Barbara was dangerously drained of that fighting spark. That country girl "never-say-quit" light went out of her eyes. They looked dull to me. I wasn't going to say anything to Milo; he had enough to worry about. Barbara never wanted to get up in the morning, never wanted to unzip the sleeping bag. When she did get going, she dragged at a speed so slow I wondered if I was losing my mind. Maybe Barbara was having a breakdown. Her face had lost its color; even her hair, which usually shone, seemed to get brittle and limp. Maybe she had a cold or the beginnings of the flu. Surely we'll fight it off. I made her take double doses of vitamins. I tried to slow down to almost a crawl. She still lagged far behind me. We could see the Three Sisters far off in the blue light of the coming of night. They were three mountains, the first major peaks of the Cascades we would be crossing, all over 10,000 feet in elevation. If Barbara could barely walk on this flat ground, there was no way she could walk across those. What was wrong? It tore at me. It was as if the plug had been pulled on B.J. I wanted to cry over the defeated look in her eyes.

I guess Milo had been watching her closely because he pulled me aside in the small town of Sisters, at the base of the mountains. "Peter, I think there's something wrong with Barbara. Do you think we should take her to a doctor?"

"Yes, I do." I was afraid it was exhaustion from the cold, physical and mental. She had been through as much as any pioneer woman from 100 years ago.

"I have a good friend, Dr. Elon Wood. He treated all our kids all their lives. He's back in Prineville, but I think that we should go to someone that I know. He'll tell us straight. Besides, he's got a daughter that climbs mountains and he can understand this kind of walk. He knows all about that exposure and exhaustion stuff."

Barbara was so weak now she couldn't eat. She said she felt sick to her stomach. We walked into the waiting room of Dr. Wood's office. He was a trim man, balding, in his early sixties and didn't say much to us. He looked worried. Milo said that he'd seen every injury known to man and woman since he treated a lot of ranchers, loggers and all that. He rushed Barbara into the back as soon as we got there. Milo tried to act as if he weren't worried, but he was quiet and that meant he was worried. I gripped my hands, sweated a lot and couldn't stay seated. There were plenty of magazines, but I couldn't concentrate on them. The other people in the bright waiting room watched my anxiety and looked as though they felt sorry for me, as if something were wrong with me. If something was wrong with Barbara, then something was wrong with me.

It seemed as though Barbara was with that doctor an hour. Milo and I couldn't think of anything to talk about. We sat in silence until, finally, the doctor came out of the examining room. Barbara was with him.

She was obviously waiting for him to tell me something. I wasn't sure I wanted to know.

"Son, we checked over Barbara. Gave her a few tests. Looks like you are going to be a father in about eight months."

I sat there a moment. So did Milo. Then it all hit us. We both jumped to our feet, grabbed each other and started dancing around that waiting room. I ran over to Barbara and kissed her. I hugged her and saw her smile, weakly, for the first time in a while. The doctor said that he wanted to speak to Barbara and me privately in his office. There he asked me if we planned to finish the walk. I asked him if he thought it was possible now that Barbara was pregnant. He said that he believed, because of his experience with his daughter and his faith in what a woman could do, Barbara could make it. We would have to be sensitive to her feelings. Her emotions would shift dramatically, he said. But if we paced ourselves, and with Milo's and God's help, we should be able to make it. We all left Dr. Woods's office, feeling a mountain was off our backs. The real mountains, though, were still waiting for us to walk across them.

Knowing Barbara was pregnant changed things for us. We weren't worried anymore, but it didn't stop her from feeling sick.

"Honey," I said to her as we walked upward, constantly up, high into the uninhabited Cascades laden with snow, "do you think you can make it over these mountains?"

"Peter, don't ask me. Just keep going. I'm too ill to think straight, but all I know is that we've got to make it. I'll do it if I have to crawl." That pinpoint squint was back in her eyes. I knew she would give it her best shot, but I was worried it might hurt the tiny baby that was growing inside her. This surrounding cold, the falling snow and below-zero temperatures would take its toll on a healthy man or woman, much less a pregnant woman. Yet the doctor back in Prineville said that she'd be all right. I hoped he knew what he was talking about. Our unborn child was more important than finishing this walk.

Milo was more determined than ever. We'd made it this far since leaving John Day. Through Dayville, past Milo's old ranch where he raised his large family, through the Ochoco Divide into Prineville. We'd made it through Redmond, past

Grizzly Mountain. We were plowing through our personal snowdrifts toward Santiam Pass. Milo said once we got there, it would be easy.

"Once you pass Three Fingered Jack Mountain, you'll get on the other side of the Cascades. It's warmer, more temperate over on the west side. No snow. And I've called one of my best friends, Warren Cornelius. He lives in Springfield with his wife, Reba...I married them a few years back, and he's a fine rancher and preacher, too. They'll be ready once you get there. They will follow you and help you all the way to the Pacific if you need them. They're the best kind of people; they'll do whatever needs to be done."

But we still had the snow to walk over, the east side of the Cascades to finish. Barbara understood why she felt so terrible, but that did not stop her emotions from running haywire several times a day. It didn't stop her from feeling sick to her stomach and very tired and weak. It didn't stop her from throwing up.

One time Barbara was walking with her head down, her face as pale as the white snow, and straining to put one foot in front of the other when Milo called over to her from his car across the road. "Barbara! You walk, and I'll throw up!"

Another day, when there had been a dozen logging trucks passing by and throwing slush all over us, Milo could see that Barbara was giving out. She looked as if she would drop in her tracks. He stopped the car, turned up some gospel music and hollered at her. "Barbara. Look. Look at me." He jumped out of the car and got down on his hands and knees in a foot of fresh snow.

"Whoop-e-ee, I feel like Cooper today. Watch me roll in the snow." He rolled over on his back, back and forth. Barbara just looked over at him and managed a weak smile. "Whoo-o-e-e-e. God's gonna get you through, Barbara," Milo said to her, his eyes dancing with a heavenly energy.

A few days before, I called our friends back in Dallas, Texas. Don and Sarah Stevens had stored everything we owned in their house since we'd left Dallas more than two years ago. They took care of all our mail, phone calls, and would send us our equipment to General Delivery, Anywhere, U.S.A.

They had been like silent partners, always there. I told them about Barbara being pregnant and that we needed an extra sleeping bag and a warmer down vest and jacket.

Don said he would have the gear in the mail tomorrow. Without their help we would never have made it. They had come out to see us several times on the road; they came to see us in New Mexico and Colorado, too. Don and Sarah, along with their two small children, Douglas Glenn and Sara Lee, had become more than friends. They were like blood family. All they wanted was to help.

Now Milo was the same way. All he wanted to do was help us, and without him, we would not have made it out of central Oregon.

On January 4 we made it to where there was no more snow. Milo went home to his wife and his church. Milo and Evelyn would be coming back to walk the last mile with us, and so would Mike and Mary Lou. Milo knew that saying good-bye was going to be very emotional, so he told us that all of our thanks should go to God. There was no way we could express what we felt about Milo. We were just glad that we'd see him again in a couple of weeks.

Sure enough, once we got down to Blue River, there was no more snow. It was like a completely different world. Everything was lushly green, the way it was supposed to be in the picture books. Moss hung from Sitka spruce trees. Rocks lay covered with moss among the jungly growth. Just as Milo said, Warren and Reba Cornelius were waiting for us.

In only a couple of days we were walking through Eugene. Another few days and we were through the mellow valley where all the big cities of Oregon were. There was another mountain range before we got to the Pacific, called the Coast Range, but it was more like hills after what we'd seen lately. Everything was dull gold, green, wet and misting rain. As we got closer to the coast, we said good-bye to Warren and Reba. Now we were on our own. I thought I smelled the ocean a couple of times. At last we walked into the seaside town of Florence, Oregon.

Paul M. Breeden

Florence

4,751
MILES

SON, YOU'RE
GONNA BE
A FATHER

WHOOPEE!

Prineville
John Day

THE LAST MILE · JANUARY 18, 1979

Twin Falls

OREGON   IDAHO

W.T. WILLIAMS RANCH

MAP 3
Lake City
to
Florence

39

One More Mile

Barbara

She walked between Peter and me, holding each of our hands, singing a church hymn from long ago called "The Last Mile of the Way." Her voice was squeaky and high but sounded as sweet to me as the slapping ocean waves that were just over the ridge ahead of us. Grandma's eighty-three-year-old hands were wrinkled, little and frail, but she held to us with a firm grip, walking in brisk steps. She wasn't even five feet tall and weighed a light eighty-five pounds, but her tiny steps led the way, setting the pace for all of our friends behind us. She wore a head scarf tied in a knot under her chin and a heavy coat to keep off the chilly wind. She said her blood didn't circulate the way it used to and she got cold easily.

One mile. It seemed painfully short. Only minutes of walking and not hours, or days, or weeks, or years. The seconds ticked away too fast and weren't willing to slow down for this occasion that had taken so long to reach. We walked forward, savoring each step and each feeling that rushed down to our toes and back up to our hearts again. This was not the time to hurry, to push ourselves. Oh, please slow down. There were no more towns to reach, no more nights to set up the tent, no more meals of apples and nuts, no more new bends in the road, no more sunrises peeking in our tent to wake us up. No more.

A feeling of grief swept over me, a sense of loss, a sense of sadness that I didn't want to be there. Oh, I wished that I had it all to do over again; maybe I would have been a better adventuress, more in tune with all that I had done. But I was so full of rich experiences that it would take years to absorb everything, I reasoned, trying to make the unhappiness go away.

> If I walk in the pathway of duty,
> If I work till the close of the day,
> I shall see the great King in His beauty
> When I've gone the last mile of the way.

Grandma's voice fluted and sang as she walked toward the ocean. How special this was for me to see my only living grandparent leading Peter and me, and singing so triumphantly, giving us all her gladness and energy. She would have shouted out the hymn if her old soprano voice had been stronger. Instead, she sparkled and smiled up at everyone taller than she was, smiling as brightly as the winter sun did that shone down on all of us on this crisp, clear January day.

When Grandma wrote us from her home in Phoenix accepting our invitation to come and walk the last mile with us, she told us her doctor said she could come, it would be good for her. Her doctor would write a note telling the airlines she had heart trouble, but she had his permission to fly. "I'm planning on making the trip...I'm going to think positive about it. I'm so thankful to both of you for wanting me to share it with you. I believe God has answered my prayers to protect you. I've never been to Oregon, but I'll see you there."

The great blue waters of the Pacific were just ahead. I could hear its roar, its clapping, and feel its approval. Grandma stopped, halting the train of friends behind us and pulled her little bottle of nitroglycerin pills out of her pocket. She popped one in her mouth. She said she needed it to get her over the last sand dune that separated us from the ocean.

Everything around me faded when we topped the knoll and I laid my eyes on the open stretches of whitecaps and blue waters that touched the clear sky. Everything before me was wide open and endless. It had taken Peter over five years to reach this journey's end and almost three years for me.

My emotions slipped and swirled like the white foam that rolled onto the beach, then rushed back to the ocean. The people, their voices, and everything around were growing dim. I remember Peter dropped Grandma's hand and grabbed mine. With one gentle tug we left everyone behind and hurried down the sand dune, toward the flat beach, toward the spaciousness of the water, the sky and eternity. I didn't look back. There was no one or nothing important enough for me to turn my head or my heart back. Peter was the only person I could share this moment with and he was wrapped in his own feelings, just like me. Neither of us could feel what the other one was experiencing, but we were sharing the end, just as we had shared all the dangers, adventures, hardships, new people, fun and years of being together on the road. If only time would stop. If only we could hold onto this.

The crowd had spread along the beach and half a dozen people followed Peter and me into the sea, where we were almost waist-deep. The groups of people on the beach cheered.

My body reached out to the deep, as the cold salt waters hugged my legs and sent shivers up my back. I wanted to speak, but words would not come out of my mouth. Everything in my soul shouted praise and glory. What a land voyage this had been! My heart thanked God Almighty as I threw up my arms toward the sky in victory.

Peter. My daring, strong, funny, loving husband pulled me next to him as the Pacific Ocean pushed at us and the undertow pulled us as though to coax us farther out. But we couldn't go any farther. I knew the walk was over. The unborn baby inside me reminded me that a whole new life was about to begin.

It wasn't just a nice day. It was a perfect day. Almost everyone had told Barbara and me that during the winter it rained on the coast every day. All day. Today the sky was bluer than the ocean just a mile away. The sun was here to congratulate *us* for having made it. Our families were here. My mom and dad, five brothers and sisters had scraped the money together, somehow, to fly out. Barbara's folks and her sister, Vicky, and husband, Sunny, were here. Barbara's mother refused to get on an airplane, so they had all driven from Missouri through three killer blizzards. Our only living grandparent from either side of the family, Viola Pennell, came all the way from Phoenix. She was eighty-three and said she wouldn't have missed this for anything. Even if she had to be pushed in a wheelchair. She walked every day for exercise, so she would set the pace for the hundreds of people who were here. We were shocked at how many had come here to Oregon to walk the last mile with us.

Friends of ours from New Orleans had driven for over a week, skirting snowstorms and blizzards to get here. Mary Elizabeth, Eric and Margaurite took their first plane trip to be here. They flew out of Atlanta. M.C. and Miss Margaret and Packy came from Orrville, Alabama, with their neighbor farmers, the Hendersons. M.C. had on his dress cowboy hat. Packy had grown a foot since I walked through Alabama. Don and Sarah, their two children, oilmen from the Panhandle and our pastor said they were here " 'cause they loved this country and this walk celebrated that." "Wouldn't have missed it for nothin'," Jack Gross said. Perk and Emma Jean came from Lake City; so did the town deputy and his wife, Jean.

We started walking toward the dunes and the Pacific. Barbara's grandmother walked between us; we held her hands. My folks walked to our right; Barbara's folks walked to our left. We hadn't gone a hundred yards before everyone was mingling together, comparing stories about how they'd met us. I heard Mary Elizabeth telling someone about how I looked when I put on a fluorescent green suit and went to church with them. Her mother, Margaurite, couldn't see, but I heard her laugh. I overheard Perk telling my dad that he just had to come to the Vickers ranch soon. "Ain't no mountains like ours."

I caught a glimpse of Lucy Ramsey talking to some people from *National Geographic* while Jack talked to my sister Betsi. W. T. Williams, Viola and Billy were all here dressed

Friends and family join us on the last mile to the Pacific! LEFT TO RIGHT, FRONT ROW: *Peter's sister, Betsi; Peter's mother, Mary Elizabeth; Mark Arden; Peter; Barbara's grandmother, Viola; Barbara; Barbara's sister, Vicky.* SECOND ROW: *Skip Yowell; Peter's father, Fred; Peter's brother, Freddy; Carl Henderson, neighbor of*

M. C. Jenkins; Peter's cousin, Morgan; Mary Elizabeth's mother, Margaurite; Barbara's mother, Betty; Mary Elizabeth from Murphy, North Carolina

in their ranchers' Sunday finest. The transmission in their car had fallen out on the way over from Idaho, but they got it repaired fast and just made it. Billy hadn't worn his cattle-drivin' hat, but I heard him telling Barbara's dad about the time we drove the herd back up Cottonwood Canyon. Ernie invited Billy to come to Missouri anytime. Our editor, Pat Golbitz, invited Milo to come to the Big Apple. Milo didn't know where the Big Apple was. Everyone was inviting everyone else to come to his own part of the country.

Many of the shier people just walked in the powerful, surrounding stillness that exists this close to the Pacific. It was very hard for me to say anything. There would be time for that later, after we had walked our last mile. It was all I could do to keep walking because of the overwhelming surges of feeling. I wanted to scream, to release my thrills of having finally made it. I wanted to cry for the same reason. I wanted to hug and kiss everyone who was here who meant so much to me, but I couldn't yet. I wanted to slow it all down, slower than slow motion, to savor every foot, and I wanted to speed it up so that it would be over. The emotion of it all was tremendous. These were the most powerful moments of my life. All that I'd seen and felt was coming back all at once.

Flashes of Cooper, the Appalachians, Homer, Smokey Hollow, my nickname, Albino. I could feel the sultry heat of the Deep South and sweet home Alabama. The first time I saw Barbara's face. The offshore oil rig and "Will You Go with This Man?" Alligators, shrimp and Texas. Windmills, Homer and Ruby, the Rockies blasting from the prairies. Idaho, the northwest. What an *incredible* country I'd found. . . .

I was interrupted. There, ahead, was a huge sand dune. Barbara's grandmother had stopped all of us. She would have to take a small pill before she could walk over that imposing dune. Oh, no. It was her heart medicine. Don't tell me she's going to have a heart attack.

They all moved as if they were one, up that dune. There was little talking now among the hundreds who were with us. Everyone could hear the ocean. Emotion and the roars of the waves took over.

Barbara and I broke from the rest. There was only fifty yards of beach left and then the ocean. We couldn't stop; we walked into the Pacific. We held our hands up. I was crying. If all that I felt could come out of me, I don't think I could have expressed it. The water may have been cold; a wave hit us and almost knocked us over. It may have knocked some of the others over. I reached for Barbara; we hugged because we had to share some of this moment in the surf. There was no land left to walk. I was glad it was over and I was sad. What this walk meant to me would take a lifetime to understand.

Epilogue

It had been more than a year and a half since we walked our last mile. Rebekah, our daughter, had just turned one year old, on August 18. She was standing in the middle of our den watching Mr. Rogers on TV. I was going over some of the pages and pages of notes I'd made, sitting in my favorite brown chair. The ceiling fans were whirling above me and Barbara was cooking lunch. Barbara loved to cook, country-style. Moments before, a covey of quail had walked through our backyard, which was coated with pine needles.

I was facing the front yard, deep in thought, when I heard a knock on the back door. I hadn't noticed anyone coming. Rebekah ran to me, saying my favorite word, "Da-da." She is such a beautiful and smart little girl. Everyone says she has curly dark hair like Barbara's and round eyes like mine. I turned to see a young man standing at our back door. He had a backpack on. Very early yesterday morning a guy had telephoned to tell us about a young man who was walking across America with his dog, Sheba. When he got to the Mississippi coastline, the same route I had walked, someone told him where I lived. Now he was here.

He said his name was Chad Hamman and he was from Indiana. He and Sheba came inside the house. The dog was part husky with a white mask, she curled up, leaning on Chad's legs just the way Cooper used to do. It was as if I were looking in a mirror, a reflection of me and Cooper seven years ago.

Chad was about my height, his body as hard as the road he walked. Just the way mine had been. His eyes gleamed with adventure and he had a thousand questions to ask. He was searching for everything.

Before Chad left, he told us he was out of money and needed a job. We fed him and he ate like I used to, three plates full, with a half gallon of iced tea and lemonade. I called a friend in New Orleans who worked for a shipyard. My friend got Chad a job.

I continued writing my book and Chad worked until he saved up enough money to keep walking. He headed out for Texas and the winding road. The circle is never broken.

Rebekah Pennell Jenkins, born August 18, 1979

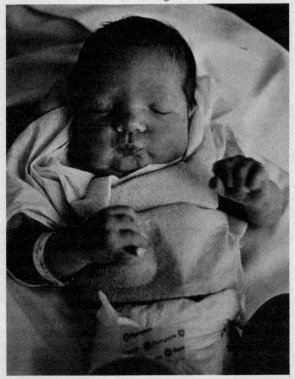